On a Cliff

A History of Third Cliff in Scituate, Massachusetts

Lyle Nyberg

Published by Lyle Nyberg, www.lylenyberg.com
Scituate, Massachusetts, 2021

ISBN: 978-1-7354745-3-3 (paperback)
ISBN: 978-1-7354745-4-0 (Kindle)
ISBN: 978-1-7354745-5-7 (hardcover)
Library of Congress Control Number: 2021923909

Cover: Design by Susannah Green using (1) Thomas Buford Meteyard, *Scituate Bay: The White Cliff*, c. 1894–1900, watercolor, author's collection [design copyright Lyle Nyberg], and (2) aerial photo of Third Cliff by G. Banks/W. Richardson 2017.

Inside: Map illustration by John Roman, www.johnromanillustration.com, [illustration copyright Lyle Nyberg]. Author photo by Kjeld Mahoney. Most images are edited for clarity and size, and converted to black and white (grayscale).

Editors: Janet Paraschos and Alix Stuart.

Special acknowledgment is made to Vernon Woodworth and the Woodworth family, for permission to share their historical photo album that opens up Rivermoor's past.

CONTENTS

PREFACE

This book is the result of a project that grew out of control. It started as a short paper about my neighborhood. Ten pages, two months, tops. Now here it is, six years later, with enough pages for this book and two others. It just goes to show how far curiosity can drive me.

More than that, it shows how much history there is in just our back yard. We are lucky to live in an area with centuries of history. Rev. Samuel Deane covered the early centuries in his history of Scituate published in 1831. Later books covered certain aspects of the town, including more recent histories of First Cliff, Fourth Cliff, the town's fire department, and town water services.

But the books leave gaps. They do not say much about the transformation of farmland into summer estates and summer colonies, features for which Scituate has been particularly noted. So even with all these books, there is still much history to unearth.

I like to dig new ground. So I dug diligently and up came a wealth of material, along with a rich stream of amazing people who lived here.

The book taps a robust set of sources, including historical maps, plans, directories, deeds, tax assessor's records, photos, residents' personal reminiscences, and picture postcards. Postcards and other images in this book are extensive, totaling more than 140. They show the area's fascinating landscapes, many houses (some of which have lasted over 200 years), and people who lived here. These sources are documented in detail in the book's Notes and Notes on Sources. They reflect, I think, an approach that was scholarly, extensive, and thoroughly researched.

Neighbors had stories and VHS videotapes. The neighborhood association has a great archive. The Scituate Historical Society is a town treasure. Google's search engine and other tools were invaluable in my explorations. The internet was a huge help, giving access to primary source documents and genealogical records, even late at night, and even during the pandemic. I relied heavily on recorded deeds, which are online at the Plymouth County Registry of Deeds back to the 1600s.[1]

I enjoyed every trip to the Scituate town archives. It has the big green, bound books with the town's tax valuation lists, prepared each year to collect taxes on the value of personal and real property. As you may suspect, tax collectors were thorough, their records detailed and complete. That allowed accurate location of many houses on the cliff, as well as dates of their construction. Here is a sample from 1917, listing names of houses owned by George Welch, lot numbers, and valuations.[2]

Scituate   APRIL 1, 1917.

	Buildings of all kinds, described by naming their uses.	Value of buildings exclusive of land.	Description, by name or otherwise, of each and every lot of land owned by each person.	Number of acres or feet in each lot of land.		Value of same.	Total value of each parcel of real estate.	Aggregate value of real estate.
				Acres.	Feet.			
1	House Hathaly F	2000	House Lot # 58 Plan 1			260	2260	
2	" Stanley 3d Cliff	1800	" " Plan 2		21780	225	2025	
3			Lot 190. 182 Plan 2			300	300	
4	Twin House F	1500						
5	House Fretwood F	1800	Lots 3d Cliff		32640	775	4425	
6	Barn in rear	250	Beach + upland			500		
7	House (Marguerite) F	2500	Lots 1 + 2 Rivermoor			300	2800	
8	" (Nicula) F	2250	" 9 + 10 "			325	2575	
9	" (Stevens) F	2000	" 11 + 12			325	2325	
10	" (Talbot) F	2000	" 27 + 28			325	2325	
11	" (Millen) F	2250	" 29 + 52			325	2575	
12	" (Hall) F	2000	" 49 + 50			325	2325	
13	" (Russell) F	1800	" 72 + 93			300	2100	
14	" (Myrtle) F	1800	" 77			225	2025	
15	" (Maidstone) F	1800	" 79			225	2025	
16	" (Mayfair) F	1800	" 81			225	2025	
17	" (Melody) F	1800	" 83			225	2025	
18	" (Moorfield) F	1800	" 85			225	2025	
19	" (Mereside) F	2250	" 87 + 88			325	2575	
20	" (Lavender) F	2000				325	2425	
21	Garage	100	Lots 115 + 116					
22	" (Unayo)	2250	" 117 + 118			325	2575	
23	" (Indian Knoll)	2500	" 123 + 124			325	2825	
24	" (Linnet)	1800	" 131 + 132					

1917 Valuation List, George Welch, p. 96, (detail). Line 7 lists the house Marguerite valued at $2,500 on Lots 1 & 2 in Rivermoor. Line 23 lists Indian Knoll at $2,500 on Lots 123 & 124.

In addition, maps were a valuable source of information. The Sanborn Map Company created detailed maps for fire insurance purposes. They showed streets and individual buildings in many American cities and towns. They covered parts of Scituate, including Third Cliff, in 1909, 1918, 1926, and 1939. They even labeled some houses with names, like those in the tax valuation lists. The houses were most likely named by developer George Welch. Appendix A lists their names.[3]

An additional resource was the online Massachusetts Cultural Resource Information System (MACRIS). I used it and added to it, documenting many houses mentioned in this book and the people who lived in them. The MACRIS forms require a description of a building's architecture, so I had to learn architectural terminology. In addition, my research took me to an expanding number of topics, such as town planning, paleogeography, antique bottles, meteorology, ship construction, windmill design, and how to date old postcards.

In addition to learning *concepts*, I had to learn *facts*, and this project turned me into a history detective. My process included finding names of former property owners, tracking down their grandchildren, and asking them for old family photo albums.

I described this to someone at the gym one day. He said, "You're quite nosy, aren't you?"

Yes, I am. At least for this project. However, I did not cover every property owner and every descendant.

With my nosing around, the scope of the project ballooned. First, it grew from just my neighborhood (Rivermoor) to all of Third Cliff, the subject of this book. Then it grew to cover all of seacoast Scituate, a subject for a future book. In the process, it spun off my book *Summer Suffragists* about the women's suffrage movement and the surprising number of nationally recognized suffragists who spent summers in Scituate, including on Third Cliff. So this went way beyond the original "ten pages, two months, tops."

But this is where it all started, my neighborhood, my cliff. I am grateful to live in this place by the ocean, with its natural beauty, great history, and amazing people.

You might think that being out of the way, this area was provincial. That is far from true. This book brings out the amazing people who were attracted here, with great ambitions and accomplishments that spanned the globe.

This book should interest anyone who lives or visits here. It should also interest anyone who likes old houses, or wants to learn about the growth of a New England coastal neighborhood, the rise of a summer colony, historic preservation, and important but overlooked parts of the history of this old town and its amazing people.

Lyle Nyberg
Third Cliff, Scituate, Massachusetts
December 2021

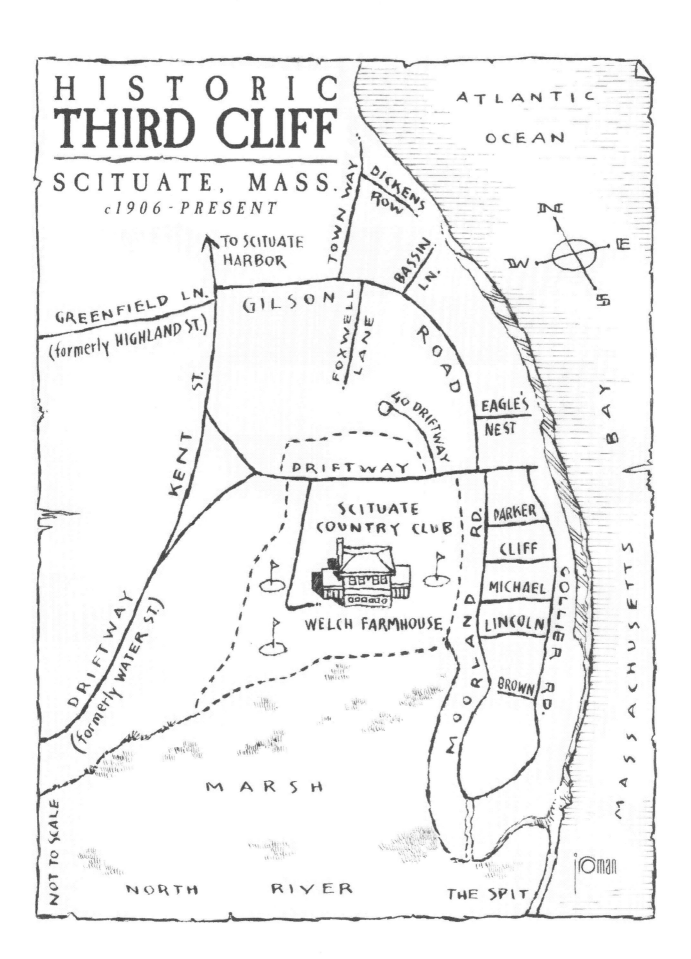

INTRODUCTION

Scituate is an old seacoast town about 25 miles southeast of Boston. It is historic and quaint, and off the beaten track. Since its founding in the 1630s, Scituate has been known for its old-time charm, beaches, and four cliffs facing Massachusetts Bay. The cliffs were named First through Fourth, north to south.

Scituate's history is the history of New England. The town's colonial records are exceptionally complete and extensive. Its extant seventeenth-century records occupy about 800 pages, more than twice as many as those of Plymouth.[4]

Likewise, Third Cliff's history is Scituate's history. For here were planting grounds of Native Americans and farms of the town's English colonists. Here were farmers, fishermen, and Irish mossers who boosted the town's economy. Here was the earliest windmill in Plymouth Colony, pirate treasure, shorebirds, and shorebird hunters. Here were summer residents, attracted to seaside Scituate to enjoy its beaches and its summer colony cottages, with their wraparound piazzas. And here lived amazing people — farmers, Irish mossers, lifesavers, builders, summer colonists, artists, golfers, suffragists, and reformers. Third Cliff is an integral part of Scituate's history, a lens through which to view its history, and a fascinating part of America's history.

In addition, Third Cliff has remarkable scenic views, including ocean, beaches, streams, rivers, and marshes.

Third Cliff evolved from farmland and a few fishermen's cottages. Now it is a community of interesting residents, a mix of blue-collar and white-collar people, like the town itself, and a mix of oldtimers and newcomers who can afford today's high cost of buying and living here. It is populated with houses, streets, and a country club with a golf course.

Why and how did this happen?

In the nineteenth century, Americans developed an appetite for summer vacations, especially by the seashore.[5] Coastal Scituate became an attractive summer destination, easily accessible after the railroad arrived in 1871. Several stations served Scituate, including the Greenbush station close to Third Cliff. While some visitors stayed in the town's inns, hotels, or boarding houses, others rented or built cottages. The wealthy built summer

2

estates. Then, from the late 1800s to the early 1920s, developers built "summer colonies" that attracted upper-class vacationers from Boston and other cities.

"Railroad Station, Greenbush, Mass.," postcard, early 1900s (37202, Webb & Litchfield, Greenbush, Mass. [printed in Germany]).
Courtesy of Scituate Historical Society (Twomey/Jacobson collection).

Third Cliff attracted vacationers, but two factors accelerated its growth — the summer colony of Rivermoor, begun in 1906 on the southern end of Third Cliff, and the Scituate Country Club, established in 1919 on Third Cliff. Rivermoor is a prime example of a summer colony. George Welch developed Rivermoor on his family's farmland at Third Cliff, and with the help of his family's Welch Company. The Country Club developed on the family's farmland. In a sense, this book is a biography of the Welch family, the Welch Company, and the Scituate Country Club.

In addition, this book takes a look at how the appearance of this area has changed —or not changed —over the years.

While this book covers a specific area, it explores broader themes in American life, including the:

- transformation of farmland into housing
- growth of summer vacations by the sea
- impact of the railroad and popularity of automobiles

- housing architecture and trends
- expansion of infrastructure (roads, telephone, sewer, water)
- impact of the World Wars on a New England town
- post-war housing boom, and
- impact of growth on a seaside environment.

This book flows more or less chronologically. While it covers pre-history and colonial times, it focuses on the early decades of the 1900s. Because of this, it describes housing development on older streets and only briefly mentions later residences such as the townhouse condominiums at 40 Driftway.

The Driftway and other roads and features are shown on the map above. Below is a general idea of the book's geographical scope, followed by an overview of Third Cliff's history.

View of Third Cliff

Third Cliff has different facets, depending on how you look at it.

Viewed from the east is the face of the cliff. It is one of four cliffs, named by English colonists First Cliff, Second Cliff, Third Cliff, and Fourth Cliff. They are separate, but not far apart. The cliffs rise above the sea, Massachusetts Bay in the Atlantic Ocean. This may be how early English colonists first viewed Scituate, from the water.

The cliffs are sea cliffs, like the famous White Cliffs of Dover, England. The sea batters such cliffs and tries to devour them. The cliffs we see today in Scituate have retreated as much as 1,600–3,000 feet since colonial times.

They are not white, like Dover's, nor are they continuous. A beach connects First Cliff and Second Cliff. Peggotty Beach connects Second Cliff and Third Cliff. A cobblestone beach once connected Third Cliff with Fourth Cliff. The storm of 1898 washed the beach away, and the North River broke through to separate the cliffs. The storm left a sandy beach and a spit of land (called "the Spit") at the southern end of Third Cliff. The cliff has sandy beaches north and south.

Southern Third Cliff was always home to the meandering North River and its First Herring Brook tributary. The river and brook helped create extensive marshes. Thanks to the 1898 storm, the usually placid river and brook become turbulent as their currents join the currents of the South River and then exit to the sea. This part of the North River is considered an estuary, where the river's freshwater and ocean's seawater mix.

Viewed from the west, as when one is driving along the Driftway toward the ocean, Third Cliff looks like a hill. It is a hill, except for its cliff face. "Bluff" is maybe a better description of Third Cliff, and probably First Cliff and Second Cliff too. But the cliff names were given in the 1630s and they have stuck.

Third Cliff, late 1800s (?), unknown artist/photographer. Close examination reveals fisherman in boat in cove (center), and steamship (left, horizon).
Courtesy of Scituate Historical Society.

Third Cliff Extent

Third Cliff has the most area and the most year-round residents of the three cliffs that connect with Scituate's mainland. Third Cliff may be the tallest, with a maximum elevation of about 85 feet.[6]

While the boundaries of Third Cliff are fluid and subjective, this book takes an expansive view for a number of reasons.[7]

Early farms ran all the way from the Colman Hills to the North River marshes that were south and west of Third Cliff, and some farms probably extended to the cliff itself.[8] We must consider the farms in their totality. In addition, it is important to consider the cliff's margins. East are beaches, marshes, and the ocean. West, beyond New Kent Street, were Turner Farms, Pitcock Farm, and the Colman Hills. In these margins, history was made.

Overview of History

Third Cliff was pastoral farmland for centuries. In the middle of the 1800s it became home to fishermen and Irish mossers. Then, with the advent of summer vacationers, housing spread on previously undeveloped Third Cliff. One Scituate family, the Welches, made the most of these development opportunities. They transformed the land on the cliff from farming to summer housing. George Welch developed its Rivermoor summer colony, opening the area to city dwellers, and the colony later became year-round housing.

We explore this evolution, emphasizing the rise of Rivermoor, and the roles of the Welch family: Michael Welch, his son E. Parker Welch, and E. Parker's son George F. Welch. The Welches left their mark on Third Cliff and Scituate that endures to this day. Third Cliff is now a lovely and historical residential area next to the ocean and the North River.

Rivermoor stands as a prime example of an American summer colony of the early 1900s. George Welch's 1906 plan still defines title to most plots of land. The area and streets developed mostly according to that plan. One might call it a planned community. Although planned for summers, its houses were adapted for year-round use. We look at its streetscapes and its "Welch houses," many of which remain. Architecturally, they were not cutting-edge, but they were sturdy and attractive examples of Colonial Revival architecture.

This book explores some of the people who lived on Third Cliff (including the Welches): farmers, fishermen, mossers, entrepreneurs, real estate developers, golfers, artists, professors, suffragists, reformers, dentists, the first American to manufacture prefabricated houses, the leader of tobacco company Philip Morris, and a famous world explorer. The book also covers a female doctor, a virtuoso violinist, a "visual psychologist," a furrier, and a farrier. Even pirates, because the skeptical historian found data to show they were once here.

These people lived at a splendid place — Third Cliff in Scituate. We explore the origins of that name, and then describe life in and around Third Cliff. We do not neglect other parts of town, for Third Cliff and the town have been inextricably intertwined since before the founding of Scituate in 1636.

1

EARLY HISTORY

Scituate's four cliffs have long figured prominently in the town's history and appearance. A cliff appears on the town seal.

However, things looked different to the early English settlers. First Cliff was an island at the mouth of the harbor. Cedar Point (Lighthouse Point) was also an island. As historian Robert Fraser wrote:

> The first settlers who came to Scituate in 1623 found the harbor a large bay with two islands at the entrance. The north island was low and covered with cedar trees while the south isle was a high treeless hump. … In time, tides and storms joined these two islands to the land. The cedar-covered isle was joined to the Sand Hills by a spit by 1793, and it became known as Cedar Point. Then, a few years later, the south island joined with the highlands to the south, and, after storms had washed it considerably, it became known as First Cliff.[9]

Even Second Cliff may have appeared as an island to early settlers.

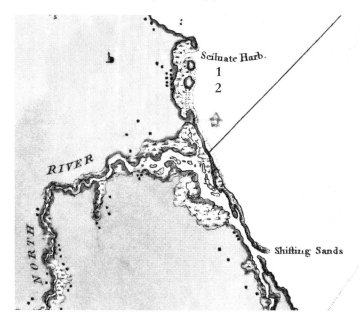

At left is a detail of an interesting old map that emphasizes First and Second Cliffs as islands, outboard of the shoreline.[10]

Detail of Des Barres, *A Chart of Massachusetts Bay* (1776), published in the 1802 edition of *Atlantic Neptune.* Harvard Map Collection, Harvard Library; image by Lyle Nyberg, adding cliff numbers.

That would mean that the beaches now connecting First Cliff to Second Cliff, and Second Cliff to Third Cliff (Peggotty Beach), are *tombolos*, a term for sand or gravel bars connecting an island with the mainland or another island. Perhaps their island past presages the future of these cliffs from rising sea levels.

It was actually about 1630 (not 1623) that colonists, many from Kent, England, settled in Scituate. They engaged in farming. They named the town based on the Native American word for Satuit Brook, meaning "cold brook," which flows into Scituate's harbor.[11]

Scituate was then within lands of the Massachuset (Mattakeesett) tribe, for which the Commonwealth of Massachusetts was named.[12] However, in the early 1600s the Massachuset rapidly dwindled in population, and it ceased to exist as a separate tribe by 1640. Scituate then became Mashpee Wampanoag territory.[13]

Native Americans evidently farmed Third Cliff before the English colonists arrived.[14] They planted corn, squash, and beans.[15] An 1845 account said cornfields of Native Americans covered the cliffs.[16]

Native Americans' concept of land was much different from that of the colonists. The colonists conceived of land as private property — to be owned, bought and sold — rather than to be shared as public commons.[17] In keeping with their concept, and likely as an afterthought, the colonists obtained a deed or deeds for the land of Scituate from Massachuset leader Josias Wampatuck in 1653.[18]

Deeds — records of land ownership — began early, and Plymouth Colony soon developed systems to record them. Land records of Scituate from as early as 1634 refer to the cliffs, including Third Cliff.[19]

These land records also refer to roads, many of which still exist with their original names. They include the Driftway, leading inland across Third Cliff, roughly east-west.[20] As one historian says, "According to the *Oxford English Dictionary*, a Driftway was a way specifically for driving cattle to pasture."[21]

Another early road was Kent Street. It was named for the English county from which early settlers came. It intersected the Driftway, as it does today, heading north into the settlement at Scituate Harbor.[22]

Bassin Lane on Third Cliff was named later. It is near Peggotty Beach, which was earlier named Bassing Cove. Perhaps Bassing Cove was a good place to fish for bass, and perhaps Bassin is a short form of Bassing. Bassin Lane should not be confused with Bassing Beach in Scituate at Cohasset Harbor.[23]

Scituate Harbor is where most settlers built houses, on the western uphill side of Kent Street. That gave them leeway from high tides and floods. The cliffs, on the other hand, were more suited to farming, as well as harvesting of salt marsh hay. Settlers valued the different kinds of marsh hay and marsh grass for roof thatch, house insulation, and forage for animals. Settlers could feed their cows and sheep with marsh hay from day one, instead of spending years cutting down trees and creating meadows.[24]

We know of 171 people who lived in Scituate between 1633 and 1639. They included William Gillson, Timothy Hatherly and his wife, Nathaniel Tilden and two daughters, five Turners, and Joseph Coleman (also spelled Colman). Colman's name attached to the Colman Hills, sand and gravel drumlins left by the glaciers, southwest of Scituate Harbor and west of Third Cliff.[25]

Third Cliff was the site of William Gillson's windmill. It was the earliest windmill in Plymouth Colony, used for milling corn.[26] Corn was the most important crop for Native Americans and the English settlers.[27]

A fort or palisade was located on the eastern side of Kent Street at the western edge of Third Cliff.[28] English settlers may have erected it out of concern about relations with Native Americans. Relations were tentative at first, then mostly friendly, until King Philip's War in 1675–1676.[29]

Early roads of Plymouth Colony were probably based on Native American trails. These included a 1600s "'Indian path,' so called, which led from Scituate to the Mattakeeset settlements at Indian head ponds by 'the Cornet's mill,' on the third Herring brook." These ponds, which feed the North River, are south-southwest of Scituate in what today is the Broadway and West Elm Street area of Hanover and Pembroke. It appears the path followed present East Street in Hanover to River Street in Norwell, and then along some of Route 123 (at Parker and Cross Streets).[30]

Based on this description, the "Indian path" intersected three main colonial roads leading north from Plymouth. Furthest to the west was the Bay Path, corresponding to parts of today's Route 3, Route 3A, and Route 53. Next came the Country Road, perhaps now Route 53 and/or Scituate's Country Way. (Today, Country Way is the longest town road.) To the east was the Pilgrim Trail. It came up through Marshfield to White's Ferry, at the site of today's Bridgewaye Inn. Then it crossed the river to Humarock (Fourth Cliff). The trail went up Fourth Cliff and across the narrow barrier beach that connected Fourth Cliff with Third Cliff.[31]

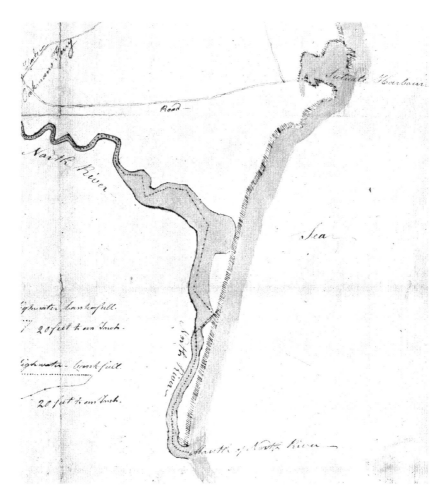

1801 map (detail). Massachusetts State Archives, No. 1586. Fourth
Cliff appears as almost an island, just below "Sea" in the center.

The Pilgrim Trail's path along the beach between the cliffs was called a "highway" in the
1800s. Upon reaching Third Cliff, travelers could take the Driftway across the cliff to
connect with either the Country Road leading north or Kent Street leading into the
settlement at Scituate Harbor.[32]

The connecting beach was so narrow between Third Cliff and Fourth Cliff that it barely
merited a pencil line on an 1801 map (see above). It was sturdy enough, however, to
prevent the North River from reaching the sea there. The river there took a right turn and
headed south, belying its name. Much further south, the river exited to the sea. Thus, Third
Cliff was far from the river's mouth. The storm of 1898 obliterated the connecting beach
between Third Cliff and Fourth Cliff. The river broke through at that point. Since then,
the North River ran directly to the sea between the two cliffs, next to Third Cliff. The
former southern reach of the river became part of the South River, which (belying *its* name)
flowed north to join the North River as it exited to the sea.[33]

Sea roads may have been just as important as pathways, roads, and activities like farming on the land. The sea joined England with its colonies in America. The sea joined Scituate with early colonies in Plymouth, Duxbury, Cohasset, Weymouth, and Boston. Often it was easier, faster, and safer to go among them by sea rather than land. Even in the late 1800s, after the railroad came to Scituate, some people traveled between Boston and Scituate by sailboat, and then explored coastal Duxbury and other towns by sailboat.[34]

In addition, rivers gave access to the interior from the seacoast. The North River and its tributaries ran through many towns before reaching coastal Scituate. Native Americans and colonists used the river as a highway. With portage, and stashed canoes, travelers could cross over to other rivers to travel far. A modern version of the Wampanoag passage occurred in 2012:

> Beginning on June 9, local rower Peter Kelly-Detwiler will lead a small group along the historic water route that was used by the Wampanoag Indians for generations. The Wampanoag Canoe Passage connects the North and Taunton Rivers, and Massachusetts and Narragansett Bays.
>
> This waterway runs for more than 70 miles from Scituate on Massachusetts Bay, to Dighton Rock State Park on the Taunton River as it flows into Narragansett Bay. The passage is divided into three sections of nearly equal length. The first, from Scituate to Pembroke, ends at Little Sandy Pond. The second section runs from East Bridgewater to Middleborough and ends at Camp Titicut, while the third section goes from Raynham to Berkley, ending at Dighton Rock State Park.[35]

Thus, one could travel from Massachusetts Bay on the South Shore to Narragansett Bay in Rhode Island without having to go in open ocean, around Cape Cod.[36]

Left: Theodor de Bry, "Native Americans Making Canoes," engraving, 1590, courtesy of the John Carter Brown Library at Brown University.

Plymouth Colony lasted from 1620 to 1691, when it was absorbed into the Massachusetts Province (the Massachusetts Bay Colony).

In 1930, the state recognized the tercentenary of the Massachusetts Bay Colony (1630-1930). This included 275 commemorative markers placed in various towns of the former colony, including Scituate. Scituate has nine markers, more than any other town in

Massachusetts. Third Cliff has a marker. In 2016, the town restored and reinstalled the marker, and held a rededication ceremony on the cliff.[37]

Third Cliff Tercentenary marker. Fourth Cliff in background. Note extensive rocky area in front of Fourth Cliff, indicating its possible earlier extent.
Photo by Lyle Nyberg 2016.

One historian said, "[d]uring most of [Plymouth] colony's existence, Scituate was its largest and wealthiest settlement."[38] Much of its wealth depended on farming.

2

FARMERS

The history of Scituate starts with farms and farmers, as does the history of Third Cliff. Farming continued on the cliff for over 400 years, and it continues in places there today.

Early colonial farms ran from the Colman Hills east onto the cliffs, and south and west to the North River marshes, and into the marshes.[39] Salt marsh hay harvested from the marshes was important to the early settlers. As on Boston's North Shore, "Here even the agriculture was maritime; not creaking wains [wagons] but broad-beamed 'gundalows' collected the harvest of salt hay."[40] Gundalows were flat-bottomed boats used in the Northeast since the 1600s and suited for shallow waters.[41]

Back on land, including Third Cliff, farms grew crops such as corn. Usually they were family farms, often passed down within the families for centuries. To rightly record their history requires examination of the genealogy of those families.

Below we consider the descendants of Humphrey Turner, who began a farm in Scituate in the 1630s. It is amazing that the phrase "Turner farm" was still being used as late as 1901. Then we consider a branch of the family of Robert Waterman, a farmer who settled in Marshfield in the 1630s. In later chapters, we examine closely the family and descendants of Michael Welch, who took over an ancient Turner farm in the 1830s and became highly influential in the town's government, commerce, and real estate.

With all these farming families, expect many names and many dates. We find a surprising amount of complexity in this small geographic area of Third Cliff, underscoring its significance to the broader history of the town.

Settlers built houses early in Scituate, but not on Third Cliff before 1628 (as stated in a map published in 1936). Reliable sources suggest houses did not appear on Third Cliff until much later.[42] An 1831 map showed the cliff itself as unoccupied. In fact, on all four cliffs it showed only two buildings, both on Fourth Cliff.[43]

However, it was a different story just west of Third Cliff. Farmhouses appeared there very early, mostly along the Driftway. Some were built on portions of a farm that Humphrey Turner began in the 1630s.[44]

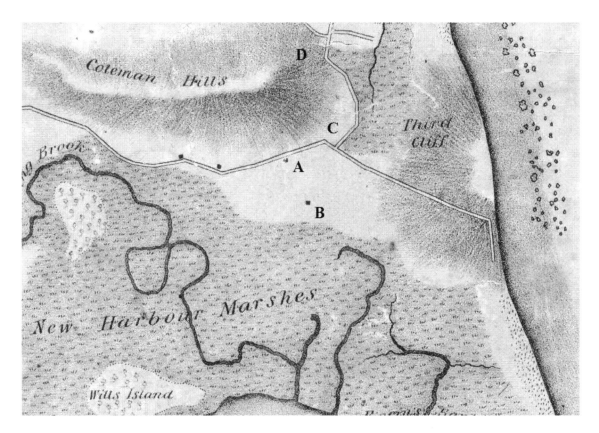

Robbins & Turner, *Map of Scituate* (1831), detail, Harvard Map Collection. Driftway runs across upper center, intersecting Old Kent Street (at **C**) going north to Scituate Harbor. Marks added for farms: **A**. Nathaniel Turner-William Waterman. **B**. James Turner-Michael Welch. **C**. Old Abbey. **D**. Pitcock Farm. Note rocks off coast and narrow beach to Fourth Cliff (lower right, dotted area, left of black shoreline).

Ancient Turner Farms

Humphrey Turner (c. 1593–1673) farmed land southeast of the Colman Hills. In 1634, town fathers transferred to him a 26-acre parcel of upland on the southwest corner of Third Cliff, and he later received other parcels. A descendant claimed that the Native Americans gave him the land out of love and gratitude. That is unlikely. As historian Bangs noted, Native Americans were likely decimated by the plague, and they neither opposed nor welcomed the English settlers. Colonists just appropriated the land and carved it up. When they later obtained any deed from the Native Americans, it was likely an afterthought.[45]

We have a pretty good idea of the location of Humphrey Turner's farm. His Third Cliff parcel "extended from the hills to the 'New Harbour Marshes' [of the North River]."[46] (See above detail of the 1831 map.) Turner built a house there and a tannery in 1636.[47] The exact location of his house is unknown. Historian Deane said in 1831:

The farm … on which he resided, was east of Colman's hills, near the spot occupied by his descendant James Turner. The house was on the side of the road next [to] the hill.[48]

A later genealogist said, "His house was on the side of the road next [to] the hill [Colman Hills], a little east of that of his descendant Samuel Turner now W. W. Waterman's, later Sand & Gravel Co."[49]

An intriguing 1921 report of the tannery's remains said:

To make use of these skins [of wild animals] a tanner was needed, and here was Humphrey Turner, an English tanner, who erected a tannery on his farm east of Colman's Hills, traces of which have been found very recently. This was started as early as 1636.[50]

According to a later source, about 1942:

[T]his house and the tannery near it were on the north side of the way, now called 'the Driftway,' nearly opposite to the house now owned by the Boston Sand and Gravel Co., in which several descendants of his grandson Samuel Turner had formerly lived.[51]

The Turner-Waterman house (the later Boston Sand and Gravel Company house) is discussed below as the Nathaniel Turner house, with the later address of 141 Driftway. The Boston Sand and Gravel Company began mining operations along the Driftway in the Colman Hills in 1914, lasting until 1963. The company owned the reported site of Humphrey Turner's house, if it was north of the Driftway, and it is now part of the municipal Widow's Walk golf course.[52]

Humphrey Turner had countless descendants. The family name fills many town records of Scituate and Norwell, and volumes of genealogical records.[53] It delights, frustrates, and confuses genealogists and historians.

Humphrey Turner's ancient farm along the Driftway should not be confused with his 80-acre farm along the North River near the Union Bridge, which lay in the part of Scituate that later became Norwell. That was also an ancient farm that his descendants occupied.[54] In addition, Humphrey Turner's farm along the Driftway should not be confused with the Turner farm on Turner Avenue between Shore Acres and Sand Hills. There were many Turners.

To simplify, and to focus on Humphrey Turner's farm along the Driftway, we look at the line that leads from Humphrey to Nathaniel to Samuel to James, and then to James Turner (1733–1803) in the fifth generation. These are the descendants who kept the farm going. The children of James Turner in the fifth generation included Nathaniel (1765-1846) and

James (1778–1835). (Nathaniel and James were common names in the Turner family.) We cover Nathaniel, then James.[55]

Nathaniel Turner Farm

Nathaniel Turner (1765-1846) evidently inherited the southwest portion of the Humphrey Turner farm from his father James in 1792. He married Sarah James. "They lived on the ancient Turner farm under Colman hills in the house now [1942] owned by the Scituate Sand & Gravel Co." Evidently, their children (Mary, Lydia, Nathaniel, Mercy, and Samuel Humphrey) also lived there.[56]

Nathaniel Turner had a sister Sally, born in 1792, who wound up marrying Augustus Cole. Cole had an adjacent farm, and he was likewise descended from an early settler of Scituate.[57] It would not be the first time, nor the last, that children of neighboring farmers married each other.

Nathaniel Turner's new "Dwelling House" (as stated in his deed) must have been close to that of his father James. In 1804, the year after his father died, Nathaniel granted a right of passage to grantees including his brother James, and "to all persons living in the dwelling House in which my late honored father James Turner of said Scituate lived … across the Westerly end of the field in which my dwelling house stands and in front of the same."[58] The location of the James Turner house is unknown. It disappeared and is not shown on the 1831 map.[59]

Nathaniel Turner's son Samuel Humphrey Turner (1811–1893) and his family were the last Turner generation to live in the Nathaniel Turner house.[60] Samuel Humphrey Turner was a mason, according to the 1860 and 1880 US census reports. Appropriately enough, he was also a Mason with a capital M. After his death in 1893, and the death of Samuel Humphrey Turner's unmarried son Samuel Humphrey Turner (1836–?), the old farm was sold outside the family. But farming continued there.[61]

William W. Waterman (1866–1928) was the next owner of the farm, from 1895 to 1927. An 1894 directory already listed him as a farmer.[62] According to 1895 tax records, he owned a house, a barn, and various parcels of property including "Old Abbey [Field]," two acres, and "Abbey Pasture," eight acres. In addition, he owned a carriage, three horses, one cow, two "2 years old" (perhaps horses), and two hogs. He and his family lived in the old Nathaniel Turner farmhouse, which would later have the address of 141 Driftway. A 1918 directory listed him as a market gardener, which means one who grows produce for sale in the market to produce cash (profit), and generally one who uses a hoe on a smaller parcel instead of a plow on a larger parcel.[63] Interestingly, by 1926, William Waterman owned two houses and two barns.[64]

William Waterman was a ninth-generation descendant of Robert Waterman, who settled before 1638 in Scituate's neighboring town of Marshfield. William was the son of Andrew James Waterman (1833–1906) and Lucia Day Stevens (1840–1921). His older brother Andrew (1863–1934) married a woman in Maine and moved there. His younger brother Charles (1870–1939) married a local Litchfield girl and "lived in Scituate, where he was a member of the School Committee and Board of Selectmen. In 1912 he represented the district in the State Legislature." As for William, the farmer, he married Lottie Scott Torrey (1871–1951) of Scituate in 1894. They had two children: Frederick Torrey Waterman (1897–1960) and Grace Day Waterman (1900–1965).[65]

Grace appears as a child in two photos of the Waterman farmhouse from the early 1900s. Each shows three females: an older woman, a child, and a middle-aged woman. One photo shows them seated in front of the house, about 1910. The other shows them with a cart and pony, and a woman and a girl are wearing cloche hats, which were fashionable starting about 1908. In the second photo (not copied here), the tree in front is taller, so the photo may have been taken a few years after 1910. The photos are from Waterman-Vines family archives.[66]

These early 1900s photos are instructive. They both show the lane leading southeast toward the Welch farm (discussed in more detail below). The lane appears on early maps as a road that traverses the southern part of Third Cliff almost to the ocean. The lane appears on the 1903 map as a road, and on a 1919 plan as a driveway. Part of the lane still runs from the Welch farmhouse (now the Scituate Country Club's clubhouse) over to Michael Avenue. In the photo with the pony, the Driftway (a dirt road) leads to the left (north side) of the house. Both photos show the house's west side, which is remarkably similar to its later appearance. In the distance to the east is farmland, the Driftway, and Third Cliff with some houses on top. The scenes are bucolic. They show no sign of the Rivermoor summer colony that was emerging in southern Third Cliff.[67]

Some detective work revealed the names and relationships of the women in the photos.

Accompanying the photos is a handwritten note: "Our Farm — Ma, Grandma Waterman & me. Driftway — Scituate about 1910." Based on the Waterman genealogy, and the apparent ages of the women, the seated women must be (left to right): "Grandma" Lucia Waterman (1840–1921), Grace Waterman (1900–1965), and Lottie Waterman (1871–1951). These were William Waterman's mother, wife, and daughter Grace. Grace appears to be about ten years old. Grace would have been the one who wrote the note.

A copy of the second photo is marked on the back "Lottie — Susan — Grace." Susan is probably Susan Vines, wife of Daniel Vines.[68] They were neighbors of the Watermans and had children, including a son named Fred who was close in age to Grace.

Three females in front of Turner-Waterman house, 141 Driftway, with Third Cliff in background. Photo probably from Waterman-Vines family archives, c. 1910.

Daniel Vines was superintendent of the Boston Sand and Gravel Company in Scituate. He came from South Portland, Maine. He married Susan, born in Maine about 1885. Their oldest son Fred D. (1902–1965) was born in Maine. After the Vines family moved to Scituate, they were neighbors of the Waterman family, and the families appeared only one page apart (alphabetically) in period directories. The Vines family lived five houses away from the Waterman family on the Driftway, according to the 1920 US census. This was probably west of the Watermans, because the census taker considered dwellings east of the Watermans to be Third Cliff, not the Driftway. The 1920 US census lists Daniel A. Vines (then age 42) as "Supt. Sand & Gravel Co." renting a house on the Driftway. The 1926 directory lists Daniel A. Vines (wife Susan G.) as superintendent BSG (presumably Boston Sand and Gravel), with a home on the Driftway.[69]

Grace Day Waterman, the little girl in the photos, married her neighbor Fred D. Vines on July 5, 1927.[70]

Less than two months after Grace and Fred married, William Waterman sold the farmhouse and its eight-acre parcel to the Boston Sand and Gravel Company. Within a year, William Waterman died. The company's superintendent, Daniel Vines, and his family may have moved into the Waterman farmhouse. The 1928 tax records' first property listed for the company was "House-Vines" followed by "Garage-Vines."[71]

Of course, it could have been a different house, since the company owned a number of houses along the Driftway by that time. An old-timer reported, "He [Daniel Vines] and his family lived in a new house on the north side of Water Street [Driftway]." The 1930 US census shows five households all renting on "Sand & Gravel Road," including the family of Daniel Vines, the family of Henry Vines (a son of Daniel and Susan Vines), and the family of Duncan Graham, a watchman for the company. Lottie Waterman lived then in a house she owned on Brook Street in Scituate Harbor.[72]

In 1933, Daniel Vines was on the town's Board of Selectmen.[73]

Eventually, in 1944, the company sold the old farmhouse and its parcel to Daniel Vines and his wife Susie. (Relevant deeds use "Susie" rather than Susan.) Daniel would have been age 66 and perhaps ready to retire from the company. He may have had a sentimental attachment to the old farmhouse, with its Waterman connection. Including the company's ownership (since its superintendent was Daniel Vines), the old Nathaniel Turner farmhouse effectively stayed in the Waterman-Vines family from 1895 until 1950. Then the family sold the property. It passed through a succession of owners to Audrie Burton, who was the owner of record for a number of years.[74]

141 Driftway, start of demolition. Photo by Lyle Nyberg, January 2021.

The farmhouse at the property was left unoccupied since about 1970. Outside, it appeared remarkably as it did in the early 1900s photos. The west (left) side kept its window placements, while the two chimneys were replaced by a central chimney and dormers were added in the front. However, the house had suffered from neglect, and it was demolished in early 2021.[75]

As for Grace Waterman, the little girl in the old photos, she and Fred Vines moved to the Midwest, where Fred worked as an electrical engineer. They had four children: Elizabeth (born 1928), a baby (died 1930), Richard (born 1933), and William (1935). Grace and the children moved back to Scituate about 1950, where her mother Lottie lived until her death in 1951. In 1952, Grace and Fred divorced, after 25 years of marriage. Oldest chile Elizabeth had entered a religious order, Sisters of Divine Providence, and became Sister Elizabeth. William went to Scituate High School, where he was president and valedictorian of his class, and captain of his varsity basketball team. William and Richard married women from Scituate. It appears that both men were engineers like their father. Richard and his wife Diane (and her brother Fred Waterman) were active in the Scituate Historical Society. All of Grace and Fred's children are deceased.[76]

James Turner Farm

Jumping back a few generations, we turn to Nathaniel Turner's brother, James Turner (1778–1835).

While Nathaniel had the southwest portion of the ancient Humphrey Turner farm, James inherited or acquired the farm's southeast portion. It included the area that later became Rivermoor and the main part of the Scituate Country Club south of the Driftway on Third Cliff. "James Turner built the original house on the so called Welch farm, where he died 24 Jan. 1835."[77] This house was near the location of the house of his ancestor Humphrey Turner.[78]

James Turner married Ruth Stockbridge (1793–1852) in 1826. In early 1836, after James died, his widow Ruth sold the property to Michael Welch.[79] The James Turner house became the farmhouse for Michael Welch's family and descendants, and they farmed the land until 1920.

Thus, the Welches and the Watermans continued farming Humphrey Turner's land on Third Cliff for centuries after his time in the 1630s. Farm crops and practices changed over time, although we cannot be certain what happened on Turner's land specifically. In general, the system of farming crops for the farmer's family, or for local barter, changed here about the 1880s. Then it became cash farming, garden farming, or farming for the market, particularly the Boston market. Crops expanded from corn, originally, to include beans, potatoes, apples, cauliflower, cucumbers, tomatoes, and lettuce. Those who continued traditional farming had many fields with "a rotation of four or five years of hay, one year of corn, one year of rye, then hay again."[80] Even William Waterman, who as late as 1919 had 20 acres of land on Third Cliff evidently devoted to growing corn, was considered a market gardener.[81]

To sum up, Humphrey Turner's farmland south of the Driftway continued being farmed by his descendants Nathaniel and James in the early 1800s. James Turner's property then continued being farmed by the Welch family. The Welch family sold or gave part to George Welch in 1902 to become the Rivermoor summer colony, and they sold the remaining 40-acre farm to the Scituate Country Club in 1919. At the same time, William Waterman sold his adjacent 20-acre farm to the Scituate Country Club.

William Waterman kept farming Nathaniel Turner's property until he sold it to the Boston Sand and Gravel Company in 1927. The sale included a small field called Old Abbey. Below, we meander around Old Abbey and explore Boston Sand and Gravel's activities around there. Note that William Waterman's sale in 1927 did not mark the end of farming on Third Cliff.

Floods, Guzzles, Tide Mills, and a Canal

Third Cliff has a long history of flooding in its low areas west of the cliff. This has limited development in those areas. However, the same areas would have made a good place for a canal. A canal was proposed several times but it never came to pass. We wade into these topics below.

Low areas subject to incursion by water, like seawater, are called guzzles. Guzzles have been a part of Scituate's history, and even part of modern land use decisions by the town. Such a guzzle lies east of the Old Abbey Field, and it has been the scene of historic flooding.[82]

Samuel Deane's 1831 history of Scituate said:

> The tides of extraordinary height flow through this proposed route [of a canal, never built, between Scituate Harbor and the North River], as has happened in October 1829, and several times before. Stetson's tide mill at the harbour was swept through this route, and carried to Marshfield shore in the great snow storm Nov. 1786.[83]

The 1786 storm carried the tide mill (a mill powered by the tides) from Scituate Harbor along the inland sides of Second and Third Cliffs until it reached the North River, more than a mile and a half away.[84]

Something similar happened in 1851:

> The great storm of 1851 [in mid-April] was of especial fury along the coast from Portland to New York. …Scituate Harbor had been damaged to the extent of $5,000, and the oldest inhabitant said the tide had not been as high since Wednesday, December 16, 1786, a period of sixty-five years. The greatest damage was along the wharves and the lumber yard of Howland & Edwin Otis, who carried on the business at the old mill and shipyard. Front and Kent Streets were flooded and filled with wreckage from the lumber yard, which was carried by the wind and tide to the farms of Michael Welch and Samuel Turner, destroying walls and fences on its way.85

Based on this description, the 1851 storm carried wreckage from Scituate Harbor along the inland sides of the cliffs, to the Welch and Turner farms on Third Cliff. This was a distance of one and a half miles, or even more if the wreckage kept going into the North River and Marshfield, as in the 1786 gale.

John Stilgoe described this area in anonymous terms in his 1994 book *Alongshore*. It is a guzzle, simply a low spot or ditch, "properly called a gutter."

> Such a guzzle lies at the foot of a cornfield, well inland — and downhill — from great cliffs that face the sea. Half a mile inland from the cliff, past expensive summer and year-round homes, then (slightly lower) past some new condominiums, the walker heading away from the sea encounters a golf course running down to a tiny drainage ditch, some scruffy trees, and a poorly paved road that crosses a diminutive culvert. Then the walker starts uphill, perhaps wondering how a cornfield first planted in the 1630s endures surrounded by upscale resort architecture. Nothing in the scene hints at the sea, for the sea is obscured by rising land and by mature juniper, beech, maple, and pine trees, and what water lies stagnant in the ditch is not even brackish. To be sure, the air often smells of the sea, and during great gales the sound of the surf striking the outer ledges, and the base of the cliff, booms everywhere, but nothing maritime marks the place. And all that is odd is the cornfield, lingering ghostlike from a colonial agricultural past.86

With a history of water flowing through here, the guzzle, or gutter, would have made a natural place for a canal between Scituate Harbor and the North River. In fact, the concept was considered as early as 1802, and several efforts were made to create a canal there later in the century.

Here we must take a short detour to explain tide mills in Scituate Harbor, before returning to our discussion of canals. Tide-powered mills go back well over a thousand years.87

The storm of 1786 swept away Stetson's tide mill. It was replaced. A "Tide Gristmill" appears at the southwest corner of the harbor on the great Turner map of 1795. It was next to the main creek, probably at the mouth of Satuit Brook. By 1802, Jesse Dunbar owned the mill at this location. Dunbar's mill was powered by tides using a dam that crossed Mill Creek, evidently the outlet of Satuit Brook. Dunbar proposed to build another dam nearby to cross Main Creek. That would use the tides that flowed through Main Creek for additional power to the mill. In 1802, the town meeting directed a committee to decide on a place for Jesse Dunbar's proposed mill dam in Scituate Harbor, and "to make a Reserve for a Canal from the waters in Said Harbour to the North River if it Should any time hereafter be wanted."[88]

Jesse Dunbar then petitioned the state legislature and received legislation authorizing him to erect a dam in the harbor for his grist mill, subject to making a passage for vessels at least twenty feet wide in the deepest water. This would have made room for a canal. Maps of the time show the proposed dam crossing Main (or Maine) Creek on the east side of a marshy island in the middle of the harbor. They also show another dam (probably Dunbar's) already crossing Mill Creek on the west side of the island, near Front Street between Beal Place and Otis Place.[89]

Jesse Dunbar probably built the proposed second mill dam across Main Creek. Later, however, only a single dam was required to cross both Main Creek and Mill Creek. In other words, a single dam captured the outlet of Satuit Brook as well as the tides running through the marshy southern end of the harbor. Evidently, the marshy harbor's configuration had changed, perhaps with some strategic filling. The single dam is probably shown on close examination of the 1831 map, where an asterisk indicates a mill. A dam appears in crisp detail on an 1879 map, extending from a grist mill off Front Street then owned by C. A. Cole. The mill was in use until around 1890.[90]

The 1879 map does not show any outlet for a canal. By then, a bridge went over Main Creek toward First and Second Cliffs. A bridge is there now, and the power of Main Creek is evident in summertime at high tide, when kids ignore the danger and jump off the bridge.[91]

A 1903 deed conveyed the mill with this illuminating language:

> … a certain property known as Scituate Harbor Tide mill situated at Scituate Harbor consisting of building, wharf, dock etc. together with all the privileges, rights and appurtenance thereto belonging, also a piece of salt marsh known as Mill Island marsh bounded as follows: northerly by marsh land formerly of Brown and Lovell, easterly by Main Creek so called, southerly and westerly by the mill pond and creek, containing five acres more or less, …[92]

Postcards from the early 1900s show a straight line or lines of posts or pilings from a building on the mainland to a marshy island in the harbor. That was likely the mill dam, or what remained of it.[93]

"Old Stone Wharf, Scituate, Mass.," postcard, postmarked 1910. Published by Chas. N. Frye. Murphy's *Irish Mossers* book, p. 55, shows larger image of same photo, late 1800s, identified as remains of the mill dam. In the distance off to the right is Second Cliff. Courtesy of Scituate Historical Society.

Returning to our discussion of a canal, and turning back in time, the idea for a canal to connect Scituate Harbor and the North River came up again in 1828. Citizens petitioned Congress for the improvement of navigation of the North River.[94] Congress appropriated $180 to survey the North River to ascertain the expediency of removing obstructions at the river's mouth.[95]

Samuel Deane, in his history of Scituate, viewed the survey's scope as including a possible canal to the harbor, estimated to cost $15,000; he said the survey was completed in July 1829 and he was awaiting the result.[96] The survey itself was completed, but it took a while for the report of the survey to appear.[97] The report was not completed until February 1830, and Congress had it printed December 23, 1830. Perhaps this was too late for Deane to describe in his 1831 history.[98]

As Deane surmised, the 1830 report recommended the excavation of a channel between the North River and Scituate Harbor, at an estimated cost of $16,283.02. This was the best alternative to the difficulty and expense of removing the bar and shoals at the mouth of the river, which at that time exited to the ocean several miles south of the current mouth. (The shoals there were labeled "Shifting Sands" on the 1776 Des Barres map, a detail of which appears at the start of chapter 1.) Another alternative was equally difficult, a cut through the shingle beach (one covered by flattened cobblestones) that connected Third Cliff and Fourth Cliff. The 1830 report recommended a new channel inland of the cliffs, providing a direct route from the river to the harbor. The report said:

> This [shipping] business of the river is more or less connected with that of the harbor, and would reap great advantages by having a direct and safe communication with it. …
>
> Hence, it is obvious that the business of the harbor and that of the river would be materially benefitted by a direct communication with each other, instead of taking the circuitous route by the mouth of the river; there would be a saving in distance of nearly eight miles, besides eluding the dangers of the navigation.[99]

The proposed channel would run 9,720 feet from the river to the tide mill dam in the harbor (at Satuit Brook). It would be 8 feet deep and 36 feet wide at the water line. It would be easy to excavate, and would be kept clear of obstructions by the ebb and flow of the tide. It would eliminate miles of ship passages, including ocean voyages.[100]

Evidently, nothing came of the 1830 report.

In 1852, the proposed canal again came before Congress. Citizens petitioned for the improvement of Scituate Harbor.[101] Congress authorized $1,000 "For a survey in reference to the improvement of the harbor of Scituate, in connection with the North River, Massachusetts."[102] Connection was the key word, as the survey was intended to consider a connection between the North River and Scituate Harbor.

US Army engineers worked on the survey in 1853. They first considered dredging the harbor. Their report looked with some favor on Scituate as a harbor of refuge, a harbor where a vessel could safely moor in case of bad storms or heavy seas. Scituate Harbor would require dredging and a breakwater, a barrier built out into the water to protect the coast or harbor from the force of waves. The breakwater alone accounted for almost half of the $250,000 cost estimate for the whole project. The report then discussed the possible canal, which would run 8,500 feet at a depth of about 7 ½ to 10 feet. It would essentially cause the North River to branch north into Scituate Harbor. The route showed "trifling deviations from a dead-level, caused somewhat by an attempt to fill up a portion of the meadow for cultivation." The canal was similar to the one proposed in the 1830 report, with one *big* difference. It would be 130 feet wide near the water line, not 36 feet. The amount of excavated material would be 500,000 cubic yards, not 88,375.[103]

Below, a detail of the 1831 map is marked up to show the route of the 1853 proposed canal, as well as the cliff numbers.

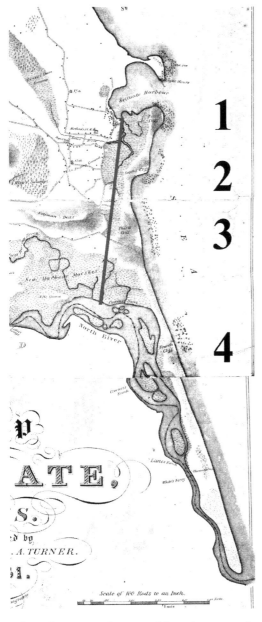

The 1853 survey was conducted by Henry P. Andrews, who reported his findings to Major J. G. Barnard, US Army Corps of Engineers. Barnard wrote Hon. E. P. Little on August 22, 1853, with information on the survey. Little, born in Marshfield, was a member of Congress representing Scituate and Marshfield from 1852 to 1853. Barnard then sent his report to his superior, the Chief Engineer, Gen. Joseph G. Totten, on November 16, 1853. Totten sent the report to Secretary of War Jefferson Davis. Davis sent the report to Congress by letter of January 20, 1854.[104]

Many of the people involved in the 1854 report were nationally recognized military men. Gen. Totten (1788-1864) was a commanding figure in Army engineering. He was involved in the design of the Minot's Ledge Light replacement, offshore from Scituate, completed in 1850. Sec. Jefferson Davis, of course, later led the Confederacy in the Civil War. The report's author, Henry P. Andrews, and its recipient, J. G. Barnard, along with Gen. Totten, all served in the Union Army in the Civil War. J. G. Barnard, born in Massachusetts, became a General, and he was one of the nation's most respected and distinguished engineers. Years after the war, in 1879, he would visit Scituate when it was under consideration as a designated harbor of refuge.[105]

Despite these reports, no canal was ever built. There was vocal local opposition. Such a canal would have separated the cliffs from the mainland. It would have been 130 feet wide, much wider than any major road. It would have run nearly alongside Kent Street. And it would have added an interesting water hazard for the later Scituate Country Club's golf course.

Nature was not through with this area. The storm of 1898 demolished camps and cottages at Sand Hills. Their ruins traveled a mile across the harbor and they piled up on the Welch Company's wharf in the harbor. Other wreckage floated a mile and a half from the harbor past the cliffs to the Welch farm, on the path the proposed canal would have taken.[106]

The area's history of flooding has discouraged building. As Stilgoe's book says, "tales of where the sea had once reached kept even condominium-builders away from the cornfield [at the bottom of the hills]."[107] The cornfield, probably Old Abbey Field, now grows beans. Despite the area's pastoral appearance, the danger of flooding remains. The area is in a designated flood plain.[108]

Pitcock Farm and Other Farms

Pitcock Farm was another farm on Third Cliff — more accurately, west of Third Cliff. This was just up Kent Street from the Old Abbey Field. Alfredo and Alice Gomes acquired the property in 1945 in two deeds, one of which called the property Pitcock Field and Pitcock Swamp.[109]

The name Pitcock came from an earlier deed in 1916 and showed up in tax valuation lists for Henry T. and Angeline Cole in 1906. But the name goes back even further, to George Pitcock (or Pidcock), who married Sarah Richards in 1640 in Scituate and lived there for many years. It is likely he farmed the site. His successor got 77 acres of upland and 5 acres of swamp.[110]

The Gomes family, of Cape Verdean ancestry, grew flowers, corn, cucumbers, tomatoes, and beans on the farm. The farm had several greenhouses, the family's house, at least one shed, and a farm stand. The farm stand was strategically located at a sharp turn in Kent Street as it curved to meet the Driftway. This is where New Kent Street later connected the Driftway directly to Kent Street and Scituate Harbor. In addition to operating the farm, Alfredo Gomes (and later John Lopes) raised beans on the two-acre patch known as the Old Abbey Field.[111]

In the early 1980s, the Roman Catholic Archdiocese of Boston bought Pitcock Farm, described as "a property consisting of 8.68 acres of land, a family home, greenhouses and a fruit and vegetable stand." The church wanted to turn the property into a mixed-income housing development. It is now a 64-unit affordable housing community in eight buildings, called Kent Village, set back from the street on the north side of Kent Street.[112]

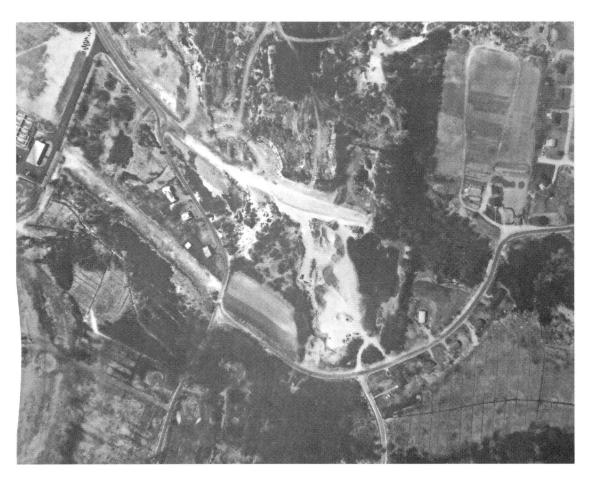

Aerial photo of New Kent Street (starting top left) under construction, 1968. Pitcock Farm at upper right. Old Abbey Field (striped) just below center. Source: Town of Scituate.

Aerial photo of Pitcock Farm, 1975, after completion of New Kent Street in 1968. Courtesy of Gomes family.

Across Kent Street is a remaining Gomes family property. In the late 1980s, Alfredo Gomes had extensive gardens there, with collard beans, shell beans, lima beans, beets, watermelons, and cantaloupes. The zinnias and other flowers were super-sized. Fertilizer was the key. "I know what to put in to make it grow," said Gomes. Today, near the front yard of the house is a blueberry patch, formerly a field of strawberries. That is about all that remains of Pitcock Farm.[113]

Disappearing Farmland

That blueberry patch across from the former Pitcock Farm, and Old Abbey Field, are about all the farmland left on or near Third Cliff, in a town that began almost exclusively as a farming town.

Farmland is disappearing in the rest of the town. Once upon a time, Rufus Clapp had a farm in the heart of Scituate Harbor Village, on the southerly side of Willow Street (now First Parish Road). It was turned into house lots in 1903. Bulrush Farm in North Scituate dated back to the late 1800s, if not earlier. It closed in 1959 after growing cantaloupes, as well as apples from its 500 apple trees, and providing milk from its 25-cow dairy herd. Brushy Hill Farm on Country Way flourished for more than 100 years starting in the middle or late 1800s until it closed. It was the largest working farm in Scituate in its heyday. A 1961 newspaper account reported farming "not long ago at the farms of the Tildens, Damon, Young, Prouty, Briggs, Andrade, Litchfield, Alves and others."[114]

In 1974, Prouty's Farm at 405 First Parish Road advertised, "We've been in town since 1651." A garden center was at that location in recent years, but it has been inactive as a farm site.[115]

Northey Farm dated back to 1675 and was family-owned for generations. Its owners lived in the Old Oaken Bucket Homestead at Walnut Tree Hill. The Northey name lives on in Northey Farm Road, off of Rte. 123, as the site of a housing development from the early 2000s.[116]

Since 1648, the Curtis family farmed a site on what is now Ann Vinal Road. As of 2018, the property was being transformed into a housing development called Curtis Estates. Another farm, the historic Tilden Farm, traced back to Nathaniel Tilden of the 1630s. In the 1880s, its crops were harvested for cash in the Boston market: cauliflower, cucumbers, tomatoes, and later lettuce and rhubarb. In the recent past, it consisted of ten acres on Tilden Road, known as the Sam Tilden Farm. About 2006, farming ended there and the land was subdivided for housing. The Tilden farm was one of the oldest farms in the United States to be continuously operated by one family.[117]

Farms still exist in Scituate. Simons Greenhouse and Farmstand on the north side of Route 123, just west of the Route 3A rotary, boasts four generations of family farming. They farm 85 acres, including the Old Abbey field (lima beans), the Steverman farm on the west side of Country Way, the former Wade farm on the east side of Country Way (now owned by Wade descendant Stephen Litchfield), and two 25-acre parcels on Union Street in Norwell. Ron Simon and his father farmed Pitcock Farm for eight years, before it was sold for housing. The Simons farm on Route 123 had been the Webster farm in the 1920s and 1930s, and may have been part of the original Northey Farm.[118]

Antonio's Farm Stand is on First Parish Road just east of Town Hall. Its sign says it is a four-acre farm continuously farmed since 1740 on land the King of England gave to the Jackson family for fighting in King Philip's War.[119]

Many of the old implements that these farmers would have used are now in museums, such as the barn at the Scituate Historical Society's Mann Farmhouse, not far from Third Cliff. It has many objects that people of today would be hard-pressed to identify or know how to use. Fortunately, labels accompany most objects. They include a rock sled for removing rocks from fields, a spring-tooth harrow for breaking up hard soil, part of a feed cutter, a post hole spoon (also called a cistern shovel), cultivators, a cultivating/harrowing beam plow, a one-horse walking weeder, blades for a field mower, a field rake, scythes, and a potato fork.[120]

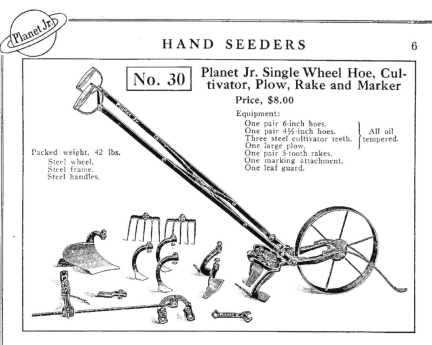

Single-wheel hoe, from Planet Jr. farm implement catalog, 1915.

Richard Mann, who came to Scituate in 1636, began the farm on the land where his farmhouse stands. His descendants farmed it, and three generations lived in the existing farmhouse. Farming there ended with the death of Percy Mann, a seventh generation descendant of Richard Mann, in 1968 at the age of 93.[121]

It is fascinating that names of farms such as Pitcock, Tilden, Northey, and Mann survived for centuries, from the 1600s until recent times.

Old Abbey and Mining

Today there is a two-acre field at the intersection of the Driftway and Kent Street, where farmers grow green beans or lima beans. This spare field gives no hint of its historical significance, and few such hints are in the historical record. Below, we excavate its long and interesting history. It was farmed, probably since colonial times. Later, related parts of the field were mined for sand and gravel in the 1900s. The field may be some of the last remaining old farmland in Scituate.

Origins

The two-acre field has had the name "Abbey" since at least 1841. It has long been associated with the parcel adjoining it to the northwest, whether eight acres (as in the past) or five acres (as today). That parcel has been called the Old Abbey pasture or meadow, Abbey Pasture, or even Abbey Place, southeast of Colman Hills. Today it is a wooded area. Both Old Abbey Field and Abbey Pasture are owned by the Scituate Housing Authority.[122]

Deane's 1831 history of Scituate does not mention Old Abbey. An 1831 map does not show any house at this location. However, a map created in the 1920s or 1930s to depict historical Scituate, and used for a 1936 Tercentenary booklet, shows "The 'Old Abbey'" at this location, northwest of the Driftway and Kent Street intersection.[123]

The Driftway had no abbey, meaning a church with attached buildings for monks or nuns. The name Old Abbey may have referred to an old house, whose ruins resembled an abbey. A historian who attempted to find out the name's origin speculated in 1950:

> In early days there was a house that stood on the westerly corner lot at the junction of Kent Street and the Driftway, which was later to become known as "The Old Abbey." …

> We do not seem to be able to find out what happened to the house. It may have been burned or it may have been let go to decay and "tumbled in" as many of the old houses were let to do.

Mr. Audery Totman, of Greenbush, says that when he was a boy, about 75 years ago, all that was left to mark the spot where the [house] had stood was a small pile of brick where a chimney had stood and a row of lilac bushes.

Mr. James W. Turner says that his grandmother, who was ninety five (95) years old when she died in 1895, told him that when she was a young girl, that the story of the house was lost and that only the ruins of the chimney and a row of lilac bushes remained.

The general opinion seems to be that a person by the name of Abigail, either Litchfield or Vinal, lived there a great number of years. No one is sure of the last name and no one will say if she was a widow or a spinster.

We learned from several sources that in the olden days that the town folks and neighbors spoke of going over to see "Old Abbey" or that they were going over to "Old Abby's" house and from this it would seem that she was a well known and liked person.

As time went by the place known as "Old Abby's" House became contracted into "The Old Abbey" and so spoken of even today. The lot of land on which the house stood is known as the Old Abbey Field.

The row of lilac bushes are still alive today, where they were planted over three hundred (300) years ago and are the only mark to show where "Old Abbys" house stood.[124]

Old Abbey may have been part of the ancient Humphrey Turner farm. It later had a tangled ownership history.[125] Any one or more of the following could have been owners: Ephraim Young, Thomas Young, Joshua Young, Jesse Dunbar, Elisha James, Lucy Otis, and Augustus Cole. The earliest mention of Old Abbey in a deed seems to be in 1841. That referred only to a field. No house was shown there in a map from the 1870s.[126]

At times, the field was owned separately from the pasture. In any event, both parts seem to have come together through acquisitions by Samuel Humphrey Turner (1811–1893). Perhaps he was enlarging the farm of his father Nathaniel Turner.[127] An informed guess is that he acquired Old Abbey Field in 1859 and Abbey Pasture in 1883.

After Samuel Humphrey Turner died in 1893, his estate sold the parcel containing Old Abbey Field and Abbey Pasture to William Waterman in 1895, along with the Nathaniel Turner farm (discussed above) and many other properties.[128] After buying this land, farmer Waterman appears to have been an astute seller.

Mining

In 1900, Waterman sold 34 acres of land to Burleigh N. Crockett of New Hampshire. The deed's remarkably short description said the land was "known as a part of Coleman's Hill so called, bounded and described as follows: Beginning at the southwest corner of Water Street [Driftway] thence with Water Street to the corner of Old Abbey Field… ." The sale evidently included the Old Abbey pasture but not the two-acre Old Abbey field. In 1901, Burleigh Crockett turned around and sold the same parcel to the Consumers Sand Company of Maine.[129] This was among a number of companies that formed in America in the early 1900s to mine sand and gravel. Sand is the single most mined commodity in the world.[130]

The Consumers Sand Company later sold the 34-acre parcel, and other land, to the Boston Sand and Gravel Company in 1914. The deed described the parcel as bounded by Old Abbey Field, following a wall along a jagged course "as the wall now stands to a corner … ." Perhaps this was a stone wall that replaced the "fence" described in deeds of the 1800s and 1900. After all, stone walls last longer than wood fences, as early settlers discovered.[131]

This 1914 deed marks the start of mining the Colman Hills. The Boston Sand and Gravel Company was a new company, having just started in business that year. "They were the first business of any size to come to Scituate."[132]

The Old Abbey area is nicely shown in a picture postcard entitled "Coleman Hills, Scituate, Mass." It is postmarked 1921, but is probably from the "divided back" era of 1907–1915 (without a white border). It is a view looking northwest up the Driftway with the Colman Hills in the background. In the foreground are fields of the Welch farm, before it became a golf course in 1919-1920. On the left is the road entering the Welch farmhouse (now the Scituate Country Club clubhouse). In the middle distance is Kent Street leading to the right, beyond which must be Old Abbey Field. Beyond that is what appears to be a fence or stone wall that wraps around the field and continues along the Driftway. This appears to enclose what must have been the Abbey Pasture. That area is steep and has no visible trees. Its rise toward the northwest is similar to the topography of the site today, minus some depressions due probably to mining operations.[133]

The fence or stone wall shown in the postcard could be the "wall" mentioned in the 1914 deed to the Boston Sand and Gravel Company.

A 1919 plan shows a stone wall on the north boundary of Old Abbey Field, and along parts of Kent Street. When the land was a pasture, a fence or stone wall would have been necessary to keep animals grazing in the pasture from eating crops in the field. Today, there is no fence or stone wall, only a few rocks about where the fence or stone wall would have been.[134]

In 1927, William Waterman sold the two-acre Old Abbey Field to the Boston Sand and Gravel Company, along with his eight-acre parcel with his farmhouse, then at 141 Driftway.[135] This was within two months after his daughter married the oldest son of the company's superintendent, and a year before William's death.

"Coleman Hills, Scituate, Mass." postcard, showing car at entrance to Welch farm (later Scituate Country Club), and Old Abbey Field (left of center, just above car), early 1900s. The pointy rock is still there. Author's collection.

The Boston Sand and Gravel Company acquired significant amounts of land on and around the Colman Hills, starting in 1914, which they mined extensively for its sand and gravel. On the land were houses, such as the Nathaniel Turner farmhouse, and the old Colman Heights Hotel, abandoned since the turn of the century. The company let schoolboys use the hotel for basketball in 1916. In 1918, vandals burned down the abandoned hotel in the evening of July 9.[136]

By 1928, according to town tax records, the company owned more than 460 acres, an astounding amount. Because of purchases from William Waterman, this included "Old Abby Field" and the land that had been the Abbey Pasture.[137] On town assessor's maps from 1928, the Abbey Pasture became part of a larger 31-acre parcel, adjacent to the 2.16-acre Old Abbey Field parcel.[138]

The company had a railroad track on its property to carry sand and gravel. The tracks could be moved. At times, they led from a spur of the main railroad line at Greenbush, running along the Driftway's northern side to the company's North River yard. Mostly, the tracks were used to carry sand to the conveyor belt over the Driftway to the company's barges.[139]

Postcards of that era show huge slanted conveyor belts sending sand and gravel from the hills, across the Driftway, over to loading areas on the First Herring Brook. There, barges were filled and then made their way out to the North River, Massachusetts Bay, and eventually Boston.[140]

Boston Sand & Gravel Co.,
Scituate, Mass.

"Boston Sand & Gravel Co., Scituate, Mass.," postcard, c. 1920 (pub. Martha G. Seaverns). Conveyor belt moved sand over the Driftway (at the house) to ships. Author's collection.

From 1922 to 1931, the company removed 6,148,000 tons of sand and gravel, an average of 2,000 tons per day.[141] It was quite an industrial production.

Mining sand and gravel had supplanted farming crops.

The company's mining operations continued from 1914 until 1963. The sand and gravel was removed by barges from wharves at North River tributaries, and later by trucks and trains. By 1963, the company had removed more than 14 million tons of sand and gravel.[142]

Then, on July 18, 1963, the company's buildings caught fire, in a huge conflagration. That caused the end of the company's operations there. The remains of its old wharves are still visible at the boat launching area off the Driftway.[143]

Posts remain from old Boston Sand and Gravel wharves. Photo by Lyle Nyberg, June 2017.

Later Activity

In the late 1960s, the town developed a road through the Boston Sand and Gravel Company property. It was a kind of shortcut or bypass between Kent Street and the Driftway. It made a smoothly curved main road connecting Greenbush and Scituate Harbor. The road curved in deference to the ancient Colman Hills, even though mining had greatly reduced them. With the bypass, motorists no longer needed to make a sharp turn at the right-angle intersection of the Driftway and Kent Street (or old Kent Street), or to meander down Stockbridge Road. In 1969, the town accepted the new road as a public road, called New Kent Street.[144]

In 1975, the town acquired much property from the Boston Sand and Gravel Company by eminent domain. This included a parcel called Parcel 3, which included the Old Abbey site. It contained seven acres: two acres of the Abbey Field, and five acres of the eight-acre parcel once known as Abbey Pasture or Old Abbey Pasture. The town acquired the other three of the original eight acres, likely land on and/or north of New Kent Street on what is today part of the Widow's Walk golf course.[145]

The town operated a landfill on or near the Boston Sand and Gravel Company property before acquiring it. Access was by a road that ran between Stockbridge Road and the Driftway. By 1974, the town was considering establishing a solid waste transfer facility, and this eventually went in at the west end of the former sand and gravel operation, with access off the Driftway. The facility stands about where the old Colman Heights Hotel was, except the area is now much lower than its original 150 feet. Abandoned paths and roadways on the old Boston Sand and Gravel property, including what later became New Kent Street, were the site of teenage vandalism and romantic dates in cars ("parking"). The town later established the Widow's Walk golf course covering much of the sand and gravel property.[146]

In 1993, the town meeting approved transfer of Parcel 3 (including the Old Abbey site) to the Scituate Housing Authority.[147] The transfer occurred in 1995.[148] In the same year, the Authority made plans to create a park there to be "known as Abbey Park in the first step toward plans for affordable housing construction."[149] The plans took awhile for action.

In 2007, the Scituate Housing Authority received Community Preservation Act funding for site testing and analysis of the seven-acre Parcel 3, as part of an Affordable Housing Initiative.[150] The Authority then pursued a project known as "New Abbey Park" for a multi-family development involving 20 affordable rental units at this location. They changed the project from rental to homeownership "due to existing concentrations of rental housing near this location."[151] This project did not go forward at the time.

In 2013, the Scituate Housing Authority developed conceptual plans for up to 30 housing units of affordable senior housing at the Old Abbey site.[152] In 2014, they sought public input for the project.[153]

Also in 2014, some Third Cliff residents applied for Community Preservation Act funding for a competing project called "Cedar Hollow" at this location. (The application had no mention of "Old Abbey.") The project would have involved designing trails, adding scenic or historical markers, and preserving the working field for farming in perpetuity. The application described detriments of the Housing Authority's plan to develop housing on the property.[154]

The application described the following kinds of wildlife that could be protected:

> Red Tailed Hawk nesting area, Foxes & Coyote dens, Woodchucks, Cardinals, Yellow Finches, Robins, Doves, Turkey vulture, Turkeys, Owl, Baltimore Oriole, Blue Jays, Toads, Deer, Squirrels, Chipmunks, etc.[155]

The application noted that area residents had cleared from the site invasive vines that would have destroyed the trees. The application proposed markers including "another historic sign about Farmer Alfred Gomes [of Pitcock Farm] who farmed that land until he was about 95." The application requested funding of $450,000 to purchase the land from the Scituate Housing Authority.[156]

The Community Preservation Committee did not approve the application. The Scituate Housing Authority's 2013-2014 project of affordable housing at the site also did not go forward at the time.

According to the 2015 Scituate Housing Production Plan, the Old Abbey site:

> has long been zoned for the development of affordable multi-family housing and has been confirmed suitable for development of up to 30 housing units based on updated predevelopment engineering work.[157]

In 2017, the town proposed the Old Abbey site as site three of four possible sites for a senior center.[158] The town's consultant gave a presentation on all four possible sites. The presentation included two options, A and B, for development of the center on the Old Abbey site.[159] Scituate selectmen voted unanimously for a different site, next to the former Gates Intermediate School.[160] The project there was approved, and the town opened the new senior center in early 2021.[161]

The Old Abbey Field was still being farmed in 2021.[162] This must be the place pictured in a newspaper photo from 2012 captioned "Farmers tend a field of beans off the Driftway in Scituate."[163]

The field is considered a "farmland of statewide importance" as defined and mapped by the USDA's Natural Resources Conservation Service. This is farmland that does not meet the criteria for prime or unique farmland but meets specific state criteria for soil and environmental characteristics favorable for the production of food, feed, fiber, forage, and oilseed crops.[164]

The Old Abbey Field may be one of the last parcels in town that have been continuously farmed since the 1600s.

Farming at Old Abbey Field. Photo by Lyle Nyberg, June 2018.

Welch Farm

Let us turn back to a time when farming was highly important in Scituate. Recall that Ruth Turner, the widow of James Turner (1778–1835), in early 1836 sold the farm and farmhouse to Michael Welch. Welch (1803–1892) continued the James Turner farm.[165]

Michael Welch started with buildings valued at $350, and 22 livestock, plus the following lands, according to the 1836 Valuation List:

62 acres	Fields
7 acres	F. [Fresh?] Meadow
5 acres	S. [Salt?] Meadow
14 acres	Pasture
19 acres	Unimp. [Unimproved][166]
[107 acres	Total]

Michael Welch moved with his family into the farmhouse on Third Cliff. This was still called the James Turner farm in deeds by Michael Welch's son in 1901.[167] By that time, though, the original 40 acres or so of the James Turner farm had grown to 158 acres.[168] It appears part of this increase was by purchasing the ancient James Cole farm, in addition to James Turner's part of the ancient Humphrey Turner farm.[169] Through the Turner farm and later purchases, Michael Welch must have owned much of Third Cliff, and he continued to farm it.

Welch family house on Third Cliff. From Duncan Bates Todd, *The Fourteenth Lot.*

The farmhouse itself was long thought to have been built about 1779. It is shown on an 1879 map as being owned by "M. Welsh" with a note "House 100 yrs. old." Indeed, a house there had already appeared on an 1831 map.[170] However, genealogical notes on file in the Scituate Historical Society tell a somewhat different story:

> James Turner built the original house on the so called Welch farm, where he died 24 Jan. 1835 age 57. A few years after his death, his widow Ruth [Stockbridge] sold this east portion of the ancient Humphrey Turner farm, including the present Rivermoor estates to Michael Welch from Chelsea, who had been the Steward of the Chelsea Marine Hospital under Dr. [Edmond, stricken through] Parker, and who married Sally Brown, dau. Jonathan & Sarah (Mann) who had been a nurse in the hospital. They came to Scituate, and lived for a short time in the original part of the house of E. P. Joseph on Cross St. where their son E. [Edmond, stricken through] Parker Welch was

> born 5 Nov. 1833. Michael Welch bought the James Turner farm in 1836, where his daughters Sarah Ellen & Susan Augusta were born.[171]

James Turner (1778–1835) thus would have been too young to build the house in 1779, so it seems he built it in the early 1800s. The value of his buildings remained the same on the town's tax valuation lists at $350 in 1821, 1825, and 1831. This was the same amount listed for Michael Welch in 1836. Before 1821, the available tax records only show each owner's total value of real property and total value of personal property, and they do not break out a value for buildings. These records show that the house was built by 1821.[172]

The Turner-Welch house may have been built by 1804. A deed that year granted James Turner passage along what evidently is the lane from Nathaniel Turner's house on the Driftway to what became the Welch farmhouse.[173]

Michael Welch's original last name was Welsh rather than Welch.[174] He was born in 1803 in Killarney, County Kerry, Ireland. He left Ireland as a boy and came to Canada, then America. He was employed for four years at the United States Marine Hospital in Chelsea, Massachusetts, a hospital for sick and disabled seamen. Some reports say he was the hospital's chief steward, evidently responsible to assist the surgeon in minor surgical procedures, dispense medicines, supervise attendants, and other administrative tasks. He settled in South Scituate (which later became Norwell) about 1830 and bought a small farm there. He married Scituate native Sarah Brown in 1831. According to family lore (and the genealogical note quoted above), he had been the chief steward at the Chelsea Marine Hospital, and she had been the chief nurse there. They had three children born in Scituate: E. [Edmond] Parker (1833), Sarah (1836), and Susan (1840).[175]

The genealogical note reported that Michael Welch served at the Chelsea Marine Hospital under Dr. Edmond Parker.[176] However, the only Dr. Parker there at the time was Dr. Willard Parker (1800–1884), who served as intern there from 1827–1829. He was the son of a farmer and later became "one of the most eminent surgeons of his day."[177] It is likely he was the inspiration for the name of the Welches' son E. Parker Welch, born in 1833.[178]

Hon. Charles Turner, Jr. (1760–1839), sometime member of Congress, was appointed Steward of the US Marine Hospital in Chelsea in 1824, and he held that position for 14 years.[179] During that time, Michael and Sarah Welch worked at the hospital and got married. Charles just happened to have a residence in Scituate and was a descendant of Humphrey Turner, who began the farm that Michael Welch bought.[180] So, it is conceivable that Charles Turner was a matchmaker for the Welches in marriage, and then in property.[181]

We discuss Michael and Sarah Welch's family and descendants later in detail.

Welch farm, early 1900s. Courtesy of Scituate Historical Society.

The Welch farm was in a beautiful location next to the North River, as described in Deane's 1831 history of Scituate:

> … there is a wide expanse of marsh, anciently called the "New Harbour marshes." The scenery here is on a sublime scale, when viewed from Colman's hills, or from the fourth cliff. The broad marshes are surrounded by a distant theatre of hills, and the River expands and embraces many islands in its bosom. Here it approaches the sea, as if to burst through the beach, but turns almost at right angles to the East, and runs parallel with the sea shore, for nearly three miles before it finds its outlet, leaving a beach next the sea of twenty rods width, composed chiefly of round and polished pebbles, excepting only the fourth cliff, a half mile in length, which comprises many acres of excellent arable land.[182]

The Welch farm and its surroundings are shown in a photo from the early 1900s in chapter 11, in the section on Henry Welch's farm.

Third Cliff, like Fourth Cliff, was arable, and remained mostly farmland. However, a few families built houses there, closer to the ocean than the Welch farmhouse. And those houses were not for farmers. They were for fishermen, and another kind of farmer — "farmers under the sea" of Irish moss.

3

IRISH MOSSERS

Third Cliff was home to fishermen who worked Scituate's waters. When fishing was at a low ebb in the mid-1800s, a new industry arose. Scituate became a national center for gathering seaweed known as Irish moss. Most sources say Irish mossing was founded by two Irishmen who lived in Scituate: Daniel Ward and Miles O'Brien. The industry would last in Scituate until 1997. For a more extensive discussion, see Barbara Murphy's excellent book, *Irish Mossers and Scituate Harbour Village*.[183]

For the purposes of this book, we explore the important role Third Cliff played in the mossing industry. But first, a look at Daniel Ward's house — the first on Third Cliff — and his background.

Irish immigrants Daniel Ward (1809–1881) and his partner Miles O'Brien (c. 1797–1850) moved from Boston to Scituate with their families in 1847. While little is known about O'Brien, records show that Ward was born in County Derry, in the north, at the opposite end of Ireland from Michael Welch's birthplace. He came to America in 1831. After moving to Scituate in their fishing schooner, Ward and O'Brien "were very successful fishermen. For a year both families made their home in the Ephraim Young house on Highland Street, occupied later by the Misses Lewis."[184]

They built a double house on Michael Welch's land at the northern end of Third Cliff by 1850. Ward paid taxes on the property in 1849, but it was not until December 1850 that he obtained a deed from Welch. Ward paid him $23.52, according to the deed. This was for the land under the western side of the house, with the property line going "through the centre of the dwelling house owned by the late Miles O. Brian [sic] and said Daniel Ward." O'Brien never had a recorded deed for his side of the lot, and title probably remained in Michael Welch's name. O'Brien died in July 1850, just before the 1850 census was taken, leaving his daughter Roxanna and a niece living in the double house. His wife had previously died.[185]

The double house was on what is now Dickens Row. Dickens Row overlooks Peggotty Beach, which curves like a moon's crescent from Third Cliff north to Second Cliff. It is a lovely beach. But where did it get its unusual name?

Peggotty is the name of a character in a popular Charles Dickens novel, *David Copperfield*, published in 1850. The double house also got Dickensian names. One side was called Bleak House. The other side on the east was called East side (descriptive), and perhaps East End (Dickensian). It is no wonder there is a road called Dickens Row. Indeed, a cottage on Dickens Row was named Trotwood, another character in *David Copperfield*.[186]

Peggotty Beach must have received its name soon after the 1850 Dickens novel. The name shows up in a published travel guide by 1873,[187] and two paintings by Frank Henry Shapleigh from 1878 and 1879 included Peggotty (or Peggoty) Beach in their titles.[188]Some writers said Francesca Lunt, a local girl, named the beach.[189] However, this is unlikely as she was not born until 1869, and her family did not move to Scituate until about 1877.[190]

Ward's house has been called the first dwelling built on Third Cliff.[191] Of course, the historical Turner farmhouse purchased by the Welch family was older, but it was inland from the cliff itself.

In late 1859, Ward sold his house and property on Third Cliff to Michael Welch's son E. Parker Welch. The price was $300. The property, including both sides of the double house, remained in the Welch family for decades. E. Parker Welch's son George Welch owned the property as late as 1916.[192]

The Ward-O'Brien house lasted for more than a century. In 1985, the house was demolished and replaced by the house now at 6 Dickens Row. The new house appears to occupy the same 54' by 28' footprint as the original house, except for the addition of decks.[193]

The location of Daniel Ward's house enabled him to see and take advantage of the many shipwrecks off Third Cliff and neighboring Peggotty Beach. Some were packet ships, medium sized ships designed to carry freight and passengers on a regular, scheduled service. One particularly important one was the London packet ship *Forest Queen*, which wrecked near Third Cliff in 1853. It was said, "the cargo was very valuable, and of great variety, from gold watches to pig iron and steel. … Vast quantities of ale, wine, gin, and liquors were thrown up on the beach and sampled on the spot."[194]

Daniel Ward salvaged the wreck and used the profits and items from the ship, including a staircase, to build a new house on First Cliff in 1854. This was called the "Big House." That gives him the distinction of having the first house on Third Cliff and the first house on First Cliff. The house on First Cliff held the first Catholic religious services, before a Catholic church was established in Scituate.[195]

Daniel Ward and his wife Charlotte had seven children. Their sons built houses nearby. The sons and sons-in-law were all mariners, fishermen, and/or mossers. The descendants were numerous. Daniel Ward's "Big House" on First Cliff still stands, at 6 Roberts Drive.[196]

Daniel Ward was well-positioned to understand and exploit the potential of Irish moss. His home county in Ireland was adjacent to County Donegal, apparently the home of Irish moss harvesting since at least the 1400s. Ward may have been one of the first to realize that Scituate had the same kind of moss. A year after Ward arrived in 1847, Scituate began "farming under the sea" according to an 1879 news item.[197]

Ward's mossing endeavors gave rise to an industry that attracted many to Scituate. Irish moss was gathered in other communities along Boston's South Shore, Cape Cod, and Block Island (Rhode Island). However, it was Scituate that acquired a reputation as the American capital of Irish moss.[198]

Left: drawing of Chondrus crispus (Irish moss) by Ernst Haeckel in *Kunstformen der Natur (1904)*.

Irish moss is a variety of red seaweed, different from kelp. The scientific or Latin name for Irish moss is *chondrus crispus*, and the Irish name is "carraigín" meaning "little rock." Its extract, carrageenan, is commonly thought to have been used as a food additive in Ireland since the 1400s. It may have been used in China as early as 600 B.C. and in Ireland as early as 400 A.D. It is still used as a food additive.[199]

To harvest Irish moss, mossers used small rakes with long handles to pull moss into dories (a type of boat). After harvesting, they spread the Irish moss on the beach to bleach and dry it. That process could take two weeks. In case of rain, it had to be gathered in and covered because rain would dissolve it. After bleaching, it was processed to make a gelatinous substance (carrageenan or carrageen) that was used in sizing cloth. It was, and still is, used in making beer, and as a thickener in toothpaste, cosmetics, medicine, and food including chocolate pudding and ice cream.[200]

Irish moss was offered as a "health giving dessert" by drugstores, including G. S. Cheney's in the North End of Boston.[201]

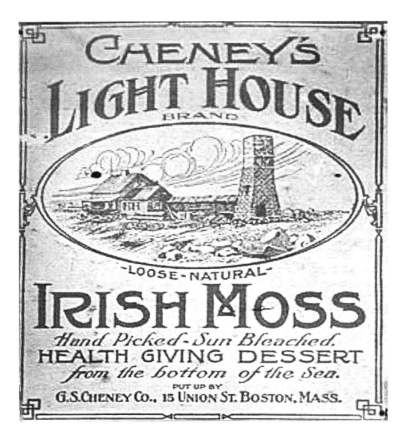

Ad for Cheney's Light House Irish Moss, probably late
1800s. The lighthouse is clearly the Scituate Light.
Courtesy of *Smithsonian Magazine.*

Daniel Ward may not deserve all the credit for starting the mossing industry. Starting in 1884, a federal government agency published an enormous study of American fisheries. It dated the Irish mossing industry to 1835, when Dr. J. V. C. Smith, a Boston doctor, told others that the plentiful moss on the shores around Boston was the same as that being imported at a high price. Turning to Scituate, the study said, "Mr. Augustus Cole, of Scituate, was the first person to pay much attention to it at this place. Starting in 1853, he and his son, Charles A. Cole, have followed the business to the present time." The study was based on information from Charles Cole. It did not mention Daniel Ward's earlier mossing or earlier accounts crediting Ward for starting the mossing industry.[202]

The study described Scituate as the New England headquarters for Irish mossing, with fisheries for cod, mackerel, and other species being "carried on to a small extent." It concluded that, as of 1879, "The number of persons employed on the vessels was 39 [fishermen], and on shore or in boat fisheries [lobstermen, mossers], 333; making a total of 372, of which number 335 were Irish, and the rest Americans."[203]

In the 1970s, when Irish mossing was in full swing in Scituate, one source listed these requirements to be a "Seamosser"''

1. Like to get sopping wet.
2. Like to get up at 4 A. M.
3. Like to be sore all over
4. Like Crabs, fish & eels in your clothes & boots
5. Enjoy long rows.
6. Like to smell seamoss
7. Doesn't get seasick
8. Doesn't mind Blisters
9. Doesn't mind waiting for Lucien to unload ..
10. Like Competition with other seamossers
11. Like to work for nothing some times[204]

Daniel Ward and other mossers of Irish descent began the rise of Scituate as an Irish enclave. According to the 2010 US census, Scituate was the most Irish town in America. It had the highest percentage, almost 50%, of persons of Irish descent of any town in the country.[205]

Third Cliff, where many Irish fishermen and mossers originally lived, has had its share of Irish surnames among homeowners. For example, in the 1930s, almost half the owners on Gilson Road had Irish surnames. That percentage dropped in recent years to about 18%, compared with 30% in Rivermoor.[206]

Ireland is not the only influence on Third Cliff. Residents have come from a diversity of countries, in addition to the early Native Americans, English and later Irish. Several residents were Mayflower descendants. Some were born or lived in Argentina, Chile, China, Cuba, France, Germany, Japan, Rumania, Thailand, Tunisia, Uganda, and Uruguay, among other countries.[207]

4

EARLY HOUSES

Early Houses [to 1879]

In addition to Daniel Ward's house, other early houses on Third Cliff included 20 Town Way (near Daniel Ward's house), built in 1854 and since replaced. Five other houses are still standing: the Captain Frederick Stanley House, 14 Bassin Lane (1826 or 1873); the James Quinn-Martin Welch House, 122 Gilson Road (c. 1858/1870); the Martin or John Curran House, 137 Gilson Road (1857–1866); the Stephen Joyce House, 138 Gilson Road (c. 1874); and the Nee Cottage, 34 Driftway (1872). At least four original owners or occupants of these houses were mossers: James Quinn, John Curran, Martin Curran (owner of the Stephen Joyce house) and Festus Nee. Three more old houses still stand on Bassin Lane (3, 6, and 9), all built in 1900, according to town records. The house at 15 Bassin Lane, also built in 1900, was replaced in 2020.[208]

Capt. Fred Stanley, who lived at what is now 14 Bassin Lane, was the keeper of the Fourth Cliff United States Life Saving Station. He was instrumental in rescuing the crew of eight on the three-masted schooner *Minnie Rowan*, which was stranded off First Cliff for 24 hours in 1894. In addition, he led the rescue of the crew of the schooner *Helena*, which crashed on the rocks of Fourth Cliff in a snowstorm in 1909. In 1915, Stanley retired at age 73 after heading the Fourth Cliff station since 1880.[209]

Stanley was a notable figure in town. His son William, it is believed, operated the Stanley House (Hotel Stanley) in the village of Scituate Harbor about 1900. The former Sea Street bridge from Marshfield to Humarock was renamed for Capt. Fred Stanley in 1998.[210]

Historical maps reflect the spread of these early houses on Third Cliff, and some show names of their occupants. An 1831 map shows no houses near the ocean.[211] An 1857 map shows two houses at the north end of the cliff (marked "M. Hoar" and "J. Butterly"). It also shows four houses clustered near the ocean, three north of the Driftway and one south of it ("T. Kneel," "P. Rogan," "D. Ward," and "M. Welch" — probably Michael Welch).[212] Most of these names (Hoar, Butterly, Ward, Rogan/Regan, and perhaps Kneel/O'Neil) were names of mossers.[213]

As on the 1857 map, an 1871 map shows four houses, without names, at the end of the

Driftway where it met the ocean and curved south.[214] Even more houses appear on an 1879 map, discussed below.

First Cliff has received the most attention for mossing. The founder of the mossing industry, Daniel Ward, and his family lived there for many years. (He previously lived on Third Cliff.) In addition, the book about Irish mossers by Barbara Murphy, a descendant of Ward, focuses on First Cliff. The book lists mossers named in the census for 1870, a high-water time for mossing.[215]

However, Third Cliff deserves more attention regarding mossers. It was an ideal home for them, since they harvested Irish moss from the ocean there and could spread it out to dry on beaches at both ends of the cliff. Compare the mossers listed for 1870 with names of house owners on an old map like the one from 1879. Based on this, more mossers lived on Third Cliff (about 20) than on First Cliff (about 7 to 14).[216]

Houses on the 1879 Map

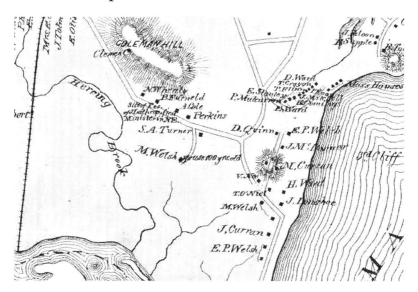

1879 Atlas of Plymouth County by Geo. H. Walker & Co.,
page 33, detail of Third Cliff. State Library of Massachusetts.

The 1879 map has some additional interesting features relating to Third Cliff.

In a business listing, of 28 persons in Scituate, only two were summer residents, and only one person ran a summer boarding house.[217] Scituate had not yet become a summer vacation mecca. But Third Cliff had an increasing number of houses, especially for Irish mossers.

At the north end of Peggotty Beach, the 1879 map lists "D. Ward" (probably Daniel Ward, founder of the Irish mossing industry) with others, next to a series of about a dozen huts labeled "Moss Houses."

The map also shows the origins of what would become Gilson Road that runs along the spine of Third Cliff. At the cliff's north end, the map shows a dead-end road leading northeast off Kent Street opposite Highland Street (now Greenfield Lane). This was probably the road the town approved in April 1877. A June 1877 Boston newspaper reported, "Hyland street has been extended to the north end of the 'third cliff' at Scituate Harbor." This dead-end road later became the north part of Gilson Road. South of it on the 1879 map was a private road (so mentioned in an 1882 deed), running north off of the Driftway. The two roads were eventually connected, making the road continuous. Later it was called County Road or County Highway, and eventually Gilson Road, named for an early settler.[218]

The 1879 map shows 14 houses on the main part of Third Cliff, along what became the south end of Gilson Road. Houses on that road were marked (north to south) with the names D. Quinn, E. P. Welsh (probably E. Parker Welch), J. McDonner, M. Curran (more than one house), H. Ward, J. Donahoe, V. Nee, and T. O'Niel. Houses further south, on the Driftway and on its turn to the south, were marked M. Welsh (probably Michael Welch, two houses), J. Curran, E. P. Welsh (probably E. Parker Welch, two houses). Again, many were names of mossers, and many were Irish.[219]

The connection between Ireland and Massachusetts runs much deeper than mossing. The two places were together as part of the same continent long ago. Just ask a paleogeographer![220]

One of the Third Cliff cottages housed a future Medal of Honor winner. As a child in 1880, George H. Nee lived in the cottage of V. Nee (probably Festus Nee) and would go on to win the prestigious medal for his bravery in the Spanish-American War in 1898. In the early 1920s, he secured a Civil War cannon that was placed in front of the G. A. R. Hall in Scituate. He and his wife lived in Boston and summered on Third Cliff.[221]

The J. Curran house shown on the 1879 map was built by 1863, when E. Parker Welch deeded the land to John Curran; it was later sold to John Flaherty and appears on the 1903 map discussed below, on Water Street (Driftway) as it turned south.[222] Also on the 1879 map, the M. [Martin] Curran house to the east evidently became 137 Gilson Road. Martin's brother John Curran made it his homestead, according to later deeds, and raised 8 to 12 children there. John's son Charles P. Curran had an ownership interest in the property up to 1951, marking almost a century of ownership within the same family.[223]

The 1879 map also shows the increase of Welch family houses or structures on Third Cliff. This reflected the Welch family's rising influence.

The Welch Family Grows on Third Cliff, 1858–1867

We return to the Welch family farm. In 1858, the Welches' son E. Parker Welch married Scituate native Mary L. [Lincoln] Collier. They had six children: Charles P. [Parker] (1858), George F. [Francis] (1859), William H. [Henry] (1862), twin girls Mary Emerson and Minnie L. (1865), and Sarah Edith (1867).[224]

George, who would go on to bring the family greater renown, was born in Scituate near the harbor, in the historic Benjamin Turner house, later known as Bayside or the Meeting House Inn. Soon afterward, in 1861, E. Parker Welch and his growing family moved in with his parents at the family farmhouse on Third Cliff.[225]

Michael Welch and his son E. Parker Welch owned much farmland on Third Cliff, and they acquired more. The *1850 Valuation List* shows Michael owned buildings valued at $645. In addition, he owned the following:

19 acres	Field
36 acres	Pasture house lots
15 acres	" 3d Cliff
[70 acres	Subtotal]
12 acres	Salt Marsh

By 1859, Michael had buildings valued at $1,000 and a new house valued at $150, plus:

20 acres	Field
48 acres	Pasture
13 acres	Pasture
[81 acres	Subtotal]
25 acres	Salt Marsh

In addition, in 1859, E. Parker Welch had:

5 ½ acres	Field
20 acres	Pasture
3 acres	Pasture
[28 ½ acres	Subtotal]
2 ½ acres	Salt Marsh

The fields were for growing crops. The pastures were for cows, horses, or perhaps sheep. The salt marshes were a source of hay to feed the animals. In 1873, Michael Welch owned four horses, two cows, two oxen, two hogs, two yearlings, two 2-year-olds, and a hen house. The horses were probably used for farm work and for transportation (including carriages). Cows were used for farm work and for milk. Much later, a neighbor said the cows there were a source of fresh milk.[226]

5

RISE OF WELCH FAMILY AND WELCH COMPANY

The Welch family grew beyond farming, and their influence expanded well beyond their homestead on Third Cliff. They built several houses on Third Cliff and rented them out, the start of a large future real estate domain. E. Parker Welch and his son George started the Welch Company that supplied lumber and everything needed for building and furnishing a house. It became Scituate's most prominent and enduring business.

E. Parker Welch. *Biographical Review* (1897), p. 399.

The Welch Family Expands on Third Cliff

E. Parker Welch expanded housing on Third Cliff beyond the family's farmhouse. On the 1879 map, the two adjacent "E. P. Welsh" houses at the southern end of Third Cliff must have been those owned by E. Parker. These property holdings represented a reach beyond that of his father Michael.

At first, in 1869 and 1870, E. Parker Welch owned "½ house" (and a "New Barn" and various lots), according to town tax records. Starting in 1871, this grew to "2 Houses," and the 1879 map shows two adjacent houses for E. P. Welch, along with a third one farther north. Later tax records listed "2 Cliff Houses" from at least 1882 until 1896, when they were valued at $875 for both. In 1897, they appeared as "Cliff House 'Bijou'" and "Cliff House 'Parker,'" valued at $500 and $1,000, respectively. Presumably, the higher values reflected improvements to the two cliff houses in the intervening years.[227]

Bijou and Parker were rented out for the summers by 1900. For example, Bijou was rented in 1891 to Mr. Harry C. Snell of Milford. The houses would become centerpieces of the Rivermoor development by E. Parker Welch's son George. Given the 1871 dates, they were by far the earliest houses built in what would become Rivermoor. In addition, they represented a business model for summer rentals.[228]

According to the 1880 US census, Michael Welch (age 76) lived at the farmhouse on Third Cliff. With him was his wife Sarah (82), along with their daughter Sarah (43), milliner; their son E. Parker (46), farmer; and E. Parker's wife Mary (47). Also living there were Mary and E. Parker's children — Charles (22), farmer; George (21), lumber dealer; William (18), farmer; Emma Mary (14); Minnie (14); and Sarah Edith (13) — along with three boarders who were farm laborers.[229]

As a boy, George helped his grandfather Michael sell the vegetables, potatoes, apples, and other produce from the family farm. There is no indication he had more than a high school education. In 1882, George married Hattie [Harriet] Marshall Brown (1857–1943) of Scituate, his second cousin. They had two daughters, Marion and Edith. George and his family later moved to a house in the village of Scituate Harbor, at 28 Otis Place. The house dated to 1740.[230] That was even older than the Welch family farmhouse.

George's brother William H. [Henry] Welch stayed on at the farm and was a market gardener there as late as 1918.[231]

The Welches were Methodists. Michael Welch and E. Parker Welch were stewards of the Methodist church in Scituate, and George Welch and his family played leading roles in that church.[232]

The Welch Company Rises

George Welch was a young, industrious entrepreneur. At the age of 20, along with his father, he established the Welch Company on Front Street in Scituate Harbor in 1879. As early as 1865, E. Parker Welch had acquired property on Front Street, some of which backed up to the harbor and contained wharves, and these would be used in the new business.[233]

At the time, Scituate had become a backwater. The town's commercial fishing industry had collapsed by 1854. Scituate's shipbuilding activities ended by 1864 at the harbor and by 1871 at the North River. Scituate's shoemaking enterprises were outstripped by those in other towns such as Rockland. In the latter decades of the 1800s, Scituate's economy was in the doldrums, and its population numbers were flat.[234]

Things had not changed much since an 1854 report that portrayed the dismal scene in the harbor:

> … The trade of Scituate is now confined to two or three small vessels, which make a trip weekly to Boston, and a very few schooners employed in the lumber trade; besides these, and the occasional visit of a fishing vessel, nothing is left of a fleet which, not thirty years since, numbered some seventy sail, and all which were owned at this place.
>
> It is believed that much can be done to restore this business, and at the same time make the harbor available to large vessels in times of great necessity; and it is more particularly to effect the latter purpose that the petitioners pray for its improvement. Those with whom it originated — and the great majority of those have no local interest — are chiefly from abroad, merchants in Boston and elsewhere, insurance companies, the Boston pilots, &c., &c.[235]

In 1888, the harbor was still quiet. That year, only 13 vessels arrived in Scituate, according to the Plymouth-based collector of customs, compared to 114 in Plymouth itself. Eight of the Scituate vessels carried some 350,000 feet of lumber, impressive for a small town, although dwarfed by the 2,700,000 feet that entered Plymouth's harbor.[236]

The Welch Company must have intended to improve this situation. It started in 1879 as a lumber and coal company with wharves in the harbor for receiving shipments of lumber. Two- and three-masted schooners delivered lumber to the Welch Company wharves. They came from as far away as Nova Scotia and South Carolina. The company supplied lumber and coal to its customers.[237]

An early 1900s postcard shows a schooner with lumber at Welch Co. wharves. It appears stuck in mud at low tide. Postcard for English Gift Shop & Tea Room, Hatherly Road. Courtesy of Sue Logan. On file, Scituate Historical Society.

In 1891, E. Parker Welch retired and his son George assumed full charge.[238] With George in charge, the company built buildings at Scituate Harbor. This included the main store building on Front Street that has been identified with the Welch Company for more than a century. This building seems to be the "Store Building" valued at a hefty $4,000 that first appeared in 1898 tax records.[239]

The success of this young company was so important to the town, but its buildings next to the harbor were at risk of fire and floods. One historian reported this scene:

> About where the woodworking mill now stands [now the site of the Mill Wharf restaurant] there was a large shed housing cement, unslacked [unslaked] lime and plaster. Along comes the big storm of 1893, burying the town in snow and the sea running wild got into the lime shed, boiling up the lime and setting fire to the building and spreading the stock piles of lumber from one end of the harbor to the other. However, this misfortune was taken with the stolidness of our Pioneer folks, and approximately about 1900 the store which is now the main building was built and the Welch Company expanded to a real country general store.[240]

Welch Company main building, early 1900s. Note telephone poles, and sign for
Glenwood Ranges. Russell Fish papers, courtesy of Sue Logan.
On file, Scituate Historical Society.

The Portland Gale of 1898 created more risks to the buildings, including the main general store built earlier that year. When fires broke out, the town historically hired people for fighting (or "watching") fires. The town report for 1898 records about $30 paid to 10 people for four smaller fires, and a whopping $326 to 32 people for the "fire at Geo. F. Welch's" company. This was under the general heading of "Expense Caused by the Great Storm of November 27, 1898." In addition, the town paid George F. Welch $50.36 for lumber and $29.15 for tools involved in fighting the storm. Such expense would have made sense in order to protect the company's brand new main store, as well as its many other nearby buildings between Front Street and the harbor. Evidently they survived the storm and fires, and the company began to thrive.[241]

Lumber arrived at the Welch Company in several modes. Schooners delivered lumber to the wharves until about 1925. The schooners would have had a tricky time maneuvering through the harbor, with its many marshy areas, mud, and islands. A 1919 plan updated in 1923 (below) shows islands in the harbor next to the Welch wharves. Lumber also came by rail. The 1903 map shows a Welch store house on a siding at the train station on First Parish Road. And by 1915, the Welch Company was using trucks.[242]

Over time, the Welch Company expanded to supply hardware, furniture, carpets, and stoves — everything for the home. The Welch Company's main building on Front Street became a three-story department store. There were additional buildings, a shipyard, a lumber wharf and other wharves, and a lumber mill.[243] This was at a time when lumber, moldings and millwork, hardware, and furniture were sold separately by individual companies. The Welch Company brought these all together in one store. This was long before the rise of home improvement stores offering all these items.

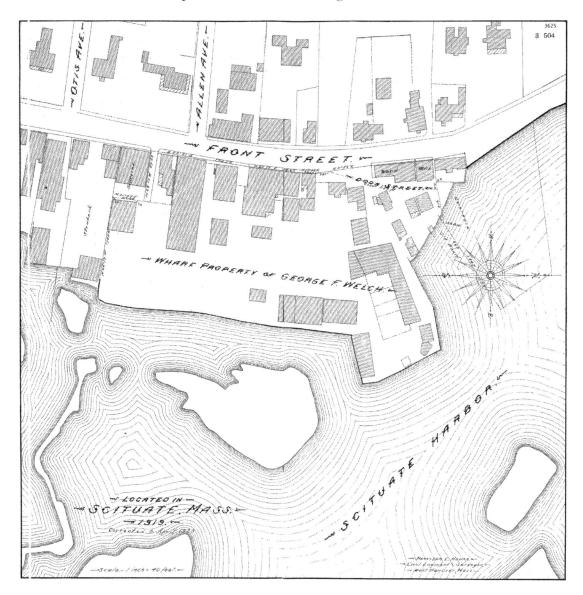

Plan of wharf property of George F. Welch, by
Harrison L. House, 1919, updated 1923.

Welch Co. card with Christmas decorations and photos of old buildings, undated. Sign for Harrison's Town and Country Ready Mixed Paints (sold in late 1800s). Russell Fish papers, courtesy of Sue Logan.
On file, Scituate Historical Society.

The Welch Company prospered under George's leadership, and this helped lift the Scituate economy out of its doldrums. Welch incorporated the company in 1914 and brought in additional management. Later, Russell Fish led the company. It added a gift shop and restaurant. For many, many decades, it was the biggest business in town. A 1941 newspaper article about the company said, "The town's biggest business is directed by Russell L. Fish, 35, who claims his firm can build, furnish and heat a home."[244]

The company, in altered form, still exists in Scituate on Front Street, now offering gifts and items for the home.[245]

Welches About Town

The Welches undertook important roles in the town's governance. Starting about 1897, George obtained various town appointments related to his work at the Welch Company: Measurer of Wood and Bark; Weigher of Hay, Coal, Grain, Moss; Surveyor of Lumber; and Public Weigher.[246] His father E. Parker had once held some of those positions and in his retirement was elected Selectman (along with other positions) about 1906, serving in that capacity for a number of years before his death in 1917.[247]

Meanwhile, in 1888, George Welch's sister Mary married an up-and-coming Harvard graduate and Boston lawyer named George G. Walbach. Walbach was raised in the home of his grandfather, a Boston lawyer, and summered in Scituate. He graduated from Harvard in 1873, Harvard Law School in 1879, and was admitted to practice law in 1880.[248]

Walbach had invested in much property on First Cliff starting in late 1886. This included a house at 179 Edward Foster Road (demolished in 2016). Walbach also had a grand Georgian Colonial house built at 30 Circuit Avenue, at the center of First Cliff. It had panoramic views of the ocean and Scituate Harbor, and it still exists. That was where the married couple lived. During their time there, two cannon balls were discovered on the property that may have come from British warships during the War of 1812.[249]

The Welch Company and its main store are the accomplishments for which people most often remember George Welch. However, he is overlooked as a major real estate owner and developer, as was his father. Their stories as developers are told in later chapters, after a discussion of their roles as rescuers.

Welches and the Humane Society of Massachusetts

The Welch family played a large role in rescuing shipwreck survivors along the coast, as volunteers, under the aegis of the Humane Society of the Commonwealth of Massachusetts. The society was established in 1786 to prevent drowning of people and reward lifesavers. (Unlike modern humane societies, it did not deal with humane treatment of animals.)

The Humane Society brought a unique presence to coastal sites such as Third Cliff. At first, it built huts ("houses of refuge") for shipwreck survivors. One of its first three huts, built in 1787, was at "Scituate Beach." Some have reported this to be at the base of Third Cliff, and others, accurately, at Fourth Cliff (Humarock). The hut no longer exists.[250]

The Humane Society later established along the coast a number of lifeboat stations with rescue boats. E. Parker Welch was a keeper of several rescue stations, and was personally involved in rescues reported for 1878 and 1886. He and his son George received awards for their lifesaving efforts from the Humane Society in 1894. E. Parker Welch's son Henry (William H. Welch) also aided in rescues.[251]

The 1878 rescue involved a packet ship, the *William P. Nettleton*, which was stranded at the northern end of Third Cliff. One account (written, years later, by E. Parker Welch's daughter-in-law, Harriet M. Welch) said:

> A volunteer crew of the Humane Society rescued the crew. There was no
> modern gear in use in Scituate at that time, but a line was sent ashore from

the packet and made secure on land, and the crew came ashore on this line. When the captain reached the shore, he said in a low tone to Mr. E. Parker Welch, who received him, "Are you a Mason?" Mr. Welch replied, "No, I'm a Methodist." "Just as good, just as good," said the captain.[252]

In addition to lifeboat (surfboat) stations, the Humane Society established mortar (gun) stations with mortars that shot lines (ropes) out to distressed vessels. The lines allowed crew and passengers to reach shore. Two stations — a surfboat station and a gun station — were established at the base of Third Cliff by January 1886, with E. Parker Welch as keeper. Third Cliff had a station into at least the 1920s.[253]

The work begun by the Humane Society was later supplemented by the US Life-Saving Service (USLS). The USLS built and equipped stations for lifeboats, including some in Scituate, but not on Third Cliff. The USLS was incorporated into the new US Coast Guard in 1915. Some people confuse the organizations, but it was the Humane Society that was present on Third Cliff for 45 years.[254]

Massachusetts Humane Society Captains, June 4, 1912, from *1911–1912 Report of the Humane Society*. In back row, E. Parker Welch is 5th from left, and Christopher O'Neil is 7th from left (far right). Courtesy of Elizabeth Nilsson of the Humane Society.

In 1917, Humane Society volunteers rescued the captain and all six crewmembers of the three-masted schooner *Henry Withington* when it floundered and then wrecked off Third Cliff. The *Boston Globe*, in a front-page story, called it "a thrilling and picturesque rescue this afternoon, watched by hundreds on shore." Volunteer Thomas J. Flynn, who lived on

Third Cliff, had been working at the Welch hardware store in town when he heard the Humane Society guns go off. He asked what was going on, and was told, "Why you damn fool, there's a vessel ashore right at your front door." Flynn hustled back to Third Cliff, and with other lifesavers shot lines to the vessel so the crew could crawl hand over hand to land. Flynn helped the rescued crew into the cottage next door to his. Interviewed later at his cottage, Flynn said, "Their captain, Devereaux by name, had my room upstairs in this house." Volunteers Michael Welch, Henry Welch, and Chris O'Neil led the rescue.[255]

O'Neils

Jane and Christopher O'Neil, Sr. Photo courtesy of Ray Zucker.

E. Parker Welch served as keeper of the Third Cliff station (and other stations) from 1885 to 1917, when he was 84 years old. His successor was Christopher O'Neil (1852-1937). O'Neil, a mosser, lived on Gilson Road on Third Cliff with his wife Jane (c. 1852–1935). He had received numerous awards from the Humane Society, including for his rescue efforts with the grounded "leviathan" steamship *Devonian* on Third Cliff in 1906. In his volunteer work for the Humane Society, "Capt O'Neil participated in or directed a number of thrilling rescues, always at hazard to himself and his companions." He served as keeper of the Third Cliff station until 1936, when the Humane Society sold the site, as it discontinued its lifeboat stations. Like E. Parker Welch, Christopher O'Neil was about 84 when his duties ended.[256]

Christopher O'Neil and his wife Jane had a daughter Margaret, who married Walter Haynes of Scituate and Third Cliff, and a son Christopher O'Neil, Jr., also of Third Cliff. Christopher O'Neil, Jr., bought a house over on Second Cliff, at what today would seem to be 38 Peggotty Beach Road, in 1919.[257] He and his wife Mary had five children: Rose, Walter, Fred, George, and Jane, born from about 1919 to 1930.[258]

Walter "Doc" O'Neil became a clam warden and lobsterman in Scituate, and was included in a 1948 *LIFE* magazine article on Mayflower descendants. Like previous O'Neils, both Walter and his brother Fred lived on Gilson Road on Third Cliff.[259] According to Jack Farley, a friend of Walter, the family used to rent out their house on Gilson in the summer, and they would move into a small shanty on Peggotty Beach (probably used for storing Irish moss), where they had "squatters' rights."[260]

At one point, the Christopher O'Neils owned four dogs, according to town registries: Toga (a brown and white hound), Bessie (a black and white setter), Pally (a black and fawn police dog), and Laddie (also a black and fawn police dog). Perhaps Toga was the dog Togo, "Mayor of Scituate," featured in Will Irwin's 1914 magazine article. The article also featured the O'Neils.[261]

O'Neil descendants still live on Gilson Road, marking more than 150 years that the family has been on Third Cliff.[262]

6

SUMMER COTTAGES, COLONIES, AND SUBDIVISIONS

After the Civil War, bathing and beachgoing became popular in America. Scituate joined in the trend, a welcome relief after the loss of its shipbuilding industry and decline of its fishing industry. Early visitors stayed in hotels or boarding houses. Later, cottages for rent or purchase become popular. Still later, in the late 1800s and early 1900s, collections of cottages known as summer colonies appeared. These involved dividing large parcels of farms and other property into smaller house lots, resulting in "subdivisions."

"Peggotty Beach, Third Cliff in Distance, Scituate, Mass.," Tichnor Brothers postcard, early 1900s. Note continuation of beach around Third Cliff. Author's collection.

Scituate as Summer Destination

Gradually, starting in the 1870s, Scituate became more popular for summer visitors. A travel guide of the time called Scituate "a quiet old marine village looking out on the ocean through a wide harbor-mouth," noting its "singular and desolate bluffs." It said, "No district in America yields such quantities of Irish moss as do the shores of Cohasset and Scituate," and it said Peggotty Beach had "good bathing."[263] An 1877 travel guide to American summer resorts called Scituate "a quaint old seaport with a summer hotel and good bathing (on Peggotty Beach)."[264]

Peggotty Beach, between Second Cliff and Third Cliff, was an obvious attraction for summer visitors. In June 1877, a Boston newspaper in its "Watering Place Notes" reported Bostonians arriving at Scituate cottages or staying in hotels like the Mitchell House in Scituate Neck (North Scituate), or the South Shore House in Scituate Harbor. The latter was described as "a cosy, quiet hotel, conveniently near to the cliffs and other places of resort at Scituate Harbor." The newspaper also reported:

> The Americus Club of this city [Boston], composed of well known professional people, actors, artists, &c., will encamp in six large tents on the "second cliff," Scituate harbor, about the 28th. A wooden cook-house is being built and a tall flagstaff erected.
>
> ...
>
> ... The professional members of the Boston Americus Club will study astronomy and other things at their new and splendid camp on the second cliff, Scituate.[265]

In 1878, *Harper's Magazine* reported on the South Shore. It recounted the historical tales of Scituate, mentioning its "Army of Two," how Egypt got its name, the Barker house, the Stockbridge grist mill, the gathering of Irish moss, the Old Oaken Bucket House, and Scituate's four "bastion-like" cliffs. This must have helped Scituate's national popularity.[266]

An 1893 history of the Old Colony Railroad said:

> This fine old shore town is becoming famous as a resort for high-class professional people, several of whom have elegant summer homes here. ...There are fine locations along the shore for summer camping, with good boating, bathing and fishing in the bay.[267]

An 1886 letter by a long-time Scituate resident describes Scituate as a summer destination:

> The village of Scituate Harbor remains much the same as it has for 50 years. ... In these years Scituate Harbor was one of the most important fishing ports on the coast, the fishing interest and the shipbuilding interest, creating and maintaining a lively business. For the last 30 years however, it has been dead except as during the past few years, the coast has been built up with summer residences, and the village hotels, the "South Shore House," and the "Satuit House," are filled with summer boarders, and the few stores with customers.[268]

An 1898 guide book to the South Shore included photos of Scituate, describing Scituate Harbor as:

> a trim little village of permanent residents, and a place much sought after by the summer tourists. This village is noted for its quaintness, its old-time streets and drives, and its fine sea coast; here also we find an abandoned lighthouse.[269]

In addition, the book contained full-page advertisements for The Cliff [hotel] in North Scituate Beach, with spacious piazzas and a public telephone, and the Hotel Stanley in Scituate Harbor. The book noted the town's cliffs, the town's attractiveness as a summer resort, the boats of fishermen, and the gatherers of Irish moss.

Summer residents of the Glades enclave had outings to Peggotty Beach, including one on August 29, 1891. Family photos showed "kelpers," as they called the mossers (although kelp is a different kind of seaweed from Irish moss). The mossers had a four-wheel horse-drawn cart on the beach to collect the Irish moss. Other photos show the "dorries" (dories, a kind of fishing boat) and mossing sheds that the mossers used. One photo shows Third Cliff in the background, faintly.[270]

The Irish mossers were picturesque. They gave Scituate a national distinction. A 1905 *National Geographic* issue featured them in a short article and two photos, showing them gathering and bleaching the moss.[271]

Scituate attracted buyers of summer cottages in the 1880s. The number of nonresidents owning houses nearly doubled in the early 1880s. The northern Scituate coastline was at first more desirable than the southern, and it attracted the wealthy and cultured families of Boston. The cottages in the north had distinctly higher tax valuations than those in the south, according to an analysis of town records and an 1894 directory. That directory was the first comprehensive listing of summer residents. In addition, by 1900, nonresident property owners grew to a remarkable 70% of registered voters, this in a town whose population had remained flat for so many years before.[272]

By 1900, a Boston newspaper described the summer scenes at Scituate shores as follows:

> It has been a pleasant week, fine weather for out-of door sports, bathing and boating at their best, and heartily enjoyed by large numbers.
>
> Picnic parties were also numerous, many of whom spent a day on the sands of the beach, enjoying their dinner from huge well-filled baskets, then rolling about on the sands, gathering sunburned cheeks and freckles to carry home as souvenirs of their visit.

> Dan, the Indian basket maker, and his family, one of the standbys of the beach, arrived this week and camped at the Sand Hills beach.[273]

The railroad helped the rising tide of summer visitors to the South Shore. A later study said:

> By 1900 another result of the railroad was noticeable — the rise in summer visitors. The beaches of the South Shore were becoming resort towns. Old-fashioned boarding houses for weekends or part of the summer were particularly prevalent along Nantasket. Those who could afford it built summer homes. Cottages sprang up throughout Hull and Humarock. Many of the affluent chose the cliffs of Cohasset for their homes but estates could be found throughout the study area.[274]

Another study said, "The railroad avoided the town [Norwell] and there was little of the resort development [in Norwell] that enabled Scituate to survive in the latter portion of the 19th century."[275]

Summer Colonies

Summer resorts at first featured hotels, then cottages, then collections of cottages called summer colonies.

Summer resort hotels flourished in New England through the 1800s and the turn of the century. Railroads promoted them, counting on increased traffic from the vacationers. However, the popularity of summer resort hotels began to decline in the years immediately before World War I. This was largely due to changes in leisure-time patterns and the rise of the automobile, which offered more mobility to summer resorts.[276] There was also a move to "privatization" of leisure space, with an early and notable example in Newport, Rhode Island:

> Newport's tourist boom, which had reached its peak during the 1850s, subsided during the years following the Civil War, resulting in the decline of the local resort hotel business. The major reason for this was the development of the exclusive, upscale "cottage" community accessed by Bellevue and Ocean avenues.[277]

With these changes came a flowering of summer colonies well beyond Newport.

The term "summer colony" described communities at some of America's elite destinations. Railroad promotional publications used the term by at least 1884. Newspapers used the term by at least 1887, usually in society columns describing where wealthy or influential people were spending their summers. Magazines used the term by at least 1898. Books used the term widely from 1900 to 1920, spiking in 1917. The term is still used, although infrequently, and mostly referring to the past.[278]

The word "colony" was apt in basic ways. It implies settlers from the same place who bring their culture to a new land, perhaps unpopulated or lightly populated. One dictionary defines "colony" as "a body of people living in a new territory but retaining ties with the parent state." Summer colonists certainly brought their city culture to remote areas. Surprisingly, many were already neighbors in their hometowns. A good example is the group of Winchester neighbors who summered on Third Cliff, also as neighbors.[279]

Other implications of "colony" are not so apt. "Colony" implies that colonists build their own settlement. Summer colonists, however, had their housing and services ready for them in advance. Moreover, their colony was part of an existing town, where they could take advantage of its places of entertainment and houses of worship. Further, "colony" implies a permanent settlement, so the word had to be qualified by "summer" since these colonists visited temporarily — for the summer, or for part of the summer, or even (as in a hotel) for a few days. And "summer" meant they were going at the most pleasant time. This was very different from the bitter winters, hard work, dangers, and starvation that the first English colonists in Plymouth Colony encountered.[280]

Instead, summer colonists typically left urban areas to escape their heat, bad air, and crowding. They went to more remote summer places for pleasure, to enjoy nature, fresh air, and the company of others of their social class. This fit with another definition of a colony as "a group of individuals or things with common characteristics or interests situated in close association (an artist colony)."[281]

Hot summers in the city were ample reason to get away for a vacation in the early 1900s. Summers were hot in Boston during the late 1800s and early 1900s, although not quite as hot as summers today. Home air conditioning was not introduced until 1926, and then adopted slowly. By 1965, still only 10% of American homes had air conditioning. The seashore and the mountains offered cooler temperatures and cooling breezes.[282]

Beachgoing gradually became more popular in the late 1800s. America's first public beach, in Revere, Massachusetts, opened July 12, 1896.[283]

At first, seashores were for breezes on the beach, or perhaps wading or "bathing" in the water. Not swimming. In an old-time account of New England that included Cape Cod, the word "swim" applied only to a bear, fishes, and eels, not people. To be socially acceptable, beachgoers were fully dressed, as shown in period postcards. After the turn of the century, people wore beach garments. They were voluminous. People waded or took a short dip in the ocean. Children, too, were fully dressed, even toddlers, as shown in a 1912 photo of children at Rivermoor's beach.[284]

Woodworth children at Rivermoor beach, c. 1912. Woodworth family photo
album, courtesy of Woodworth family, copy on file, Scituate Historical Society.

Times were changing, and only a few years later those children were wearing bathing suits
(providing full coverage) at the same beach. Writer James O'Connell and historian John
Stilgoe have described that scene and traced its transition to the beach scene and beach
fashions of later years.[285]

Woodworth children at Rivermoor beach, c. 1914, Third Cliff at left in
background. Woodworth family photo album.

As vacationing by the seashore became more popular, and with some people wanting to spend the whole summer there, the supply of housing had to increase. For towns with resort hotels that filled up, and for towns with limited hotel space like Scituate, an obvious solution was to build summer cottages or houses on available land. Often, this land had been farmland. In the past, single houses were built independently. Now, to develop land for summer residential use, the first step was to hire a surveyor and have a parcel of land subdivided into multiple house lots. The surveyor's plan was then filed with the county registry of deeds.

These subdivisions, or "developments," began appearing in the following Massachusetts coastal resort towns:

- Nahant, 1828 and about 1870,[286]
- Oak Bluffs, Martha's Vineyard, 1866, following the religious camp meeting movement that started there in 1835,[287]
- Falmouth Heights on Cape Cod, 1870, and Falmouth area, 1880s,[288]
- Hingham (Downer Landing, or Downer's Landing, now called Crow Point), 1870,[289]
- Salisbury Beach, 1870s–1880s,[290]
- Hull (Nantasket), 1870s–1880s,[291]
- Hingham (World's End), 1890 (threatened subdivision),[292]
- Revere, late 1800s,[293]
- Cohasset, 1915 or later,[294] and
- Eastham on Cape Cod, about 1923.[295]

In 1901, a *Boston Globe* article about the "watering holes" (not called colonies), to which "sweltering city people" escaped, mentioned many of these communities: Buzzards Bay, White Horse Beach, Chatham, Onset, Marion, Cohasset, Brant Rock and Ocean Bluff in Marshfield.[296]

And yes, the article mentioned North Scituate Beach and Scituate, including Third Cliff cottages.

Scituate's Subdivisions and Developments

Subdivisions appeared in coastal Scituate in the late 1800s, after a few earlier examples in the 1870s at Second Cliff and Mann Hill.

North Scituate Beach was one of the earliest and best-known subdivisions. It was not far down the coast from the exclusive, private Glades Club. An 1891 plan laid out 119 lots there.[297] Already by the 1890s, "many wealthy and influential people from Boston had started to build summer homes at North Scituate Beach."[298]

An 1893 newspaper article described North Scituate Beach:

> The popularity of this beach as a summer resort increases each year as its true worth becomes known. Its scenery is unsurpassed, embracing as it does high, rocky cliffs and rugged shores, with shady groves, the white, sandy beach of smooth pebbles made so by the constant wash and wear of ages. The health-giving air at this beach has become so far famed that the best building lots are fast being bought and fine residences erected for private use.[299]

The prestige of North Scituate Beach was further enhanced when the Cliff House (later called the Cliff Hotel) was constructed in 1898. Despite its name, the hotel was built not on a cliff but on a small bluff overlooking the ocean. On the 1903 map, the "breakwater" or sea wall started at Beach Street (now Gannett Road) and followed the shore north almost to Bailey's Causeway. The Cliff Hotel was at the center of the breakwater.[300]

The development of North Scituate Beach was a success and a likely inspiration to develop other places near the seashore. In 1900, the Scituate Beach Land Association (SBLA) was formed. George F. Welch was one of its early trustees. It focused on developing land around Hatherly Road. It had a plan for lots there, north of the harbor, and it had another plan, south of the harbor on Third Cliff.[301]

Gilson Road

The SBLA laid plans to develop Gilson Road on Third Cliff. In addition to its 1900 subdivision plan around Hatherly Road (Plan 1) for 216 lots, the SBLA had a 1900 subdivision plan (Plan 2) to develop 70 lots it owned on County Way (now Gilson Road) on Third Cliff. On his own, apart from the SBLA, George Welch's earliest real estate sales were of lots on County Way and Town Way on the cliff's north end. Now, the SBLA started selling lots on the large central part of County Way.[302]

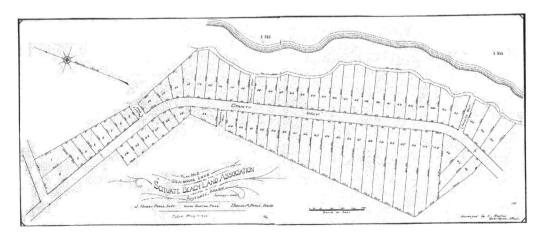

"Plan No. 2, Seashore Lots, Owned by the Scituate Beach Land Association," L. Barton, surveyor, January 1, 1900, PCRD, plan book 1, page 215. North end of Gilson Rd.

The SBLA County Way subdivision of 1900 was perhaps overshadowed by the SBLA's larger development around Hatherly Road. However, it should be considered the first real estate development on Third Cliff.

Joseph Flynn, born about 1857 in Ireland, already had a home on Third Cliff by 1894. In 1901, he bought property from E. Parker Welch with the later address of 72 Gilson Road. Thus, Flynn became an early buyer in the Gilson Road subdivision (Plan No. 2). Unlike other buyers there, he was not a new summer resident from out of town. He was a surfman at the US Life Saving Service station on Fourth Cliff. In 1884, on patrol north from the station, he saw a house on fire at the northern end of Third Cliff. He went to the house and roused the residents, and three of their neighbors lent them a hand to put out the fire. This saved five or six dwellings, according to US Life-Saving Service reports.[303]

The great storm of 1898 separated Third and Fourth Cliffs. This would have had a big impact on Joseph Flynn and Capt. Fred Stanley. They both worked at the US Life Saving Station. No longer was there a road leading from Third Cliff where they lived to Fourth Cliff where they worked. The road was called "the highway leading to the beach or sea" in an 1884 deed. Flynn and Stanley would now have a much longer commute to work on Fourth Cliff. Later, Flynn was listed as a fisherman, mosser, and lobster fisherman. In 1901, when Flynn bought his property on the inside of the northern bend of Gilson Road, he moved into a new house there. A house appears with his name at or near there on the 1903 map. He owned it until his death, with his estate selling it in 1944.[304]

The Gilson Road development lacked infrastructure. It is not clear how good or complete the road was. Town sewer would not arrive until decades later. Town water would not arrive for years. Buyers could be consoled with fresh water, evidently from a spring just behind Joseph Flynn's property, and perhaps from what some deeds called "the falls." Buyers also had the advantage of oceanfront property, with excellent views.[305]

Despite this activity, the 1903 map showed no subdivisions for Third Cliff, not even the Gilson Road subdivision plan of 1900. Families had built only a few more single homes on Third Cliff since those shown on the 1879 map. These homes again catered to mossers rather than summer residents. Only a few families summered on Third Cliff.[306]

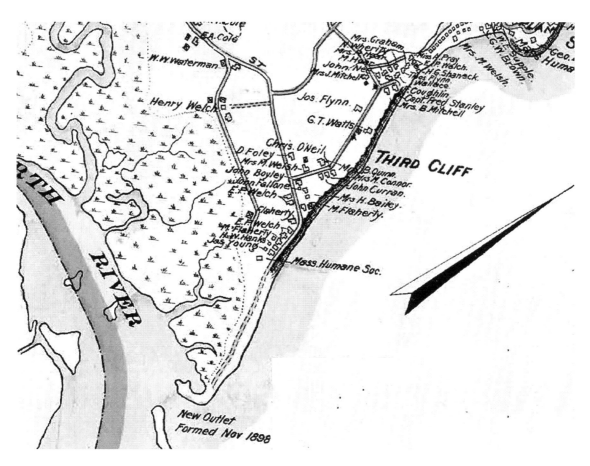

1903 map, detail of Third Cliff, edited. Welch farm is in ovalish area in center, bounded on the right by Water Street (Driftway) running down to the tip of the cliff.
Source: State Library of Massachusetts.

7

RIVERMOOR'S SITE

The site that would become Rivermoor, at the southern end of Third Cliff, was pastoral. Farm animals grazed in pastures. Beachgoers went elsewhere. The site was also historical and dynamic.

Rivermoor's Dynamic Site

George Welch's Rivermoor site held promise and risk. Proximity to the ocean breezes held promise. Nature was a risk. Storms, water, and erosion had battered the site in the past.

The site was the southern end of Third Cliff, a peninsula with the ocean to the east and marshland to the west. To the west and south was the North River, with its new mouth (since the storm of 1898) spilling out into the ocean, as shown on the 1903 map. The land sloped south toward the river's outlet, giving the lots in the subdivision beautiful views.

The site was dynamic. Water was on view on most sides and it had historic impacts on Third Cliff. A storm in 1786 swept into Scituate Harbor, forcing Stetson's tide mill at the far end of the harbor south "across the marshes to the Marshfield shore." The water must have burst through the marshes inland of the cliffs, behind Second Cliff and Third Cliff. Today that area contains marshes, small creeks or trickles of water and parts of the Scituate Country Club. But the historic storm carried Stetson's tide mill even further, all the way across the North River to the Marshfield shore.[307]

The sea was always a concern. Samuel Deane's 1831 history of Scituate, said:

> The cliffs have gradually wasted by the attrition of the tides and storms. Comparing the third cliff with the number of acres of planting land originally laid out, we find that it is reduced nearly one half in two centuries. … The beach between the third and fourth cliff, is composed of sand and pebbles, and resists the attrition of the tides more than the cliffs: yet it is slowly wasting, and the river probably will eventually find its outlet between those cliffs.[308]

An 1833 town report said:

> The action of the sea and frost, upon the steep bank of the [Third] Cliff, causes a portion of it annually to fall off, and the highway [presumably the eastern end of Water Street and the road leading to Fourth Cliff] gradually becomes more narrow and dangerous.[309]

An 1845 book said:

> In some past century these cliffs were long promontories, jutting out into the ocean waves. Storm after storm has beat upon them, and now, more than two thirds of their soil has fallen, and been washed away. Twenty years ago, I remember riding on firm soil, at a safe distance from the then peaceful brink of one of the cliffs, more than an hundred feet beyond the present reach of the fierce waves.[310]

An 1854 report said:

> The whole extent of the coast bears evidence of the great encroachments made by the sea. Records extant show that, at the time of the settlement of the country, two hundred years ago, the four cliffs were much more extensive, and that the wearing away has more than averaged one foot per year.[311]

The sea also encroached the coast up at North Scituate Beach. A 1912 history said:

> When the public road was extended to the beach about 1843, the extension was located as Beach Street [now Gannett Road] now runs, but the road on the cliff was originally considerably further east than it now is. The cliff formerly extended much farther eastward than it does at the present time, and there have been several different roads east of Cliff Road of to-day.

> An interesting item of evidence as to the recession of the cliff is a statement, reported by Mr. John B. Damon, that there was a time when between the old Collier house now standing at the corner of Beach Street and Cliff Road [now Glades Road], where it was originally built, and the sea, fifty-six rows of corn were planted.[312]

Back at Third Cliff, deeds reflected the ocean's encroachment. An 1863 deed for property near Water Street and the ocean reserved "all rights of the Beach on the sea-shore opposite said granted land however the same may hereafter be moved by the inroads of the sea on or over said granted land."[313] Water Street (earlier and later called the Driftway) was really an appropriate name for its Third Cliff properties.

Deeds for property near the shore were careful to disclaim the dangers of the sea. A 1905 deed for property on Third Cliff said, "Only reserving the beach as the land may wash away by the action of the sea."[314]

Much later, a 1931 deed conveyed a lot on Bassin Lane at the northern end of Third Cliff "of which area a portion in the Ocean side has been washed away."[315]

The title of a 1910 *Boston Globe* article was descriptive: "How the Sea Eats Away Third Cliff, Scituate." It said:

> Cottages stood on the bluff where now there is no bluff at all. At a point near where the two rocks are seen in the water on the right of the picture, the cliff stood within the memory of middle-aged men, and a road here ran along it.[316]

The cliffs also eroded internally, due to underground watercourses, seepage, frost, and springs. About the early 1900s, waterfalls flowed from the cliff. Women who lived on the cliff gathered their own laundry and linens, and gathered those of other people for pay. Then they washed them in the waterfalls and spread them out on the rocks below to dry.[317]

Beach Between Third Cliff and Fourth Cliff

The major dynamic event at Third Cliff was the great storm of 1898, the Portland Gale. Its most significant physical impact here was to destroy the narrow beach and road that connected Third Cliff and Fourth Cliff.

In the past, travelers coming up the Pilgrim Trail from Plymouth or other towns would go up to White's Ferry in Marshfield, make the short crossing across the river to Humarock (Fourth Cliff), travel up the narrow Fourth Cliff, and then travel up the road on the narrow shingle pebble beach that connected Fourth Cliff and Third Cliff. This was the beach described in 1831 by historian Samuel Deane, who accurately predicted its demise. This was also the location dismissed by an 1854 Congressional report as not feasible for an outlet of the North River between Third and Fourth Cliffs. In 1889, a geologist described the beach as follows: "between the Third and Fourth Cliffs an excellently developed shingle beach extends nearly one mile, with its crest about fifteen feet above mean tide."[318]

However, Briggs' 1889 book had an ominous warning. This was the beach "where the high tides now often connect the river with the ocean far above its natural mouth."[319]

The beach became more susceptible to ocean erosion as beachgoers removed rocks or stones. The town tried to help, as Deane reported in his 1831 history, by repeatedly forbidding these thefts.[320]

The shingle beach with flat cobblestones and a road allowed for travel between the cliffs. On Third Cliff, at the ocean end of the Driftway, a road turned south to go to Fourth Cliff. It was called "the highway leading to the beach or sea" in an 1884 deed.[321]

One resident said his great-grandparents used to hitch up a horse and buggy, and travel down the Driftway to the ocean and over the road to Fourth Cliff. They went there because they thought the water was warmer in Humarock.[322]

"View of 'fourth Cliff from 'Third Cliff.'' Scituate, Mass. 1892," photograph of connecting beach with road. Courtesy of Jon Bond.

The photo below shows the beach and the road, with a good view of early Third Cliff. There is a small structure at the foot of the cliff, before the road rises, at the center of the photo. It is probably the lifesaving station of the Humane Society of Massachusetts. Above it are houses on the cliff, precursors of the Rivermoor summer colony soon to come.

The storm of 1898 obliterated the shingle beach, destroying the old highway along it next to the water. It created the new mouth of the North River, separating the two cliffs. It tore away parts of Third Cliff facing the ocean.[323]

John Flynn and Bill Flynn watched as the storm hammered the cliff and part of it fell into the ocean, according to a long-time resident who spoke with the men years later.[324]

This was high drama. The storm's action in destroying the barrier beach connecting the cliffs, and creating the new mouth of the North River, would be documented in the 1903 map.[325]

The effect must have been much like that in modern times, described in vivid terms, with aerial photos, in an article about the changes to the Nauset-Monomoy barrier system off Chatham, Massachusetts.[326]

Photograph of beach connecting Third and Fourth Cliffs, and road, before 1898 storm, view from Fourth Cliff. Courtesy of Historical Research Associates.

Barrier beaches are changeable and changing.

The Spit, Beaches, Seawalls

The storm of 1898 left a narrow spit of land at the southern end of Third Cliff, a remnant of the shingle beach. Since then, ocean waves nudged the spit westward up the North River, and inland over the marsh. Some reports say the spit moved 300 feet, but its southern tip may have whipped around as much as 3,000 feet. The tip of the spit curls like Cape Cod, another spit, although much larger.[327]

The ocean and storms kept eroding the cliff.[328] The erosion noted in the 1854 report of more than one foot per year accelerated [329]. A 1924 survey by Henry Litchfield showed the cliff had "narrowed by dropping into the sea 64 feet in 17 years," almost four feet a year, compared to the 1906 Rivermoor plan by Stephen Litchfield.[330] Later, it was estimated that some 300 feet of the cliff was lost to erosion from 1879 to 1984, about three feet a year.[331]

For a while, in the early 1900s, this erosion nourished a fronting beach at the bottom of the cliff. The beach was rather wide, depending on the tides. It appears in a number of postcards of the early 1900s. The beach was like a continuation of Peggotty Beach, and it wrapped all the way around the cliff. Steps led down to it.[332]

"Steps on Third Cliff to the Beach, Scituate, Mass.," postcard, early 1900s (55249 A. S. Burbank, Plymouth, MA [printed in Germany]). Peggotty Beach is in the background. Courtesy of Scituate Historical Society (Twomey/Jacobson collection).

"Third Cliff Showing Second Cliff in Distance, Scituate, Mass.," postcard, early 1900s. Courtesy of Scituate Historical Society (Twomey/Jacobson collection).

Then came seawalls. They hug the shore, unlike breakwaters or jetties, which extend out into the waters. . In 1906, the state legislature directed the board of harbor and land commissioners to build certain seawalls in Scituate. These included "a concrete wall in extension of the present wall near Surfside road," "a concrete wall between first and second cliffs," and "a jetty, sea wall or breakwater at the southerly end of the third cliff." It is not clear whether or when these were built, or even why they were directed. But a breakwater was authorized and seawalls were built on Third Cliff starting as early as 1919.[333]

Seawalls stretched around Third Cliff as far south as about Lincoln Avenue. After the Blizzard of 1978, a revetment was built around most of Third Cliff as well as around First and Second Cliffs. The revetment is a tall seawall with a flat top, built of rocks angled toward the ocean to reduce the impact of waves. This armoring kept Third Cliff relatively well-protected, but contributed to eliminating the fronting beach and moving sand south toward the Spit.[334]

In recent times, storm waters have sometimes affected parts of the Scituate Country Club and adjacent marshes west of Rivermoor. The tides sweep a long way up and down the North River. Along the river, acres of marsh have eroded, but a wide buffer of marsh, along with the revetment, continues to protect the developed portion of Third Cliff.[335]

Rocky Shore

Scituate was long known for its rocky shores. Many ships foundered and wrecked on the rocks, including around Third Cliff. Rocks were always a notable feature, even after Scituate became known for its beaches.

Other beaches in Scituate have long strands of sand. Third Cliff's beaches have sand and many rocks. They appear in early photos and postcards of beachgoers at Third Cliff.

Woman and Woodworth child at Rivermoor
beach, c. 1914. Woodworth family photo album.

Woodworth children and friends on rocks at
Rivermoor beach, houses in background, 1913.
Woodworth family photo album.

ALONG THE ROCKY SHORE, THIRD CLIFF, SCITUATE, MASS. *1920*

"Along The Rocky Shore, Third Cliff, Scituate, Mass.," postcard postmarked 1920, Second
Cliff in far background. Courtesy of Sally Rossi-Ormon.

Despite the rocks, there was and still is room around Third Cliff for beaches. They could
be narrow, wider, or submerged, depending on the tides and the seasons. In the early
1900s, the Rivermoor beach — where the Woodworth children played — was at the
bottom of Collier Road, opposite Lincoln Avenue, next to the house of Harriet Miller.
(The Woodworths and Millers are discussed later.)

Rocks predominate along the shore now. We may deplore them, but they have been a feature for a long time.

At low tide, close to the seawall, large black rocks emerge from the waters. South of the seawall to the Spit is mostly a field of rocks, round and smooth. Sometimes they give way to a ribbon of sandy beach, or large and scattered areas of sand. The rocks form a ridge, but waves have thrown sheets of sand over the ridge and onto the inland marshy area. This natural area, along with the Spit, is large. It mimics the size and shape of the developed portion of Third Cliff.[336]

"Southerly end, Third Cliff, Scituate Harbor, Mass." postcard with view of rocky shore, steep face of Third Cliff, and Rivermoor looking north up Collier Road, with 33 Collier at left, c. 1910–1920 (C. Frye 1202[?]).
Courtesy of Scituate Historical Society (Twomey/Jacobson collection).

Margins, Channels, Ditches, Beaches, Peat

Third Cliff is interesting at its margins, which have been shaped by nature and history and humans. They offer more than just rocks.

Marshlands to the west appear as grassy meadows at low tide, like an extension of the golf course. Or they appear as a large lake when covered by a high tide, especially a king tide.[337]

During a king tide, the North River rises to flood the marshes at Cliff's End.
Photo by Lyle Nyberg, October 19, 2016.

The marshlands, and the shore to the east, have channels or ditches dug into them. They are curious features that appear to be far too straight and regular to be natural.

Some people think workers for the Works Projects Administration dug the marsh channels in the 1930s. The WPA supposedly dug the channels to drain the marshes, to keep mosquitoes from breeding. Actually, they go back much further.

Native Americans may have originally dug the channels to help harvest salt marsh hay, perhaps in canoes. Early settlers also valued the marsh hay, and they dug ditches to mark their property boundaries. The ditches are referred to in deeds from the late 1700s into the 1800s. Later owners dug small side ditches for drainage. These may be what the town voted in 1784, "to ditch the flats." The ditches and channels appear here in art works by Thomas Buford Meteyard in the late 1800s, and in town maps from 1922, long before the WPA projects.[338]

The marsh channels are not unique to Third Cliff, although they are easy to see there. Aerial photos and Google Maps/Satellite Views show such channels in countless other marshy places along the coast, including west of Fourth Cliff, west of Second Cliff (next to Kent Street), and west of Glades Road in North Scituate Beach. The channels also appear in the Back River/Mill River area of Weymouth and Hingham, and in the Great Marsh along the North Shore of Massachusetts.[339]

Example of channels in North River marshes, view from lower Moorland.
Photo by Lyle Nyberg, July 2021.

Somewhat different are the channels and other features on the seashore east of Rivermoor, south of the seawall. At very low tide, you can see them. Then you can also walk halfway to Fourth Cliff without swimming in the North River (which would not be safe), on land that is normally underwater.

At low tide, beaches and sandy areas appear at the seashore. They hint at what the beach looked like 100 years ago when the Woodworth children played there.

The sandy areas that appear at low tide are accompanied at the water's edge by protrusions of peat. The peat is brown, slippery, and on the very firm side of spongy. It is probably compressed remains of old marshes and botanical debris, left from the North River marshes back when they were protected by the shingle beach connecting Third Cliff and Fourth Cliff. The same material appears elsewhere, including at nearby Peggotty Beach.[340]

Beach south of seawall, very low tide, peat at water's edge at far center, rocks behind and to the right, with the Spit, North River, and Fourth Cliff in the distance.
Photo by Lyle Nyberg, June 2021.

At Rivermoor, the peat is carved with long channels. One channel, close to the end of the seawall, was named the "Grand Canyon of Rivermoor" by the local historian. From a distance, the channels look like a series of mini-cliffs, like the seacliffs of Ireland.

Peat formations at base of Third Cliff. Photo by Lyle Nyberg 2016.

Canyon-like peat formation, Rivermoor beach. Photo by Lyle Nyberg 2016.

The ocean may have carved the channels. But some are too precise, straight, and geometric to be other than man-made. They suggest that hunters dug drainage channels around their huts, or created pools of water to attract their waterfowl targets.

Channel, Rivermoor beach. Photo by Lyle Nyberg 2016.

Today, pieces of wooden boards, like jagged teeth, stick straight up near these channels at Rivermoor beach. (See photo at left, by Lyle Nyberg 2016.) Perhaps the boards are remnants of hunters' huts, fishers' huts, mossers' huts, or cottages. The structures sprouted along the shingle beach that once connected Third and Fourth Cliff. Or they could even be remnants of the Humane Society lifeboat station and its house for "Boat & Mortar" as shown on the 1879 map at the point of Third Cliff. The station seems to appear on an old photo of the beach connecting Third and Fourth Cliffs before the storm of 1898. The channels, and the pieces of wooden boards, are vestiges of the shore's past.[341]

Gunners at the Shore

While other beaches attracted bathers, Third Cliff's beaches and marshes attracted hunters, called "gunners." Their prey — shorebirds. These included sandpipers, curlews, and plovers. All are small birds with thin bills and skinny legs. Gunners also went after ducks, geese, and grouse. Shorebirds abounded since the earliest colonial days, particularly at salt marshes, where migratory waterfowl landed during their spring and fall migrations. Hunting, and overhunting, started with the earliest European settlers.[342]

The history continued to the 1830s, when Daniel Webster hunted along Cape Cod Bay. In Webster's hometown of Marshfield, an 1898 book said, "Marshfield shores are very attractive to sportsmen. Sea ducks and shore birds abound." Hunters hunted for sustenance, for sale to metropolitan fowl markets, or for sport.[343]

Gunners could be local, or from elsewhere. The Henderson brothers of Marshfield hunted "yellow legs," ducks, coot, and "peeps" (sandpipers) to sell in the market in the 1890s.[344]

"So. River Gunning Shanty"
Richard Clapp, Everett Clapp, Wm. H. Clapp
(all brothers)

Clapp family hunters with birds they bagged, at South River gunning shanty.
Clapp Family book, page 29, Scituate Town Library.

In 1884, erring gunners not far from Third Cliff drew the wrath of Margaret Cole Bonney's grandfather:

> … my grandfather wrote in his diary that "shore bird hunters staying at Mr. Eaton's hotel had shot holes in his hay-boat." Grandpa owned a landing on the river at the foot of Colman's Hills. He kept the flat-bottomed boat which he used to get salt hay and black hay, tied up to his small pier. One day he discovered his boat had sunk at the mooring and upon retrieving it found many gun shot holes in it. He complained to Mr. Eaton but I do not know who paid for the repairs.[345]

"Gunning Rock" appears on the 1903 map, just off Cedar Point, which then had many summer cottages.[346]

90

By 1915, one Cape Cod old-timer noticed some hunters and said:

> They're about forty years too late for first class sport. Why, when I was a boy, you could go down on the ma'shes and get a back-load of birds in a little while — plover and curlew and snipes and such. Oh, Lord, yes! all you had to do was to get behind a stone wall and shoot 'em.[347]

In the late 1800s, "it was not uncommon for a proficient hunter to kill thirty birds with a shot and bring home a bag of over a hundred shorebirds."[348] A newspaper reported in 1883 on a champion hunter in Scituate:

> Eddie Edson is champion so far this season at Scituate, having killed 41 coots last Tuesday. Twice he has killed the same number, and once 50. He also killed a pair of loons at one shot, which is very seldom done.[349]

Third Cliff was no exception to the interest in hunting. Even when the storm of November 1898 threatened, four gunners near Third and Fourth Cliffs kept hunting instead of seeking shelter. They included two of the Henderson brothers. When the storm hit, all four perished, paying with their lives.[350]

In the early 1900s, public sentiment began to shift towards protecting birds, and this resulted in various game laws to protect songbirds and limit hunting of birds for sale in the market. Sport hunting continued.[351]

By 1904, Third Cliff was "dotted with gunners' huts, and enlivened by the flight of sea fowl overhead," and the gunners' shots could be heard from morning until night.[352] Perhaps it was not much different at Cedar Point, where coot hunting was a favorite pastime in the early 1900s.[353] As a hunters' destination, Third Cliff was like Revere Beach back in the 1830s, or like nearby Brant Rock in Marshfield (brant being a particular kind of shore goose), or like Eastham on Cape Cod in the 1890s and early 1900s, as hunters moved to more remote locations.[354]

The huts appeared in works by an Impressionist artist who lived and worked in Scituate in the late 1800s and early 1900s, Thomas Buford Meteyard. He painted many landscapes of Scituate, the North River, and the Third Cliff marshes. His works' titles sometimes mention "fishers' huts" and "mossers' huts" rather than gunners' huts, but these huts may well have been used for hunting.[355]

Some of the gunners' huts (or gunners' stations or camps) at Third Cliff may later have been turned into cottages, like the tiny "Cedar Camp" that remains at 77 Collier Road.[356]

Cedar Camp and Jack the Wild Man

The history of gunners at Third Cliff lived on. A tiny cottage at 77 Collier, down at the southern point of Third Cliff near the entrance to the Spit, is likely a former gunners' hut. It is one of the earliest cottages in Rivermoor. Its story requires a few detours, including to the neighboring town of Norwell.

Cedar Camp Cottage. Photo by Lyle Nyberg, March 2019.

First, we must throw cold water on a story that some locals tell — that a married man built the cottage next door for his sister because his wife did not get along with her.

The history does not seem to support this scenario. George Welch sold the property to two brothers in 1908. Charles W. Thomas (born 1866) and Alpheus W. Thomas (born 1861) of Norwell were sons of Alpheus Thomas (died 1909) of Norwell. The property did not show up on the tax rolls until 1910, when the cottage — called "Cedar Camp" (not "House") — was valued at $500, along with a stable valued at $100. The Thomas brothers held the property until 1937, when they sold it to Rachel W. Cartland, a librarian. Welch sold the adjacent property at 79 Collier in 1910 to Ernest L. Loring, who held the property until 1942. Loring and Charles Thomas were friends, but no brother-sister connection could be found of Loring and the Thomases (or Rachel Cartland).[357]

The use of the word "camp" for the cottage suggests that it was a hunters' shack or "gunners' camp." The tiny cottage is called "Cedar Camp" on a 1918 map. The cottage was still there as of 2021. To its side is what appears to be a cedar tree. Cedar Camp is the smallest cottage on Third Cliff, having only 532 square feet. It is a rustic, two-room cottage, unlike any other on the cliff. It has an open porch that wraps around the building. The porch roof is supported by posts that look like old tree trunks with their branches cut off.[358]

Thomas family on back porch of Cedar Camp, c. 1928. Courtesy of Phyllis Haskell.

This could be the last hunter's shack remaining from the days when Third Cliff was a mecca for hunters. The Thomas brothers were already familiar with these hunting grounds by the late 1800s. A diary that Alpheus Thomas's wife Maria kept said Alpheus and Charles used to go gunning in the late 1800s at the marsh between Third Cliff and Fourth Cliff.[359]

The granddaughter of Charles W. Thomas thinks that Cedar Camp as a hunting shack is "very plausible due to the fact that all the male members of the family were hunters. Charles went on to be 'C. W. Thomas, Guns & Ammunition' of Accord." Charles, his friend Ernest Loring, and others from the area maintained a hunting "blind" on Accord Pond at the Norwell-Hingham line. In addition, Charles was a decoy "whittler" of some renown and was a friend of Joe Lincoln, the great decoy duck carver.[360]

C. W. Thomas, Guns & Ammunition shop in
Accord, with C. W. Thomas (probable), c. 1920s.
Courtesy of Phyllis Haskell.

Charles W. Thomas's gun shop was on the east side of Washington Street (Rte. 53) at Queen Anne's Corner at the border between Norwell and Hingham. His building appears there on the 1903 map, plate 17. A 1997 history of the area said "Thomas eventually moved his shop to High Street where his son Clem [Clement] Thomas and later his son-in-law, "Red" Haskell ran it until the late 1950s. The building is still there." But now the building is gone, replaced by a building with a liquor store and a drug store.[361]

Cedar Camp remains. It is the last of the hunters' cottages (or gunners' camps) that were moved up from the beach, according to Valerie Vitali, who knew the later owner Rachel Cartland.[362]

Alpheus Thomas was an important name in Norwell. In the late 1800s and early 1900s, Alpheus Thomas (probably the father) was a selectman, town moderator, and assessor. He was an alternate representative for Massachusetts in 1905 at the national encampment of the Grand Army of the Republic. In 1892, he was an incorporator of the Plymouth County

94

Railroad Company, which was authorized to run a line from East Weymouth through Norwell to Brant Rock in Marshfield. (It appears nothing came of this plan.)[363]

Then there was the "Jack the Wild Man" incident.

In 1891, a nearly naked, hairy creature suddenly appeared and frightened residents of Norwell. The newspaper story called Norwell "perhaps the most lonely village in Massachusetts after dark." Alpheus Thomas was the constable who led a team that discovered a large tree trunk in the woods near the Valley Swamp that was the hiding place of "Jack the Wild Man." Then a search party went out, armed with guns, pitchforks, and pistols, but they were unsuccessful in finding him. The next day, a second search party was formed, including several Boston people summering in Scituate, and they carried shotguns. What happened then is told in the bold headlines of the *Boston Globe*'s 5 o'clock extra edition:

> He Wore Pants. Wild Man of Norwell Sighted Today. Driven from the Underbrush by Boston Searchers. He Fled Like a Deer and Escaped. Probably Deacon Clapp's Missing [farm hand] Mike. Frightened Women Still Bar Doors and Windows.[364]

The "Wild Man" incident must have made for great stories by the time Alpheus and Charles Thomas moved to Cedar Camp in Rivermoor.

E. Parker Welch and George Welch as Early Developers

At the turn of the century, George Welch and his father owned quite a few properties in town, including those of the burgeoning Welch Company. Their properties in the town valuation lists took up at least a full page or two, at 50 lines per page. Their properties were notably on Allen Place in Scituate Harbor. These were in addition to the lots being sold on County Way (Gilson Road) by the SBLA, with which the Welches were associated. George Welch was the only Scituate member of the SBLA trustees, serving from 1900 to 1906.[365]

The 1903 map shows the Welches owning property on Water Street on Third Cliff. (Water Street was originally named the Driftway, and its former name was restored in 1915.) Off Water Street, near the coast, a road headed north. It was unnamed on the map but was clearly County Way (now Gilson Road). It connected the southern end of the cliff to the road and houses at the north end of the cliff. It followed the curve of the cliff. At the south end of County Way (Gilson), just north of Water Street, a "Mrs. M. Welsh" (unrelated to George Welch and his father) owned a house, probably the Stephen Joyce house. Water Street (Driftway) continued east, then turned south as it reached the ocean. For a short distance, it had a few houses to the west, with the ocean to the east. It continued as a road or pathway to the southern end of the cliff. The land south of Water Street would soon host the second development on Third Cliff.[366]

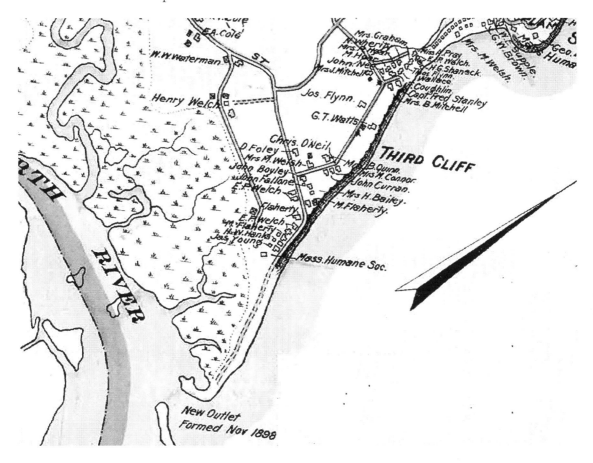

1903 map, detail of Third Cliff, edited. Source: State Library of Massachusetts.

By the early 1900s, E. Parker Welch had moved from the family farm to a house in Scituate Harbor. He distributed large parts of the family farm to his children. In 1901, he conveyed his home farm to his son William H. (Henry) Welch and his daughter Minnie L. Welch, each receiving an undivided one-half interest. This was a parcel of about 40 acres of "field, pasture, meadow and orchard land, with the buildings thereon … known as the James Turner farm." It included the Welch farmhouse. The deed also included unspecified acreage of a number of marshland meadow pastures with various names.[367]

In 1902, E. Parker Welch conveyed to his son George a large amount of the farmland and fields on the southern end of Third Cliff. This was to become the summer colony of Rivermoor. The deed described the tract as "about thirty five (35) acres of field and Pasture land and also about fifty (50) acres of Marsh and Beach land adjoining and near said upland," east of the Home Farm. The tract included two barns. The deed reserved for the Humane Society of Massachusetts the right to use the land where its building stood, rent-free, for five years.[368]

After acquiring this tract on Third Cliff, George arranged for the town to build a new road there in 1905. The road was soon named Collier Road. Collier ran south, to a point east of the old lifesaving station of the Humane Society of Massachusetts, just south of where Michael Avenue would be built.[369]

Until then, George's focus had been on selling lots. By engaging with the town political process and arranging for infrastructure improvements on Third Cliff, Welch demonstrated that he was prepared to be more than a pure land speculator strictly interested in selling vacant lots.[370] Of course, it helped that his father was a town selectman at times during 1906–1917, and that his brother-in-law Ansel F. Servan, was a selectman during 1916–1921.[371]

The landowner or land developer who started a summer colony faced a number of concerns. He needed adequate infrastructure. He needed well-structured arrangements with early renters or lessees. Early buyers would be concerned about who else was allowed to buy in to the summer colony. Perhaps the buyers would create a homeowners association. Both landowners and summer colonists would need to deal with the permanent residents of the town. All these concerns were noted in a 1908 magazine article.[372]

By 1906, Scituate's tax valuation list revealed major changes in land ownership. More than a third of all property owners were now nonresidents.[373] And with the change in ownership came a change in land use. Now, nonresident owners played a major role, particularly wealthy men like Thomas Lawson and John W. Graham, who had influence in town decisions and had their own ideas about land use. Now, land was bought for uses other than farming, with an emphasis on summer vacations by the shore.

It did not take long for George Welch to add Third Cliff to the subdivision frenzy. In 1906, he laid out a subdivision plan named Rivermoor.[374]

Third Cliff would no longer house only a small group of mossers.

8

RIVERMOOR'S BEGINNING

When George Welch acquired this dynamic site from his father in 1902, it was mostly pasture, with few houses. Within four years George was ready to turn this into a summer colony with 222 numbered lots, houses, roads, marketing materials, and services.

1906 Rivermoor Plan

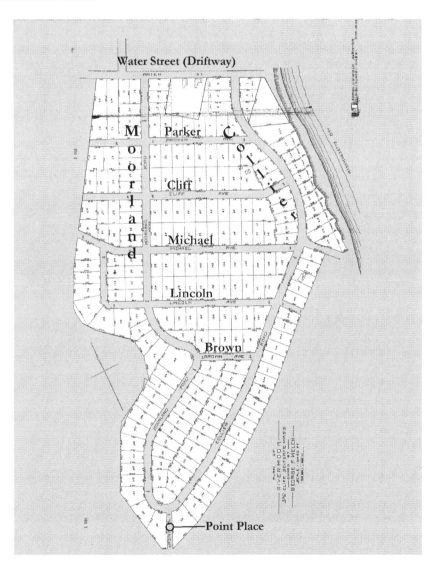

1906 Rivermoor plan, rotated so north is almost up, shaded to emphasize roads, with road names enlarged.

Most lots on Welch's 1906 plan were 50 feet by 100 feet, 5,000 square feet, a bit more than a tenth of an acre. All lots were south of Water Street (the Driftway). The plan showed roads and few structures.

As Water Street reached the ocean, the road turned south. A good part of the road had crumbled into the ocean with the 1898 storm. The 1903 map still showed about five houses west of and facing that road. The 1906 plan, however, had Water Street just ending at the ocean. The five houses would now be facing the edge of the cliff, if they were still there at all. Their back entrances would be facing the new Collier Road that snaked south parallel to the ocean.[375]

The 1906 plan laid out a logical series of roads. Collier Road had already been approved by the town and built in 1905 much of the way south from Water Street. The 1906 plan extended Collier further south, where it looped sharply around to meet Moorland Road that headed north to Water Street. Avenues ran between Collier and Moorland, roughly east-west, parallel to Water Street. They were (north to south) Parker, Cliff, Michael, Lincoln, and Brown. Two avenues, Michael and Lincoln, had extensions beyond Collier leading east toward the ocean. A similar road (Point Pl.) led toward the cliff's southern point. Off Moorland, Michael also extended west toward the Welch farm. This connected with a road or pathway to the Welch farmhouse shown on other maps. Also off Moorland was a short extension of Lincoln that turned to join the extension of Michael.[376]

Thus did George impose a grid on Third Cliff meadowland.

The 1906 plan disclosed some interesting information. In fine detail, some boundary lines had connected ovals, indicating stone walls. They included walls (1) along Water Street and the north side of the Michael Avenue extension, remnants of which still exist, (2) along many of the lots next to the marsh, and (3) from Water Street (Driftway) most of the way to the marsh, as mentioned in the 1902 deed ("Water Street near the Nee Cottage with a stone wall to the Marsh"). In addition, the plan showed a large boulder at the southern end of Moorland Road (between lots 168 and 169), which still exists and stands about 6 feet tall and 12 feet wide.[377]

Further, the plan had what appeared to be a stream (perhaps underground) running to the ocean. It looked like a smudged line running between Water Street and Parker Avenue.

The plan showed few existing structures. One was at lot 209 on the ocean side of Collier Road, between Michael and Lincoln Avenues. It was probably the Humane Society of Massachusetts lifeboat station. It ran parallel to the ocean, almost filling the 50-foot frontage of the lot. In 1910, Welch conveyed the adjacent lot (208) to the Society, and the station was moved or established there.[378]

Of the other structures on the 1906 plan, two houses on Water Street were on lots without numbers, so not really part of Rivermoor. They were evidently owned by George Welch's brother. Two more structures were on lot 42, the smaller one straddling lots 43 (the later 10 Cliff Avenue), 42, 39, and 38. Both structures had Xs, probably to indicate they were barns or stables (as on the 1903 map's key). At least one of these structures was almost certainly removed soon after George sold lot 43 in 1911.[379]

The plan omitted additional structures, including the two barns mentioned in the 1902 deed, one of which was likely the structure shown with an "X" through it on the 1903 map. It did not show a house on what became lot 41 (18 Collier) that George had just sold in 1905. It did not show gunners' huts, which might have been on or just outside the numbered lots. It did not even show Bijou (lot 222) and Parker (lot 39), two Welch houses built in 1871 that lasted into the early decades of the 1900s.[380]

For George, the Rivermoor plan was a clean slate to write on.

Rivermoor Names

George Welch named most Rivermoor roads after family members: his father Parker (who now got a street as well as a house named for him), his grandfather Michael, his grandmother's (and wife's) maiden name Brown, his mother's maiden name Collier, and his mother's family name Lincoln. All were natives of Scituate, except for Michael, who was born in Ireland. The other roads reflected natural features: Moorland, Cliff and Point Place.

Another development in Scituate, Shore Acres, had already named its roads after early Pilgrim settlers and a Native American they met: Samoset, Priscilla, Alden, Brewster, Winslow, Bradford, Carver, Standish.[381]

When it came time to select a name for his summer colony, one of its main streets, and house names, Welch turned to British names.

The word "moor" in "Rivermoor" and "Moorland" was apt, with all the site's meadows. The word describes a place with open, rolling landscapes, low-growing vegetation, and few human inhabitants. The word evokes a place primeval and unspoiled. In addition, the word added a touch of British class that may have been attractive to Welch's customers.[382]

Surely his customers would be reminded of the romantic and mysterious scenes in Emily Brontë's *Wuthering Heights* (1847), and Arthur Conan Doyle's *The Hound of the Baskervilles* (1902), featuring detective Sherlock Holmes and the moors of Dartmoor in Devon. Charles Dickens used "moor" in his enormously popular 1843 novella *A Christmas Carol*. There was even a "Moor's cottage" on Third Cliff as early as 1901.[383]

While his customers might not have been aware of it, the Rivermoor names had historical resonance. Scituate was founded by English people from Kent, where moors are not uncommon.[384]

Americans at this time were borrowing British words to name places and streets. In Boston, for example, the Back Bay was filled in starting in the mid-1800s, creating new streets. The cross streets were named for English lords, starting with Arlington and Berkeley in 1859. The streets, with these aristocratic and anglophilic names, were in alphabetical order. Boston's Back Bay became a fashionable district in Boston.[385]

Boston landmaking then turned to what is now called the Fens. This was a filthy, marshy area with sewer outlets. Famed landscape architect Frederick Law Olmsted designed a plan in 1879 to improve this area, with the plan originally named Back Bay Park. Work lasted from 1880 to 1894. In 1888, Olmsted got the name changed to the Back Bay Fens. The road encircling it was named The Fenway. The word "fen" means a low wetland fed by groundwater or surface water. It is Old English in origin, and similar words appeared in the West Frisian, Dutch, Norwegian, and German languages. Longfellow used the word in an 1842 poem.[386]

The Fenway would supply the name for baseball's Fenway Park, established in 1912.

If Bostonians could adopt an Old English word for the Fens, then George Welch could adopt the British word moor for Rivermoor and Moorland. His target customers would come from the Boston area. For example, Dr. Frederick S. Burns of 237 Marlborough Street in Boston's Back Bay stayed at "The Marshes" in Rivermoor in 1915. That was an appropriate name for a house that was near the North River marshes, marshes that could be considered a fen.[387]

Prospective customers for Rivermoor lots would have taken advantage of the cultural institutions that had recently sprouted in the Fenway area, including the Massachusetts Historical Society (1899), Symphony Hall (1900), Horticultural Hall (1900), Simmons College (1904), and the Museum of Fine Arts (1909).[388]

Starting in the early 1900s, people were also moving out from the Back Bay and other parts of Boston to the city's suburbs. No new houses were built in the Back Bay after 1917. The electric trolley and automobiles made it possible to live outside the city. Automobiles made it possible to spend summers farther outside the city, in places like Rivermoor.[389]

George Welch and his customers did not likely delve into the origins and other meanings of "moor." If so, they might have been repelled. A moor is defined as an extensive area of waste ground, from the Old English word for morass or swamp, open and uncultivated, a marshy kind of low wetland perhaps less fertile than a marsh; its origins include words for mud.[390]

A moor is often described as bleak, wild or desolate. As one writer said:

> In fact, heath and moor are different names for a similar terrain, namely, a desolate, sandy-soiled place, where dead vegetation piles up and accumulates into peat. The difference between a heath and a moor is the greater amount of rainfall on the moor, which, unlike the heath, is characteristically boggy and marshy. Hardy remarks both on the similarity of and transition from the one to the other in a passage from *The Return of the Native* where "they wandered onward till they reached the nether end of the margin of the heath, where it became marshy, and merged in moorland."[391]

These darker meanings of "moor" were probably not on most people's minds, and they do not fit the description of Rivermoor in the 1902 deed, which calls this "field and Pasture land." Instead of a mysterious and threatening Baskerville hound roaming the moor, there would have been cows and maybe horses, later replaced by automobiles.

George picked a good marketing name for Rivermoor. Most people regarded a moor as a romantic, interesting place with upscale connotations. In any event, the houses to be built were on Rivermoor's meadowy slopes, above the marshy areas.

The houses, too, would be given British names, like "Mereside." This was a feature of other summer colonies in Massachusetts shore towns in the early 1900s.[392]

Marketing and Building Rivermoor

With his attractive development name and street names, George Welch quickly began building residences in Rivermoor. In a Boston newspaper advertisement of June 20, 1906, he offered a new house for rent in Rivermoor for the summer:

TO LET AT RIVERMOOR, THIRD CLIFF
SCITUATE, MASS

> New 11-room house, including 8 bedrooms and bath. Piazza all round house, balcony piazza on second story. Plastered throughout with 5-foot stained green dado finish. Furnished with new mission furniture. Beaver Dam water and stable. A marvelous sea, river and inland view, not to be equaled on this shore. Best of bathing, boating and fishing close by. Two smaller cottages same place, completely furnished. Fine location on high land. Address for further particulars, George F. Welch, Scituate, Mass.[393]

The advertisement highlights a most characteristic feature of a "Welch colonial" of that era — the wraparound covered porch. This ran along the front and either one or both sides of the house on the first story. The second story porch ran along either the center one-third or the entire front of the house's main structure. This was either open or screened in, and was considered a sleeping porch. On the first story, a porch was called a "piazza," a term used in describing summer resort hotels on the New England seacoast from at least the early nineteenth century. Porches allowed residents to enjoy the cooling ocean breezes in the summer.[394]

COTTAGES AND POST OFFICE, THIRD CLIFF, SCITUATE, MASS.

"Cottages and Post Office, Third Cliff, Scituate, Mass.," postcard, c. 1910–1912. Upper Collier Road. Courtesy of Scituate Historical Society (Twomey/Jacobson Collection.

A typical Welch colonial in Rivermoor was roughly square, about 22 or 26 feet by 30 feet, plus the wraparound porches. It was two stories high plus an attic. A brick chimney occupied the center. Many had a hip roof (one that slopes up from all four sides) and dormer windows. The roof's slope became gentler in the last few feet from the edge: a flared roofline. Other Welch colonials had gable or gambrel roofs, also with dormers. In many respects, a typical Welch colonial was a junior version of the Welch family's farmhouse on Third Cliff. The farmhouse was bigger, about 36 feet by 38 feet, plus porches. Architectural historians call the Rivermoor house style "Colonial Revival," a style that flourished from 1880 to 1955.[395]

The house at 10 Cliff was a rare departure from the Colonial Revival style. It was built 1912–1914 for the Eames family. An early photo of the house (copied in chapter 11) shows a low-slung cottage, with a full-width front porch having a deeply overhanging roof and four columns. It has a hipped dormer window over the front door, and a chimney on the right. Its style is Bungalow, associated with the Arts and Crafts movement of the late 1800s and early 1900s. The cottage appears in the center of an old picture postcard entitled "Rivermoor Colony, Third Cliff, Scituate, Mass." which looks north from the rocky beach. A copy is in chapter 11.[396]

Welch colonials often had a distinctive window on the first floor with diamond panes. Examples still exist at 18 Michael (1909) and 74 Collier (1912).[397]

Typical diamond pane window, 18
Michael. Photo by Lyle Nyberg 2017.

Welch colonial foundations were made of concrete block, sometimes covered (parged) with cement on the exterior. Concrete blocks came into widespread use during the first decade of the 1900s.[398]

Turning to interior features of the Welch colonial, a picture window offered views south to the water, and the kitchen was in the cool part of the house, in back. In many houses, the staircase down from the second floor split at an intermediate landing, turning one way toward the kitchen, and the opposite way toward the living room.[399]

Split staircase, 18 Michael. Photo by Lyle Nyberg 2017.

The green dado finish mentioned in the ad was probably beadboard, wood paneling that features narrow planks with grooves or beading. It was used as wainscoting on walls, with beads running up about five or six feet. Above it might be horizontal beadboard. Beadboard was common in cottage interiors. The alternative, plaster, could crack if left unheated in the winter. Remaining examples of Welch colonials have beadboard walls and ceilings. The beadboard was likely milled by the Welch Company at its lumber mill. The green stain, too, was an item carried by the Welch Company. So was mission-style furniture, popular at the time. George Welch provided such furniture in his cottages.[400]

If the summer resident lacked for anything, he or she could probably buy it at the Welch Company store. George apparently looked for as much synergy as possible between his store, his lumber business, and his housing business.

Living room with beadboard behind (and above) mission-
style armchair, Indian Knoll (36 Moorland), 1912.
Woodworth family photo album.

Water and Services for Rivermoor

As promised in the newspaper ad, George supplied his summer homes with bottled water from Beaver Dam. The springs at Beaver Dam were a little over two miles north-northwest of Third Cliff. This was the home of the Beaver Dam Spring Bottling Works, as shown on the 1903 map, next to the railroad tracks on the north side of Willow Street (now Beaver Dam Road). This was near the start of Satuit Brook, which wound its way south into Scituate Harbor.[401]

The Beaver Dam Spring bottling company operated from the late 1800s until at least 1913. During its heyday, the company produced bottled soda (soft drinks, tonic, or carbonated beverages) in addition to supplying drinking water. A bottle from the company was discovered not long ago. It has a colorful paper label featuring an illustration of a beaver. The boldest part of the label says "Vanilla," suggesting the company provided a range of soda flavors.[402]

Left: Beaver Dam Spring Bottling Company bottle. Photo by Lyle Nyberg, April 2018.

Water pipes from a private water company reached Third Cliff by 1904, although it is not clear if the water reached all the way to Rivermoor at that time. As the *Boston Globe* reported in 1904,

> The Scituate water company have decided to extend their pipe line from the Third cliff along the beach to the southerly end of the Second cliff, where there are quite a number of summer cottages, the pipe for this extension having arrived.[403]

Turning to other possible services at the time of George Welch's 1906 ad for Rivermoor, the Town of Scituate had no paved roads or public lights. But Front Street in Scituate Harbor, in 1908, had the Welch Company stores, and a cobbler, bakery, Chinese laundry, tailor store, pool hall, bowling alley, meat store, Joseph Ward's fish market, barber, drug store, the Satuit Tavern, and an undertaker.[404] Right there in town, one could amuse oneself, dress well, eat well, and drink well. What more could one ask for?

The Welch Company offered many other things in this 1910 ad:

> If you want to buy a house-lot or a house; if you want to build a Summer home or to furnish a new house all ready built; if you need a new dory with which to go fishing, or a farm machinery for the better cultivation of farm and garden; or if may be you are planning to give the home buildings a coat of paint. For all these things, as well as the necessity of fuel — where can you go better than to W E L C H' S at the Harbor.[405]

An early 1900s photo of the Welch Company buildings on Front Street, copied in chapter 5, showed this sign on the front of one of the buildings, in large capital letters:

> Doors Windows Frames & Blinds
> Gutters Mouldings Stair Posts Rails & Balusters
> All Kinds of Turned Piazza Work[406]

Scituate became known as an attractive place for the summer. A 1910 Boston newspaper article said:

> Midsummer is at hand, and fully the usual number of summer visitors are quartered here; while the whole South shore is well patronized this season, this quaint old town has a very large and representative summer colony.
>
> Railroad facilities the present season are by far the best the Scituates have ever enjoyed; there are hourly trains between here and the "Hub" from early morning till midnight.
>
> Many transients are now spending their vacations here; bathing parties are all the rage, and hundreds enjoy their daily plunge in the breakers.[407]

"Rivermoor, Scituate, Mass.," (Chas. W. Frye, Pub.). The Parker is just left of center (two-deck, open porches), Bijou is the wide hip-roofed house with two men standing in front, and behind it (just to its right) is the Marguerite with hip roof and dormers. Author's collection.

The postcard above, postmarked 1910, shows the houses Parker, Bijou, and Marguerite, at the upper end of Collier Road, the "high land" noted in Welch's 1906 ad.

Another early 1900s photo view including (left to right) Lamprey (16 Collier), Parker (1871, 14 Collier, two-story open porch), 2 Collier, P.O., Marguerite (1908, 3 Driftway, dormer windows), and Bijou (1871, wide building with hip roof). Courtesy of John L. Sullivan.

By 1910, Rivermoor was a growing success. A newspaper reported that as early as March, "George F. Welch has let [rented] about all of his cottages on the Third cliff so early and has contracted for the building of several new cottages."[408]

9

THIRD CLIFF IN THE EARLY 1900S

Third Cliff was still secluded in the early 1900s. It had enough open space to accommodate a whole cavalry squadron of the state militia that camped overnight on August 20, 1907, on George Welch's land. It was called "Camp Welch," and the *Boston Globe* reported:

> The arrival of the troops at the cliff was characterized by a display of patriotism, seldom seen in a little community, almost every cottage displaying the national emblem, several large flags being strung across the streets.
>
> …
>
> The camp is beautifully located on the bluff overlooking the Atlantic, and is on land owned by George F. Welch of Scituate, who kindly loans its use to Maj. Perrins and his command, and he was here to welcome the squadron and was instrumental in getting all the cottagers to decorate.[409]

It seems Third Cliff had hosted the militia as early as 1900.[410]

Third Cliff had permanent residents as well. As of 1910, about 80 people lived in some 20 houses scattered around the cliff. Most were mossers and lobster fishermen. A few women were laundresses working from home: Catherine Hoar, Mary Graham, Bridget Mitchell, and Sarah Mitchell. They washed the laundry perhaps using the waterfalls at the cliff.[411]

Mary E. (Quinn) Welch lived at 138 Gilson Road. She was married to John Welch, a fisherman who was not related to George Welch. Some say he built a house for the family on Peggotty Beach but it proved to be too vulnerable to the ocean and storms, so they moved up on Gilson Road. On November 18, 1896, John Welch went out in his boat to go lobstering. A boom on the mast knocked him into the water. Unfortunately, he could not swim, and he drowned. Mary Welch, about age 37, was left to take care of at least six children (some sources say nine).[412]

Mary Welch owned the house and a shed, a house on the beach (probably Peggotty Beach), and a moss house (probably also on Peggotty Beach). One or both of her sons James and Martin were fishermen and mossers, again probably mossing off Peggotty Beach. It was said they had a main house on Third Cliff that they rented out during the summer, staying in the small cottage at 138 Gilson Road. The cramped loft upstairs was the bedroom for four or five of the boys, and the girls were downstairs.[413]

Mary's daughter Sabina was born in that cottage in 1895, less than half a year before her father died. She was the youngest of the children. To make ends meet, she recalled,

> … my brother Mark [who had infantile paralysis and used crutches] and I had a store on Gilson Road. We sold ice cream and bread and milk and other things people might run out of. Our family kept a horse and a cow….[414]

Sabina Welch later worked in Boston at R. H. Stearns and other department stores. She was a labor organizer at Gilchrist's department store. Her sister Delia also worked with her at R. H. Stearns, in the men's department on the first floor. When living in Scituate, Sabina Welch would take the train, probably from the Greenbush station, into Boston, where she would stay during the workweek. She recalled seeing early commuters walking down the cliff with their lanterns, which they left at the train station until their return from Boston. She recalled:

> We walked everywhere. … We would walk to the North Scituate life saving station and to the cemetery in Cohasset to watch the flag raising ceremony.
> …
> We used to go to the church on Meeting House Lane early in the morning in Lent. And we would see the women coming from First Cliff across the bridge, with lanterns in their hands. People would turn down their lanterns and leave them in the vestibule to be picked up when they came out.[415]

Sabina's church, the Roman Catholic Church of the Nativity, was then on the northern side of Meeting House Lane, next to the cemetery. For a while, Sabina lived in Dorchester, where the family's main home was, but in 1960, she moved back into the cottage at 138 Gilson. She received a pension from R. H. Stearns of $19 per month.[416]

Years later, owners of 138 Gilson found a hand painted sign in the barn behind the cottage. It read, "The Roadside Tea House: Sandwiches, Salads, Home Cooked Foods, Lobsters, Live + Boiled. …E. F. Welch …" This was probably Elizabeth F. Welch, married to George's brother William H. (Henry) Welch, an entirely different Welch family from Sabina's. Elizabeth F. Welch (1868–1930) lived at the original Welch family farmhouse until 1919, when her husband Henry sold the land to the Scituate Country Club. Then she lived on First Parish Road in Scituate. The tea house was on that road, a main thoroughfare, rather than at the farmhouse, or the residential Gilson Road. Elizabeth and Henry's daughter Elinore M. Welch lived with them on First Parish Road and ran an art shop there in 1926. Perhaps Elinore was the one who painted the sign. It is not clear how it wound up at Gilson Road.[417]

The later owners of 138 Gilson also found a solid silver medallion in the rock wall at the property. Research found it was a medal presented to Martin Quinn by the Humane Society of Massachusetts for assisting in the rescue of the schooner *Ulrica*, which wrecked at Nantasket in 1896.[418] Based on census records in 1900, Martin Quinn, age 36, a mosser, was the son of Bridget Quinn, and both lived next door to Sabina Welch's family on Gilson. (Sabina Welch's mother was a Quinn.) Further research confirmed that the Humane Society awarded Martin Quinn a silver medal, and he earned monetary awards from the Society in 1905, 1906, and 1907 for his other lifesaving actions.[419]

Humane Society of Massachusetts silver medal for Martin Quinn, 1896.
Photos by Lyle Nyberg 2017.

Third Cliff's seclusion in the early 1900s is well documented. A painting from about 1899 by Scituate artist Mariquita Gill shows an oceanside meadow with a wood fence and no houses at what is likely Third Cliff. (The artist painted scenes of the North River marshes at Third Cliff.) A photo taken before 1913 by Scituate artist Alice Beckington shows an empty path heading south along the edge of Third Cliff, uphill toward the top, where the cliff was crumbling, with only a lone house or two standing at the crest. A lip of grass sticks out over the edge of the cliff.[420]

Third Cliff was nearly bare, with just a few solitary houses at the top, as shown in a Frederick Damon photo from about 1900 of Peggotty Beach, with the twin house of Daniel Ward and Miles O'Brien. A copy of the photo is in Barbara Murphy's book *Irish Mossers*, page 3. Many postcards from that era show just a few solitary houses on the cliff.[421]

Apple orchards covered both sides of the Driftway up to the top of the cliff. At least one apple tree is still there. The top of the cliff also had cow pastures.[422]

Alice Beckington, "Crest of Third Cliff," *School Arts Book*, 1911–1912.
Thanks to Boston Public Library.

"The Third Cliff, Scituate, Mass.," postcard published by Souther-Mears Co., Boston.
Courtesy of Scituate Historical Society.

Access to Third Cliff required a bit of backtracking. At the western edge of Scituate, at Greenbush, many roads met. The Driftway was not one of them, as shown on the 1903 map. One had to go north on Country Way, take the bridge over the railroad tracks, and then turn south to reach the Driftway. Starting in 1914, one would then have to pass by operations of the Boston Sand and Gravel Company in the Colman Hills along the Driftway. On the Driftway, the company's large chute or conveyor belt passed over the Driftway to reach barges waiting to be filled with sand and gravel on a tributary of the North River. Even then, the Driftway did not lead directly into the village of Scituate Harbor. One had to negotiate a right curve, then a dangerous sharp right curve where the road narrowed. Then, a choice: make a left turn onto Kent Street to reach the village, or stay on the Driftway to the secluded Third Cliff. It was probably much easier to reach Scituate Harbor using Stockbridge Road.[423]

It was not until 1968 that one could travel straight through from Greenbush to Scituate Harbor along the Driftway and New Kent Street, which eliminated all those curves and turns. An aerial photo of the new street under construction is in the Pitcock Farm section in chapter 2.[424]

***

To this secluded spot of Third Cliff came a woman from North Scituate. Helen M. Bailey bought land at the eastern end of the Driftway starting in 1900. A dwelling marked "Mrs. H. Bailey" appears on the 1903 map. A descendant, Dr. Ruth Bailey, later lived there, at 8 Driftway. How Dr. Ruth Bailey wound up there is traced as follows.

Helen Bailey, a member of the Seaverns family, was related by marriage to the extensive Bailey family of North Scituate. Her husband was Jotham W. Bailey, a carpenter, builder, and merchant in North Scituate. Their son Willard L. Bailey made and supplied wood moldings.[425]

Helen Bailey first purchased the King Cottage parcel from E. Parker Welch. This was a one-acre parcel with a dwelling house known as King Cottage that had 86 feet of frontage on Water Street (now Driftway). It was bounded by P. Rogan's house lot, John Donahue's house lot, and 220 feet along a stone wall running westerly. That wall was likely the long stone wall that appears in a 1909 postcard view of "The Marguerite" built in 1908 at 3 Driftway, across the road from Helen Bailey. The parcel evidently became 10 Driftway. Soon after acquiring this parcel, she acquired a nearby (or adjacent) parcel that eventually became 8 Driftway. This parcel of three-fourths of an acre was described as "bounded Southerly on said Water Street, westerly on land now or late of the heirs of Dennis Ward, northerly by said Dennis Ward's land, and easterly by the Falls so called." It was next to cow pastures at the edge of the cliff.[426]

The Marguerite stands at the top of Third Cliff in the center of this postcard, postmarked 1909. View looking southwest, with Fourth Cliff and Marshfield hills in the background. Note the cow pastures enclosed by stone walls, and the stairway leading down the face of the cliff to the beach below.
Courtesy of Scituate Historical Society (Twomey/Jacobson Collection).

After Helen M. Bailey's death, her Third Cliff parcels were divided in 1920–1921. The King Cottage parcel went to one of her three heirs, H. Miriam Agnew. The parcel next to the Falls went to another heir, Willard L. Bailey, Ruth's father. In 1934, that parcel went to Ruth and her mother.[427] Dr. Ruth Bailey became a legendary local and she is profiled later in chapter 19.

10

THIRD CLIFF'S NORTH END DEVELOPS

As George Welch developed Rivermoor on the southern end of Third Cliff, development continued on the cliff's northern end.

Some of the sales were made by the Welch family. For example, E. Parker Welch sold property in 1900 at the north end of the cliff, probably along Town Way. The deed referred to house lots of Edward Cummings and Patrick Mulkern, and related deeds in 1900 conveyed the land with buildings thereon "situate in said Scituate on the Third Cliff."[428]

But much of the sales activity occurred through the Scituate Beach Land Association (SBLA), with which the Welches were associated. Since it was formed in 1900, the SBLA sold lots on the northern end of Third Cliff.

Early Sales by SBLA

In 1908, the SBLA sold lot 9, at the intersection of Gilson Road and Bassin Lane, the site of today's 1 Bassin Lane. A cottage was built there by 1909. In 1921, John S. Gill bought the lot "together with the Buildings and improvements thereon." Gill was originally from Connemara, Ireland. He was a leader, since at least 1909, in organizing a union at the *Boston Globe*. Gill's work in the art department involved dealing daily with dangerous chemicals. At least, said Gill:

> The fine summer days "have came," and most everyone has that desire to take a trip to the country or seashore. Boston and vicinity has many fine country and shore resorts, where the tired photo engraver can go to breathe God's fresh air and forget about shop for a week or two.[429]

In 1922, the *Boston Globe* reported that more than 25 of the "boys" in its art department had a party at Gill's cottage to celebrate the 50th birthday of their colleague, John "Father" Gill. Gill's cottage was named "Barbara." The party included swimming and foot-racing contests (including the 100-yard dash), and a clambake and games on the beach.[430]

In 1923, John Gill was credited in the *Boston Sunday Globe* magazine for a photo of the old Collier House at North Scituate.[431]

John Gill sold the property in 1927. In 1938, his wife (perhaps then his widow) spent her summer on Third Cliff. By 1939, the lot was empty, according to a plan made that year. The 1939 plan appeared to adopt the same lot numbering system as the SBLA's 1900 Plan 2.[432]

In 1909, the SBLA sold lots that were reported as being on the easterly side of County Way (Gilson) and "extending to Cliff walk." It is unclear if there ever was a walkway along the cliff.[433]

The SBLA also sold lots 4 through 7 to Catherine Nee in separate deeds from 1909 to 1912. These lots along Gilson Road were between Town Way and Bassin Lane. As was customary, the deed mentioned no building. However, the 1939 plan showed a house on lot 6 (today's 53 Gilson) with a garage on lot 7. The house may go back to 1912.[434]

The SBLA sold more lots along Gilson Road. On some lots, houses were built in the early 1900s, mostly cottages for summer vacationers. These were built at lots on Gilson Road corresponding to the following street numbers used later: 49, 53, 76, 87, 91, 93, and 113. Of these, the following appear to have been replaced later: 49, 76, and 87. The house at 87 was evidently named "Watson" for the person who originally occupied it from approximately 1900 to 1911, George F. Watson. In 1900, he and his family were reported to be "at their new house on third cliff." The house at 93 Gilson had the name "Seaholme." Olive P. Gore, of #8 Beacon Street, Room 48, Boston, owned this house from 1909 to 1959, although her husband Harry W. Gore was indicated as owning "Seaholme" in the 1915 directory. Also in that directory was Clarence E. Brier, who owned a summer house with the pretentious name "Vue De L'Eau." It is not clear where that house was, but from 1921 to 1943, his wife Florence owned lots 49-52, equivalent to today's 100-104 Gilson.[435]

Sales by the SBLA on Gilson Road started slowly. By 1912, however, only 15 of the original 70 lots were left for sale. By 1920, only 6 of the original 70 lots remained unsold.[436]

Dickens Row

Off Gilson Road is Town Way, and off Town Way is Dickens Row, at the far north of Third Cliff. Today's 6 Dickens Row was the site of the first home on Third Cliff itself. This was the home of Daniel Ward, the Irish mossing entrepreneur. It was a twin house, later called Bleak House and East End. Three other homes were built on Dickens Row in the first decades of the 1900s, all of which had names: Prey, Trotwood, and Shannock. They are shown, without names (except for Antoinette Pray's property), on a 1918 plan. They are discussed in more detail below.[437]

Starting in numerical order, 1 Dickens Row was the home of Harumichi Yatsuhashi (Yatsuhashi Harumichi) (1886–1982) of Brookline, an important and distinguished Asian art dealer. In 1931, he purchased two parcels comprising the property. It appears to have stayed in his family until 1984, not long after his death. A house remains there, said by the assessors to have been built in 1922.[438]

Contemporary view of Third Cliff looking south, across marshes. At left are backs of Peggotty Beach cottages, which face the ocean. Photo by Lyle Nyberg 2017.

At 2 Dickens Row, where it meets Town Way, Antoinette Pray bought a small lot of 4,400 square feet from George F. Welch in 1901. The house there was built in 1902, and "A. Pray" is shown as the owner on the 1903 map. In 1920, she sold the land and buildings to Marion Brown, wife of Capen Brown of Boston. On the *1921 Valuation List*, the house was named "Prey." The name probably came from the prior owner's last name, Antoinette Pray. She had moved into a historical house near Greenbush at Scituate's border with Norwell. The new owners of the Pray house then evidently renamed it. In 1922, the *Boston Globe* reported, "The 'Rookery' cottage on Dickens Row is being occupied by Mr and Mrs Capen Brown." Marion Brown later moved from Boston to Scituate, where she owned property and lived on Dickens Row, perhaps at The Rookery. The original house at 2 Dickens Row no longer exists.[439]

At 4 Dickens Row, a house named "Trostwood" (also called "Trotwood" or "Trottwood") was built about 1902–1903. The 1903 map shows E. Parker Welch as the owner of two houses here, almost certainly 4 Dickens Row and 6 Dickens Row. The house at 6 Dickens Row is the historical Daniel Ward double house. Despite the 1903 map's marking, it was actually E. Parker Welch's son George who owned the Daniel Ward house, from 1897 to at least 1902, and he sold the property by 1919. By 1919, Trotwood at 4 Dickens Row was owned by William E. and Bessie W. McCoy of Wellesley. Bessie McCoy continued to own the property for decades. The house has had major alterations.[440]

At 10 Dickens Row, a house named "Shannock" was built by 1901. There was some confusion about the name. Herman G. Shaneck of 106 Saratoga, East Boston, was the owner, according to the town's valuation list, and he was listed in the 1915 and 1918 directories as a summer resident. Herman Shaneck had his own firm and was a director of the Columbia Trust Company. Back in 1879, he had changed his name from the Germanic Herman G. Schnück to the more English Shaneck. It turned into the homophonic "Shannock" name for the house, just like Antoinette Pray's name turned into "Prey."[441]

Third Cliff looking south from Peggotty Beach, c. 1919. Shaneck house is at far right.
Compare to like Damon photo, early 1900s, in *Irish Mossers*, p. 3.
Courtesy of Scituate Historical Society.

George Welch had sold the property to Herman Shaneck in 1900. The deed contained an early and simple example of restrictions that would later be expanded:

> This conveyance is made however subject to the restriction that no dwelling house shall be erected on said lot except it be on a line with the dwelling house of the said grantor now standing on the adjoining lot.[442]

The house on the adjoining lot was the double house of Daniel Ward, owned by George Welch. An early photo (above) of Peggotty Beach and Third Cliff shows the Shaneck house at the far right. Off the photo to the right would have been the double house, as shown in an early Damon photo with a similar view, from the early 1900s, copied in *Irish Mossers*. In addition, the Shaneck house was featured in a drawing by Tom Eames, discussed in chapter 13.[443]

Herman Shaneck owned the property from 1900 to 1919, and the house name lived on even after he sold the property to Charles E. Holt, who is discussed in chapter 13. The house was at the southern end of Peggotty Beach, where Third Cliff starts its rise as a cliff. The house was replaced in 1954, according to town records.[444]

But George was now turning from selling individual lots to developing various areas of Scituate and Third Cliff.

Off Gilson Road, and just north of his Rivermoor houses, George owned property in 1911 along Eagles Nest Road on Third Cliff. This was outside the Gilson Road Plan 2 of the SBLA, in which Welch participated. George also built houses in Scituate near the harbor, and on Jericho Road, Barker Road, Allen Street, and Hazel Avenue. He was a major partner in Allen Associates that transformed the Barker Farm area. Then he developed Porter Road, starting in 1916 with two houses named Marion and Edith, the names of his daughters.[445]

By 1915, George Welch opened a real estate office on Front Street in Scituate, which he operated as a private business separate from the Welch Company.[446]

11

THE RIVERMOOR COLONY'S DEVELOPMENT

Early Years

Until the early 1900s, the southern end of Third Cliff contained fields and meadows. They appear in an interesting photo (below) taken by 1910. A large house overlooks fields, meadows, and marshes.

"Rivermoor, Scituate, Mass." photograph, c. 1910. The house, later called "Indian Knoll," was on the west side of Rivermoor overlooking the North River and its marshes (36 Moorland). The photo also appeared on postcards, including one postmarked 1910.
Courtesy of Nancy Howell.

"Rivermoor, Scituate, Mass.," shows a large house, one of the earliest built by George Welch in Rivermoor. The house stood on the west side of Moorland (at today's 36 Moorland), between Michael and Lincoln. By 1912, it was named "Indian Knoll," so the photo's title "Rivermoor" likely refers to the whole new development rather than the house. Looking south, the view takes in large meadows, stone walls running east-west (perhaps marking Michael and the curve in Moorland), the house (sitting on a knoll), a distant boulder (site of a later house named "Boulder"), about four distant houses at the southern edge of Collier, and the North River and Marshfield in the background. The meadows predominate, and fill most of Rivermoor. It is a pastoral scene.[447]

Having named this secluded area Rivermoor, George Welch then laid roads through the meadows and built houses, turning the area into a summer colony.

Consider a Latin origin of the word "colony" — "to cultivate."[448] The origin fits. Here, Welch was "cultivating" a colony of summer residences. Even better, he was cultivating on former farmland. (Ironically, he was cultivating the colony on what he named a moor, which is uncultivated land.)

In this way, George took on the role of developer/builder of a planned community. We do not know if he studied the growing field of planned developments. That field went back to Olmsted and Vaux's well-publicized 1869 plan for Riverside, Illinois. Their plan was curvilinear, not in rectilinear grids. Welch's 1906 plan for Rivermoor had plenty of curves, and his deeds carried restrictions such as minimum setbacks from the road, characteristic of planned developments.[449]

George reportedly used workers and supplies from the Welch Company's lumber business, building houses (on speculation) in the winter when the lumber business was slow. We do not know what role Welch played in actually building the houses, whether he swung a hammer, or sawed boards. We do know that he took pride in his handiwork. He signed his name on boards installed in his Rivermoor houses, and at least two of these survive.[450]

George Welch signature on plank from house at 7 Lincoln. Photo by Lyle Nyberg 2016.

George's business approach in Rivermoor was later described this way: "Each year five of the distinct summer houses would be built in this planned resort community. When rented, he would build five more." This description has much truth.[451]

By 1909, George Welch already owned many buildings and houses. He owned the numerous buildings of the Welch Company, his own house in town at Otis Place, several houses in the development around Hatherly Road, four houses on Hazel Avenue, and four other houses. In addition, he owned four older houses on Third Cliff, some previously owned by his father E. Parker. Three were in Rivermoor — Bijou (built in 1871), Parker (1871), and Lamprey/Lamphrey (by 1900, per *Boston Globe* articles). In addition, Trotwood (1902–1903) was at the northern end of Third Cliff. All four of these houses were rented for summers. The first three are now gone, and Trotwood has been extensively altered.[452]

In 1905, even before his Rivermoor plan was drafted, George Welch sold a lot at the northwest corner of Collier and Cliff on which a house had been or would soon be built.[453]

The Marguerite

Then, in 1908 (or perhaps earlier), George Welch built an important new house in Rivermoor, "The Marguerite." It was on Water Street (Driftway) at the north end of Collier Road, a key intersection. It had an impressive position high on the cliff, with a commanding view of the ocean, the North River, the other cliffs, and the entire southern end of Third Cliff. The source of the house's name is unknown, but it is not the name of either of Welch's daughters.[454]

"View from Third Cliff, Looking South, SCITUATE, Mass." Postcard.
Courtesy of Scituate Historical Society.

The Marguerite stands at the top of Third Cliff on the above postcard, postmarked August 1908 (Souther-Mears Co., Boston). Fourth Cliff and Marshfield hills are in the background, separated from Third Cliff by the North River. Note the beach and road at the bottom, the site of later seawalls.

George reportedly gave The Marguerite to his daughter Marion as a wedding present. That report appears inaccurate. Welch retained ownership of the Marguerite and rented the house to others until he sold it in 1918.[455]

In 1907, Marion married Dr. T. Branch Alexander, a local physician who served as the school doctor. George provided the newlyweds with a newly renovated house on Central Street (later called First Parish Road). It still exists at 29 First Parish Road, and has been passed down in the family.[456]

The Marguerite was a reference point for photos and postcards of the era. It was a big cube of a house, with hipped dormer windows of the tall attic sticking out in all four directions, and double windows on the dormer facing south. With its porches ("piazzas"), it was a virtual step-pyramid of a house. It was a classic example of the "American Four-Square" house form used in Colonial Revival and other house styles. The Marguerite stood at 3 Driftway until it was demolished on January 2, 2019. A house built on the site is now 3 Collier Road.[457]

The Marguerite stood at the end of the Driftway at Collier. View looking northeast.
Photo by Lyle Nyberg, August 2016.

Further Development, Phase 1

After building the Marguerite, George continued developing Rivermoor. With the nucleus of houses already at the upper end of Collier, he focused on Michael and then Lincoln, as discussed in more detail below.[458] At the southern end of Collier, he sold lots, some including cottages, at 77 Collier (1908), 78 Moorland (at the very southern point of Rivermoor) (1909), and 79 Collier (1910).[459]

George built an impressive number of the town's new houses. The data is too sketchy to quantify specific years, except for 1909. In that year, George built 10 houses in Rivermoor, on Michael and on Collier. This was an impressive one-fourth of the town's total increase of 43 houses that year.[460]

That year of 1909 marked George's first big move in Rivermoor. He built five houses on Michael in 1909–1910, ready to rent for the summer of 1910. Each house had a name, and each name began with "M." Names may have been helpful, because houses had no street numbers until decades later. The houses on Michael were: Myrtle (later #6), Maidstone (10), Mayfair (14), Melody (18), and Moorfield (22). Each was set back 30 feet from the road on the road's northern side. Each had views of the ocean and the mouth of the North River. All five were two-and-one-half-story Colonial Revival houses with similar sizes, appearances, hip roofs, and open wraparound porches with balustrades. Two or three had garages for automobiles.[461]

Welch built a similar house called Mereside in line with the five houses on Michael. Because it was west of them on the other side of Moorland, it later took the address of 28 Moorland. It was built in 1911, ready to rent for that summer.[462]

The first renters of Mereside were Dr. & Mrs. Harvey P. Towle (and Alice M. Buswell) of Boston. In 1910, they had rented Maidstone in Rivermoor They appear in Scituate in the 1911 Summer Social Register, with no house name.[463] They are listed in the 1912 and 1913 Summer Social Registers at Mereside in Rivermoor, with a phone number of 67-3.[464] Dr. Towle of 453 Marlborough Street in Boston was a noted dermatologist, associated with Massachusetts General Hospital, and a former professor at Dartmouth Medical School.[465]

Period postcards show the houses on Michael and other Rivermoor houses such as Mereside. They reveal the similarities of the houses, along with other features of the area during these times.

One postcard (below, original in color) is entitled "Rivermoor Colony, Third Cliff, Scituate, Mass.," copyright W. N. Seaver It looks north from the rocky beach, with the cliff dropping to the ocean on the right. About 20 houses are inland. Just to the right of center is a white two-story structure (33 Collier) next to the rocky shore. At left is a red shed, probably the lifeboat station of the Humane Society of Massachusetts. Near the center is the one-story bungalow with a low-pitched roof at 10 Cliff, discussed in chapters 8 and 13.[466]

The Seaver postcard shows four adjacent houses on the north side of Michael Avenue, all with two stories and hip roofs, which George Welch built in 1909.[467]

"Rivermoor Colony, Third Cliff, Scituate, Mass." postcard with view of Rivermoor looking north, c. 1910–1920 (Detroit Publishing, copyright W. N. Seaver). The Marguerite is at right. Four hip-roofed houses at left are at eastern end of Michael (from left, #18, 14, 10, 6). Courtesy of Scituate Historical Society (Twomey/Jacobson collection).

The Scituate Historical Society has a rare postcard with a view similar to that in the Seaver postcard, "Southerly End, Third Cliff, Scituate Harbor, Mass." The four hip-roofed houses on Michael are more pronounced. The Human Society lifeboat shed is oriented differently, or maybe it is a different shed. The two-story house at 33 Collier is shown with more detail than on the Seaver postcard. Likewise, there is more detail of Collier running up the cliff to the right, as well as the houses on that road that face the ocean.

"Southerly End, Third Cliff, Scituate Harbor, Mass." postcard with view of Rivermoor looking north, c. 1910–1920 (C. Frye 1199). Four houses on Michael Avenue appear at left, with shed in front. Courtesy of Scituate Historical Society (Twomey/Jacobson collection).

The Michael Avenue houses and streetscape were characteristic of Rivermoor. Along with Mereside (28 Moorland), in line with these houses, they comprise 6 of 17 hip-roofed houses in Rivermoor. They still exist today, but they have additions that doubled the footprints of the houses. Despite the changes, Michael Avenue is the most complete remaining example of an original Rivermoor streetscape.

Left: "Michael Ave., Rivermoor, Scituate, Mass." postcard, c. 1910–1920 (Chas. W. Frye, Pub.). Three hip-roofed houses are at eastern end of Michael (from left, #14, 10, 6), with 33 Collier at right. Courtesy of Scituate Historical Society (Twomey/Jacobson collection).

Further Development, Phase 2

George's next big move was building five houses on Lincoln, 1911–1912, plus a few on other roads: 24 Cliff (about 1911); 55 Moorland ("The Marshes") (1911); and 59 Moorland ("Boulder") (1912, reconstructed about 2000).[468] In a departure from the Michael Avenue scheme, he built houses on both sides of Lincoln.

A photo from about 1912 shows 74 Collier ("Clyde") (1912) and 59 Moorland ("Boulder") (1912).[469] In the background are three or four cottages along the southern point of Collier, perhaps including 79 Collier (1910), or perhaps they are fishing or hunting huts, later replaced. "Boulder" was named for the big boulder in its yard, visible in this photo near the house, and in the 1910 photo of "Indian Knoll" (36 Moorland). The big boulder is still there.

View from Indian Knoll (36 Moorland) of "Clyde" (74 Collier) at left with laundry on line, and "Boulder" (59 Moorland) with boulder in yard, and other cottages at southern end of Third Cliff, c. 1912. Note Woodworth boy (left) and high tide covering marshes. Woodworth family photo album.

Some people bought property in Rivermoor rather than renting a cottage. Examples include the Hunt sisters, and the Thomas brothers of Norwell, who bought the tiny cottage ("Cedar Camp") at 77 Collier in 1908, as discussed in chapter 7.

In 1908, Margaret C. (Hunt) Colgate of Rockland, MA, bought lot 71 and part of lot 70 from George Welch, today's 20 Collier Road.[470] A house was there by 1909, perhaps earlier.[471] Margaret Colgate had a sister, Susan L. Hunt of Boston.[472] In the same month of 1908 that Margaret bought her property, Susan bought parts of lots 73 and 74 (and evidently lot 75 at the corner of Michael Avenue). This was approximately today's 28 Collier, and practically next door to her sister's cottage.[473] There was no cottage then, but there was by 1910.[474]

Susan Hunt's cottage was named "San.-Souci" on the 1926 Sanborn map. (Perhaps this was a play on the owner's name, Susie.) The name means "without worries" or "carefree," and probably arose from the famous collection of colorful Prussian palaces in Potsdam, Germany. The 1918 directory lists a Susie L. Hunt on Collier Road as a summer resident, with home address of 91 Linden, Allston. This was the same address listed in 1896 for her sister Margaret C. Hunt, as a teacher at the Washington Allston School in the Boston Public Schools.[475]

Margaret C. Hunt married Dr. Charles Colgate of Rockland. Dr. Colgate was a graduate of Harvard College, class of 1898, and received his M.D. degree from Boston University in 1901. Margaret's middle name was Campbell. This explains the cottage's name — "Campbell" — on the 1926 Sanborn map. Margaret was a supporter of the women's suffrage movement.[476]

Sisters Margaret Colgate and Susan Hunt owned their cottages for 20 years, 1908–1928.[477] Both cottages have since been demolished (Margaret's in 2017) and replaced.

By 1912, quite a colony of houses had been built, including a cluster at the southern end of Rivermoor.

The Scituate Historical Society has a rare postcard showing this cluster. It is postmarked June 4, 1912, from Rivermoor. On the back, the anonymous writer says:

> This is where I am situated. X marks the house. We are only 2 min. from the shore. At high tide the marshes are nearly submerged. Fell down a flight of stairs today and feel quite bruised up about it. The water is too cold yet for bathing. A few have tried it but found it mighty cold.

"View of Third Cliff Scituate," postcard, postmarked 1912. Southern end of Rivermoor.
Courtesy of Scituate Historical Society (Twomey/Jacobson collection).

The view is disorienting to us today because of its perspective, age, and the lack of trees.
Here is a best guess of what it shows, including cottages. The road running across the
center is Moorland. At left is Indian Knoll (1910, 36 Moorland). Just to its right, behind
and above it, is Talbot (1912, 21 Parker). Directly to the right of Indian Knoll, with the X,
is Mereside (1911, 28 Moorland). Just behind and above Mereside is Mitton (1912, 12
Moorland). The larger (closer) houses at the right are (left to right) Mayo (1912, 18
Lincoln), Lavender (1912, 14 Lincoln) (across the street from Linnet), and Linnet (1911,
15 Lincoln) (gable roof). The houses farther back are mostly those along Michael Avenue
(Moorfield, Melody, Mayfair) and one on Cliff (west end). In the center (on close
inspection) is a boulder at the corner of Lincoln and Moorland.

The boulder, Mereside, Mayo, and Linnet are all still there.

Given the X marking the house, the message, and the 1912 postmark, the writer must have
been a member or friend of the family of Dr. Harvey Towle, who rented Mereside in 1911
and 1912.

House Names

By 1909, George Welch rented out at least five houses in Rivermoor for the summer. Like the Marguerite, the "Campbell," and the five houses on Michael Avenue, the houses had names. The *Boston Globe* reported these summer residents:

> Mrs. Albert W. Quinn of Brookline occupies the "Hazlemere," William B. Wood of Milton, Jerome D. Greene of Cambridge, Dr. F. E. Garland and Dr. D. C. Greene of Boston at "The Rivermore," Thomas S. Childs of Holyoke at "The Parker," Dr. A. M. Clarke of Boston at "The Tichnor," A. L. Russell of Hyde Park at "The Russell," U. Urquhart of Brighton at the "Bijou," F. S. Eggleston of Boston at "The Lamprey," Henry E. Hammond of Boston at "The Marguerite," … C. E. Holt of Boston at the "Trotwood," C. N. Page of Boston at "Bleak House," ….[478]

Most named houses were in Rivermoor, and all can be traced to current addresses, except for "The Rivermore" and "The Tichnor."[479]

The "Hazelmere" was a new house built by George, not on Third Cliff, but at Hatherly Road and Turner Road, just north of the development around Hatherly Road in which Welch was involved. "The Parker" was, appropriately enough, at the end of Parker Avenue (14 Collier). Next to it, further south, was "The Lamprey," sometimes called "The Lamphrey" after one of its early tenants, and later called "Eastview" (16 Collier). A bit further south was "The Russell" (22 Collier). These three houses have been replaced. "The Marguerite" was at the top of Collier Road (3 Driftway).[480]

The houses were probably named by the Welches. The names appear in several places. Parker, Lamprey, and Bijou (11 Collier) appeared in town tax valuation lists. Those lists included their lot numbers from the 1906 plan of Rivermoor. That made them traceable to the town assessor's maps, which used the same lot numbers. The detailed maps of the Sanborn Map Company also included names for some houses in Rivermoor. Apart from Rivermoor, names for houses on Third Cliff are difficult to find. This is largely due to the multiplicity of owners during this period (compared with George Welch's dominant ownership of Rivermoor properties), and evidently because fewer houses there had names. "Trotwood" and "Bleak House" were located on Dickens Row at the northern end of Third Cliff. They are discussed in chapters 3, 10 and 13.[481]

A 1910 newspaper article said, "Edw. Bailey of Reading is at Viola cottage" (8 Driftway, since replaced), and "John Tilton and family of Needham are at Edgecliff cottage on Third cliff" (4 Collier, since replaced). Both cottages were on Third Cliff.[482]

Picture Postcards

About 1905 to 1918, picture postcards appeared, showing houses and residential life in places like Third Cliff.[483] Some postcards were in color, though these were likely black and white photos colored by hand, because commercial color photography was in its infancy.[484]

In Scituate, postcards were often published by postmasters, presumably for sale at post offices, including those at Third Cliff. These postmasters included Charles W. Frye on Front Street in Scituate Harbor, members of the Seaverns family (Martha, A. A., or H. F.) in North Scituate, and Edna A. Litchfield in Egypt. Others who were photographers, not postmasters, also published postcards in the early 1900s. The most prominent was the excellent photographer Frederick Damon. His cards, black and white, carry the imprint "Published by the F. N. Damon Curio Co., The Museum, Scituate, Mass." E. Feola also published a few postcards.[485]

Postcards had pictured most Scituate hotels and inns, so why not homes? Postcards for Rivermoor show hip-roofed houses with piazzas, roads with the occasional horse-drawn carriage or automobile, and views of the ocean unobstructed by trees. Some postcards show steps leading down the face of the cliff to the beach. Some of their captions refer to Rivermoor as a "colony."[486]

A nice example of these postcards, shown in chapter 8 and copied below, is entitled "Cottages and Post Office, Third Cliff, Scituate, Mass." It looks north on upper Collier Road, depicting about 10 houses and a horse-drawn carriage with two elegantly dressed women. The house on the far right is The Marguerite built by George Welch by 1908. Other houses include the "Lamprey" and "Parker" built by 1901. The house second from the left is Margaret Colgate's "Campbell" (1909, 20 Collier, demolished in late 2017).[487]

COTTAGES AND POST OFFICE, THIRD CLIFF, SCITUATE, MASS.

Left: "Cottages and Post Office, Third Cliff, Scituate, Mass." postcard, c. 1910–1912, view looking north on Collier Road. At far right is The Marguerite. Courtesy of Scituate Historical Society (Twomey/Jacobson Collection).

Same view looking north
on Collier Road, 2016.
Photo by Lyle Nyberg.

In another postcard entitled "Rivermoor, Scituate, Mass." the conveyance is not a horse — it is a red convertible touring car. It motors up narrow Moorland with telephone poles on one side, and about 10 two-story, hip-roofed houses on the other side. The view looks out to the river and the ocean. Very few trees are to be seen, and then only short ones.[488]

RIVERMOOR, SCITUATE. MASS.

"Rivermoor, Scituate, Mass.," postcard, postmarked June 1917. Original is in color with red convertible. View looking south, Moorland Road in foreground, and North River in background. Courtesy of Gail Ledwig.

This postcard with the red convertible shows houses just built in 1917. As an educated guess, it shows 24 Cliff at left, with two houses on the north side of Michael, two houses with hip roofs on the north side of Lincoln, three houses on the south side of Lincoln, and houses at 51 Moorland (built 1914), 55 Moorland (1917, "The Marshes"), and 50 Moorland (1912, "Boulder"). The white area near the center may be a tennis court, which appears in the Woodworth family photo album.

The picture postcards and photos from 100 years ago show an open landscape for the Scituate coast that surprises modern eyes. This view existed partly because summer colonies were developed on pastures, with low vegetation. Then residents added landscaping, and the trees and shrubs grew up. The ocean views in the old scenes are now often obscured by this growth.[489]

Picture postcards must have helped in marketing Rivermoor. The Rivermoor post office, attached to or part of a general store, probably sold the cards. Summer residents and visitors could write to their friends and relatives and entice others with scenes of seaside living.

COTTAGES LOOKING WEST FROM THIRD CLIFF, SCITUATE, MASS.

"Cottages Looking West from Third Cliff," postcard view of Lincoln Ave., running to the right (west) off Collier Rd. (left), early 1900s. Courtesy of Gail Ledwig.

The postcards and early photos show that the roads were only dirt. They feature houses on Collier Road (laid out in 1905) and Michael Avenue because those roads were some of the earliest laid out. Echoing this, later, the first Rivermoor streets that the town accepted were Collier (and Moorland) in parts in 1905, 1921, and 1924 (final part); Michael in 1921; Lincoln in 1921; Parker in 1925; and Cliff in 1929.[490]

With all these streets and houses and telephone poles, the term "moor" was no longer an apt description of Rivermoor.

The Telephone

The presence of telephone poles in these early postcards may surprise. However, the telephone was invented in 1876 by Alexander Graham Bell in Boston, just 25 miles from Scituate. By 1910, the Bell System had 5.8 million telephones across the country, reaching west and south from Boston, and it enabled transcontinental calls by 1914.[491]

Starting in 1898, Scituate selectmen authorized the Southern Massachusetts Telephone Company to erect telephone poles along most of the town's public ways. The telephone company did not have to obtain private easements from individuals for these poles. The earliest streets to get telephone service included Front Street from Brook Street to Richardson's store.[492]

William P. Richardson's pharmacy had existed since the late 1800s.[493] Later called W. H. Richardson's, it was located on Front Street, opposite Beal Place.[494] The 2 ½-story building was built in 1883 by the P. Y. O. C. (Paddle Your Own Canoe) Society to house a library on the first floor. They rented part of the building to a store (probably Richardson's) and a hall, until the Society dissolved and sold the building in 1891. Then, the building held Richardson's pharmacy on the first floor and a Music Hall on the second floor, "to let for dances, entertainments, &c." The Music Hall later became the Idle Hour Theater, Scituate's first moving picture theater.[495]

Richardson's pharmacy probably had a telegraph office by the late 1880s, and an 1894 ad said, "telegraph office in store."[496] Even before Richardson's, Scituate had a telegraph office, listed in an 1860 business directory as "Charles Young, Operator, Herald Office."[497] Since telephones were an outgrowth of telegraphs, it was logical for Richardson's to expand into telephone service.[498] In 1899, the town paid Wm. P. Richardson and another person "for telephoning town business."[499]

George Welch was an early adopter of this new technology. In 1901, the George F. Welch hardware store was one of only four subscribers in town to have telephones, and they were public pay stations. The others were D. J. Bates, Grocer, C. H. Davis, Physician, and W. F. Richardson, Druggist.[500]

Early telephone lines ran to some of the town's hotels: the Hotel Minot (in 1902) and the Grand View Hotel (in 1903).[501] It may be that summer hotels like these, and summer communities, drove the development of the country's telephone infrastructure. By the time of a 1906 social register, the South Shore had telephone pay stations at Buzzard's Bay, Duxbury, Falmouth, and North Scituate. The North Scituate central location had the following branch locations in town:

- Central Office, Gannett's Block, Gannett Street
- Egypt, Thos. J. Newcomb
- Greenbush, Webb & Litchfield
- North Scituate, J. R. Ainslee and D. J. Bates
- North Scituate Beach, Mitchell Hotel and Sea View House
- Sand Hills, Jonathan Hatch
- Scituate, Grand View House"
- Scituate Centre, C. H. Davis
- Scituate Harbor, W. P. Richardson[502]

Daisy Carpenter (probably the former Daisy L. Graves) was one of the town's earliest telephone operators at the turn of the century, and she served from 1903 until 1927. She later was interviewed for a newspaper story:

… Daisy recalls that the first telephone office in Scituate was in Richardson's Drug Store at the Harbor. That was located in what is now the Coveney Block. Mr. Richardson was a civic minded man and was a town officer for many years. He also was a former telegraph operator which might explain why the first phone was in his store … about the turn of the century.

… About 1902 business must have been growing as larger quarters were needed, so, the "Company" was moved to the second floor of what is now Gates Store where it was to stay for eight years.

… From the Summer of 1903 to 1906 she [Daisy] worked Summers and part time for the company and from then on full time.

… When Daisy started work in 1908 there was a one-position board with about 40 lines and 3 to 5 out side lines. [In the same year, up to four operators serviced 350 lines for the US Capitol.[503]] One of the factors in installing a two-position board was the increase of summer people.

… In the next 20 years, nine more positions were added and there were 12 positions and 18 operators. There was only one line out to Third Cliff and as there were not many families on the Cliff it was sufficient until the summer colony began to take shape there. In the Summer, there were often as many as 20 parties on the line. … One longtime Third Cliff resident recalls that the service was always very good "Way out There."[504]

The telephone came to Third Cliff and to key town residents. On August 20, 1906, poles were authorized along Highland Street (Gilson Road) from Kent Street to Water Street (Driftway), and then along Water Street, and this covered the northern half of Third Cliff.[505] Later in 1906, the town authorized telephone poles on Otis Place in Scituate Harbor from Front Street to the residence of George F. Welch.[506]

In 1909–1910, the town arranged for telephone service for its selectmen, the superintendent of schools, and other town officials.[507] In 1914, the selectmen authorized additional telephone poles along Water Street (Driftway), westerly from the company's existing telephone poles.[508]

By this time, telephone service had reached Rivermoor in the southern half of Third Cliff. The 1911 Summer Social Register listed Dr. Harvey Towle with a phone number of 67-3. The 1912 Summer Social Register listed him with the same number, at "Mereside" in Rivermoor (now 28 Moorland).[509] His cottage and some others included telephones, as stated in George's 1915 ad for Rivermoor, copied in chapter 13.

In 1912, a telephone was installed in the high school, in a building that is now the home of the Scituate Historical Society.[510]

In 1916, two telephone booths were installed in Harry Macdonald's drug store in Scituate Harbor.[511] (Perhaps Macdonald had taken over Richardson's drug store.) Also in that year:

> Complaints were made about the amount of telephone ringing at the Hatherly School. The four-party line, which included two stores, was changed to a two-party line with no store sharing it.[512]

Margaret Cole Bonney recalled picking up a telephone on a party line in 1915, when she was seven years old, and carrying on nice conversations with a friendly voice. Margaret later learned the voice was that of Edna Litchfield. Edna F. Litchfield was the "day operator" and Olive Litchfield was the "night operator." Edna lived near the telephone office, which was in a building on Country Way near Branch Street.[513]

Daisy L. Graves (probably the same as the above-mentioned Daisy L. Carpenter) was the chief operator of the telephone company's Scituate Exchange on Country Way, according to a 1918 directory listing for the New England Telephone and Telegraph Company.[514]

Magneto wall telephone 1917, open to
show magneto and local battery.
Source: Wikimedia Commons.

That 1918 directory had about 550 listings in Scituate. Some were for businesses, as well as individuals. But considering there were about 1,570 dwellings in town, this was a remarkably dense communications network.[515]

The 1918 directory had 22 listings for town functions, including the police station, fire stations, schools, and selectmen (office and residences). Some people had more than one listing. George F. Welch's residence was number 95-3, and his real estate business on Front Street was 95-4. (The dashes may have indicated a shared party line.) The George F. Welch Company was 16, with a star designating a Branch Exchange System, presumably for its multiple buildings and offices. George's brother Henry, on the family's Third Cliff farm, was not listed, but Henry's farmer neighbor across the Driftway, W. W. Waterman, was listed. George's son-in-law, Dr. T. Branch Alexander, was 26. Thomas Lawson was 39 and his Dreamwold farm was 38. Even some summer residents had telephones, like Dr. Towle in Rivermoor.[516]

The 1918 telephone directory had advice for users (which may or may not still be valid):

> Because of the personal touch it affords, the telephone is superior to all other means of communication.
>
> …
>
> Make advance appointments by telephone to better utilize your time.
>
> …
>
> Time never was at such a premium and the telephone is the greatest time saver the world has ever known.
>
> …
>
> The telephone has become an indispensable aid to merchandising and, in fact, to business of every nature.[517]

Henry Welch Farm

As George Welch was building up Rivermoor, his brother Henry kept operating the family farm on Third Cliff. The farm's focus as a market garden, with apples and a few milk cows, must have helped sustain it while other New England farms declined through the Industrial Revolution. By 1911, the farm had two cows, two swine, three horses, and 30 fowl. George, living in town, had 20 horses, which he could have kept on the pastures on the cliff. Perhaps to rein in the livestock and horses, the Welch family covered its farmland with stone walls and wooden fences. Wooden fences were used in early colonial times and mostly gave way to stone walls, since they required less maintenance and could make use of rocks turned up in plowing.[518]

Welch farmhouse overlooking North River marshes, covered at high tide, 1912–1913. Orchards lead down to water. Colman Hills in distance, topped by Colman Heights Hotel. Woodworth family photo album.

12

Notable Summer Residents

Ernest Hodgson — Inventor, Builder

An important summer resident of Scituate was noted in the *Boston Globe*, August 10, 1909: "Ernest F. Hodgson of Boston has just completed and is occupying a fine cottage on Third cliff."[519] His cottage was at 60 Collier Road on Third Cliff.

Ernest F. and Florence (Stowell) Hodgson, 1939, about 41st wedding anniversary, photo by Bachrach Studios, Boston (detail). Courtesy of Dover Historical Society, Hodgson family, and Bachrach Studios.

His name is largely forgotten today, but Ernest Franklin Hodgson (1871–1948) was the first American to manufacture prefabricated houses. He founded his company in 1892, and established manufacturing operations in his hometown of Dover, Massachusetts. The company first made small structures like hen houses, then garages for automobiles about 1900, which proved timely and popular. In 1902, the company started producing modular panels for summer cottages that buyers could easily assemble on-site in as little as one day. They used a bolting system patented by Hodgson. Advertisements for these cottages began in *The House Beautiful* magazine about 1911. This was evidently years before Sears, Roebuck & Company entered the market. Sears at first offered similar panelized cottages. It was only later that Sears turned to its well-known large houses sold through mail-order catalogs, typically with Victorian designs.[520]

The E. F. Hodgson Company's panelized summer cottages were popular, selling well for decades. The company delivered them throughout America and the world, often to locations with unfavorable climates, such as the coast of Maine, the mountains of Vermont, Messina in Italy, and what had been the ancient city of Troy in Turkey.[521]

The company wrote persuasive ads. One ad in the 1920 *Clark's Boston Blue Book* showed its upper social class readers an image of the company's Army and Navy canteen building on Boston Common, saying:

> During War or Peace the HODGSON Portable houses are extensively used by discriminating people who want the best. They are used as Summer Cottages, Lodges, Play Houses, Garages, Screened Houses, Schools, Churches, Etc.[522]

Testimonials from satisfied customers appeared in company catalogs, such as the one published in 1933:

> Forty years ago a youngster with an ingenious mind conceived the idea of building small houses in a new way — completely in sections, that could be shipped anywhere, that could be erected by anyone in a few hours' time without the use of nails — simply bolted together.[523]

These cottages could be unbolted, too, making them portable to a new location. They were modular in design, and priced based on units 10 feet wide, creating, for example, a room 10 feet by 10 feet. Prices for Hodgson Camp Houses ranged from $200 to more than $1,600. Later, the company offered kits for larger houses, still one story and modular, with units 12 feet or 18 feet wide. Prices for these ranged from about $1,565 to more than $10,000. The company's customers ranged from those of moderate means to America's wealthiest families, including Rockefeller, Astor, Frick, DuPont, Endicott, Vanderbilt, Cabot, and Lowell. Hodgson sold his interest in the company in 1944, but the company continued to sell its panelized structures into the 1960s.[524]

Ernest Hodgson was a pioneer and an American legend.

Hodgson advertisement, *The House Beautiful*, February 1921, 147

Hodgson's Scituate cottage was in Rivermoor. In 1909, George Welch sold the lot, number 180, to Hodgson's wife Florence,

> subject to the restrictions that no building to be used as a dwelling house shall be erected thereon at a value of less than Five Hundred Dollars, that no swine or fowl shall be kept on the premises herein conveyed and that no objectionable outbuildings shall be erected thereon.[525]

Such restrictions were common in Welch's Rivermoor deeds.

The Hodgsons summered there from 1909 to 1912. The cottage Hodgson built was probably one of his company's products. It had a footprint unlike any Welch-built house in Rivermoor. It was called "House (Portable)" in the *1910 Valuation List*, probably the only such description in the town's entire list. When the property was sold in 1912, Hodgson could have moved the cottage elsewhere, but the new owner received the house "now standing," and the house kept the same tax valuation. Conveniently, it was valued at $600, just higher than Welch's $500 deed requirement. After this, Hodgson's name lived on for the cottage, appearing on the *1921 Valuation List* for a later owner.[526]

The cottage may have been replaced in 1924. (The town assessor's database for 2016 says 1930.) The valuation of a house at that location jumped from $800 in 1923 to $1,500 in 1924, and stayed fairly constant for 18 years thereafter. This suggests that a new house replaced Hodgson's original 1909 house in 1924. A garage was added in 1925. On all the Sanborn maps (1918, 1926, and 1939), the cottage has the same shape: a narrow rectangle about 12 feet by 48 feet, with its narrow end facing the ocean. This corresponds to the combination of several units of Hodgson's prefabricated houses, although it was not like any single plan footprints in the Hodgson catalog.[527]

The Hodgson cottage might have been the first and only house in Rivermoor not built by George Welch or his father.

One wonders what relationship Hodgson had with Welch, who was about 12 years older. Both were Massachusetts farm boys who became self-made men and successful entrepreneurs in the housing field. Perhaps Hodgson's speed of production encouraged Welch to build more houses.

However, Hodgson's prefabricated summer houses presented possible competition with Welch's housing on Third Cliff. Not only that, but Hodgson customers could order furniture, furnishings, and even bathroom sets (tubs, toilets and sinks) from the Hodgson company, in competition with the Welch Company.

Certainly, small prefabricated cottages were not what Welch envisioned for his upscale Rivermoor community.

Welch had advantages. He owned or controlled most lots on Third Cliff. In Rivermoor, he usually built first, then rented for years before selling. When sold, the deeds contained restrictions with minimum costs for a dwelling house. The prices of Welch's houses appear to have been much lower than the comparably sized mail-order houses from the Hodgson Company or Sears, Roebuck & Company. These prices are discussed below in a detailed discussion of notional profitability of Rivermoor houses in the early decades of the 1900s.[528]

With the lower prices of Welch houses came higher value. For a later example from 1933, Hodgson Cottage No. 3329 had a basic price of $6,325. That was higher than the 1932 tax valuation of two large Rivermoor houses (Maidstone and Indian Knoll, without lots) of $5,000 or $5,500. This Hodgson cottage seemed smaller, with about approximately 2,600 square feet, all on one floor. That was comparable to only some of Welch's smaller houses, and those had two floors. Further, the prices of Hodgson's prefabricated houses did not include additional costs for construction of foundations, assembly of the house, electrical wiring, and plumbing.[529]

Perhaps Welch had little to fear from Hodgson's company. Perhaps he enjoyed the presence of Hodgson himself, a fellow builder and entrepreneur.

Suffragists

Scituate, including Third Cliff, was the summer home of a surprising number of national leaders of the movement to give women the right to vote. These suffragists were here during the critical years leading up to the adoption of the 19th Amendment in 1920. They included:

- Inez Haynes Irwin (who developed deep family roots in Scituate)
- Will Irwin
- Beatrice Forbes-Robertson Hale and Swinburne Hale
- Judith W. Smith and Sylvanus Smith
- Caro Moore
- Mary Moore Forrest
- Meyer Bloomfield

For a more detailed discussion, see my book, *Summer Suffragists: Woman Suffrage Activists in Scituate, Massachusetts* (2020). A brief summary follows.[530]

Prolific and popular author Inez Haynes Gillmore Irwin (1873–1970) made her summer home on Second Cliff, and in her later years lived there year-round. She was nationally known as a suffragist. She co-founded the College Equal Suffrage League with fellow Radcliffe student Maud Wood Park. Inez became a leader of the militant National Women's Party, and wrote a book telling the party's history. Her husband Will Irwin (1873–1948), a famous writer and journalist, was also a staunch suffragist. Both are buried in Scituate's Union Cemetery.

Others on Second Cliff included Inez's friend, actress Beatrice Forbes-Robertson Hale (1883–1967). She traveled the country giving speeches to promote women's rights. She and her husband Swinburne Hale (1884–1937), a Harvard-educated lawyer, were prominent suffragists in New York City.

At Cedar Point (Lighthouse Point) were long-time summer residents Judith Winsor Smith (1821–1921), and her husband Sylvanus Smith (1817–1901). Judith was born in Marshfield. Sylvanus was a shipbuilder who came from Duxbury and moved his family and workplace to East Boston. For decades in the late 1800s, the family spent summers at the lighthouse keeper's cottage at the abandoned Old Scituate Light. They then built a cottage near the lighthouse. Both Sylvanus and Judith were devoted suffragists. Judith was a leader in Boston-based suffrage organizations, and even into her old age, she gave public speeches promoting suffrage. She lived to vote for president in 1920.

Third Cliff Suffragists

Third Cliff was the summer home of Caro Moore (1860–1942) and her stepdaughter Mary (or Marie) H. M. [Moore] Forrest (1873–1956), both of Washington, D.C. Both played key roles in the first suffragist procession in Washington on March 3, 1913. With more than 5,000 marchers, this was the largest parade that had ever been held in the nation's capital. It was a major turning point for the suffrage movement.

Caro was married to Mary's father, Commodore (later Captain) William Sturtevant Moore (1846–1914), a native of Duxbury. A prominent supporter of suffrage for women, he was an original member of the Massachusetts Men's League for Woman Suffrage in 1910. After retiring from the Navy in 1906, he resided with Caro at his summer home in Duxbury. In 1909 and 1910 he represented the district encompassing Duxbury, Marshfield, Norwell, Pembroke, and Scituate in the Massachusetts legislature. He supported legislation to repair seawalls and breakwaters in Scituate, and he proposed legislation to prohibit the pollution of the North River and tributaries in Pembroke and adjoining towns.

William died in 1914, and later that year, Caro and Mary bought "The Bijou" at 11 Collier Road in Rivermoor on Third Cliff. In 1919, they bought an adjacent lot. They summered at the cottage, eventually selling the properties in 1921. The cottage was later demolished. Mary Forrest continued her actions for women's rights for decades as a leader of the National Women's Party.

Mary undoubtedly knew Inez Haynes Irwin, as both were leaders of the NWP. While no correspondence seems to survive between them, one can imagine them chatting and wading in the water at Peggotty Beach that connected the two cliffs where they lived.

Third Cliff was also home in the summer to Margaret Colgate of Rockland, an early resident of Rivermoor. In 1908, she bought lot 71 and part of lot 70 from George Welch, today's 20 Collier Road. A house was there by 1909, perhaps earlier. It was called "Campbell" after her middle name. She would own the property until 1928. (The house was demolished in late 2017.) During her tenure on Third Cliff, Colgate petitioned Congress in 1914 for woman suffrage legislation.

Another suffragist, Mrs. Schuyler F. Herron, was from Winchester, wife of the Winchester Superintendent of Schools. In 1918 and perhaps other years, she summered on Third Cliff.

Meyer Bloomfield — Reformer, Suffragist

One of the most prominent summer residents of Third Cliff was Meyer Bloomfield (1878–1938). He was a noted lawyer, social worker, and industrial reformer — and an early and active suffragist.

Meyer and Sylvia Bloomfield, evidently on amusement ride,
early 1900s. Courtesy of Bloomfield family.

Bloomfield was born in Bucharest, Rumania, and moved to New York City with his parents at age four. He built a glittering resume, graduating from the College of the City of New York, Harvard University, and Boston University School of Law.[531]

Bloomfield served immigrants in his early years. In 1901 he became the first director of the Civic Service House on Salem Street in Boston's North End, a settlement house serving immigrants, mostly Jewish and Italian. A volunteer there was Sylvia "Sadie" Palmer (1881–1949), an opera singer, and in 1902, Meyer married Sylvia.

Bloomfield was an early and noted suffragist. He was an original board member, the only man, of the Boston Equal Suffrage Association for Good Government (BESAGG), founded in 1901. It was quite active, and it eventually became the Boston League of Women Voters.

Bloomfield was a national pioneer in the vocational guidance movement, which led to hiring guidance counselors in schools. Later, he was a leader in the study of personnel management, which led to creating human resources departments in corporations and large organizations. He was called the founder of the science of industrial relations.[532]

In the early 1920s, the Bloomfields moved from Boston to New York, where he specialized in immigration law and consulted on labor relations. President Hoover interviewed and considered Bloomfield for US Secretary of Labor in 1930, but eventually appointed someone else.

The Civic Service House had an interesting connection to the garment industry:

148

Three teachers at the Civic Service House later became quite prominent: Therese Weil Filene, Max Perkins, and Walter Lippmann. Filene taught music at the Civic Service House. She was married to Lincoln Filene, who with his brother, Edward A. Filene, ran Filene's Department Store. [She was also a cousin to Meyer Bloomfield.][533]

It was thus not surprising that Bloomfield played a key role in the New York garment workers' "Great Revolt" in 1910, helping to end the strike on behalf of Lincoln Filene, owner of Filene's Department Store.

Meyer and Sylvia Bloomfield had three children: Catherine Pauline, Joyce Therese, and Lincoln Palmer. With a growing family, they bought The Marguerite as a summer home in 1919. It had a commanding Third Cliff location at 3 Driftway.

Bloomfield was likely acquainted with other suffragists who lived on the cliffs. Next to The Marguerite was the Bijou, home to Caro Moore and Mary Forrest. Caro's late husband (Mary's father) had been an original member with Bloomfield in 1910 of the Massachusetts Men's League for Woman Suffrage. In addition, in 1937, Sylvia Bloomfield served on a committee of the Scituate Women's Betterment Club with Inez Irwin's sister Edith Thompson and Inez's sister-in-law Mrs. Harry E. Haynes.[534]

The Marguerite, Bloomfield summer home 1919–1944, c. 1930s.
Courtesy of Bloomfield family.

The Marguerite must have provided a quiet respite from the Bloomfields' life during the rest of the year in the heart of New York City. They renamed the cottage "On the Cliff."

Meyer Bloomfield died in 1938. Sylvia continued to own the house until 1944.[535]

J. Colby Bassett

J. [Josiah] Colby Bassett (1873–1940) was a prominent and frequent summer resident of Rivermoor. He was a descendant of a Bassett who came from England to Plymouth in 1621 on the *Fortune*, the second English ship (after the *Mayflower*) destined for Plymouth Colony. He received degrees from Colby College in 1895, Harvard Law School in 1900 (L.L.B.), and Harvard Graduate School in 1901 (A.M.). He became a partner and later senior partner (from 1929) of the law firm of Powers and Hall in Boston. He was a director of many companies, including the New England Telephone and Telegraph Company.[536]

His brothers George and Norman also became lawyers after attending Colby College and Harvard Law School. Norman taught at Colby College and later served on the college's board of trustees (1916–1931). In addition, the brothers' uncle, Leslie Colby Cornish, class of 1875, was also a trustee of the college from 1888–1926 and chairman of the board from 1907–1926. Given this background and Bassett's middle name, it is likely they were related to Gardner Colby, for whom Colby College is named.[537]

In 1915, J. Colby Bassett and his wife Josephine left their home at 6 Louisburg Square on Beacon Hill in Boston to summer at "The Melody" (18 Michael) in Rivermoor. In 1918, they rented on Moorland, probably at the "Boulder Cottage" (59 Moorland), where they also stayed in 1920.[538]

Hermon Holt Jr.

Hermon Holt Jr. (c. 1876-1968) was another notable resident, listed in the 1938 Social Register. His summer residence was on Moorland and Cliff, probably on the northeast corner, in a house that is no longer there. His winter residence was at 45 Pleasant Street in Newton Centre. He graduated from Dartmouth College, class of 1897, and Harvard Law School, class of 1901. (Perhaps he knew J. Colby Bassett, Harvard Law class of 1900.) He was a partner in the law firm of Powers, Holt and Foster. He was also a trustee and director of the Massachusetts Savings Bank. His wife Marian was a Mayflower descendant.[539]

Colonel Charles W. Furlong

Colonel Charles Wellington Furlong (1874–1967) was a famous American explorer, US Army intelligence officer in World War I, and aide to President Wilson during the Paris Peace Conference. In addition, he was an artist, cowboy, college professor, scientist,

150

author, and lecturer. He was a good friend of Theodore Roosevelt. In the early 1900s he explored Tierra del Fuego, the southernmost point of South America. He later explored French Guiana, the Near East, Surinam, Venezuela, and Bolivia. In 1929–1930, he explored Kenya, Tanganyika, the Belgian Congo, Uganda, and the Sudan. On that trip, newspapers reported, "Col Furlong covered some 7000 miles, visited the pigmy country and had numerous adventures with wild beasts."[540]

Soon after his Africa trip, he bought the house at 18 Collier Road on Third Cliff. He owned it from 1931 to 1942.[541]

This must have been a summer residence. Since 1928, he had owned another house in the Sherman's Corner/West End area of Scituate, close to the Norwell line. This house, at 304 Old Oaken Bucket Road, was built about 1781. He called it "Six Gables" and added buildings on the lot. It was later documented as "Eight Gables." The house still exists.[542]

Furlong was instrumental in arranging the donation of Henry Turner Bailey's papers to the University of Oregon Library. Bailey (1865–1931) had been Furlong's art teacher and was a noted son of Scituate.[543]

Although Furlong was born in Cambridge and later lived in Newton, Massachusetts, he could also be considered a noted son of Scituate. He visited the town often from the age of four and even stayed in the historic Bates House, as he explained in a speech on "The Influence of Scituate in the Life of an Explorer."[544]

For the town's tercentenary celebration in 1936, Furlong was one of four people on the booklet committee, along with noted writer Will Irwin. The committee produced a fine history of Scituate, with text by Irwin and photos by Furlong.[545]

Left: Furlong in safari gear, early 1900s. Right: map by Furlong, *Geographical Review* 3:3 (1917), 177. Both courtesy of Wikimedia Commons.

13

RIVERMOOR'S CONTINUED RISE

George Welch did his part to attract summer colonists to Third Cliff's Rivermoor.

A June 21, 1914, Boston newspaper article reported, "At Rivermoor the cottages are nearly all occupied." Cottages had been built and given names, and Rivermoor was getting municipal services. In just eight years since its start, Rivermoor had taken its place as a premier summer destination on the South Shore.[546]

The term "cottage" today implies a small dwelling, as it did long ago. A hundred or so years ago, however, the term could mean a summer home of any size, even including the grand mansions of Newport, Rhode Island. Postcards of Rivermoor houses called them cottages.[547]

To get an idea of the size of Welch colonials of a hundred years ago, look at two existing examples. They have two stories and mostly original layouts, with about 2,738 square feet of living area (12 Parker), and 1,848 (18 Cliff, as of 2016, since expanded). Both were two or three times the size of the average house at the time, about 1,000 square feet. The average size of a new US single-family house later grew to 1,660 square feet in 1973 (the earliest figure available from the Census Bureau), and 2,687 square feet in 2015. In other words, it took one hundred years for the average US house to grow to the size of a Rivermoor "cottage."[548]

The seaside cottages were built on land that was once cheap. By 1914, the *Boston Globe* marveled at how expensive the land had become in 55 years, based on tax valuations. Americans now wanted to spend summers by the shore and that land had become valuable.[549]

House Names Again

Houses in Rivermoor kept being named, probably by George Welch. Newspaper reports used house names to say where summer residents were staying. They did not use street addresses (numbers), which were not in use at the time.

A 1914 Boston newspaper article, for example, named 22 cottages, including The Marguerite. It included all four houses on the north side of Michael Avenue: "the Myrtle," "Mayfair," "the Melody," and "the Moorfield." (Later, a smaller cottage was built on the south side of Michael Avenue named "Midget.") The article also included houses on Lincoln Avenue: "the Linden," "Lavender," and "the Linnet." Alliteration ran rampant. Some cottages, however, were named after their occupants. For example, in 1914, the newspaper reported, "the Mayo" was rented to George H. Mayo of New York. The name of the Mayo did not start with an L, like the others on Lincoln Avenue.[550]

George H. Mayo (?–1927) was evidently an 1894 graduate of Boston English High School. He became an executive of the United States Rubber Company in New York, while retaining his ties to the Boston area.[551]

The 1914 newspaper article reported that "Mitten Cottage" on Moorland was rented to Arthur G. "Mitten" of Brookline. It had earlier reported that George "Miton" had stayed in Rivermoor in 1911, perhaps in the same cottage. In 1915, evidently correcting its spelling, the newspaper reported that "Mitton" cottage was rented, but to someone other than Arthur G. Mitton.[552]

Newspaper readers at the time might have recognized a renter like Arthur G. Mitton as being from a prominent family. Mitton family members led the famed Boston department store Jordan Marsh for most of the first seven decades of the 1900s.

Arthur Mitton himself was a prominent Boston attorney, a senior partner in Hemenway & Barnes. He represented Jordan Marsh in at least one case.[553]

His father was Edward J. Mitton, and his brother was George W. Mitton.[554] Edward J. Mitton (1847–1913) was an early partner and vice president of Jordan Marsh, and George W. Mitton (1869–1947) was president of Jordan Marsh from 1916 to 1930; George W. Mitton's son Edward R. Mitton (1896–1973) became president of Jordan Marsh in 1937 and later chairman, serving until 1968.[555] For many people, "Mitton" was synonymous with Jordan Marsh.

The Mitton family typically appears to have summered, at the turn of the century, in Swampscott on the North Shore, rather than Scituate on the South Shore. Perhaps the Mittons were drawn to the North Shore because Eben D. Jordan, founder of Jordan Marsh and Company, built a summer estate called "The Rocks" about 1905 at West Manchester.[556]

However briefly Arthur and George Mitton occupied the Rivermoor cottage on Moorland, its name stuck for years. Town tax valuations listed "Mitton" until George Welch sold it in 1919. Even afterwards, the cottage's association with Jordan Marsh endured so long that at least one local resident mentioned it in 2016.[557]

This was not the only example of a cottage named for an owner or renter. The cottage at 22 Collier was known as "The Russell" for years after A. L. Russell of Hyde Park rented it for a short term in 1909. Later renters of "The Russell" eventually had the cottage named after their family, the Leonards.[558]

Even with an occupant's name on the cottage, there was turnover. For example, a year after the 1914 newspaper article, at least 10 of the 22 cottages (including "Mitton") had different summer residents.[559]

Naming the cottages was a good marketing strategy by George Welch, and it was a custom of the era, now somewhat quaint. Naming houses such as those in Rivermoor was a practice that flourished in the early 1900s, then apparently faded away in the 1920s. By the mid-1930s, house addresses in Scituate used street numbers.[560] Some house names survived, like "Cliff's End," discussed in chapter 19. And some — like "Laurel" and "Mereside" — have been revived by their owners from historical documents (with some help by the local historian). The names are now displayed on carved wooden signs.[561]

Some Third Cliff residents have more recently given their houses names such as "Cliffhanger," "Seagrass," Seabiscuit," "Cheers," "Wild Edge," "Salty Dog," "Topgallant," "Rosecliff," — even "Rivermoor" (at least two such signs) — or the owner's name. The names appear on carved wooden signs, based on ship quarterboards. The practice is widespread in Scituate. The town is fortunate to have had skilled woodcarvers such as Paul McCarthy, Paul Kukstis, and others.[562]

The practice of naming houses extends to automobile license plates, with names like "CLIFF," "RVRMOR," and "BYDSEA." A neighborhood resident even had a boat named "Rivermoor'd."

Quarterboard by Paul McCarthy, c. 1970s. Image by Lyle Nyberg.

Services Available for Rivermoor

By 1915, George Welch had retired from active participation in the Welch Company, turning his attention to real estate, including Rivermoor. He continued to own the Welch Company's properties in Scituate Harbor, which were quite extensive.[563]

Perhaps this was a good time to be in real estate, because as one source reported, "the building trade [in Massachusetts] is especially active at this time, which has caused an increased demand for building materials of all kinds."[564]

The year 1915 also marked the town's big push to attract summer tourists. It added a pier, and the *Gurnet* boat service began between Boston and Scituate. George Welch placed national ads (example copied below) to promote the Rivermoor colony.

Rivermoor by that time had town water service, from the private Scituate Water Company. By 1918, the town's average daily consumption of water swelled from 200,000 gallons in winter to 500,000 gallons in summer, indicating the surge of summer residents at places like Rivermoor.[565]

Rivermoor also had its own post office serving Third Cliff. Mail arrived there twice a day, and departed twice a day. Thus, summer residents could get away for the season, yet still stay connected to others. Mail was not delivered to each house. Instead, residents picked up their mail at the post office.[566]

The Rivermoor post office had three locations over the years. Each post office was prominently located at the entrance to Rivermoor. Originally, it was on the east (ocean) side of Collier Road, between Water Street (Driftway) and Parker Avenue. At first, it was operated by storeowner Charles W. Frye (see discussion below). Then it was operated by postmistress Beatrice H. Flaherty from about 1915 to 1918. Old photos show this as a shed barely wide enough for a doorway and window, confined on both sides by other structures.[567]

Left: original Rivermoor post office, c. 1915–1918. Courtesy of Nancy Howell.

Between 1918 and 1926, the post office moved around the corner to a place on Water Street (Driftway), close to Gilson Road (as it was later called). There, the Fallon family ran the post office, a general store, and a gasoline pump. The family kept residences on Gilson Road and Eagles Nest Road.[568]

The Fallon family's two-story house held the post office and a general store on the first floor. It burned down in 1935. By 1939, a new structure appeared nearby as the post office, along with an adjoining structure (probably the store). It was at the Gilson-Driftway intersection, replacing an earlier structure. Ellen H. Fallon was the Rivermoor postmaster, according to 1926 and 1938 directories. The post office was in operation as late as 1949. It closed in the late 1950s. The structure was demolished and replaced by a home in 2010, when its address of 22 Driftway changed to 149 Gilson.[569]

Rivermoor also had a general store, at least in the summer. It was probably always connected with the post office operation. In 1909, George Welch sold a part of Rivermoor lot 3 with its buildings to Charles W. Frye, who operated a general store and post office on Front Street in Scituate Harbor. Lot 3 was east of Collier Road, a little south of the Driftway. A structure here marked "S." appeared on the 1918 Sanborn map. Perhaps this was a store, next to which was the narrow shed housing the original post office. With Frye's involvement, both could have been in use since his 1909 purchase. A 1915 directory listed Charles W. Frye as having a general store on Front Street and in Rivermoor. Perhaps Welch convinced the owner of Frye's store to establish a branch in Rivermoor. Welch's 1915 ad for Rivermoor mentions a "branch store." By 1918, Frye no longer had a store in Rivermoor, and the Fallon family operated a store there along with the post office.[570]

Residents in 1918 could have their laundry done in Scituate Harbor at two businesses near each other: Meadow Brook Laundry (where Hennessey News is now, at 5 Brook Street), or the smaller Chinese laundry (just north of where Maria's Submarine Sandwich Shop is now, at 47 Front Street).[571]

For recreation, residents had ready access to Rivermoor's beach, at the foot of Third Cliff, with swimming and foot-racing for the children on the beach. Some residents set up a tennis court at the western end of Michael or Lincoln Avenues, across Moorland from "Indian Knoll." Residents played croquet on their lawns.[572]

Left: playing croquet in Rivermoor, 1913. Tennis court in background. Right: foot-racing on Rivermoor beach (detail), 1913. Woodworth family photo album.

Marketing Rivermoor

George Welch continued his promotional actions. He placed this advertisement in Nebraska's *Omaha Bee*, May 19, 1915:

Summer Resorts
RIVERMOOR
A Select Colony On
The South Shore
Scituate, Massachusetts

This lovely shore resort is located at the end of the road on the southerly end of Third Cliff, Scituate, Mass.

It is about a mile from the station and the town, directly on the ocean front, and commands an unobstructed view up and down the coast and out to sea. There are grassy uplands all around and hills in the distance. Boating, bathing and fishing may be enjoyed and canoes and motor boats are used on the North river, where trips up the river for fifteen miles may be taken. A branch store and post-office are located here, and many of the cottages have telephones.

The town has good stores where all supplies may be obtained. Fresh fish and lobsters can be bought at any time. Summer train service gives a train every hour and the livery stable service is good.

All the cottages are new, with modern conveniences, including excellent town water, baths, fireplaces, sleeping porches and garages. The houses are large, with large rooms having windows on two and three sides.

All floors are of the best hard pine, well finished. The rooms are fully furnished except for bed and table linen and silver. The furniture is of the plain mission type. All beds are of plan [plain] white iron with best National springs and combination mattresses. Blankets, quilts and pillows are supplied. The pantry and kitchen are generously furnished, the range is a Cabinet Glenwood, and the china a set of matched willow ware.

There are no houses to compare with these in cleanliness, equipment, comfort and convenience.

Rentals range from $300 to $600, for a four months' lease.

No dissatisfied tenants have ever summered here. The houses will be shown at any time.

Apply to the Owner,
GEORGE F. WELCH
SCITUATE, MASS.[573]

So George had gone from offering one house for rent in 1906, to a whole resort colony in 1915. Other places could offer "no houses to compare" with those to be rented in Rivermoor.

Note how his ad emphasized recreational opportunities at or on the water, and how, above all, it offered the latest household conveniences, such as Glenwood stoves. The ad did not trade on any historical New England quaintness, as Nantucket did in the late 1800s.[574]

Glenwood was a leading brand of stoves that the Welch Company carried. In an old photo, copied in chapter 5, the main Welch Company building on Front Street had a sign on the side: "Glenwood Ranges & Heaters [nearly illegible two lines, likely "Make Housekeeping Easy" and "For Sale By"] Geo. F. Welch."[575]

Glenwood ranges and heaters were designed and made by the Weir Stove Co. in Taunton, Massachusetts. The company was active from 1879 into the 1920s and beyond, shutting down in 1949.[576]

Cabinet Glenwood stove ad, *Boston Globe*, Oct. 28, 1915, 3 (detail).

The $300–$600 rent for the summer in the 1915 ad seems competitive. Back in the 1870s, a cottage in high-end Newport, Rhode Island, could cost $3,000 for the summer, and lesser accommodations at less exclusive resorts could be as low as $15 a week. In 1914, a ten-room cottage in Nantasket with ocean and lake view was offered for $325 for the year. In 1915, a seven-room cottage on Sagamore Hill in Nantasket was offered at $300 "for long season." In 1918, a ten-room bungalow in Annisquam (Gloucester), north of Boston, could be had for $300 for the summer, and a six-room cottage on Cape Cod went for $150 for the season. A typical house in Rivermoor could have eight or nine rooms.[577]

Left: willow ware example (original in blue and white). Photo by Lyle Nyberg.

It is not clear how "select" the Rivermoor colony was. It was, like the summer colonies of Buzzards Bay, "a rung or two beneath the social exclusiveness of Bar Harbor, Southampton, and Newport" of the late 1800s.[578]

It was also a rung or two below Oyster Harbors on Great Island at Cape Cod:

"You cannot visit the club unless you know the management or are introduced by a member. You cannot buy property on the island or rent a house unless you are a Christian with a sizable bank account."[579]

Oyster Harbors, opened in 1927, had a windmill for a gatehouse where visitors had to check in.[580] Rivermoor had nothing similar. Rivermoor was not that exclusive and not a gated community. But it attracted mostly upper-class professionals and businessmen from the Boston area.

Summer Colonists Drawn to Rivermoor Cottages

Rivermoor was evidently full of summer colonists in 1915.

On June 20, the *Boston Globe* reported these summer residents: Mr. and Mrs. C. M. Moore of Washington, DC, at the Bijou, Mr. and Mrs. Robert Leonard of Brookline at the Russell cottage, Mr. and Mrs. Colby Bassett of Boston at "The Melody," William B. Coffin and family of Boston at a Rivermoor cottage, Mrs. E. Farnsworth of Boston at Moorfield cottage, C. E. Goodrich and family of Boston at the Jennings cottage, and Mr. and Mrs. Arthur Woodworth of Boston at Indian Knoll cottage. Dr. Frederick Burns and family of Boston were at "Livermoor," a misprint for Rivermoor, because his name appears in the 1915 directory as staying at "The Marshes," which is on Moorland Road in Rivermoor.[581]

The *Boston Globe* was careful to report the new summer arrivals separately for each summer colony: Shore Acres, Third Cliff, Rivermoor, etc. Each evidently had its own distinctiveness and perhaps social standing.

Just a week later, on June 27, 1915, the paper reported the following:

Down on the southerly end of Third Cliff, known as "Rivermoor," there is quite a colony of Summer visitors, including George C. Scott and family of Framingham at "Mereside," H. A. Macgowan of Worcester at the "Wheeler," Mrs. F. A. Walker of Brookline at the "Sunshine," Cyrus Brewer of Brookline at "Maidstone," George C. Coit of Boston at the "Mayfair," A. W. Jackson of Boston at the "Moorfield," W. D. Dexter of Boston at the "Laurel," C. S. Whiting of Cambridge at the "Marguerite," J. S. Miller Jr. of Chicago at the "Linden," G. S. Gillis of Hyde Park at the "Linnet," Barton Leonard of Boston at the "Russell," A. W. Gregory of Hartford, Conn. at the "Gregory," and J. C. Hunsaker of Brookline at the "Myrtle."[582]

These summer residents alone rented at least 40% of the houses then in Rivermoor.[583]

Rivermoor attracted notable renters in 1916. Among them was Mr. John A. Trott, who rented the "Sunshine." He was the treasurer and general manager of the Riverside Boiler Works in Cambridge, Massachusetts. The company manufactured boilers and expansion tanks since 1896. No connection could be found for Mr. Trott with George Welch's early-1900s cottage on Third Cliff named Trotwood, Trottwood, or Trostwood. Probably the cottage was named for Betsey Trotwood, a character in Charles Dickens' 1850 novel *David Copperfield*, thus adding another Dickensian name on Third Cliff's north side.[584]

In addition, "Mr. C. H. Blackall has rented the 'Primrose' and the 'Mitten' cottage at Rivermoor for the coming season." Clarence Howard Blackall (1857–1942) was a renowned theater architect. His work includes Boston landmarks such as the Colonial Theatre, the Wilbur Theatre, the Modern, and the Metropolitan (now the Wang Theater), as well as Boston's first steel frame structure, the Winthrop Building (1892).[585]

Scituate was among the South Shore towns that attracted some of Boston's social elite for summers. The 1920 Social Register's summer edition had 9 entries for Scituate, 16 for Duxbury, and 36 for Cohasset.[586]

Rivermoor's Uniqueness

How unique was Rivermoor? It is difficult to say. Both Rivermoor and North Scituate Beach, at opposite ends of Scituate, are representative of seaside residential communities that developed around coastal New England during the late nineteenth and early twentieth centuries.[587]

Both areas attracted the attention of the Sanborn Map Company. The company created surveys and detailed maps to assess fire risks for insurance purposes. The company surveyed properties in the Scituate Harbor business area, and summer resort areas in Scituate, but generally not other established areas in town.[588]

The Welch houses in Rivermoor were very well built, according to a builder who has renovated and expanded many of those houses. Houses at North Scituate Beach were of equal or better quality and higher in architectural style. The houses in both places had names. For every "Marguerite" or "Bijou" in Rivermoor, there was a "Briny Rest" or "Cliff Haven" at North Scituate Beach. Rivermoor's lot sizes were comparable to those at North Scituate Beach and Shore Acres. Rivermoor's beach access was equivalent to that at other seaside summer resorts. Post offices were located at both Rivermoor and North Scituate Beach. Both had public water service.[589]

North Scituate Beach had advantages. It appears to have had a public sewer early, in 1899, more than 100 years before Rivermoor. North Scituate Beach had a water system by 1902, more than ten years before Rivermoor had one. North Scituate Beach had electricity early, perhaps by 1908. North Scituate Beach had the Cliff House and other places to stay, while Rivermoor had no hotel. Rivermoor lacked proximity to a private golf course until 1919, compared to North Scituate Beach, with its Hatherly Country Club, founded in 1899.[590]

North Scituate Beach was created and became an established area early, and that held an attraction for summer visitors. It also offered places for religious services. The Seaside Chapel was built in 1894 at the northeast corner of Collier Avenue and Ocean Avenue. It was operated by the Baptists, and later the Episcopalians. In 1903, a Roman Catholic summer chapel was built nearby on Cleveland Avenue (now named Whitcomb Road).[591]

For more earthly desires, according to a 1912 account, North Scituate Beach had lobster fishermen to supply lobsters "for the gratification of the critical tastes and eager appetites of Beach residents and visitors."

Left: Capt. [Charles] Pratt, right, with Woodworth family and friends, c. 1909. Woodworth family photo album.

In addition, the 1912 account boosted North Scituate Beach with this statement:

> Captain Charles Pratt, with whose upright figure we are all familiar, with his good sloop, the Thomas B. Reed, has furnished summer-long opportunities for the enjoyment of pleasure sailing and deep sea fishing."[592]

Rivermoor, however, had other advantages. It was newer than its nearby rivals. Rivermoor alone had rolling hills, and this allowed more houses to have ocean views. All four cliffs were hilly, but Third Cliff had the largest area for a summer colony. Perhaps the cliff location provided protection against the devastation of lower seaside areas. The Portland Gale of 1898 had moved and more or less wrecked every house at North Scituate's Rocky Beach and many cottages at Sand Hills. In addition, Rivermoor residents could easily drive to Scituate Harbor or even North Scituate Beach for sailing and deep-sea fishing, since automobiles were becoming more popular. Rivermoor had a single developer and builder in George Welch. He had access to lumber, supplies, and furniture from his Welch Company business. He seemed to have been a talented marketer as well.[593]

The Woodworth family offers a telling example. For years, they summered at the Alice Place Cottage on Collier Avenue in North Scituate Beach. By the summer of 1912, they moved to the newly built "Indian Knoll" cottage in Rivermoor. They eventually purchased the property, in 1919.[594]

A 1916 guidebook to New England highlighted Third Cliff and not North Scituate Beach. It called Scituate "an ancient town settled in 1628 whose appearance has been greatly modernized by the advent of summer residents." It reported, "The Third Cliff has some all-the-year-round homes and many summer cottages" while dismissing Scituate's Shore Acres as "an unpretentious cottage colony." The book also said, "The old town of Scituate, or Satuit, has retained much of its oldtime atmosphere and simple beauty, and is the summer resort of many literary and artistic people [listing many who lived on Second Cliff]."[595]

An Artists' Colony?

Some sources say that Third Cliff — like Second Cliff — also had a summer colony of artists. The main source for this is Margaret Cole Bonney's book *My Scituate*. Perhaps Bonney mistakenly wrote Third Cliff when she meant Second Cliff. The evidence for such a colony on Third Cliff is meager.[596]

It is true that Joseph Henry Hatfield (1863–1928), an artist who studied in Paris and Giverny and settled in Canton, Massachusetts, had some connection to Third Cliff and is pictured there in a 1918 photo.[597]

Other artists lived near Third Cliff, and some painted scenes of the cliff.

Josephine Miles Lewis (1865–1959), an artist who also studied in Paris and Giverny, summered in Scituate at Elm Park with her sister Matilda Lewis. Elm Park was off Highland Street (later named Greenfield Lane), within walking distance of Third Cliff.[598]

Mariquita Gill (1861-1915), another artist who studied in Giverny, also lived in Scituate and painted scenes of Scituate cliffs and the North River marshes at Third Cliff. She had married Arthur Murray Cobb, another wealthy expatriate and artist from Boston who studied painting in Giverny. They both had paintings exhibited in the 1893 World's Columbian Exposition in Chicago. They divorced by 1895.[599]

Thomas Buford Meteyard (1865–1928) also had paintings in the 1893 World's Columbian Exposition. He painted landscapes at Third Cliff, particularly the marshlands along the North River. He did not live on Third Cliff, but he had his own "colony" at his studio and home on nearby Meeting House Lane at the turn of the century. He had painted in Monet's Giverny, as had his friends Mariquita Gill and Alice Beckington (1868–1942). Meteyard had proposed marriage to Beckington, but she turned him down.[600]

Beckington was a miniaturist who had a studio, the "Barn," on Kent Street near Meeting House Lane, also within walking distance of Third Cliff. Beckington painted a landscape of Third Cliff showing the old Nathaniel Turner (Waterman) farmhouse (formerly at 141 Driftway), which is discussed in chapter 2. In addition, she took a photo of the lip of Third Cliff that is copied in chapter 9.[601]

Dawson Dawson-Watson (1864–1939) was another artist in Meteyard's circle on Meeting House Lane, near Third Cliff, who had worked with Meteyard in Giverny.[602]

A contemporary of these artists was Eleanor Richards (1865–1950). She lived across the North River on Spring Street in Marshfield, about four miles from Third Cliff. She studied painting at the Academie Julian in Paris, the same school where Josephine Miles Lewis, Alice Beckington, and Mariquita Gill studied. She painted a portrait of her father, Lysander Salmon Richards (1835–1926), on display at the Marshfield Historical Society headquarters. She painted a portrait of her sister-in-law Fanny Richards (1868–1958), in the collection of the Chevy Chase Historical Society. The Historic Winslow House Association in Marshfield has her paintings of members of the historic Winslow family.[603]

Sears Gallagher (1869–1955), an artist originally from Boston, summered on Fourth Cliff (Humarock) in 1918. He also visited nearby Sea View in Marshfield frequently in the early 1900s. He was a lover of golf whose artistry was critiqued by Howard R. Guild in 1920. Guild owned much property in Rivermoor, and perhaps Sears Gallagher visited him and painted at the Scituate Country Club's new golf course there. Sears Gallagher created a watercolor of Third Cliff that was exhibited in a gallery in 2009.[604]

Other sources of information fail to show an artists' colony on Third Cliff. A 1915 business directory listed only two artists, and both were from Marshfield. An art student who summered on Third Cliff died young in 1928. The Scituate Historical Society files on artists mention 81 artists, including those listed in a 1938 local paper. Only two of them appear to have lived on Third Cliff. One was Frank L. Nason, employed full-time as a sales manager for an electrical equipment manufacturer for much of his life, according to US census reports. Another — Joyce Bloomfield — was only about 19 years old at the time of the 1938 list, according to US census reports. However, she was later noted as a gifted painter.[605]

Artist Mrs. Clarence Brier owned property on Gilson Road and evidently lived on Highland (now Greenfield Lane), just west of Third Cliff.[606]

Also on the fringe of Third Cliff was another artist, who lived at 119 Kent Street, the former home of the Scituate Hospital. Elizabeth Davey was an artist for some of America's and England's leading greeting card companies, in addition to being one of the country's foremost bulldog artists.[607]

In the 1960s, Claudia and Stephen Edgell of Winchester bought property on Third Cliff, first on Gilson Road, then on Collier Road. Claudia was an artist and Stephen was a photographer. The Edgells were known more on Third Cliff, however, for holding dog shows on their lawn.[608]

Not far from the Edgell's house lived Bill Sexton, a cartoonist in the late 1970s and in the 1980s when he lived at 14 Driftway. His cartoons appeared regularly in the *Scituate Mariner*.[609]

Haumans and Tom Eames

Before dismissing Third Cliff as an artists' colony, consider the team of George Hauman (1890–1961) and Doris (Holt) Hauman (1897–1984). Doris's family was from the Boston area, renting in West Somerville and later owning a house in Lexington. Her father Charles Holt (born 1870) appears to be the C. E. Holt reported in a 1906 social register and a 1909 *Boston Globe* article as staying at the "Trotwood" on Dickens Row (#4) on Third Cliff. He and his wife Caroline (born 1872) summered on Third Cliff thereafter, and in 1920 he bought the Shaneck cottage on Dickens Row (#10). Since Caroline's father was born in Germany, perhaps there was a connection with former owner Herman Shaneck, who was also born in Germany.[610]

We don't know when Doris Holt met George Hauman. He was a talented artist early on. In 1909, he won first prize in a competition with pupils of the high schools of Greater Boston. At Revere High School, he was the class-day essayist, speaking on "The Influence of the Cartoon." George and Doris married in 1924 and lived next door to her parents in Lexington. They also summered on Dickens Row. They helped found the Arts and Crafts Society of Lexington.[611]

Doris and George Hauman, c. 1920s.
Courtesy of Kirk Hauman.

The Haumans wrote and illustrated several books, including *Happy Harbor: A Seashore Story*, a delightful story published in 1938 that takes place in a seaside town that could only be Scituate. They also illustrated the popular 1954 edition of *The Little Engine That Could*.[612]

A news article reported:

> In their heyday, the Haumans were a remarkable pair of artists. They worked out of a studio in their Scituate home and cranked out hundreds of illustrations for children's books. They worked for the major publishing firms of the 1930s, '40s and '50s, including Platt and Munk, Houghton Mifflin and Little Brown.[613]

George Hauman died in 1961, and Doris Hauman died in Scituate in 1984.[614]

In their early years, the Haumans had a friend who was a talented young cartoonist, Thomas H. Eames (1902–1975). He gave the couple a seven-foot scroll of watercolor sketches (cartoons) showing scenes of Front Street, Third Cliff, and other places in Scituate. It has great value as historical documentation, and it has funny comments by the people shown in the scenes. They include cartoons of Charles Frye, Capt. [Fred] Stanley, George Welch, Will Irwin, and other local notables of the era. The scenes take place roughly about 1915. The Scituate Historical Society reprinted the scenes from the Eames scroll in a calendar for 2000. The calendar attributes the scenes to Tom Eames of Cohasset.[615]

One scene shows "Tom" (the artist) hitching a ride in front of Severn's drug store and the Stenbeck market on Front Street. To Tom's right is "Doris" eating an ice cream cone while a Scottish voice from below says "Little girl, ye'll fen [fain = gladly] marry a nartist" (which Doris Holt did). In front of Tom and Doris is a man showing a picture and saying, "It's a impression pitcher by the Hauman kid." Another scene shows a poster in Curran's shop window announcing an exhibition "by the boy wonder George Hauman" at Allen Memorial Library.[616]

Yet another scene shows Third Cliff with the twin houses of Daniel Ward and the "Shannok" house next door, on Dickens Row, and the "Graham" house behind them. All these houses appear on the 1903 map. Their current addresses would be 24 Town Way (Graham) and 10 Dickens Row (Shaneck). Herman G. Shaneck owned the latter property from 1900 to 1919. It was often called "Shannock." In 1920, it was sold to Doris Hauman's father Charles Holt. The site is still in the Hauman family, although a new house was built there in 1954.[617]

A little detective work reveals the Third Cliff connection between the Holt family (including Doris) and the family of Tom the artist.

Tom's family lived in Somerville and spent summers in Rivermoor on Third Cliff. His father, Henry H. Eames, was one of the first buyers in Rivermoor, buying lot 211 (33 Collier) from George Welch in 1906 and building a house there by early 1908. Then the family bought lot 43 (10 Cliff) in 1911 and moved there by 1914. They bought adjacent lot 44 in 1919. They must have known the Holt family (and daughter Doris), who summered on the northern end of Third Cliff since about 1906. The Eames family must have spent summers at their home on Cliff Avenue until 1937, when they sold the property.[618]

The house at 10 Cliff remains, with alterations.

Eames Bungalow, Third Cliff, 10 Cliff Ave., c. 1914.
Courtesy of Scituate Historical Society.

Thomas H. Eames became a "visual psychologist" (appropriately enough for a cartoonist) and ophthalmologist specializing in instruction of children with reading problems. He was on the faculty of Boston University's School of Education and published an astonishing 153 scholarly articles. He and his wife Marjorie lived in Cohasset. It is not known if he kept up his illustration work.[619]

The Eames family had neighbors on Cliff Avenue. The Thomas J. Edwards family owned the house at 18 Cliff, built by 1918. A native of Wales, Edwards had founded a Boston engraving and die business in 1901. The house remains, but has been extensively modernized and expanded.[620]

Edwards House, 18 Cliff Ave., c. 1912–1918.
Courtesy of Scituate Historical Society.

Whether or not the Haumans and all of the above-mentioned artists added up to an artists' colony on Third Cliff, the cliff would have been a wonderful and scenic place for a colony of artists. And it still is. Several artists have lived and worked there, including Nancy Howell, Valerie Vitali, and the late Joanne Papandrea.[621]

Home of Pirate Treasure?

If Third Cliff held no artists' colony, what about buried pirate treasure? This claim is not as extravagant as it may seem. Third Cliff has legendary associations with pirates.

Some sources say Capt. Kidd or other pirates buried treasure on the cliff, supposedly at a large rock at what is now the southern intersection of Collier and Moorland. Edward Rowe Snow, part historian and part showman, and a resident of Scituate's neighboring town of Marshfield, wrote many popular books about buried treasure along the Massachusetts coast. This included 1953's *True Tales of Pirates and Their Gold*. Chapter XVIII "Treasure on the Third Cliff" tells the story of William Holmes, purportedly of Scituate (others say he was from Scotland). Holmes signed on to a privateer ship that captured another ship near Cadiz, Spain, in the early 1800s. He then participated in killing two of his officers, stealing the captured ship, and sailing it across the Atlantic to Scituate. He and his mates buried the ship's treasure at Third Cliff. He was caught, tried and convicted in Boston. He was sentenced to death as a pirate. The defendants' appeal to the US Supreme Court was denied. In 1820, near the corner of Washington Street and Dover Street in Boston, Holmes and his two mates were hanged.[622]

Edward Rowe Snow, who uncovered this information, had a "traveling museum" of artifacts that included the skeleton of Holmes.[623]

This much is based on court records at the federal district court in Boston. Snow's book goes on to say that two coins, possibly from the treasure, were found at Third Cliff in 1951–1952, and the book says more of the treasure could gradually surface. Some of this pirate treasure was reportedly hidden in the historic Mann House in Scituate, according to reports in the 1980s. All this provides some basis to believe Third Cliff had (and may still have) buried pirate treasure.[624]

Rivermoor Attracts Summer Residents and Buyers

Rivermoor had attractions beyond artistic appeal and possible pirate plunder, and it developed rapidly. By 1918, Rivermoor had about 47 houses. More than half had small detached garages for an automobile. This was at a time when only one in thirteen families owned an automobile. The days of access to Scituate exclusively by railroad or horse-drawn carriage had ended. Professional men could house their families at the shore for the summer, visiting them by automobile on weekends and holidays. People wanted a summer break despite, or possibly because of, America's entry into war in early 1917.[625]

Those who could afford an automobile could travel from Boston on "fine macadam all the way" to Plymouth. The official *Automobile Blue Book* of 1915 offered two routes to Plymouth, both passing through the Scituate area. One was Route 264, "the direct route via the Parkway system." (This appears to have been the ancestor of today's Route 3.) The second was Route 263, which "while longer than Route 264, is the more interesting." (Evidently the ancestor of today's Route 3A.)[626]

A map at the beginning of a 1916 guidebook simply showed a road along the South Shore. Later on in the book, however, were detailed driving directions for that area.[627]

1916 key map (detail) in Sargent, *A Handbook of New England*, shows
a road (in red in original) along the shore to Provincetown. Scituate,
unmarked, is halfway between Boston and Plymouth.

Some residents of Scituate were early adopters of the automobile. The postcard entitled "Rivermoor, Scituate, Mass." (copied in chapter 11) shows a red convertible touring car that looks like the Mitchell Little Six owned by George Welch's son-in-law, Dr. T. Branch Alexander. Dr. Alexander extolled the car in a 1916 *Boston Globe* article. He had driven it 1,000 miles up north through New Hampshire to Quebec and back through the Green Mountains of Vermont. That was not his first automobile. Dr. Alexander had offered for sale a 1907 Maxwell Model L with top, lights, "Storm Shield" and "Extra Tubes."[628]

Left: Example of license plate, 1914 (blue on white in original), at Mann Farm House, Scituate Historical Society.
Photo by Lyle Nyberg 2016.

Ad for Mitchell Little Six, *Automobile Topics*,
January 3, 1914, p. 639 (portion).

The automobile provided a fun and interesting way of traveling to seaside towns like Scituate. Whatever the mode of travel, the visitors came. They might want to rent or buy property, and this was a good opportunity for George Welch. By 1918, he had a significant investment in real estate, as well as furniture for the houses he was renting.[629]

In Rivermoor, Welch had begun by renting houses. Now, it was time to sell them. In a typical deed, he included the following restrictions, presumably designed to maintain an upscale community:

> The above premises are conveyed subject to the following restrictions I No building to be used as a dwelling shall be erected at a cost less than $1,000.00. II No objectionable outbuildings shall be placed upon the premises III No swine or fowl shall be kept upon the premises.[630]

Such private deed restrictions were often used in the subdivisions of developer/builders that began in the mid-1800s, and these planned neighborhoods were widespread by the early 1900s. Such restrictions were the origin of later public zoning bylaws.[631]

As residents moved from renting to buying houses, Rivermoor was undergoing the same ownership transition as the North Scituate Beach community. The transition began with the occasional vacationer hiring a cottage (implying a short stay), or boarding (shorter term). It progressed to leasing for summer housekeeping, implying a longer-term commitment. An example is the four-month lease mentioned in George's 1915 newspaper ad. The next step was buying one's own summer house.[632]

By 1918, George began to turn his focus to selling houses.

14

Rivermoor's Boom Year of 1919

The year 1919 was significant for the country and for Rivermoor.

After the armistice ending the World War was signed November 11, 1918, cities and towns welcomed returning soldiers and sailors with various ceremonies. Scituate held a day-long welcome-home program on July 4. Thomas W. Lawson, the "Copper King," hosted the event at his Dreamwold estate, where the riding academy could accommodate 3,000–5,000 people. Lawson, chairman of the Scituate Welcome-Home Committee, addressed the audience, as did Samuel W. McCall, the Massachusetts "War Governor" who served from 1916 to early 1919.[633]

On January 16, 1919, America ratified the constitutional amendment prohibiting alcoholic beverages. It took effect one year later, but saloons in some towns like Rockland closed in July.[634]

The year 1919 also marked a boom for George Welch's real estate development business. After a few slow years, sales in Rivermoor spiked in 1919. In that year alone, Welch sold half of the 222 Rivermoor lots.[635]

This was good timing. Most of these sales occurred before the worst storm since 1898 hit the South Shore late in the year, causing damage to cottages and to the Welch Company's coal and lumber wharf.[636]

The spike in home sales had two key causes. First, with the end of the World War, Americans looked forward to a more prosperous future, with more time for summer vacations and leisure activities. Second, golf had become popular, and it came to Third Cliff.

Scituate Country Club is Founded

In 1919, summer residents of the cliffs (First, Second and Third) purchased the Welch farm and built the Scituate Country Club there, with a nine-hole golf course. The original home of the Welch family became the clubhouse, and it survives today along with the golf course.[637]

The concept of a country club was invented when The Country Club in Brookline, Massachusetts, was established in 1882. Most people now associate a country club with golf, but The Country Club was first organized around horses and horse races. It was not until 1892 that golf was even proposed at that club. At the Hunt Club on the North Shore, golf was not formally introduced until 1894. The Hatherly Country Club in North Scituate was founded in 1899. It included tennis courts, a baseball field, a golf course of six holes, and a clubhouse that was to be called "The Casino." [638]

Establishment of a country club along with a summer resort was considered a crowning achievement. As one historian noted, country clubs were one of "the most important barometers of power and prestige in elite circles" at the turn of the century. They "were first and foremost social instruments and only secondarily dedicated to sport and leisure pursuits." [639]

Golf grew quickly in popularity and, as one writer stated:

> The date when golf became a truly popular American sport was 1913 and the scene was The Country Club, for then an unknown ex-caddy, Francis Ouimet, defeated in the National Open two celebrated professionals, Harry Vardon and Ted Ray. [640]

The Scituate Country Club would ride this wave of popularity. Its founders included four Massachusetts residents as officers:

- S. Harold Greene, president, of Newton, who had rented a summer house on Parker Avenue in 1918 and whose wife later bought a house and lots on Moorland Road
- James H. Stedman, vice-president, of Braintree, who owned a house on First Cliff
- Ellis L. Gates, secretary, of Waban (Newton), who later bought a house on Lincoln Avenue, and
- Clarence C. Miller, treasurer, of Winchester, who had rented a house on Michael Avenue in 1918 that he bought in 1919 along with other nearby lots.

In addition, Henry H. Wilder served (along with S. Harold Greene and Clarence C. Miller) on the committee that secured the land for the club. Wilder had rented a summer house on Lincoln Avenue in 1918, and later took leadership roles in the US Golf Association. These men loved golf and thus invested in Third Cliff. [641]

On August 30, 1919, the two key landowners agreed to sell their property for the golf course. William W. Waterman agreed to sell his 20 acres on the north side of the Driftway. The other seller was William Henry Welch, George's brother. He had continued to operate the family farm on the south side of the Driftway, but then agreed to sell his farm of 40 acres, including the farmhouse. Both sellers agreed that preparations for the golf course could commence immediately.[642]

Within days, the news of the coming golf course hit the front page of the local newspaper. The sales of the properties to the country club were concluded on November 14. By then, George Welch had sold many Rivermoor lots, including to leaders of the new Scituate Country Club.[643]

The old Welch farmhouse was altered significantly to become the clubhouse for the country club, as indicated by period photos and postcards. The changes included additions of a screened front porch that extended more than the full length of the building, an enclosed porch or addition on the east side providing a side entry, and the tennis courts on the east side. These alterations also appeared to include moving the two interior chimneys to the building's west and east exteriors.[644]

Work on the clubhouse was nearly complete by the end of May 1920. The new club boasted two clay tennis courts. During construction of the golf links, the workmen unearthed a wealth of domestic implements from Native Americans, who were the earliest inhabitants of Third Cliff.[645]

"Country Club Showing Tennis Courts, Scituate, Mass." postcard, early 1920s
(pub. Tichnor). Author's collection.

174

"View of Country Club Showing Golf Links and Tennis Courts, Scituate, Mass." postcard, early 1920s. Note the Driftway going across image. Courtesy of Scituate Historical Society.

The Scituate Country Club flourished from the start. A Boston newspaper reported that the club and its rival, the Hatherly Country Club, both had full membership lists in 1922. In 1923, a joint tournament was held between the Scituate Country Club and the Plymouth Country Club. The star of the tournament was Francis Ouimet, hero of American amateur golf. He partnered with Scituate Country Club's S. Harold Greene, who was also president of the new Charles River Country Club in Newton Centre, which opened in 1921. Ouimet returned to the Scituate Country Club for an exhibition match in 1926.[646]

Early members of the Scituate Country Club included "The Clarence Briers', the Frank Nasons, F. Britain Kennedy and family, the Englishs', Harold Green [Greene], Dr. Arthur V. Rogers, and Pearly Barbour, Mayor of Quincy."[647]

A detailed history said:

> The summer people on the cliffs and the Norwell group started the Club. The Drapers, First cliff; the doctors & dentists of 3rd cliff; the Foggs (Norwell), Barnards (Norwell), 3rd cliff Dr. Rogers & Sargent & Hagars (Marshfield) — were officers and members. All bought shares. As building got underway, and expenses soared, Yacht Club members bought in and the "natives" were encouraged to join …. Two tennis courts were built on high spot east of club, but wind on the hill was such that courts were later

discontinued. …It was a busy, friendly club, and the yacht club and golf club combined activities.

… Early presidents of club — Joe Draper, Billy James, Frank Nason, Dan Killefre [?]. The first professional was Jack Leary. The greenskeeper was Pat Fitzpatrick, right from Ireland with his five boys.[648]

In 1926, summer arrivals in Scituate included members and founders of the Scituate Country Club:

Among the latest arrivals are Charles B. Stretch of Winchester, E. Frederick Cullen of Brookline, Clarence E. Brier of Chestnut Hill, S. Harold Greene of Newton and Frank L. Nason of Boston at Rivermore [sic].[649]

Likewise, in 1928:

At Rivermore [sic] are Clarence E. Brier of Chestnut Hill, E. Frederick Cullen and Robert H. Lord of Brookline, Paul Draper and Roger Williams of Canton, Clarence E. Miller and William D. Eaton of Winchester.[650]

Likewise, in 1929:

At the Rivermore [sic] are Mr. and Mrs. William D. Eaton and son, Charles, prominent amateur golfer of Winchester, and Mr. and Mrs. Clarence E. Brier of Chestnut Hill.[651]

In 1929, the club was the scene of a whippet (dog) race. The club's team also won the South Shore golf four-ball championship about 1930. A member of that team was Arthur V. Rogers, Jr., the son of dentist Arthur V. Rogers of Winchester and 10 Parker Avenue in Rivermoor; he was a prominent contender for amateur golf championships.[652]

Scituate Country Club clubhouse. Photo by Lyle Nyberg 2017.

The 1919 creation of the golf course on Third Cliff spurred the sale of houses and lots in Rivermoor. This was the year that George Welch sold half of the Rivermoor lots. He issued 24 deeds covering 111 lots to about a dozen buyers.[653]

Buyers in Rivermoor

Before 1919, buyers split into two roughly even camps: those who bought just one lot, and those who bought two lots for their house and maybe a garage. In 1919, however, a speculating boom developed. Howard R. Guild alone bought 24 lots. He had previously summered on the cliff for at least four years. William N. Ambler (evidently a real estate entrepreneur) bought 24 lots in 1919, and another 52 lots in the spring of 1920. Margaret Woodworth (discussed below) bought the "Indian Knoll" cottage along with 17 lots. Clarence Miller (also discussed below) bought 17 lots. On average, George Welch had rented the houses for seven years before selling. This allowed time for him to develop relationships with the renters, and for the renters to become accustomed to, or enamored with, their houses.[654]

Who were these first big buyers? As noted above, they shared a love of golf. In addition, they had high positions in society and business, and appeared to share social connections.

The Scituate Country Club's president, S. Harold Greene (1881–1937), was a partner and executive in the well-known industrial engineering firm Lockwood, Greene & Co. He was also president of the Lancaster Mills in Clinton from 1914 to 1925, and director of other cotton mills. His wife Lillian M. Greene bought a block of nine lots on the north end of Moorland Road. The site was the highest point of Third Cliff, very close to the golf course, and it included an existing house, the former "Mitton" cottage of Jordan Marsh fame (later 12 Moorland, replaced in 2015).[655]

Like S. Harold Greene, big buyer Howard Guild (24 lots) was a native of Providence, R.I., where he lived in 1890 and where his father had been a successful cotton broker and manufacturer. Guild therefore may have had a cotton company connection with Greene, a cotton industrialist. Both Guild and Greene were subscribers to the Museum of Fine Arts in Boston in 1918.[656]

Arthur V. [Vernon] Woodworth (1865-1950), whose wife Margaret bought "Indian Knoll" in 1919, was an 1891 graduate of Harvard University, a member of The Country Club in Brookline, a Boston stockbroker, and later a professor at the Harvard Business School.[657] Margaret K. [Kennard] Woodworth (1875-1954) was an 1898 graduate of Smith College with a B.L. degree.[658]

The Woodworth family spent summers at North Scituate Beach before renting in Rivermoor starting in 1912. They had four children: Kennard (born 1905), Alfred Skinner

(1907), Arthur Vernon, Jr. (1911), and Margaret (c. 1915). They would stay until 1933. When they sold the house, the sale excluded "1 baby's crib, mattress and pillow; 1 single iron bed; 2 bicycles; personal articles of clothing, books and family photographs." Thankfully, the photographs survived.[659]

For these people, summering in Rivermoor was a way of continuing their social ties and maximizing leisure time for golf and family. William N. Ambler, on the other hand, seems to have been a Boston real estate entrepreneur with only a financial interest in Rivermoor. He seems to have had no trouble later selling his Rivermoor lots.[660]

These were well-heeled buyers. They differed from those who bought cottages at Wesleyan Grove on Martha's Vineyard in the 1860s, who were artisans and shopkeepers "at the edge of the middle class," according to one historian.[661]

At this time, Third Cliff had two parts: one for residents and one for summer colonists. On the north were the fishermen, mossers, and workers mainly of Irish descent who worked hard, and whose modest houses were passed down within their families. On the south, in Rivermoor, were the executives, professionals, college-educated and wealthier families who were there just for the summer and for leisure and relaxation. As described by a resident of the northern half — a descendant of Third Cliff fishermen — Third Cliff ended at the Driftway.[662]

Reports in the *Boston Globe* about summer visitors to Scituate began referring mostly to Rivermoor, rather than Third Cliff, even as it kept referring to Second Cliff and First Cliff. Rivermoor had become a separate world.

In a way, this mirrored the typical divide in Scituate during its growth as a summer resort: "the dynamic summer resort and the slow paced winter country town … the refined and wealthy enclaves of the north [such as North Scituate Beach] and the common, sturdy resorts in the south."[663]

Third Cliff inverted the Scituate formula. The north held the fishermen, lobstermen, and mossers who worked the sea. The south — Rivermoor — held people who were there to relax and escape from work. Rivermoor had more than its share of doctors, dentists, insurance executives, bankers, brokers, and businessmen. It also had such distinguished summer residents as Ernest Hodgson, the first American to manufacture prefabricated houses, plus suffragists and social reformers, all as discussed in chapter 12.

15

SUMMER LIFE IN RIVERMOOR

The family of Clarence C. [Crossman] Miller, who bought many Rivermoor lots, provides a great example of summer life in Rivermoor.

Clarence Miller Family

Clarence Miller (1878–1928) was a Boston life insurance executive. He was a director of the Winchester Cooperative Bank and the Rockland Trust Company. He was a member of the council committee for the Mystic Valley Boy Scouts, covering Winchester, Woburn, and Stoneham. Like his fellow golf club founder, S. Harold Greene, and like Howard R. Guild, he was a native of Rhode Island. He was a resident of Winchester, Massachusetts, like both Thomas Lawson and the "War Governor" Samuel McCall, where they all lived within a mile of one another. He married Harriet F. Huffman in 1905. They had two sons (Robert Huffman Miller and Philip Miller) and a daughter (Harriet Miller, born 1920).[664]

CLARENCE C. MILLER

Clarence Miller, *Boston Globe*, obituary,
September 20, 1928.

179

180

Daughter Harriet later wrote of her summer childhood years at Third Cliff. She said her father bought a house there some time in the 1920s as a summer home for his family and a "refuge from Boston's heat." Actually, it was 1919 when he bought into Rivermoor. In 1922, on the way from his Boston office to South Station to take the train to his summer home, he suffered what was at first thought to be a cerebral hemorrhage, but was later determined to be a bout of heat prostration. His health problems must have existed before then. When he bought his summer home, according to his daughter, his "cardiologist would not allow him to live right on the seashore, so Dad bought the entire block across the street in order to have an unobstructed view of the ocean."[665]

In fact, Clarence Miller bought a significant 17 of the 222 lots in Rivermoor, along with part of an 18th lot. These were on the southeast side of Michael, northeast side of Lincoln, and both sides of Collier between Michael and Lincoln. Most of his purchases were in 1919 when he helped found the Scituate Country Club. His main house on Michael Avenue (10 Michael) was called "Maidstone." From there, his vacant lots really did give a sweeping and unobstructed view of the ocean to the south and east.[666]

Later, Harriet's mother (also named Harriet) decided to build a cottage near the main house on some of those vacant lots, "fronting on the beach." In 1922 or 1923, she had plans drawn up for two similar Cape Cod cottages facing each other. Between them was a path, opposite Lincoln Avenue, leading to the beach. Only one cottage was built. It was the subject of a 1923 article in *The House Beautiful* magazine, "The House That Harriet Built." The cottage was still there, at 43 Collier, until July 2018, when it was replaced.[667]

Harriet's summers were carefree and adventuresome. One night, Harriet and her brother "conceived a plan to foil that evening's landing of the bootleggers' liquor shipment on the beach below the house. We signaled frantically with our flash lights, but we never knew whether we had upset their rum shipment."[668]

1931 Ford Model A Woodie Wagon.
Courtesy of Owls Head Transportation Museum.

Harriet's family had a Ford station wagon, a "beach wagon" with wood panels. It was known as a "woody" or "woodie." The family drove the woodie to the Scituate Yacht Club, where they kept a sailboat. Yacht Club members in 1938 would include Donald Hagar (of Marshfield), Irving K. Hall (of Meeting House Lane), and the noted writer and suffragist Inez Haynes Irwin and her sister Edith Haynes Thompson.[669]

Bootlegging

Harriet Miller's adventures in Rivermoor with possible bootleggers reflected the area's history as a hotbed of liquor smuggling during Prohibition, 1919–1933. As one local writer said:

> The North River mouth was the water highway out to the mother ships that were waiting three miles out to unload their contraband into smaller boats and dories. [The smaller ships would travel by night.] Safe unloading areas were located. Bays, harbors, rivers, creeks, and other landing spots were found. Humarock was one of these safe places — or at least more safe than other harbors. Federal funding was weak and the revenuers had to spread themselves thin.[670]

Liquor was landed often on Third Cliff during Prohibition, as reported in many news articles. Some landings were accompanied by gunshots. In one instance, bootleggers abandoned 500 cases of assorted liquors on Third Cliff, and a newspaper reported,

> The Scituate police think that the landing was made at Third Cliff, because the cliff tended to deaden the sound of the operations, and that the plan was to store the liquor temporarily in one of the unoccupied cottages in that vicinity.[671]

Rum-running was not confined to Third Cliff. It extended up to the Glades in North Scituate, much to the chagrin of Navy Secretary Charles Francis Adams III, a Glades Club member, who denied any knowledge of 600 cases of liquor seized there.[672]

Bootlegging on Third Cliff continued even after repeal of Prohibition, as shown by a colorful story on the front page of the *Boston Herald* in 1936. A photo showed seized liquor being hauled up steps on the cliff to the top of Third Cliff.[673]

Diversions

Scituate offered many summer diversions. Families could watch moving pictures at the Idle Hour Theatre on Front Street in Scituate Harbor, just south of where the CVS store is now (at 100 Front Street), or at the Victoria Theatre on Gannett Road in North Scituate (open only summers). After 1921–1922, movies moved from the Idle Hour Theatre to the

Satuit Playhouse in Scituate Harbor, now the site of the Mill Wharf Cinemas. Summer residents could dance at the dance hall on Jericho Road (probably Vinton's Pastime Pavilion) or at the upper story of Charles W. Frye's store on Front Street. Afterwards, they could buy a treat at "The Sunflake Carmeled Corn Shop" on Front Street (in 1932). Or they could get ice cream at the "Chanticleer" ice cream and soda store on Front Street in Scituate Harbor, run by Doris Stenbeck and her brother Charles V. Stenbeck. They used real cream and churned it on the back porch. Near there was a bowling alley.[674]

MAIN STREET, BUSINESS SECTION, SCITUATE, MASS.

Chanticleer, ice cream and candy store, far right, next to H. T. Stenbeck & Co. Provision Market. Postcard, early 1900s. Courtesy of Elizabeth Foster.

One restaurant in Scituate Harbor was O'Hara's Restaurant. A 1938 ad offered "Fish or Lobster Dinners; Specials at Fifty Cents Up; Broiled Lobster, Chicken, Steaks or Chops." It was evidently located in the Coveney Building, now the site of a building housing Jack Conway Realty (at 80 Front Street) and other establishments.[675]

Customs

Meanwhile, in the 1920s, little Harriet Miller in Rivermoor said, "[t]here were several children in the neighborhood and all of us went to the beach for a swim every day. On the Fourth of July we children used to walk up and down the street carrying American flags." An old photo shows ten children, perhaps including Harriet, each carrying an American flag.[676]

Patriotic parade in Rivermoor, c. early 1920s. Courtesy of John L. Sullivan.

The photo shows them parading in the middle of Michael Avenue, which then was a narrow dirt road. Three houses on Michael are visible, as well as the house (Mereside) in line with them at the intersection of Michael and Moorland (in the background). Most paraders appear to be girls ranging from three years to nine years old. Two girls are blowing horns, one is beating a drum. Most are carrying flags and wearing hats, with one or two wearing dunce caps. This must have been a Fourth of July parade.

Perhaps it was a "Horribles Parade" customary in New England on the Fourth of July, or Labor Day at the end of summer. It is an old tradition: "The parades involve local children and adults dressed in comic costumes, often poking fun at political figures and current events—it's a spectacle that's more charming than horrible, for the most part."[677]

A "horribles" parade or exhibition on the Fourth of July in Scituate was noted as early as 1873.[678]

Harriet also described the Humane Society's lifeboat station on Collier Road near Lincoln Avenue, as follows:

> At the end of the street was a Life Saving Station, a barn-like building which contained a large, open boat [26-ft. lifeboat, per her marginal note] which could carry six men. One night a ship foundered off Third Cliff and the men of the Life Saving Service opened the big doors, and wheeled the boat

on its carriage to the surf and went to the rescue. We never learned the outcome of their effort.[679]

In the summer of 1928, Harriet's father became very ill, and he died in September after the family got back to their winter home in Winchester. Her mother sold their property in Scituate in the late 1930s.[680]

By then, some unique and picturesque elements of the area were changing or vanishing.

In 1936, the Humane Society sold its lifeboat station on Third Cliff, the one that Harriet described. It became a private residence. In 2016, it was demolished (along with the adjacent "Wee Cottage") and was replaced with another residence, elevated on pilings.[681]

In addition, starting in 1916, the town took steps to take by eminent domain four parcels for bathing beaches: Peggotty Beach (Bassing Cove), Sand Hills Beach, Shore Acres Beach, and Hazard Beach near the intersection of Bailey's Causeway.[682] In 1925, voters approved taking land at Peggotty Beach, allowing mossers to use the southern end without charge.[683]

Then, in 1928, the town removed Irish mossing sheds at Peggotty Beach, featured in many postcards. The owners protested to the selectmen:

> Mr. Richard Graham, Mrs. Nee, Mr. & Mrs. Fred S. Mahon with Mr. Louis E. Cole of the Park Commission appeared in regard to the removal of their mossing buildings from the Peggotty Beach Park. They wish to remain where they are as they cannot get land to move onto. Matter referred to Town Counsel Murphy.[684]

It is doubtful the protest had any success. By the 1930s, the area of the sheds became a town parking lot, with a hydrant and "Comfort Station" on Peggotty Beach.[685]

The sheds were gone, but mossing continued on Peggotty Beach and other areas of town, into the 1980s and later.[686]

During that time, some mossers would anchor their mossing dories in the cove in front of Peggotty Beach. Some would moss off the two rocks at the southern end of Peggotty Beach. The rocks appear only at low tide. The rocks are evidently those that appear in a watercolor by Thomas Buford Meteyard in the late 1800s, used on the cover of this book. The rocks appear in at least one photo of the same period, and in a book illustration by the Haumans in the 1930s. The rocks were called Martha and Arthur, at least since the time of Walter "Doc" O'Neil and his brother George in the mid-1900s. (Locals have similarly given names to the larger beach rocks east of Cedar Point [Lighthouse Point].) The rocks mark the start of Third Cliff, which was farther away for most mossers, but they considered the cliff the best place for mossing.[687]

Today, the Irish moss still grows around Peggotty Beach and Third Cliff, but it is more difficult to find.[688]

Peggotty Beach Road heads toward the ocean and then turns left to go up the hill on Second Cliff. Just before the turn, on the left, is a small cottage that once was a store that sold penny candy and other items, about the 1940s. At the turn, the road widens to provide a scenic view of Peggotty Beach. A boardwalk once ran along the beach here. This scenic spot is where the ice cream truck would park, and it may still do so. Its musical tones enticed kids to go up to the top of the beach for an ice cream treat.[689]

Behind Peggotty Beach, between the beach and the mainland, was a big creek. For decades, kids would swim in its warm water. The creek was even big enough for a sailboat, if one believes the story in the children's book *Happy Harbor* by Third Cliff authors George and Doris Hauman.[690]

Over in Rivermoor, Clarence Miller's plan for an unobstructed view of the ocean lasted from 1919 until at least 1972, when houses began to appear on the south side of Michael Avenue.[691]

16

GEORGE WELCH'S SIGNIFICANCE

George Welch was among Scituate's top three property owners in his time. The value of his real estate property holdings peaked in 1918, when Rivermoor accounted for a third of this value. The total value of his real estate holdings were $170,485 in 1918, falling to $136,400 in 1919, mostly due to sales of properties in the Gilson Road and Hatherly Road developments. His holdings plummeted even further with large sales in Rivermoor — in 1919 when he sold 111 of the Rivermoor lots (some with buildings), and in 1920 when he sold more than 50 lots to real estate entrepreneur William N. Ambler.[692]

George F. Welch, obituary, *Boston Globe*,
May 31, 1931, A20.

These sales were often to summer residents. That contributed to an increase in nonresident taxpayers in Scituate. By 1920, for the first time, there were more nonresident taxpayers than resident taxpayers.[693]

Even at George's peak property ownership, he was no match for Thomas Lawson, whose total property valuations were double those of George. Few people in the country, however, could have matched Thomas Lawson, the wealthy Copper King.[694]

But George Welch was instrumental in developing Scituate. Early on, he played a large role in the Scituate Beach Land Association. That group developed both the area around Hatherly Road, just north of Scituate Harbor, and Gilson Road on Third Cliff. Welch built countless houses in Scituate, including some 40–50 houses in Rivermoor between 1905 and the 1920s. The spike in Third Cliff housing in 1908–1911 was part of an explosive growth in Scituate housing development plans in the same years. These included Sand Hills (1908, 205 lots), Jericho Beach (1908–1910, 932 lots), and Barker Farm (1911, 99 lots). Welch was a 1/8th shareholder in the massive Jericho Beach plan.[695]

Welch's own Rivermoor summer colony introduced many well-to-do summer residents to Scituate. He and his family played crucial roles in establishing the Scituate Country Club on Third Cliff, which still exists.

The number of houses on Third Cliff, for which George was largely responsible, grew quickly from 1903 to 1926, as shown below and detailed in Appendix B. Some 23 houses in 1903 grew to almost 100. The average annual growth rate was about 10% for Rivermoor, and 7% overall for Third Cliff. Many of these houses remain, perhaps more than half, as indicated by Appendix A.

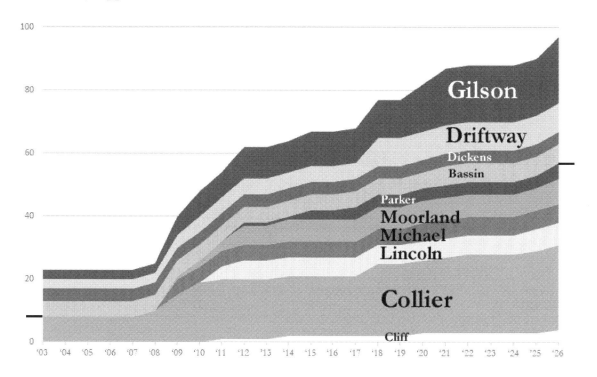

Number of houses on Third Cliff, 1903–1926, by street
(alphabetical, starting at bottom with Rivermoor streets).
Tick marks left and right indicate Rivermoor's contribution to growth.

Rivermoor Business Model

George Welch's impact on the town's development can be appreciated by looking at the fifteen years from when he created the 1906 Rivermoor plan until 1921, when he disengaged from active development. In this period, Welch accounted for about 40 new houses in Rivermoor alone. At the same time, the number of houses in town grew from 1,053 to 1,637. Based on these figures, Rivermoor accounted for about 7% of all the new houses in Scituate.[696]

George must have stood out as a builder and employer, as there were only 13 carpenters and builders listed in Scituate in a 1918 directory.[697]

George probably achieved financial success in his real estate development activities. Without access to his business records, many assumptions must be made. Some key facts and factors, however, exist and are explored in more depth below, using Rivermoor as an example.

On the surface, one would think that George Welch was quite successful. His costs should have been low. His father likely gave him the Third Cliff property at no charge. His housing construction had the benefit of reduced costs for lumber and workers from the Welch Company. In addition, George seemed to be selling in a time of increasing property values. For example, the town valued his Rivermoor properties in 1918 — 23 houses and associated garages and lots (mostly double lots) — at $59,000. Three years later, the value of these properties in the hands of their new owners had grown to $81,600, a 38% increase.[698]

George's apparent success raises the following questions.

Was this increase in value due simply to general economic factors? US housing prices were stable during the early decades of the 1900s. Inflation was high during and after World War I, with inflation of 35% from 1918–1921.[699] Adjusted for inflation, therefore, housing prices actually plunged during that time. The causes could have been the war and the Spanish Flu pandemic, both of which reduced the number of new homebuyers.[700]

Rivermoor may have sidestepped these issues. Rivermoor appealed to affluent, established homeowners who were prepared to buy a summer home, rather than to first-time homebuyers. Unlike the general plunge in housing prices, Rivermoor's rising property valuations seemed to keep pace with the 35% US inflation rate in 1918–1921. They also exceeded the 29% general increase in Scituate property valuations in 1918–1921.[701]

Did George sell at or above these rising property values? What were his sale prices? Records are sparse.

Recorded mortgages contain some clues. George took mortgages back from some of his buyers. They state some but not all terms of the loans. Those for Maidstone and Indian Knoll, for example, required payment of 6% interest, with a term of three years.[702] Presumably, payment was for interest only, without amortizing principal, with the full amount of the loan due at the end of the term. This was typical for the period, along with mortgage lengths of five to seven years.[703] The 6% interest rate was also common at the time; it was the rate for houses sold by Sears, Roebuck & Company.[704]

Left: Maidstone (10 Michael Ave.), Dec. 2016. Photo by Lyle Nyberg.
Right: Indian Knoll (36 Moorland Rd.), 1912. Woodworth family photo album.

Also typical (but not stated in the recorded mortgages) was a down payment of 20%.[705] One might make these further assumptions and calculations for Maidstone and Indian Knoll and their related lots: (1) the loan amounts stated in the recorded mortgages were 80% of the sales prices, and (2) the resulting prices were about $475 per lot. Given this, Welch sold Maidstone and its two lots for $4,750 in 1919 compared to an assessed value of $2,225 in 1918, and he sold Indian Knoll and two of its lots for $2,875 in 1919 compared to an assessed value of $2,825 in 1918. Thus, it appears that Welch was able to sell at or above the tax assessor's valuation.[706]

Did George make a profit? Let us continue with our example of the two key Rivermoor properties for which we have some good data — Maidstone and Indian Knoll. They were two of the 23 houses owned by Welch in 1918, and both sold in 1919, with their sales comprising a substantial 34 of the approximate 111 lots sold in Rivermoor that year.

To determine profit, consider George's costs. First, start with the town's 1918 valuations for these two properties. Second, adjust them to reflect Welch's cost advantages mentioned above, assuming: (a) his lots cost nothing, (b) his materials and labor for construction saved him 20% of the town's valuations. Third, adjust these further to reflect Welch's other costs. He bought furniture for his houses, and presumably included the furniture when selling the houses. The furniture was valued at $10,750 for 43 houses in the *1918 Valuation List*. He paid property taxes at a rate close to 2% per year, for the approximately seven years he rented the houses. He would have had to pay interest if he borrowed money to pay for construction. If he did not borrow the money, and used his own, then he still lost the opportunity to earn interest on his own money by spending it on the development, and this was an imputed cost to him.

Considering all these factors, it appears that George achieved financial success with these two representative properties, and thus with Rivermoor as a whole. Appendix C summarizes these factors. It appears that Welch achieved profitability just through his property rentals alone. Sales of the houses produced additional profits.

To summarize in general terms, George Welch created value. He turned empty meadows into a summer resort colony. He profited. His buyers benefited from rising property values. The town benefited by having new taxpayers and taxing them based on these rising property values. Workers in the town benefited from employment in the development of Third Cliff.

Accomplishments

George Welch's accomplishments were summarized in a 1921 advertisement profiling the Welch Company:

> … In 1891, Mr. [E. Parker] Welch, Senior, retired to the large home farm near Third Cliff, and Mr. George F., aided by many faithful employees, conducted the business alone. In 1914 he formed a corporation, admitting Mr. Herman J. Wells, and in 1918, Mr. Chas. S. Short was added to the firm.
> Mr. Welch retired as the active head upon incorporating and devoted his time to real estate. He had gradually acquired the whole usable wharf frontage, including five wharves, twenty-five store houses and sheds, and had built at the railroad station a large storehouse, for lumber. He had also been the first to build in this section a fine type of large, airy, spacious summer cottage modernly equipped, many of these being erected at Rivermoor, a colony which he developed. He was a pioneer in the use of Southern hard pine flooring and sheathing, as well as many other items of high-grade building materials. The stock carried increased in variety, until it included everything to build a house, to furnish it, as well as the lot upon which to build. The whole plant became the largest of its kind in New England. The firm has always been noted for the good quality of merchandise carried, aiming to buy the best grades of building materials. It has been a prominent factor in the growth of the town, and with the increasing population of this section it bids fair to be of even greater service to its many patrons.[707]

It was time for George to exit from business. He sold more than 160 of the 222 Rivermoor lots (72%) in 1919–1920. He disposed of the Twin Houses (Bleak House and East End) and Trotwood on Dickens Row by 1919. This might have been difficult for him, since the Twin Houses were on a house lot that his grandfather Michael once owned, which he sold to Daniel Ward in the mid-1800s. By 1921, George sold most of his remaining interests in Rivermoor. His sister Mary, widowed in 1919, sold her properties and grand house on First Cliff in 1921.[708]

In 1923, George sold his interests in the Welch Company to Marshall C. Spring of Newton Lower Falls, whose company sold building materials. On May 5, 1923, the *Boston Globe* reported: "C. H. Spring of Newton Upper Falls has purchased from George F. Welch several parcels of real estate on Front st, which include the Postoffice and buildings occupied by the Geo. F. Welch Company." The deed included wharves and other parcels that Welch had acquired as far back as 1889, along with wharf and dockage rights, and wood sawing machinery. The deed referred to a plan of the wharf property, which is copied in chapter 5.[709]

George moved to Boston between 1923 and 1925, and he bought property there through a trust, as well as property in Brookline. When he moved to Boston, his one-time rival as property king of Scituate, Thomas Lawson, had lost his fortune and his property.[710]

George supposedly lost his fortune after investing in Boston and Brookline property and encountering the Great Depression.[711]

George later returned to Scituate. Throughout his moves, though, he continued to own and sell property in Scituate's Shore Acres, carrying on what his father E. Parker Welch had done since the late 1800s.[712]

George died May 29, 1931, having developed, according to his obituary in the *Scituate Herald*, "the largest business outside of Boston in this section of the state" — the Welch Company — and leaving houses and properties in Scituate, with a flourishing residential colony on Third Cliff.[713]

As another obituary said:

> Dependable, steady and honest, George F. Welch filled a big niche in the life of Scituate. As a young man he was enthusiastic and progressive, bringing the merchandizing methods of the old firm of E. P. Welch & Son, which was just a little establishment on a coal wharf, up to the huge emporium which he managed so successfully year after year. He knew details of the stock, met his customers pleasantly and began to build trade as soon as he commenced the new partnership with his father. When he commenced to work up surpluses of lumber stocks into Rivermoor at Third Cliff he became a real estate operator and after selling out the Welch Co., his office on Front Street was quite a seat of business activity.[714]

George Welch's impact on Scituate cannot be overstated. His growth of the Welch Company, and his development of summer housing, significantly helped rescue Scituate's economy from its doldrums in the late 1800s, and they propelled the town into the 1900s.[715]

Rivermoor was his crowning achievement as a real estate developer and builder. His work charted a course for growth for the town. George created houses and neighborhoods that people still live in and talk about 100 years later.

***

Meanwhile, the Welch Company changed ownership. As noted above, in 1923 George Welch sold the Front Street wharf property occupied by the company to Marshall C. Spring, evidently behind the C. H. Spring Company that acquired the Welch Company. Welch took back a mortgage on the property, but in 1927, he conveyed it to a bank. When the Great Depression came, the C. H. Spring Company went into receivership. Marshall Spring defaulted on the mortgage of the Welch Company property, and the bank foreclosed on it in 1933. In 1939, the bank conveyed the property to the Welch Company, which was then under new ownership.[716]

In 1932–1933, Herbert G. Perry (1880–1971) bought the company for $10,000. He was a leader of A. W. Perry, Inc., a real estate investment, management, and development firm. He owned the Welch Company about as long as George Welch did. He and his wife Nell and their family summered in Rivermoor in a Welch colonial at 28 Collier, at the corner of Michael ("San Souci," since replaced). Their summer residency lasted from 1946 to at least 1969, with lasting memories for their grandchildren, some of whom live in the area.[717]

Russell L. Fish (c. 1906–1985) also became a part owner of the Welch Company in 1932–1933. He had worked there since 1922, and later gained a degree in business administration in evening courses at Boston University. He was named president of the company, a position he held for 49 years. He lived on Greenfield Lane for a number of years. He later moved to a waterfront cottage in Scituate Harbor next to the Welch Company. In 1982, the company was sold to the Warner family, with Stephen C. Warner as president.[718]

Herbert G. and Nell Perry and daughters at Third Cliff home, c. 1960s. Photo by Robert
Ledwig. Courtesy of Robert Ledwig and Jack Spurr.

17

THE 1920S AND 1930S

Third Cliff continued to attract new summer residents in the 1920s. In 1922, the *Boston Globe* reported about Scituate:

> The town is witnessing the greatest building boom in its history. There are few houses on the market. Anyone familiar with the general aspect of such sections as Hatherly Beach, Sand Hills or Shore Acres five years ago would have great difficulty in recognizing those same places today. The large tract of land at Rivermoor taken over and improved by the new Scituate Country Club has greatly changed the landscape in that vicinity for the better.[719]

Later in 1922, the *Boston Globe* reported on Scituate visitors, including these:

> Mr and Mrs Otway Chalkley and daughter Cornelia, who have just arrived from China, where Mr Otway [sic] has represented a large tobacco concern for a number of years, have taken the Riley cottage for the remainder of the season.[720]

Otway Chalkley (1883–1956) was originally from Richmond, Virginia. His family lived on Long Island, NY, after their stay in China. His wife, Rachel Florence (Riley) Chalkley, had a Boston and Scituate connection. Her mother was born in Massachusetts, and lived in Boston. Rachel Riley was born in Boston in 1880. Rachel Riley attended school in Boston, graduated from Mount Holyoke College in 1902, and worked in Boston. The Riley family had a cottage in Scituate. (Thus, the "Riley cottage" in the *Boston Globe* report above.) Rachel's mother Harriet, sister Rebecca (a high school teacher), and brother Joseph (a professor at MIT), spent summers there.[721]

It took some detective work to track down the location of the Riley cottage. In 1918, it was reported to be on Third Cliff (evidently rented), and in 1926, more specifically on Highland (Gilson). Town records and deeds place it at 111 Gilson. A cottage was there (with garage) by early 1923, and Joseph C. Riley, Rachel's brother, the MIT professor, owned the property from 1922 to 1966, when he conveyed it to Seth Riley. There, for decades up to 1950, Professor Riley hosted reunions of his class of 1890 from the Thetford School of Dorchester. The cottage was replaced in 1997.[722]

Perhaps desiring more room than the Riley cottage allowed, Otway and Rachel Chalkley summered on nearby Collier Road in 1926. With them must have been their daughter Cornelia, then almost seven years old. She graduated in 1936 from the Friends Academy, a preparatory school in Locust Valley, Long Island, New York. The Academy yearbook said she was popular, with a "brilliant mind," and "beautiful but not dumb." She went on to Sweet Briar College in Virginia, where she was head of the choir, graduating in 1940.[723]

Meanwhile, Otway Chalkley, "a lanky, reticent native of Richmond [who] had served as secretary-treasurer of Philip Morris for a dozen years," had risen to become president of the tobacco company in 1936.[724]

In 1938, he was featured on the cover of *TIME* magazine. In 1945, he became the company's chairman of the board. In 1949, he retired as chairman, but evidently continued on the board for a few years, including when Philip Morris sponsored the "I Love Lucy" show. In these years, Philip Morris was the fourth-largest cigarette maker in the United States. It is not known if Chalkley and his family kept spending summers on Third Cliff.[725]

Back in 1924, George Welch, who had named Michael Avenue after his grandfather, petitioned the town meeting to change the name to Rivermoor Road. The change was not made.[726]

Rivermoor grew to more than 60 dwellings by 1935. Many were large Welch colonials, like the one described in the 1906 ad. They went on the north side of the avenues. Smaller cottages, also with porches, later went on the south side. This left the larger houses on the north side with a better view of the ocean.[727]

Most dwellings were occupied only in the summer. Even as late as 1937, a town directory listed year-round occupants for only 8 of the 59 dwellings then on Rivermoor streets. It must have been very quiet by the seashore in the off-season.[728]

During the off-season, the town police department was careful to inspect summer cottages for possible break-ins. In 1929, the chief of police said that 1,400 vacant houses were inspected, and he reported that:

> For many years past the Town has been troubled with many of the summer homes being entered and ransacked; since the system of inspecting and marking the vacant houses and having the day and night patrol on duty this trouble has been nearly eliminated. During the fall of 1928 and the winter of 1929 only six were reported to the department and nothing of value taken; up to January 1 of this year, all houses have been inspected and no breaks found. Telephone calls and letters received from the property owners commending the department for their interest is proof that the Police Department is advancing in the right direction.[729]

In the summer, Scituate's population swelled. The population tripled from about its usual 2,500. Average daily consumption of water more than doubled.[730]

From 1918 to 1926, the number of Third Cliff houses grew steadily. The most striking increase was in ownership of summer houses in Rivermoor. In 1918, about 8 of Rivermoor's 33 summer houses were owned, not rented, comprising 24%. In 1926, that had grown to 26 out of 44, comprising 59%. Clearly, renters liked what they saw and decided to buy their summer homes in Rivermoor. This validated George Welch's acumen in the property business.[731]

Who were these summer residents? They came mainly from Boston and surrounding towns, with a few from New York. Besides tobacco executive Chalkley, there were doctors, company presidents, a lawyer-publisher, an investment banker, a Harvard Business School professor, and even a virtuoso violinist. There were so many dentists on one avenue that it was called Dentist Avenue.[732]

Rivermoor's summer residents did not want a flood of visitors and sightseers. In 1934, residents (including some of the Clarence Miller family) requested that parking of motor vehicles be prohibited on Rivermoor roads. Police Chief Stewart concurred. The Selectmen approved the prohibition, to start June 1.[733]

Summer life on the southern end of the cliff in the 1930s was not all about golfing or yachting. According to a 1930 newspaper report, the Daughters of the American Revolution held a meeting in Rivermoor and discussed subjects that included historical pageants and the local chapter's placement of historical markers on Revolutionary War graves. The paper reported:

> The Chief Justice Cushing Chapter, D. A. R. held its regular July meeting at the home of Mrs. C. B. Stretch [of Winchester, with summer home at 18 Lincoln, later a year round home] at Rivermoor, Scituate Harbor, last Wednesday afternoon. Mrs. Stretch with Mrs. Frank L. Nason [year round resident of Rivermoor on Michael Avenue], Mrs. H. R. Guild [wife of Howard R. Guild, a long-time owner of much property in Rivermoor] and Mrs. W. G. Smith were the hostesses for the day.[734]

The 1930 paper also included an ad for the Satuit Playhouse, featuring talking movies with Clara Bow, Frederic March, Fannie Brice, and Basil Rathbone.[735]

By 1936, the drive-in theater was another option for local moviegoers. Weymouth had one of the country's earliest drive-in theaters, advertised as "New England's Only Open Air Auto Theatre."[736]

Third Cliff residents joined in Scituate's celebration of its tercentenary in 1936. The town was founded 300 years before.

> THIRD CLIFF (In Scituate). **To Take Part in Celebration**. The feeling of celebration is in the air, especially since all the stores and shops are being gaily and patriotically decked. Third Cliff will be well represented in this coming celebration, the Scituate Tercentenary to be held next week. Mrs. Frank L. Nason of Michael Avenue wrote the Pageant and is assisting Miss Lois Nelson and Miss Anne Newdick in the staging. Mr. F. Brittian Kennedy has the part of the poet, Samuel Woodworth in the Old Oaken Bucket episode with Frank L. Nason as his father, Benjamin Woodworth. Mrs. Katherine Kennedy, F. Leroy Fox and W. Frederick Spence are also participating in this episode. Mr. and Mrs. Otis Andrews will appear as Mr. and Mrs. John Barker in the scene at the Cudworth House. The program for the whole celebration is of a most interesting nature and represents untiring effort on the part of the committee.[737]

The tercentenary pageant consisted of eleven parts in eleven different historical locations over two days, followed by a grand historical pageant combining the previous episodes.[738]

Tercentenary festivities included a special Scituate broadcast over Boston radio station WHDH, with text written by County Commissioner Frederic T. Bailey of North Scituate, and an in-person address by US Secretary of Labor Frances Perkins. This was one of the few times in the history of the town that a cabinet officer visited Scituate. During her visit, her old friends Inez Haynes Irwin and Will Irwin entertained her at their home on Second Cliff. Newspapers reported that Will Irwin "is a former classmate of Miss Perkins and knows her very well," and that her address said she was a descendant of the Otis family of Scituate.[739]

Left: Frances Perkins, 1936. Born and educated in Massachusetts, served as US Secretary of Labor, first woman in US Cabinet. Harris & Ewing (detail), Library of Congress Prints and Photographs Division.

Just before the tercentenary celebration, there was a newspaper report of an incident near Third Cliff involving a boat carrying loads from the Boston Sand and Gravel Company.

> **Caught in the Marsh**. On last Saturday one of the sand and gravel scows became caught on the marsh, while going down the North River on its way to Boston. The scow was tipped over on its side, thus becoming swamped

and unable to be towed further. The lighter, thru skillful manouvering turned around in mid-stream and returned to assist the disabled scow. After its cargo of gravel had been dumped it was righted and floated off. Only a slight damage resulted. The high course tide due to the nor'easter caused the scow to swing onto the marshland where the water was too shallow for its heavy bulk.[740]

The year after this excitement, in 1937, there were a few year-round residents of Rivermoor. They included the above-mentioned Mrs. Frank L. Nason (Isabelle C. Nason) and her husband, of 18 Michael Avenue. She was active in historical groups: president of the Scituate Historical Society from 1940 to 1945; Registrar General of the DAR; Secretary of the Society of Mayflower Descendants; and founder of the Women Descendants of the Ancient and Honourable Artillery Company members.[741]

Other year-round residents of Rivermoor at the time included Ethel J. Stretch (mentioned in the 1930 news item as hosting the DAR meeting) and her textile industrialist husband Charles B. Stretch of 18 Lincoln Avenue, originally from Winchester. In addition, Hazel E. and John F. Eichorn were year-round residents at 22 Collier Road. John Eichorn was a furrier, according to a 1937 list of residents. His father John was also a furrier, who died in 1908 at his country home in Newton Centre, the "oldest raw fur dealer in the United States" according to an obituary.[742]

Note that the wives owned each of these three properties (Nason, Stretch, Eichorn). This was not uncommon. Perhaps half the properties on Third Cliff were owned by women.[743]

Frank L. Nason of 18 Michael Avenue served as president of the Scituate Country Club during the Great Depression. Evidently referring to the Great Depression, he wrote to club members in 1933:

> Due to conditions that are familiar to us all, we have had many resignations from the Club. It is, therefore, necessary that a concerted effort be made for new members, and this seems to be a splendid time for this drive.[744]

The club kept operating during the Great Depression.

18

WORLD WAR II

Even before World War II started, Scituate residents were concerned about German submarines (U boats). Germany had become more aggressive, annexing Austria in March 1938. In August 1938, it was reported:

> Rumors that a U boat had arrived off the coast of Scituate and was firing on some of our vessels caused much excitement in the town and people rushed to Mann Hill and the Egypt beaches. It turned out however that some of the U. S. Naval boats were having practice. The flashes of the guns could be seen plainly.[745]

When America entered World War II in December 1941, German U boats attacked merchant marine vessels along the Atlantic coast. In 1942, a German submarine surfaced off Long Island and sent four saboteurs to land on the beach. Soon after, another submarine sent four more saboteurs to land on a Florida beach. They were all caught. The Long Island saboteurs were apprehended by the alertness and actions of a US Coast Guard patrolman.[746]

The US Coast Guard provided shore defenses. On Third Cliff, blackouts were ordered every night, the Coast Guard patrolled the cliff every four hours, and "four men [from the Coast Guard bunkered] in a foxhole on the Cliff just north of Michael Avenue." There were rumors of a spy living on the cliff and aiding German soldiers who visited.[747]

Just offshore, blimps from the Naval Air Station at South Weymouth practiced anti-submarine warfare. One of the blimps crashed in Scituate on July 31, 1943, although nobody was hurt.[748]

On nearby Fourth Cliff, the US Army installed a coastal artillery gun site with 16-inch guns capable of firing a distance of 10–20 miles, and associated radar units to guide the guns. Some of the military installation still exists, including a five-story concrete tower.[749]

Some Scituate residents volunteered to observe aircrafts for enemy activity, as members of the Army Air Forces Aircraft Warning Service. Russell Fish was one such volunteer, and he lived close to Third Cliff at 41 Greenfield Lane.[750]

Armband for Russell Fish, blue felt with orange
and white detail, US Army Aircraft Warning
Service, 1940s. Courtesy of Sue Logan.

Identification card for Russell Fish, 1940s.
Courtesy of Sue Logan.

Fish had more responsible positions during wartime. He was president of the Welch Company, president of the Massachusetts Retail Lumber Dealers Association, and a director (later president) of the Northeastern Retail Lumbermens Association. As such, Fish represented the lumber industry in dealing with government price controls, and getting business under war conditions. In addition, he was closely involved in War Production Board controls on lumber production, sales and distribution. As the board pointed out to him in a letter of August 4, 1944,

> For the past three years there has been quite a scramble for lumber among all users … However, we cannot tell exactly when the war will end, and we do know that the military demands for overseas are actually increasing. The more men we get overseas, the larger the boxing and crating demand becomes, and it is now well over one-half of our production. The uncertainty of the requirements of the invasion of Europe plus heavy drains for the Pacific Theater would simply not permit us to continue to allow all types of uses of lumber without further inventory to draw upon. [Therefore, the board had to limit the amount of civilian work the lumber yards could do.][751]

Meanwhile, according to one source, the Scituate Country Club "prospered until 1941 when World War II and gas rationing meant no more trips to summer homes — and golf courses."[752]

George Welch's son-in-law, Dr. T. Branch Alexander, was a director of the Scituate Country Club before his death in 1941.[753] His daughter recalled:

> The Club flourished even during the depression & into the 40s's. When gas rationing came any car that was found parked at the Club —the license no. was noted & their permit revoked. However, many continued to play. Some walked, others bicycled & my father Dr. Alexander would play when he had a patient on the 3rd Cliff. If he said "I'm going to see a patient on the 3rd Cliff" it meant that he'd play a little golf too. ... During World War II, Pat Fitzpatrick, greenskeeper, continued to live there & he tried to keep it up but there was less & less money — stocks became worthless ...."[754]

A more detailed history confirms the club's troubles as World War II arrived:

> This was an era of Prohibition, so liquor was not served. It was a period of afternoon tea dresses, and fancy evening gowns — all this changed when W.W. II made such a difference in life style.
>
> ...During the war, one could not use gasoline to drive to golf clubs. So "Pop" O'Brien, who owned P.J.s Country House, would walk over from Greenbush, Harry Stenbeck would bike over from the Harbour and Dr. Alexander would stop after seeing his patients. The 3 men had a private course.[755]

Driftway, entering Third Cliff, with canopy of trees. Scituate Country Club golf course on both sides of Driftway. Townhouse condominiums at 40 Driftway at left. Ocean straight ahead. Photo by Lyle Nyberg 2016.

19

AFTER WORLD WAR II

After World War II, the Scituate Country Club was revived, new houses were built on Third Cliff, and people continued to enjoy the beaches. Several notable Third Cliff residents from this era are profiled below.

Lumber in Welch Co. yards, panoramic view, perhaps early 1940s. In background is Third Cliff and bridge to Second Cliff. Photo by Samuel Kitrosser. Courtesy of David Kitrosser. Russell Fish papers, courtesy of Sue Logan, on file in Scituate Historical Society.

The pace of construction on Third Cliff rebounded after World War II, after dipping in the 1940s. The number of new houses dropped from 18 in the 1930s (4 in Rivermoor, 14 on Gilson), to 8 in the 1940s (7, 1), then increased to 20 in the 1950s (10, 10). The lumber business must have been good at the Welch Company. The postwar boom was not rivaled until the post-pandemic period of 2021: "The Federal Reserve Board says the price index of lumber and wood products almost doubled from April 2020 to February 2021, the sharpest rise since 1946, when the post-World War II housing boom kicked in."[756]

Scituate Country Club

Because of the decline in membership during World War II, Rockland Trust took over the Scituate Country Club. About 1946, the club went up for sale at auction, and Donald H. Whittemore bought it. He was a Scituate resident working in Boston as a stockbroker. He had been a Scituate summer resident in Minot (in North Scituate) since about the 1930s. He was also a golfer who won a trophy in a tournament at the historical Wianno Club in 1923. The trophy is now in the possession of the Scituate Country Club. [757]

When he bought the Scituate Country Club, it was a mess, according to his stepdaughter Ann. Clubhouse windows were broken. The tennis courts were no longer there. Ann, then a teenager, had to help at the club, including cleaning the sand traps.[758]

Don Whittemore wound up reviving the club. He also revived the town's other private golf club, the Hatherly Country Club, of which he was president from 1937 to 1948. In 1959 a group of members explored purchasing the Scituate Country Club from Whittemore, but it did not happen. There was talk of combining the golf course with a new course to be developed across the Driftway on the former sand and gravel operations (which later led to the town's Widows Walk golf course), but this did not happen. Whittemore finally sold the club to a developer in 1982, who added condominium townhouses, while the club and golf course continued.[759]

Left: Donald Whittemore, from *Boston Globe*, April 14, 1984.

The Club was a good source of income for caddies. Jack Farley said he would get $1 for eight holes, which was like he "died and went to heaven." Another caddy, in his youth, was George P. Lowder. He played golf there until his death at age 90, in 2001.[760]

Dr. Ruth Bailey

Dr. Ruth Bailey (1904–1992) was an icon on Third Cliff who made her name as the first female physician in Scituate. She was an osteopathic doctor who began her practice during World War II. She lived at 8 Driftway next to the ocean. This was her childhood home, and she lived there into the 1980s.[761]

Dr. Bailey contributed tales of early life on Third Cliff for the neighborhood association's newsletter. She came to Third Cliff in 1905 when she was 17 months old. When she was older she went over to the Welch farm daily for milk. She said her house used to be Farmer Donahue's barn. That makes sense, as it corresponds to the "J. Donahoe" listed on the 1879 map, John Donnahue (mosser) in the 1870 US census, John Donahoe (laborer) in the 1880 US census (with wife Mary, 55, and daughter Mary A., 16), and Mary B. Donahue (home, Third Cliff, summer) in the 1894 directory. Dr. Bailey's childhood home may have been the "Viola" shown on a 1918 map. The house was later replaced.[762]

Dr. Bailey had the Bailey Professional Building built at 4 Brook Street in Scituate Harbor. It replaced her previous office there in an antique Cape. She had an office in the new building, and also made house calls. She was honored as Citizen of the Year in 1977 by the Scituate Chamber of Commerce, which noted that she had delivered 838 babies.[763]

Ruth Bailey was a legendary local featured in a book, with a photo and this profile:

Dr. Ruth began her practice in 1941, and beginning in 1962, her office was in the Bailey Building on Front Street. Her specialty was as an osteopath, treating diseases by manipulating bones and muscles. She also delivered babies. …Dr. Bailey served for 35 years on the staff of the Massachusetts Osteopathic Hospital and Medical Center in Boston. …Married to Robert F. Gammon, the couple made their home at Dr. Ruth's childhood home on Third Cliff.[764]

Left: Ruth Bailey, c. 1950s?, detail, from *Legendary Locals of Scituate, Massachusetts* (2013).

A Baker's Tale

A Rivermoor neighbor recalled there were two "Frenchmen" on Lincoln Avenue, deRow and Duplain. Albert and Beatrice Duplain in 1949 bought lots 117-120, on the north side of the west end of Lincoln (18 Lincoln). Albert D. Duplain (1893-1956) of Waban (Newton) owned a well-known French bakery in Boston's South End. It was started by his father in 1878. According to the neighbor, the bakery made deliveries using the last horse-drawn carriage in Boston. The reason was that the driver could not get a license to drive an automobile.[765]

Summer Life

In the 1940s and 1950s, the cottages on the cliff had electric power, but it took a while for telephone service to reach them, according to long-time resident Paula Buckley. For refrigeration, "Mr. Eliot, the ice-man, came twice a week with as much ice as you wanted."[766]

Third Cliff was home to blueberry bushes, grape vines, and wild pheasants. Residents picked grapes from vines near Moorland and made grape jelly. Some residents went pheasant hunting on property of the Scituate Country Club. Today there are the occasional groups of wild turkeys and Canadian geese.[767]

Other residents did a lot of clamming (gathering clams) in the nearby clam beds. They said it was a great pastime. The clams were made into clam chowder, or simply steamed ("steamers") and dipped in melted butter.[768]

Rivermoor's beach took a bit of adjustment for visitors. The beach was rocky, "not what we thought of as a beach," said Alice Gallagher, who arrived in 1949. But summer residents loved Rivermoor's beach. Paula Buckley wrote, "It always was a great beach for raising a family because it was so safe, and so big, it was never crowded. The rocks scared most people away but the Cliff-Dwellers loved it![769]

Kids used to swim in the North River alongside the Boston Sand and Gravel Company barge or tug that traveled twice a day between the company's quarries at the Colman Hills and Boston. Young people also occasionally swam across the North River to Fourth Cliff in Marshfield, a dangerous practice because of tricky currents and increased boating traffic.[770]

The current advice is, "If you are not an experienced boater/swimmer, do NOT paddle past the spit into the mouth of the North River where it meets the open ocean. Changing surf conditions lead to drowning deaths every year."[771]

Historical dangers of the area led the Humane Society of Massachusetts and the US Life-Saving Service to have a presence here. But these were not the only lifesavers.

Eva Abdou

Eva Belle Morrison Abdou (1911–1985) moved to Third Cliff with her husband in 1949. She had been a world-class long-distance swimmer in the 1930s, challenging the English Channel several times. Her home at 15 Collier Road was opposite Parker Avenue, next to the ocean. She kept up her swimming and swam out to the bell buoy off Third Cliff every day. From her house, she had a good view of the ocean and any struggling swimmers. The house had a stairway down to the beach.[772]

Left: Eva Abdou holds her long-distance swimming trophy. Photo courtesy of *Patriot Ledger.*

She saved about fifty people from drowning, many of them just off Third Cliff. In one incident in May 1955,

> After telephoning for aid, Mrs. Abdou kicked off her high-heeled shoes and ran nearly a mile over rocks and sand to the beach opposite the struggling swimmers. …Mrs. Abdou reached his side and helped him the remaining 50 yards ashore with his drowning companion.[773]

Eva's 53rd rescue, also off Third Cliff, came in 1967, when she was in her 50s. The grateful family of a person she saved had flowers delivered to Abdou once a week. She gave swimming lessons at Third Cliff until the neighborhood association brought in the Red Cross for lessons. Her actions to prevent drowning fulfilled the purpose of the Humane Society of Massachusetts that began in the 1700s.[774]

Mary Jane MacKenzie, Cliff's End

At the southern end of Third Cliff, the road curves in a wide U. Collier Road going south becomes Moorland Road going north. Here is a short path, called Point Place on George Welch's 1906 plan. There is no street sign, but a walker can follow the path (a private way) to the cliff's pointy southern end, and its lowest part. Beyond it is the boardwalk and marshy path leading to the beach and the Spit.[775]

At this place is a cottage at 78 Moorland. It has a panoramic view of the marshes, Marshfield hills, and Fourth Cliff. It dates to 1909, if not earlier. Mary Jane MacKenzie bought it in 1933.[776]

It was said that MacKenzie (1883–1974) came from a high social class, and she was listed in *The South Shore Social Register and Who's Who on Cape Cod* for 1938. As a girl, she lived on the southern slope of Beacon Hill in Boston and went to the nearby Prince School on Newbury Street.[777]

She had an early stage career in New York from 1898 to 1905. Then, from 1905 to 1925, she was a drama critic and society columnist for the *New York World*, the Joseph Pulitzer newspaper. By 1940, when she was living on Third Cliff, she was not employed nor looking for work, according to the US census. She still had a pass saying, "Admit this person to any performance at a Shubert Theatre." It was signed by Lee Shubert.[778]

Mary Jane MacKenzie, New York stage publicity photos, c. 1898–1925.
Courtesy of Donald Corey.

At Third Cliff, say former neighbors, she wore old men's clothes, a hat that looked like a beekeeper hat, and a gauze surgical mask around her mouth. She loved to stand and talk with people who took the path by her cottage to the boardwalk. The boardwalk then was a series of narrow planks, laid end to end.[779]

At Third Cliff, MacKenzie had a rowboat, painted bright orange. She kept it tied to a post on her property. When the marsh waters were high enough, she launched the boat over her stone wall next to the marsh. She put on her rubber boots, also orange. Into the boat with her went her dog, a black-spotted Dalmatian.[780]

Family photos show that the marsh next to the cottage ranged from marshland to sandy beachland to watery lake, depending on the seasons and tides. They indicate that 1980 renovations found a buried bird decoy, suggesting that the cottage was used for hunting.[781]

In the winter, MacKenzie and Mrs. Fallon were the only two women in Rivermoor. She wore snowshoes to get to the grocery store.[782]

MacKenzie had a beloved cat named Mocha. When Mocha died, she had his remains made into a pelt and hung it on the wall or on the back of the door into the living room. The pelt was not the only pelt in the room.[783]

Cliff's End family photos, courtesy of Donald Corey. Top photos show pilings (for dock?) and Scituate Country Club clubhouse in distance. Bottom left two show boardwalk as narrow planks, c. 1975. (Another photo from c. 1975, not included here, shows what appears to be the Boston Sand and Gravel conveyor belt tower in the distance.) Bottom right shows rowboat, with Dalmatian and Mary Jane MacKenzie, c. 1962.

In the living room, over the fireplace mantel, was a sign, "Cliffsend." That was the name of the cottage (or "Cliff's End"). It is quite appropriate given its location. At her death in 1974, MacKenzie left instructions that her ashes be buried at Cliff's End. The property was sold in 1977. Relatives have owned it since then.[784]

Cliffsend sign on front door.
Photo by Lyle Nyberg 2021.

Jack Farley said Third Cliff had "more characters per inch" than anywhere else. He may have been exaggerating, but Mary Jane MacKenzie would certainly qualify.[785]

View of Cliff's End, North River marshes, and boardwalk. Photo by Lyle Nyberg 2016.

Reduced Winter Population

In the late 1940s (and even much later), at least 90% of Rivermoor's population consisted of summer residents.[786]

After summer residents left, Third Cliff was pretty deserted. It was so deserted that "if a cow went by, everyone went to their windows."[787] Other residents said nobody went there, buildings were a "disaster," and even as late as 1985, it was a "dump." Second Cliff was much more attractive. (Third Cliff's reputation has improved dramatically in the last 10-20 years.)

After the war, winters must have been cold and lonely. A 1956 directory shows the reduced winter population on Third Cliff streets, as follows (Rivermoor streets in italics):

Bassin Lane: 4 addresses, 9 residents (including 5 Flynns)
Brown Avenue: 1 address, 2 residents
Cliff Avenue: 7 addresses, 13 residents
Collier Road: 13 addresses, 28 residents
Dickens Row: 3 residents (including George and Doris Hauman)
Driftway (up to Scituate Country Club at #91): 4 addresses, 10 residents
Eagles Nest Road: 1 address, 2 residents
Gilson Road: 27 addresses, 58 residents (including Walter S. "Doc" O'Neil, clam warden, but not Sabina Welch, who may have only summered there)
Lincoln Avenue: 1 address (#19), 2 residents
Michael Avenue; 2 addresses (#14 and #22), 4 residents
Moorland Road: 10 addresses, 20 residents
Parker Avenue: 0 addresses, 0 residents
Town Way: 5 addresses, 11 residents (including 6 Sextons)

Total: about 77 addresses (34 in *Rivermoor*), 162 residents (69 in *Rivermoor*)[788]

For comparison, in 2016 the same streets had 250 addresses rather than 77. Of the 250 addresses, about 99 were in Rivermoor rather than 34. In other words, the number of addresses — probably equal to the number of houses — have tripled in the 60 years from 1956 to 2016. This shows how a summer resort evolved into a year-round community.[789]

20

THIRD CLIFF-RIVERMOOR IMPROVEMENT ASSOCIATION

In 1949, residents formed the Third Cliff-Rivermoor Improvement Association (TCRIA). Soon after incorporation, Donald H. Whittemore was made an honorary member. He owned the Scituate Country Club, the site of many early meetings and social events of the Association. Its first annual dinner dance was held in 1950 at the Scituate Country Club.[790]

In its early years, the Association also organized a 4th of July children's party, a Night Before the 4th Celebration, and a Labor Day party. Later events included fishing derbies.[791]

The Association worked to establish rights of residents to use the oceanside Rivermoor beach and the marshy area south of the cliff. It appears that George Welch had granted 50 acres of marsh and beach to real estate dealer Howard Guild, whose heirs granted the property to the Prebles. (The Prebles would later grant the property to the North and South Rivers Watershed Association.) The Prebles allowed use of the beach subject to restrictions. They initially forbade, but later allowed (for a few years), bulldozing of the beach to prepare it for bathing. The Association arranged for a boardwalk accessing the beach to be laid down and taken up each year. They also arranged for Red Cross swimming lessons.[792]

Residents enjoyed the natural features of the area. In the past, dunes along the beach south of the cliff were massive, high, and extensive, reaching down to the Spit. There was a tidal pool, where swimming lessons were held, with warm water. It started about where the boardwalk is now. You could jump on an inner tube and weave around through the creek to the North River. The creek itself was a good 10 feet wide.[793]

In 1968, the town of Scituate had aerial photos taken of the town. Some show how Third Cliff looked then. Google Maps/Satellite View and Google Earth can help identify later changes.[794]

In the 1968 aerial photo below, the creek appears (and maybe the pool). A storm before 1978 destroyed the pool.[795]

Aerial photo of Rivermoor and surroundings, 1968. Scituate Country Club at upper left, marsh and North River at bottom, tidal pool and creek with part of Spit at bottom right. Source: Town of Scituate (CGL-134, 136, 137, or 139).

At Third Cliff, there was a history of using woodie beach wagons, as described in chapter 15 in stories about the Clarence Miller family.

The tradition continued, and became a feature of Association activities. Dr. Bowers in Rivermoor sold a 1938 woodie station wagon for $200 to the newlywed Martinet (?) couple of Lincoln Avenue, and it held all their wedding presents as they drove away for their honeymoon. Polly Bowers was worried the car would conk out on them. It didn't. Dr. Bowers bought another woodie, a 1946 Chrysler Town and Country convertible, for $800. Less than a mile after the purchase, it conked out, but it was revived. His boys used to drive it to the Yacht Club. It is still in the family, making an appearance at the Association's Labor Day parties.[796]

Woodie, Lincoln Ave., 2017. Photo by Lyle Nyberg.

The Labor Day party was the big Association event of the year. It included cookouts and races for the children. This echoed Labor Day parties at Brant Rock in neighboring Marshfield in the early 1900s.[797] On Third Cliff, events were held at the Coolbroth's house at 18 Collier (at Cliff Avenue) until about 1961, then the Kenney's place on Eagles Nest, then the Bowers' big yard at 7 Lincoln since at least 1976 to at least 2019, after which the Covid-19 pandemic put a damper on activities.[798]

The Association published a newsletter from time to time, occasionally called "Cliff Notes." In one issue, they reported on the faux-lighthouse built by Preston Gray in the 1970s at his house at 55 Collier, on the ocean side. It was not a real lighthouse, just an architectural folly, perhaps 20 feet tall, built out of stone with a light at the top. According to Dick Sherrell of Gilson Road:

[Preston Gray] spoke of the time when he had the light on and realized a good sized schooner was coming on almost into the breakers. He (Preston) jumped into his own small boat and rowed out to warn them — they were drunk, of course, and just managed to claw off the shore before running aground.[799]

Another resident of Third Cliff said that the Coast Guard showed up one day and told Preston never to put a light in the lighthouse because seamen might think it was real.[800] A later owner, about 2014, remodeled the house and removed the lighthouse.

Lighthouse (folly) formerly at 55 Collier Road.
Photo by Lyle Nyberg, March 2014.

In the late 1980s, the Association gathered information on the history of Third Cliff and published it in one of its newsletters. As part of this collection, a long-time resident noted in 1986 that the place where the foxhole had been in World War II had eroded, and the cliff had been at least 30 to 40 feet wider then.[801]

***

In 2000, the Association held a golf tournament on the July 4th weekend, with a course of nine holes, each laid out on a resident's property. The course had special neighborhood rules such as "All flowerbeds and shrubs to be played as lateral hazard." Course designers were Bruce E. Beagley and John H. Messenger. Hole 9 at 55 Moorland had a fairway called "The Rose Garden."[802]

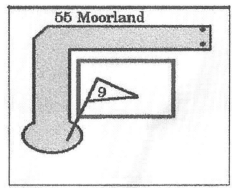

The 9th Fairway — "The Rose Garden"

Hole 9, "The Rose Garden," 2000. Detail from scorecard in TCRIA archives.

In the late 1970s and 1980s, the Association addressed some recurrent concerns.

First, it obtained legal advice and asserted rights to beach access via a de-facto right of way between the Spears and the Barnard properties, or alternatively via a legal right of way between lots 206 and 207 of the Barnard property as shown on the 1906 Rivermoor plan, at or near the end of Lincoln Avenue. This was the site of Harriet Miller's 1920s cottage at 43 Collier Road.[803]

Second, Association members cleared a path through the rocks at that right of way, and salvaged pieces of the seasonal boardwalk near there to create a new, year-round boardwalk from the neighborhood's access point at the southern end of Collier to the beach and the Spit.[804]

Third, they raised concerns about the ocean breaching and eroding Rivermoor beach, eroding its sand dunes and degrading other features. In 1980, the Association explained to local officials that the overwash was covering and choking off vegetation in the marsh behind the beach, and it had closed the creek in which residents had gone swimming. However, despite whatever action was taken after the Association raised the concerns, the ocean continued its incursions and reduced the dunes. However, the fine beach is still there.[805]

The right of way issue was not clarified until 1996. At the Association's initiative, the then-owner of the Barnard property at 43 Collier Road granted an easement on the north side of lot 207. The easement grants a right of way between Collier Road and the beach to all Rivermoor property owners ("successors and assigns of George F. Welch, who from time to time have an interest in fee [title] in and to the subdivision lots" on the 1906 Rivermoor plan). The easement acknowledged that the right of way in the 1906 plan between lots 206 and 207 was made impassable by the construction of a garage and driveway. The easement pertains to the lot at 43 Collier and people should respect the rights and privacy of other shorefront property owners. Apart from the easement, residents have historically used the way at 43 Collier, and the extension of Michael Avenue, to access the beach, along with the path leading to the boardwalk at the cliff's southern tip.[806]

Boardwalk, view toward Fourth Cliff. Photo by Lyle Nyberg 2021.

The Association is still active. It has informed residents about matters affecting them, sponsored civic contributions, organized beach and street clean-ups, and built and maintained a boardwalk leading to the beach. It has also arranged social events, such as fishing contests, yard sales, outdoor movies, lobster cookouts on the beach, and the annual end-of-summer Labor Day party. This party has included gunny-sack races, egg-toss contests, tug-of-war competitions, and the "Silly Hat" parade, echoing the old Fourth of July "Horribles Parades" in this area.[807]

Third Cliff neighbors at Labor Day party in 2016, except for
upper left (Carolyn & Skip DeBrusk, 2017) and upper right (Jack Farley, 2016).
Barbecue by Alec Graziano. Photos by Lyle Nyberg.

21

CHANGES AFTER 1950S — GROWTH, ENVIRONMENT, INFRASTRUCTURE

In the 1950s and beyond, housing expanded around Boston, including along the South Shore. This was enabled by the extension of the Southeast Expressway and construction of Route 3 in the late 1950s and early 1960s.

In the 1960s, road maps issued by gasoline stations continued to highlight Rivermoor along Scituate's coast, as well as North Scituate Beach, Shore Acres, and Sand Hills.[808]

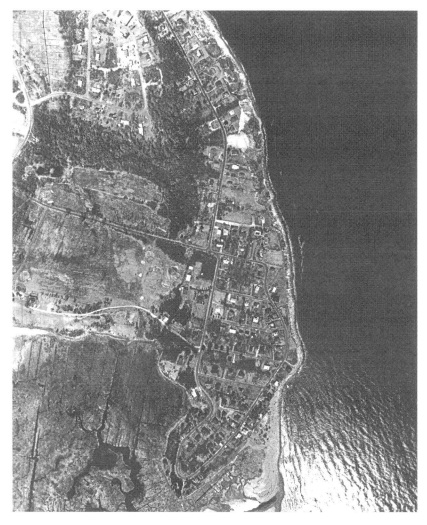

At left, this aerial photo of Third Cliff is from 1968, before condominiums were built at 40 Driftway. The Driftway runs across the center, with the Scituate Country Club on both sides.

The photo shows new roads at the top, channels in the North River marshes at the bottom, and the start of the Spit at the bottom right. (Source: Town of Scituate, Town Archives, CGL-136.)

In the early 1970s, in Scituate's coastal zone

(not the entire town), the value of residential building permits soared — from $614,150 in 1970 to $1,020,100 in 1971, $1,565,910 in 1972, and $1,368,510 in 1973. Then they fell back to $609,160 in 1974. During this time, the town accepted new streets on Third Cliff: Cobb Lane, Foxwell Lane (named after one of the town's early settlers), Hewes Road, and Town Way Extension. About the same time, Collier and Moorland became one-way streets year-round, Collier going south and Moorland going north.[809]

Concerns about the impact of development in the area led Massachusetts to pass the North River Protective Act, and to issue a North River Protective Order in 1979 to control development on or near the North River. The Act and Order limit or forbid certain development on parts of Third Cliff. The North River is the state's only scenic protected river.[810] In 1977, federal agencies designated the North and South Rivers as a National Natural Landmark.[811]

In addition, in 1985 the town designated the Driftway as a Scenic Road under the state's Scenic Road Act, protecting its trees and stone walls. The Driftway has a "canopy of trees" as the road rises to enter Third Cliff.[812]

In 1974, the town commissioned a study of the erosion of Third Cliff and possible remedial actions. The study was done by Goldberg-Zoino & Associates, Inc. (GZA). GZA's investigation included a survey of residents, an aerial survey, a land survey, a seismic survey, and test borings. GZA's investigation found the cliff was composed of (from top to bottom) glacial till containing clay, sand from possible Miocene Epoch (5.333 to 23.03 million years ago), marine clay from possible Eocene Epoch (33.9 to 56 million years ago), and bedrock that test borings reached at 70 to 90 feet. GZA's 1975 report found that the erosion on Third Cliff was not caused by the ocean, but rather by ground water seepage along its face, and massive, deep slope failures causing landslides. GZA's report did not consider the historical reports (in deeds) of waterfalls at the cliff, or the 1906 Rivermoor plan that showed what appears to be an underground stream south of the Driftway leading to the cliff. GZA's report recommended remedial action to stabilize the 3,200 feet that the firm evaluated (the portion opposite Gilson Road, out of a total 4,000 feet of the cliff). GZA proposed (1) flattening the steep upper face of the cliff to a 1 on 2 slope, (2) adding riprap to the toe (bottom) of the slope, and (3) adding relief wells and trench for drainage along the toe of the slope, to reduce the water table at the face of the cliff near its bottom. The proposed work had a total estimated cost of $1,900,000. A later report to the town deemed this remedial action ineffective and possibly counterproductive. The remedial action was not undertaken.[813]

A few years after these reports, the Blizzard of 1978 caused great damage to Scituate's shores. The existing seawalls were insufficient to protect homes, roads, and infrastructure.

As a result, First, Second, and Third Cliffs were armored with revetments. This has reduced storm damage, but its effect on cliff erosion is unclear.[814]

Seawalls or revetments are a complicated business. Property rights come into play, and engineering has evolved over the years.

Shorefront landowners generally own land to the mean low-tide mark, under colonial-era laws still in effect in Massachusetts. The intertidal area between low tide and high tide is where seawalls go. To add or maintain them, the government requires access over, and use of, private property of landowners. Often, the government seeks consent, usually written, from each landowner. A single holdout can mean no foreshore protection for a whole area including the holdout's property. Use of the seawalls, and the intertidal areas, are governed again by colonial-era laws and the Massachusetts version of the "public trust" doctrine. They allow use by the public for fishing, fowling (hunting for birds), and navigation.[815]

Peggotty Beach, start of revetment at north end of Third Cliff. Photo by Lyle Nyberg 2014.

In 1975, the town took by eminent domain much of the land of the Boston Sand and Gravel Company. The land encompassed the Colman Hills, to the west of Third Cliff, and was the site of the town's earliest farms. The company's mining operations from 1914 to 1963 had significantly reduced the hills. In the western part of the hills, in Greenbush, the town opened a sanitary landfill for waste disposal, later capped, and added a waste transfer station there. Much of the land was used to create the municipal Widow's Walk golf course that opened in 1997. It was America's first "environmental demonstration course," and it used the original terrain left over from the mining operations. The golf course and the transfer station each have an enterprise fund, reviewed every year by town meeting, with the purpose of financially self-sustaining operations.[816]

In the 1970s, various commercial businesses started or were already located in Scituate that are still around. They include Maria's Submarine Sandwich Shop (started in 1965), Rocco's Barber Shop (started in 1970), Jack Conway Realtor, Kennedy's Country Gardens, Harbour Insurance Agency, and, of course, the Welch Company. No longer around are Gates Clothing, Combs Shoe Company, Goddard's 5 & 10 (1961 to about 1994), Paul McCarthy's Carving Place, the Quarter Deck, the Grog Shop, and the Bell Buoy (casual wining and dining), among others.[817]

The Blizzard of 1978 attacked Third Cliff along with other places. Coastal towns like Scituate had to deal with exceptionally high tides as well as the intense and extended snowstorm. Joan Foster said the storm lifted her house off its cinder-block foundation and twisted it. She later had the house elevated. Alice Gallagher said the water almost reached the floor of the lower level of her house, which has one of the highest elevations on Collier. They lost power and heat, in 40-degree weather. Alice cooked in the fireplace. She was cooking beef Stroganoff in the fireplace when the power came back on, about a week after the storm.[818]

In the late 1980s, a complex of townhouse condominiums with 36 units was built at the Scituate Country Club. Originally, the complex was to be built on the ridge overlooking the North River, but that proposal faced much local opposition, based in part on the North River Protective Order. As a result, the complex was built on the club's former property north of the Driftway. That required moving the fifth and sixth holes of the golf course. The address of the complex is 40 Driftway.[819]

The Scituate Country Club golf course was sold to its current owners in 1991.[820]

In 1991, the owners of 14 Collier Road on Third Cliff (the Spencers) took steps to open a bed and breakfast in their home. It was called "Rivermoor By The Sea." Neighbors challenged it in court but were unsuccessful. The bed and breakfast did not last very long.[821]

In other developments, the town sewer system came to Third Cliff in 2005. The Scituate Wastewater Treatment Plant had become operational in November 1967. The system's expansion to Third Cliff eliminated the need for private, individual septic systems.[822]

In 2007, commuter rail service began between Scituate and Boston on the Greenbush Line, after an absence of 48 years.[823]

In 2012, the town installed a wind turbine on the west side of Third Cliff to provide energy for town-owned buildings. It is highly visible. The town considers it an economic and environmental benefit. However, some residents have complained about its noise, and this produced a controversial and close vote by the town in 2013 to continue wind turbine operations.[824]

In 2021, the town meeting approved the purchase of a parcel of almost 18 acres of open space on Border Street in northeastern Scituate. The parcel was described as a bucolic open field with stone walls, woods, and wetlands. Community Preservation funds are to be used to pay the price of more than $2 million. The town had a first refusal option to purchase the parcel and preserve the open space under the state's Chapter 61A law, which provides tax breaks for agricultural land. The alternative was that a builder would build a subdivision there with six houses. A farmer who spoke at the town meeting said that it is easier to turn a farm into a subdivision than the reverse, and "good dirt is hard to come by."[825]

The overwhelming support for the town's purchase of the Border Street land demonstrates a big change from the times when subdivisions were built on Third Cliff farmland.

22

SOUNDS AND SIGHTS OF THIRD CLIFF

It's the unusual that gets the attention of our senses. That's why we take photos of fires and floods and tend to overlook everyday landscapes, sights, and sounds. Unusual or everyday, sounds and sights are rich and diverse on Third Cliff, and give us insights into life on the cliff.

We notice sounds of helicopters at Third Cliff. They follow the shoreline, presumably taking military personnel to and from the US Air Force recreation facility on Fourth Cliff. This facility is the former US Army's World War II coastal artillery gun site.[826]

We also notice the sounds of house construction and yard maintenance — pneumatic nailers, leaf blowers, hedge trimmers.

Other sounds don't always get our attention because we have become used to them. The sea always makes sounds. Sometimes they are constant, like the steady hiss of water against the shore. Other times they are rhythmic, like crashes of waves, or thunder of surf from a storm. Some are distant, some are close.

We take the sounds of birds for granted. Yet birds abound on Third Cliff, perhaps outnumbering human residents. Robins, doves, hawks. Grackles, with their crow-like raspy croaks or caws. Some birds tweet. A few trill. One makes a singular sound like the clink of a thick drink glass in a restaurant. Other birds join in, too numerous for a non-birder and non-ornithologist to describe. The English language is inadequate to express their sounds. Bats congregate at dusk around the streetlight where Collier and Moorland meet, no doubt feasting on bugs attracted to the light.

Eagles are evidently quiet, too. One visits the top of the tree at the intersection of Collier and Moorland. It visits from its nest across the river in Marshfield.[827]

Sights on Third Cliff are interesting and often unique. Of course, there are ocean views, constantly changing in appearance, shape, and color. Storm clouds are visible for miles. Fog can collapse visibility to just part of the house next door. The setting sun in the west is beautiful, often accompanied by bright oranges and reds.

230

The setting sun colors the sky in the *east*, as well. Colors are layered above the ocean from purple, dark blue, pinks, oranges, yellowish beiges, to sky blue. It happens anywhere because dust and other fine particles in the atmosphere create the colors (by scattering light) and clouds reflect them across the sky. In addition, the path of the fading sunlight makes a difference, according to meteorologist Stephen Corfidi:

> … at sunset, the light takes a much longer path through the atmosphere to your eye than it did at noon [up to 40 times as long] …. It means that much of the blue has scattered out long before the light reaches us.[828]

Whatever the science, the sunset effect in the east can be beautiful. On a clear evening, pick a site with an unobstructed eastern horizon, like Third Cliff, and watch.[829]

In the daytime, Third Cliff is a balcony overlooking a major passageway for ships traveling to and from the port of Boston. They include freighters, ocean liners, and even a barge with a house on it. On one special day, you could have seen the aircraft carrier USS John F. Kennedy leaving Boston on its final voyage.[830]

From Third Cliff, you can see at least one feature at the tip of Cape Cod, 26 miles away — the Pilgrim Monument in Provincetown. It is interesting to walk through calculations of how this is possible. It is not as straightforward as you might think. The curvature of the earth (and the water) must be considered.

Assume a person 5 feet tall stands on the widow's walk atop a house 35 feet tall on a part of Third Cliff that is 60 feet above sea level, for a total of 100 feet above sea level. At that height, the distance to the horizon is about 13 miles. But that is only halfway to the tip of the Cape. The person on Third Cliff could only see a feature that is high above the horizon. To find out how high, assume a hypothetical observer at the tip of the Cape at an elevation of 100 feet looking back toward Third Cliff. The observer can see the horizon 13 miles away, the same as for the Third Cliff person. Together, they total the 26 miles between Third Cliff and the tip of the Cape. Any higher than 100 feet, and the hypothetical observer can see the person on Third Cliff and vice versa. So the person on Third Cliff can see most of the Pilgrim Monument because its base is about 100 feet above sea level, and it rises another 252 feet.[831]

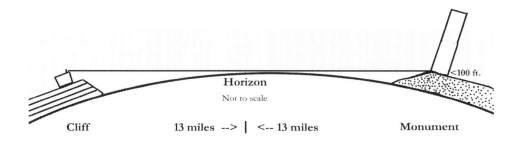

By contrast, the nearby Race Point Light is only 45 feet tall and not far above sea level, so it cannot be seen from Third Cliff, according to these calculations.[832]

Aided by a Third Cliff neighbor, the local historian was able to see the Pilgrim Monument in favorable weather and lighting conditions.

The ability to see items that lie *over* the horizon can be explained by two words: temperature inversion. Warm air that usually stays at lower altitudes moves on top of colder air. This bends the light rays down from the object (like the Pilgrim Monument) and creates a kind of optical illusion. Sailors call this "looming" over the horizon.[833]

While on the subject of light, it should be mentioned that Scituate is not immune from the growing concern over light pollution. As one amateur astronomer has said, "life has evolved over millions of years with half the time dark and half the time light, and we have now enveloped our planet in a luminous fog of light."[834] The International Dark-Sky Association warns:

> Less than 100 years ago, everyone could look up and see a spectacular starry night sky. Now, millions of children across the globe will never experience the Milky Way where they live. The increased and widespread use of artificial light at night is not only impairing our view of the universe, it is adversely affecting our environment, our safety, our energy consumption and our health.[835]

Another writer says:

> To see skies truly comparable to those which Galileo knew, you would have to travel to such places as the Australian outback and the mountains of Peru. And civilization's assault on the stars has consequences far beyond its impact on astronomers. Excessive, poorly designed outdoor lighting wastes electricity, imperils human health and safety, disturbs natural habitats, and, increasingly, deprives many of us of a direct relationship with the nighttime sky, which throughout human history has been a powerful source of reflection, inspiration, discovery, and plain old jaw-dropping wonder.[836]

Scientists have created an interactive map that shows where and how much light appears at night.[837]

Some communities on the South Shore have adopted bylaws to control outdoor lighting, but Scituate is not among them.[838]

Residents of Third Cliff experience light from street lighting, the occasional historian burning the midnight oil, nearby town centers, perhaps even metropolitan Boston. However, one presumes, the closer to the ocean, the less light pollution (and sound pollution) there is. Being on the cliff close to the ocean can cut the amount of human-generated light at night in half, as the half from the ocean is negligible. Residents can better enjoy the night sky.

Similarly, shore dwellers can enjoy the fresh air, and not just at night. Sometimes, though, the air has that "low tide smell" of decaying ocean life, kind of like rotten eggs. The smell seems to have something to do with sex by seaweeds. Visiting in summer in the old days, when cars did not have air conditioning and the car windows were rolled down, that smell told us we were nearing the cliffs.[839]

23

THIRD CLIFF TODAY

Today, as it has been for decades, Scituate is noted for its summer beaches. In particular, swimmers flock to Peggotty Beach, between Second and Third Cliffs, and will be lucky to find a parking spot there on a summer day. Surfers visit the area, too, when conditions are right. Small pleasure sailboats are rare there now. But dories still ply the waters at Peggotty Beach so that owners can pull their lobster pots (lobster traps) and harvest lobsters.[840]

The beach at Rivermoor on Third Cliff is still there. A more accurate term is beaches. They are as rocky as ever, but with the right ocean currents and tides, strings of rocks zigzag and create many sandy areas and tidal pools.

Rivermoor beach, with Fourth Cliff in background, viewed from 57 Collier Road.
Photo by Lyle Nyberg 2021.

Third Cliff still has the cooling breezes that attracted people to the shore a century ago. A neighbor says it's always nine degrees cooler here. (The local historian thinks he means in summer.)

Housing and Welch Legacy

George Welch left a significant legacy on Third Cliff. In 150 years, Third Cliff has gone from mossers' huts to mansions, thanks to Welch's ambitions and planning.

His plot plans and street layouts continue. Today's Gilson Road has grown along the lines of the 1900 plan of the Scituate Beach Land Association, of which George was a key participant. On Gilson, together with its offshoots Bassin Lane, Dickens Row, and Town Way, there are now more than 90 houses.

Similarly, today's Rivermoor looks much like George's 1906 plan, with its street names and ocean views.[841] However, it evolved to multiple lots per house, so now the 222 lots of the original plan have close to 100 houses.[842]

George Welch built most of the early Rivermoor houses. By 1930, Rivermoor had grown to about 48 dwellings. Of these, more than half still exist, which is remarkable. Some are more than 100 years old, old enough to have been shown to tenants attracted by George's ad in 1915. Michael Avenue has an impressive six Welch colonials of the surviving dwellings. Real estate agents have advertised the Welch houses here and throughout Scituate as "Welch colonials."[843]

Most owners have updated, rehabilitated, winterized, modified, and expanded their houses, including enclosing the upper porches.[844] About half of the remaining Welch houses in Rivermoor still have their characteristic hip roofs.[845] And, of course, the houses still share the cliff with the Scituate Country Club and golf course, established in 1919.

George Welch originally developed these houses to satisfy Americans' desires for summer vacation housing. Today, nearly all serve as year-round homes. The summer colony has become a neighborhood, a part of the larger Third Cliff community.

New houses — usually bigger — have been built on Third Cliff. A few have about 6,000 square feet, according to the Scituate Assessor's Database, putting them in mansion territory.

"Michael Ave., Rivermoor, Scituate, Mass.," postcard with view looking east, c. 1910–1920 (Chas. W. Frye, Pub.). Three hip-roofed houses on eastern end of Michael (from left, #14, 10, 6). Courtesy of Scituate Historical Society (Twomey/Jacobson collection).

Michael Ave. looking east, December 2016. Three hip-roofed houses on eastern end of Michael (from left, #14, 10, 6), next to new gambrel-roofed house (Collier Road address). 33 Collier is at far right (both images). Photo by Lyle Nyberg.

For all of George Welch's impact on Scituate, he has received surprisingly little attention in historical writings. Sources mention the Welch Company store but overlook the fact that Welch was a major real estate owner and developer, as was his father. Other preeminent figures and property owners of the time, such as Thomas Lawson and the Glades Club, have been the subject of published works, but George has not.[846] Thomas Lawson and George Allen, top property owners of the past, have streets named after them. George Welch does not.

Likewise, houses on Scituate's cliffs were largely overlooked in historical analyses, inventories, and documentation. At the end of 2016, Scituate had 900 or so historical buildings listed in the state's database, the Massachusetts Cultural Resource Information System (MACRIS). Only five were on Third Cliff. None was on Second Cliff, one or two were on First Cliff, and none was on Fourth Cliff (except for those in the historical area at the cliff's northern end). The Welch farmhouse on Third Cliff, now the Scituate Country Club's clubhouse, dates to the early 1800s. The Daniel Ward House, the first house on First Cliff, dates to about 1854. Neither was listed in the MACRIS database at the end of 2016. Thanks to the local historian, they were documented and added to the database, along with about 100 other overlooked historical houses on the cliffs. From 2016 to mid-2021, the list of Scituate historical buildings grew from 900 to 1043.[847]

Teardowns

We live in an age of teardowns. They represented almost 8% of single-family housing starts nationally, in recent years, particularly in long-established communities around large cities such as Boston. This is partly due to old housing stock. Recent surveys show that Massachusetts had the second-oldest stock of any state, with a median age of 56 years. The national median age for owner-occupied homes was 39 years.[848]

The housing stock on Third Cliff is particularly vulnerable to teardowns, as the median age of its homes ranged from 61 years on the northern end to 68 in Rivermoor in the most recent analysis.[849]

In the ten-year span of 2006 to 2016, at least 12 historical houses in Scituate were torn down. Nearly all were on Third Cliff. This represented a rate of one a year, a rate that is quickening. In 2015, two historical houses were demolished on Third Cliff — 22 Collier and 12 Moorland. In 2016, four houses (two considered historical) were demolished and replaced. In 2017, two more historical houses were demolished on Third Cliff — 20 Collier and 9 Driftway. In 2018, 3 Driftway (the Marguerite) was replaced by a house with the new address of 3 Collier. In 2019–2020, the house at 15 Bassin Lane (which evidently contained historical parts) was replaced. In early 2021, the old Turner farmhouse at 141 Driftway, built about 1792, was demolished.[850]

Protections for these older houses are limited. Scituate, like many other towns in Massachusetts, adopted a demolition review bylaw for old buildings. A demolition permit for a building 100 years of age or older requires a review by the Scituate Historical Commission, formed in 2006. The Commission can delay demolition for up to 12 months for a significant building. Apart from this bylaw, property owners are free to make decisions based on economic factors and personal values. Those values may not (or may) include historical preservation. Scituate has not established any local historic districts, as other towns have. Such local districts limit uses of and changes to historic properties. National Register Districts have no such limits and are mostly symbolic.[851]

Housing Construction

Construction materials and methods have changed a lot since George Welch's time. Back then, foundations were built with single concrete blocks, mortar, and days of work by masons. Now, foundation forms are set up and a continuous concrete foundation can be poured in less than a day. Back then, summer homes needed no insulation. Now, spray foam is commonly applied to all interiors for superior insulation and air sealing. Modern builders consider concepts of energy efficiency, "building envelope," and controlling "air leaks" or infiltration. For example, builders install sill gaskets between the sill plate and the foundation; in older houses, caulking that joint is recommended to reduce air infiltration. To let houses "breathe" without losing energy, there are air-to-air heat exchangers. In coastal areas prone to strong winds or hurricanes, certain construction techniques are available or required, such as metal tie-down straps that attach the roof and each floor to the house structure, storm shutters, reinforced glass windows, and garage door braces.[852]

Today's houses are arguably better built in some ways than they were 100 years ago, and they are certainly more energy efficient. Moreover, these newer technologies can be used to make older houses energy efficient.[853]

A 2013 *Boston Globe* article featured a new house at 4 Collier for its energy efficiency. It is uber-insulated, with 12-inch walls filled with spray foam. It has photovoltaic solar panels that produce 70% of the home's electricity. With all this new technology, it retains the shingle style of the original cottage it replaced.[854]

A modern trend is to prefabricate and build modular houses in factories, and then transport the house in pieces that are reconstructed on site. The factories are equipped with computer-aided design and manufacturing systems, and they borrow techniques used to manufacture consumer electronics.[855] Ernest Hodgson, the first American to make prefab houses and a former resident of Rivermoor, would be proud.

Ecosystem

Natural calamities have not alone been responsible for changes along the Northeast coast. Human-made developments on Third Cliff and elsewhere along the coast have affected the ecosystem, including impacts on clams and birds such as piping plovers. They inhabit the Spit at the southern end of Third Cliff, along the North River, accessible on foot from the cliff or by boat.

For decades, taking clams was prohibited because of polluted waters. Clamming was once again permitted in 1996 along the North River (and later along the South River), for those who obtain a clamming license from the appropriate town and follow its rules. From time to time in recent years, the state has closed the clam beds due to concerns about polluted waters. In 2020, the state closed all clamming, including recreational clamming, based on FDA rules to prevent contamination that apply to commercial clamming.[856]

Piping plovers are among the 200 migratory shorebirds that stop to nest, lay eggs and hatch them on specific spots, usually in the spring. Third Cliff is one of those spots, and it is a major migratory stopover. Due to threats from predators and beachgoers, the population of piping plovers fell dramatically by 1986. Then, both federal and state governments designated them as threatened under each of their Endangered Species Acts, and imposed restrictions designed to protect piping plovers. Since then, their numbers have recovered, and the federal government has proposed relaxing restrictions in Massachusetts. In a nod to its special ecosystem, much of the area south and west of Third Cliff is considered the Rivermoor Habitat Park. In addition, the Audubon Society listed this area as an Important Bird Area (IBA).[857]

Shorebird, Rivermoor beach. Photo by Lyle Nyberg 2016.

Changing Site

As is the case for most coastal communities, the pace of change is fast at Third Cliff's margins. Tides occur about every 12 hours, constantly transforming the scene along the

North River and the ocean shore. Green marshy meadows turn into lakes, lakes turn back into marshy meadows. At the ocean shore, rocky fields turn into sandy beaches, then back to rocky shores. The tide creates varied rock peninsulas, rock piers, rock islands, rock inlets, and rock coves. Strings of rocks separate the beach into strands of stranded sand, and rocks surround watery pools containing tiny crabs and residues of the ocean.

The rocks are solid, but they move and scuttle. Neighbors build rock cairns to mark the top of the path to the beach, and they repair their creations when the ocean damages them.

Rock cairn with sign:
"Dedicated to the spirits of the Spit."
Photo by Lyle Nyberg 2021.

Change is slower for Third Cliff's landscape. Trees and shrubs bloom as seasons dictate. Most of them were not there a century ago, when Third Cliff was mostly pasture land. Old photos and postcards show few trees and shrubs, and few houses. On land, the time scale of change is measured in decades or centuries, not tides.

Conclusion

Houses on Third Cliff have come and gone over the ages. So have people. Some of their names appeared in newspapers, directories, or deeds. For the author, the question "why did they live on Third Cliff?" always surfaced, called for research, and produced their stories. Their answers to the question ranged from farmers looking for good land, Irish mossers wanting to live near their work on the ocean, summer residents with family connections, and people who enjoyed living in a beautiful area by the ocean.

Change is even faster today with new construction. Neighbors hear the occasional crunching of a backhoe demolishing an old house, the clatter of lumber for new houses, the hammering of nails, the thwacks of nail guns, and the rumble of construction vehicles.

So, is living here like a "never-ending vacation" as one real estate ad puts it?[858]

Well, the chances may be better here than other places. Scituate is a small town, out of the way, so it can offer a vacation from big city life. Drivers learn to slow down because of bikers and walkers on the roads, throngs of summer visitors, and the archaic features of some intersections. Today, a traffic circle controls the flow of traffic at the multi-road intersection of Route 123, Old Oaken Bucket Road, Route 3A, Country Way, and the Driftway. But before the circle, it was more complicated. There was a yellow caution sign that the local historian recalls and has never seen elsewhere: "Beware of Misused Turn Signals."

Nearby are malls and large supermarkets, commonly reached by scenic country roads. In town, food shoppers have a choice of a small but well-supplied supermarket, an excellent fish market, a seasonal farmers market, and local greenhouses and farmstands. Those who engage in fishing or boating probably make up a greater proportion of residents than in other towns. Yet all are within an hour's reach of Boston.[859]

Intriguing people lived on Third Cliff, as noted in this book. The history continues. Recent residents have included university professors and people who come from or have lived in diverse foreign countries. Others are contributing to our society, its governments, and its businesses. Perhaps their stories will be written some day.

A realtor who lives in Rivermoor recently described the cliff as "breathtaking," and "the best spot in town." Another person said this area is "[o]ne of the most scenic meetings of land and sea on the East Coast."[860]

Even with all the changes in housing, changes in people, and changes wrought by nature, Third Cliff retains the charm of its older houses, along with the scenic beauty of its marsh, river, and ocean surroundings, and sounds of a bell buoy, seagulls, and ocean waves.

View of Third Cliff looking north, with Rivermoor beach, sandy areas, and beachgoers. Photo by Lyle Nyberg 2021.

APPENDICES

Appendix A. Names of Cottages in Rivermoor

#	Street	Name	YrBlt	D*
18	Cliff	Edwards	1918	
24		Hall	1911	D
4	Collier	Edgecliff	1910	D
11		Bijou	1871	D
14		Parker	1871	D
16		Lamprey (Lamphrey)	1900	D
20		Campbell	1909	D
22		Russell; Leonard	1909	D
28		San.-Souci	1909	D
59		Jennings	1909	
60		Hodgson	1909	D
67		Curtis	1910	D
74		Clyde	1912	
77		Cedar Camp	1908	
3	Driftway	Marguerite; On the Cliff	1908	D
8		Viola	1910	D
11		Maplewood	1918	D
7	Lincoln	Laurel	1911	
9		Linden	1911	D
14		Lavender	1912	D
15		Linnet	1911	
18		Mayo	1912	
6	Michael	Myrtle	1909	
10		Maidstone	1909	
14		Mayfair	1909	
15		Midget	1920	
18		Melody	1909	
22		Moorfield	1909	
12	Moorland	Mitton	1912	D
28		Mereside	1911	
36		Indian Knoll	1910	D
51		"1914"	1914	
55		The Marshes	1917	
59		Boulder	1912	
78		Cliff's End	1909	
10	Parker	Wheeler	1915	
12		Stevens	1915	
21	Parker (Ext.)	Talbot	1912	D
	Total:	38		18

Sources: Tax valuation lists; Sanborn maps; *Boston Globe*; vintage postcards
*Demolished, as of mid-2021

Appendix B. Number of Houses on Third Cliff, 1903–1926

	'03	'04	'05	'06	'07	'08	'09	'10	'11	'12	'13	'14
Cliff Ave									1	1	1	2
Collier Rd	8	8	8	8	8	10	15	19	19	19	19	19
Lincoln Ave									4	6	6	6
Michael Ave							5	5	5	5	5	5
Moorland Rd							1	2	3	6	6	7
Parker Ave									1	1	1
Rivermoor	8	8	8	8	8	10	21	26	32	38	38	40
Bassin Lane	5	5	5	5	5	5	5	5	5	5	5	5
Dickens Row	4	4	4	4	4	4	4	4	4	4	4	4
Driftway	3	3	3	3	3	3	4	5	5	5	5	6
Gilson	3	3	3	3	3	3	6	8	8	10	10	10
Total	23	23	23	23	23	25	40	48	54	62	62	64

	'15	'16	'17	'18	'19	'20	'21	'22	'23	'24	'25	'26
Cliff Ave	2	2	2	2	2	3	3	3	3	3	3	4
Collier Rd	19	19	19	23	23	23	24	25	25	25	26	27
Lincoln Ave	6	6	6	6	6	6	6	6	6	6	7	7
Michael Ave	5	5	5	5	5	6	6	6	6	6	6	6
Moorland Rd	7	7	7	7	7	7	7	7	7	7	7	8
Parker Ave	3	3	4	4	4	4	4	4	4	4	4	5
Rivermoor	42	42	43	47	47	49	50	51	51	51	53	57
Bassin Lane	5	5	5	5	5	5	6	6	6	6	6	6
Dickens Row	4	4	4	4	4	4	4	4	4	4	4	4
Driftway	5	5	5	9	9	9	9	9	9	9	9	9
Gilson	11	11	11	12	12	15	18	18	18	18	18	21
Total	67	67	68	77	77	82	87	88	88	88	90	97

Annual Average Growth Rate: 10.3% (Rivermoor), 7% (Total)

Sources: Scituate Assessor's Database; Town *Valuation Lists*; *Boston Globe;* deeds
Note: Numbers are approximate, and do not include Brown Ave (Rivermoor), Driftway above #91, and Gilson #125, 125A. Numbers in 1918 are based on 1918 Sanborn map and some of those houses might have been built earlier.

Appendix C. Notional Profitability for Two Rivermoor Properties of George Welch

	Maid-stone	Indian Knoll	Note
Year built	1909	1910	a
Tax value without lots, 1918	$ 2,000	$ 2,500	a, b
Income			
$600/year rental income, 7 years	4,200	4,200	c, d
Implied sale price with 2 lots, 1919	4,750	2,875	e
Total Income	8,950	7,075	
Costs			
Construction cost after 20% savings	1,600	2,000	f
Additional Costs			
Furniture ($10,750/43 houses, 1918)	250	250	a
Maintenance, cleaning, misc., 7 years	100	100	
2% taxes, 7 years	280	350	a
6% interest, 7 years	777	945	g
Comprehensive Cost Base	3,007	3,645	
Rental profit before sale (rent less comprehensive cost base)	1,193	555	
Profit (total income less comprehensive cost base) after sale	$ 5,943	3,430	
Return on comprehensive cost base	198%	94%	h

Notes

a	Town of Scituate Valuation Lists
b	Assume no-cost lots (gift from father)
c	1915 ad: $300–600 for 4 months
d	Assume later rented for 7 years
e	Recorded mortgage amounts, assume 20% down, etc.
f	Assume savings from Welch Co. relation
g	6% rate in recorded mortgages
h	Not adjusted for inflation or time value of money other than imputed interest at 6%, 7 years

Notes on Sources

General. Below are basic sources of information, and abbreviations, used in this book. This supplements the endnotes, which mostly attempt to follow the Chicago Manual of Style.

The endnotes link (hotlink) to many websites. This may be particularly helpful if you use the electronic version of this book. The links were good when consulted for this book and most were still good at time of publication. Unfortunately, it seems some special-interest websites last less than five years. That is less time than it took in writing this book. So some of these websites no longer work ("former" websites or "dead links"). To find or recover these websites, try a Google search, or the Internet Archive's Wayback Machine.

***

<u>Architecture</u>. Virginia Savage McAlester, *A Field Guide to American Houses: The Definitive Guide to Identifying and Understanding America's Domestic Architecture* (New York: Alfred A. Knopf, 2013). A great, helpful guide to understanding houses.

Assessor's Database (Town of Scituate). Past versions were consulted online. Current version is online at http://www.assessedvalues2.com/index.aspx?jurcode=264.

Biographical Review, Vol. XVIII: Containing Life Sketches of Leading Citizens of Plymouth County, Massachusetts (Boston: Biographical Review Publishing Co., 1897), https://archive.org/details/biographicalrevi1897biog and https://books.google.com/books?id=7qd5EML7tYYC&source=gbs_navlinks_s ("*Biographical Review*").

Boston Globe. Most citations are from www.bostonglobe.com online archives, powered by ProQuest Archiver or, more recently, Newspapers.com. The word "Daily" is omitted.

<u>Directories</u>. Key ones are:

- 1894. *Directory of Cohasset, Scituate, Marshfield, Duxbury and Norwell* (Quincy, MA: J. H. Hogan Co., 1894), Scituate Historical Society and online, https://archive.org/details/directoryhistory00quin ("*1894 Directory*");

- 1915. Harold Howard, *Resident and Business Directory of Scituate and Marshfield Massachusetts* (Harold Howard, 1915), Scituate Historical Society (Businesses file) ("*1915 Directory*");

- 1918. Harold Howard, compiler, Towns of Scituate and Marshfield Massachusetts Directory 1918: Containing an Alphabetical List of the Inhabitants, a Summer Resident Directory, Street Directory and Classified Business Directory; a List of Town Officials and Churches, Diagrams of Boston Theatres and Census of Massachusetts (Boston: Harold Howard, 1918), Scituate Historical Society ("1918 Directory");

- 1926. Harold Howard, compiler, Towns of Scituate and Marshfield Massachusetts Directory 1926: Containing Alphabetical List of Inhabitants and a Street Directory Classified Business Directory; a list of Town Officials; Churches, Schools, Teachers, Societies, Associations, Clubs, Institutions and Summer Resident Directory (Boston: Harold Howard, 1926), Scituate Historical Society ("1926 Directory").

Maps. See Sanborn and State Library, below. A key map is the 1903 map, J. E. Judson, *Topographical Atlas of Surveys: Plymouth County together with the town of Cohasset, Norfolk County, Massachusetts* (Springfield, MA: L. J. Richards & Co., 1903), plate 31 ("1903 map").

Massachusetts Cultural Resource Information System ("MACRIS"). It documents old buildings and other resources, and is a database of the Massachusetts Historical Commission, online at http://mhc-macris.net/.

North and South Rivers Watershed Association ("NSRWA").

Plymouth County Registry of Deeds ("PCRD"). Deeds and plans are online at http://www.plymouthdeeds.org/.

Sanborn Maps. They covered parts of Scituate, including Third Cliff, in 1909, 1918, 1926, and 1939. On file on microfilm at State Library of Massachusetts, Special Collections.

Scituate Historical Society ("SHS"), http://scituatehistoricalsociety.org/.

Scituate Town Archives ("Town Archives"). A great resource, located at Town Hall.

Scituate Town Library. Local history books. Website has digitized local newspapers and town reports, https://www.scituatema.gov/town-library (tab for Research/Local History & Genealogy).

Scituate Town Reports. Published annually by the Town of Scituate, they are on file in the Town Archives and the Scituate Historical Society. They are available online from Scituate

Town Library and Scituate Historical Society websites. They list printers, including The Memorial Press of Plymouth, Boundbrook Press of North Scituate, and Sanderson Brothers of North Abington, MA. Notes in this book omit the place of publishing and printing, and the year (normally the year after the one in the title).

State Library of Massachusetts. Key source for historical maps, including Sanborn maps. The library's Real Estate Atlas Digitization Project put many atlases online.

Third Cliff-Rivermoor Improvement Association ("TCRIA") archives.

US Census data. HeritageQuest Online, distributed by ProQuest, powered by Ancestry.com ("HeritageQuest"), available online from Scituate Town Library.

Valuation Lists. ("*Valuation List*," or "*VL*" in notes). Tax valuation lists were prepared each year by hand in bound ledgers, on file in the Town Archives. In addition, they were printed and published occasionally, with partial information, as part of town reports, including those for 1876, 1886, 1896, 1906 and 1927. These reports are on file in the Town Archives and at the Scituate Historical Society. Some or all are available online from the Scituate Town Library website. The one for 1896 is in the set of 1892–1898 reports, and the one for 1906 is in the set of 1906–1908 reports. Note that taxpayers are listed alphabetically only by first letter of last name, and nonresidents appear in a separate section at the end.

1896: https://archive.org/details/annualreportofto1892scit/page/n311/mode/2up

1906: https://archive.org/details/annualreportofto1906scit/page/n137/mode/2up

NOTES

[1] Deeds and plans are on file in the Plymouth County Registry of Deeds ("PCRD"), and they are online for documents back to 1686 at the registry's website, http://www.plymouthdeeds.org/. A useful document is Middlesex North District Registry of Deeds, "Guide to Registries of Deeds in Massachusetts," at website of Massachusetts Society of Genealogists, Inc., www.msoginc.org/mv/handout201402a.pdf.

[2] Tax valuation lists were *printed* and published only occasionally, as part of town reports, including those for 1876, 1886, 1896, 1906 and 1927. Some or all are online at the Scituate Town Library website. The one for 1896 is in the set of 1892–1898 reports, and the one for 1906 is in the set of 1906–1908 reports. These printed reports list values of taxpayer houses, lots (with acreage), and other property. However, more details are contained in *handwritten* tax valuation lists that assessors prepared every year from early on. After 1859, these lists were on printed and bound ledger sheet books provided by the Commonwealth of Massachusetts. They often listed lot numbers in published surveyor plans. They are on file in the Town Archives at Town Hall. Specific lists are called "*[year] Valuation List*" in this book's text, or "VL" in notes. They are the forerunner of today's Assessor's Database that is online.

[3] *Scituate, Plymouth County, Massachusetts* [map], (New York: Sanborn Map Company, September 1908), sheet 1; *Scituate, Plymouth County, Massachusetts* [map], 1 inch = 100 feet (New York: Sanborn Map Company, December 1918), sheet 8; *Scituate, Plymouth County, Massachusetts* [map], 1 inch = 100 feet (New York: Sanborn Map Company, October 1926), sheet 14; *Scituate, Plymouth County, Massachusetts* [map], 1 inch = 100 feet (New York: Sanborn Map Company, August 1939), sheet 14, all on microfilm at State Library of Massachusetts, Special Collections, film box 709, reel 37 (hereinafter "[year] Sanborn map").

[4] Jeremy Dupertuis Bangs, *The Seventeenth-Century Town Records of Scituate, Massachusetts*, vol. 1 (Boston: New England Historic Genealogical Society, 1997), 3.

[5] Catharina Slautterback, *"Always Delightfully Cool": Summer Vacations in Northern New England, 1825-1900* (Boston: The Boston Athenaeum, 2008); Cindy S. Aron, *Working At Play: A History of Vacations in the United States* (New York: Oxford University Press 1999), 21; Dona Brown, *Inventing New England: Regional Tourism in the Nineteenth Century* (Washington, DC: Smithsonian Institution Press, 1995), 74–76.

[6] Goldberg-Zoino & Associates, Inc., "Investigation of Third Cliff, Scituate, Massachusetts," report, prepared for Board of Selectmen, Scituate, Massachusetts, File No. 1361 (April 1975), 1, Scituate Town Archives.

[7] Author's review of Assessor's Database, online ("Assessor's Database"). This includes previously posted data for past fiscal years, usually updated in December. The sheets in the database are called assessor's field cards.

[8] Samuel Deane, *History of Scituate, Massachusetts, from Its First Settlement to 1831* (Boston: James Loring, 1831), 9-10, https://archive.org/details/historyofscituat00deane.

[9] Robert Fraser, "Scituate Lighthouse Stood Sentinel Duty for 49 Years; Fourteenth Oldest in the U.S.," *South Shore News*, July 6, 1961, 4.

[10] Joseph F. W. Des Barres, "A Chart of Massachusetts Bay [and Cape Cod Bay]" [1776], in Joseph F. W. Des Barres, *The Atlantic Neptune: The 1802 edition of the Atlantic Neptune, published for the use of the Royal Navy of Great Britain*, Harvard Map Collection, Harvard Library, Cambridge, Mass., Part III: New England to Gulf of Mexico (seq. 41), https://curiosity.lib.harvard.edu/scanned-maps/catalog/44-990020501850203941_FHCL:10188008; map (1776) for sale at RareMaps.com, https://www.raremaps.com/gallery/detail/59282/massachusetts-bay-with-boston-and-part-of-cape-cod-des-barres. Thanks to Donald Corey for access to a copy of the map.

[11] Deane, *History of Scituate*, 1.

[12] Howard S. Russell, *Indian New England Before the Mayflower* (Hanover, NH: University Press of New England, 1980), 23 (map entitled "4. Approximate locations of certain Southern New England Indian tribes"), https://books.google.com/books?id=noVQBAAAQBAJ&source=gbs_navlinks_s; Alan Leveillee email to author, November 2, 2016; see *Early Settlements in New England and Distribution of the Indian Tribes, 1686* [map], in W. H. DePuy, *People's Cyclopedia of Universal Knowledge: V.2* (New York: Phillips & Hunt, 1881), 1230, Maps ETC, Educational Technology Clearinghouse, FCIT, University of South Florida,

https://etc.usf.edu/maps/pages/9900/9975/9975.htm; Joseph Foster Merritt, *A Narrative History of South Scituate-Norwell, Massachusetts* (Rockland, MA, 1938), 5-6.

13 Lee Sultzman, "Massachuset History" at "First Nations Histories" website, http://www.dickshovel.com/massa.html; Massachusetts Native American Trails website, formerly http://www.massnativetrails.com/mashpee/, available at https://web.archive.org/web/20170601172855/http://www.massnativetrails.com:80/mashpee. For an excellent detailed description of interactions between Native Americans and the colonists (and later Americans), see Mark Jarzombek, "The "Indianized" Landscape of Massachusetts," *Places Journal*, February 2021, accessed 28 Nov 2021, https://placesjournal.org/article/the-indianized-landscape-of-massachusetts/, and https://doi.org/10.22269/210209.

14 Deane, *History of Scituate*, 9, 28; Will Irwin, "The Story of Scituate" in *Scituate, 1636–1936* (Scituate: Scituate Tercentenary Committee, 1936, reprinted 1973), 6 ("the workmen who built the golf links on the landward slope of Third Cliff [in 1919] unearthed a wealth of domestic implements"). See de Bry engraving after John White watercolor, *Village of Secotan*, c. 1585-1610, showing planting grounds of Algonquins in Roanoke, North Carolina; Library of Congress, https://www.loc.gov/pictures/item/2001695723/.

15 Horsley Witten Group, :Town of Scituate Open Space and Recreation Plan (February 2009)," 6, Town of Scituate website or Google search.

16 Charles T. Torrey, *Home! or the Pilgrims' Faith Revived* (Salem: John P. Jewett and Co., 2d ed., 1845), 15, https://archive.org/details/homeorpilgrimsfa00torr, quoted in L. Vernon Briggs, *History of Shipbuilding on North River, Plymouth County, Massachusetts* (Boston: Coburn Brothers, Printers, 1889), 364–365, https://archive.org/details/historyofshipbui00brigg.

17 William Cronon, *Changes in the Land: Indians, Colonists, and the Ecology of New England* (New York: Hill and Wang, 1983, first revised ed. 2003), xvi, 74-75; see also Glendon J. Buscher, Jr., "The nature and evolution of title," March 4, 2003, Mass.gov website, https://www.mass.gov/info-details/the-nature-and-evolution-of-title.

18 The Massachuset under Chickataubut, their sachem until 1633, "lived as far south as Marshfield" which is south of Scituate. Lorena Laing Hart and Francis Russell Hart, *Not All Is Changed: A Life History of Hingham* (Hingham, MA: Hingham Historical Commission, 1993), 29. Chickataubut claimed lands south to the North River, and his son and successor Josias Wampatuck may have conveyed the Scituate lands as early as 1640 or 1637. Deane, *History of Scituate*, 144–145; Stephen R. Valdespino, *Timothy Hatherly and the Plymouth Colony Pilgrims* (Scituate: Scituate Historical Society, 1987), 61. Settlers obtained a deed for the land of Scituate from Josias Wampatuck in 1653. Bangs, *Seventeenth-Century Town*, vol. 1, 11. See also Jedediah Dwelley and John F. Simmons, *History of the Town of Hanover, Massachusetts, with Family Genealogies* (Hanover, MA: Town of Hanover, 1910), 38–39, 47–48, https://archive.org/details/historyoftownofh00dwel. A wonderful summary of Native American and early colonial times in Plymouth Colony is in Thomas Spear, "The Descendants of Humphrey Turner, John Whitman, George Spear, and Related Families of Southeastern New England" (Madison, WI: by author, 2007), 6–14, on file in Scituate Historical Society ("SHS"), genealogy section, Turner Family file.

19 See Bangs, *Seventeenth-Century Town Records*, vol. 1, 76.

20 Deane, *History of Scituate*, 12, 143; see Bangs, *Seventeenth-Century Town Records*, vol. 1, 78.

21 Jeremy Dupertuis Bangs, *The Seventeenth-Century Town Records of Scituate, Massachusetts*, vol. 3 (Boston: New England Historic Genealogical Society, 2001), 18.

22 Kent Street is the unlabeled road south of item 37 in Jeremy D. Bangs' map "The Conihasset Grant," in Jeremy Dupertuis Bangs, *The Seventeenth-Century Town Records of Scituate, Massachusetts*, vol. 2 (Boston: New England Historic Genealogical Society, 1999), 28.

23 Chief Justice Cushing Chapter, Daughters of the American Revolution (DAR), *Old Scituate* (Boston: DAR, 1921), 248 (1848 report), https://archive.org/details/oldscituate00chapgoog; "Bassing Beach," Cohasset Conservation Trust website, https://cohassetconservationtrust.org/properties/properties-a-g/bassing-beach/; Kristi Funderburk, "Did Dickens inspire Peggotty Beach's name?" *Scituate Mariner* website, posted July 16, 2016, updated July 18, 2016, https://scituate.wickedlocal.com/news/20160716/did-dickens-inspire-peggotty-beachs-name.

24 Bangs, *Seventeenth-Century Town Records*, vol. 1, 15; "The North and South Rivers," in *North and South Rivers Guide* (Norwell, MA: North and South Rivers Watershed Association, Inc., 3d ed, 1997), ["NSRWA," map and guide], containing excerpts from *The Tidal North River, Issues and Recommendations, 1976–1977*, Harvard Graduate School of Design; Bethany Groff Dorau, "A Roll in the Hay," blog and e-newsletter of the Museum of Old Newbury, September 17, 2021.

25 Bangs, *Seventeenth-Century Town Records*, vol. 1, 24–26, and see 222, etc. ("Coleman"); "Moses B. Colman," *Biographical Review, Vol. XVIII: Containing Life Sketches of Leading Citizens of Plymouth County, Massachusetts* (Boston: Biographical Review Publishing Co., 1897), 581, https://archive.org/details/biographicalrevi1897biog

("*Biographical Review*"); William Gould Vinal, *Salt Haying in the North River Valley (1648-1898)* (Cohasset, MA: Vinehall, 1953), 6; Deane, *History of Scituate*, various ("Colman"); Colman Family file, SHS. See also Gregory Dicus, *Window Seat: Reading the Landscape From the Air* (San Francisco: Chronicle Books LLC, 2004), 66-67. No source clearly describes the origin of the name Colman Hills.

[26] Frederic T. Bailey [probable], *Map of Settlement of "Men of Kent" Scituate 1633* (n.p., 1936?), printed in the back of certain printings of the booklet *Scituate, 1636–1936,* and also at end of "Early Families of Scituate," SHS website, http://scituatehistoricalsociety.org/early-scituate-families/; similar but more detailed map, Frederic T. Bailey, *Historical Map of the Town of Scituate, Plymouth County, Massachusetts, Tercentenary Edition* (n.p., 1936, originally compiled in 1929), bound in the back of certain printings of the booklet *Scituate, 1636–1936*, and same, *Revised Tercentenary Edition* (copyright 1930, 1936, 1947, 1950), courtesy of Nancy Howell; "Pilgrim Village Families Sketch: William Gilson," formerly at American Ancestors website of the New England Historic Genealogical Society; Henry Whittemore, *Genealogical Guide to the Early Settlers of America* (New York, 1898), 211, https://archive.org/details/cu31924095655571/page/n49.

[27] Cronon, *Changes in the Land*, 127, 150. After 1825, the center of farming moved to the Midwest. Dicus, *Window Seat*, 37-38. Corn is currently the largest crop in the US. Tom Capehart and Susan Proper, "Corn is America's Largest Crop in 2019," US Department of Agriculture, https://www.usda.gov/media/blog/2019/07/29/corn-americas-largest-crop-2019.

[28] "Men of Kent Cemetery," National Register of Historic Places Registration Form, certified as entered in the National Register June 25, 2013, at 8, 12, available from MACRIS, SCI.800 (click on NR button). The Massachusetts Cultural Resource Information System (MACRIS) is a database of the Massachusetts Historical Commission, online at http://mhc-macris.net/. It contains forms documenting the history and architecture of buildings and other resources. Forms for Scituate are numbered with the prefix SCI. At each MACRIS inventory page summarizing the form, click on the INV link to download the complete form and any continuation sheets. Houses are typically documented on a Form B — Building. Forms and sites may be accessed through MACRIS Maps, http://maps.mhc-macris.net/. Most forms are generated locally. Many forms for Scituate are on file in the Scituate Historical Society and/or the Scituate Historical Commission. Deane's book does not mention the palisade; instead, it mentions the "block house" where there was a fort and a garrison in King Philip's War, a half mile above the Union Street bridge over the North River, now probably in the Norris Reservation in Norwell. Deane, *History of Scituate*, 20, 119, 125, 158.

[29] Nathaniel Philbrick, *Mayflower: A Story of Courage, Community, and War* (New York: Viking Press, 2006).

[30] Deane, *History of Scituate*, 125 (source of quote), and see 5 and 144; see Merritt, *A Narrative History of South Scituate-Norwell*, 5-6.; *North and South Rivers Guide*, sites 50-57 (ponds feed river).

[31] Deane, *History of Scituate*, 125 (quoted): Cynthia Hagar Krusell and Ann Hoffman Granbery, *Map of Early Pilgrim and Indian Trails of Old Plymouth Colony* (Plymouth: Plymouth-Provincetown Celebration Commission, 1971), courtesy of Skip DeBrusk; Cynthia Hagar Krusell, *Map of Early Indian and Pilgrim Trails of Old Plymouth Colony with Town Histories of Plymouth, Barnstable, Bristol and Dukes Counties,* [map], no scale (Plymouth: the author, 1978); "Journey by Land: Footpaths, Cart Roads, Post Roads & Turnpikes," formerly at Pilgrim Hall Museum website, www.pilgrimhallmuseum.org/pdf/Journey_by_Land.pdf; Nancy Braithwaite, "Pastimes: Town's history pre-dates Pilgrims," *Marshfield Mariner* website, http://marshfield.wickedlocal.com/article/20140916/news/140919037.

The Pilgrim Trail may be what was shown as an Indian trail near the coast on the "Winthrop map" from about 1633. The trail led from Plymouth to Dorchester, but the map only shows the portion from the Scituate-Cohasset border northward (using a dotted line). The map is in the Sloane manuscript collection of the British Museum. See map facsimile, courtesy of the private collection of Roy Winkelman, Maps Etc website, https://etc.usf.edu/maps/pages/8500/8527/8527.htm; Edwin Victor Bigelow, *A Narrative History of the Town of Cohasset, Massachusetts* (Cohasset: Committee on Town History, 1898), 100-101, https://www.google.com/books/edition/A_Narrative_History_of_the_Town_of_Cohas/KJsYAAAAYAAJ?hl=en&gbpv=1&bsq=map.

The "Plymouth and Bay Path" followed present Washington Street in Hanover (today's Route 53), according to Dwelley and Simmons, *History of Hanover*, 219–220. The Country Road, analogous to today's Country Way in Scituate, is item 32 in Bangs' map "The Conihasset Grant," in Bangs, *Seventeenth-Century Town Records*, vol. 1, 28. The Pilgrim Trail is shown as a dotted line in the map "Sea View Village" in Cynthia Hagar Krusell and Betty Magoun Bates, *Marshfield: A Town of Villages 1640-1990* (Marshfield Hills: Historical Research Associates, 1990), 144 (map), 150 (discussion). See also Regina Porter, "Marshfield History" formerly on Marshfield Chamber of Commerce website, http://www.southshorechamber.org/pages/MarshfieldHistory. Valdespino, *Timothy Hatherly*, 64, explains the paths differently:

254

Plymouth Colony was linked to the Massachusetts Bay by the routes known as The Country Way and the Massachusetts Path. Both converged at Hingham where they became the Plymouth and Bay Road, which then continued on to Boston. [Between 1654 and 1657, the "Old Boston Turnpike" was built to provide the most direct route from Scituate to Plymouth. including a bridge over the North River. This turnpike connected with The Country Way leading to Boston.

32 Before the storm of 1898, the road from Third Cliff ran all the way to the Fourth Cliff site of White's Ferry. WPA card file, Town Archives, under "Third Cliff, Road from, to Whites Ferry," summarizing document C-11, page 174, March 4, 1889, and same document in Town of Scituate Records (Town Meeting voted to refer to committee the relocating of the road). In 1827, the town allowed owners of meadows between Third and Fourth Cliffs to set up bars (for tolls?) across the cartway near the southern end of Third Cliff. Barbara Murphy, *Scituate: The Coming of Age of a Plymouth Colony Town* (n.p., 1985), 61. The cartway or road ran about three miles — about a mile from the highest spot on Third Cliff to the tip of Fourth Cliff, and about two miles from there to White's Ferry. A map drawn shortly after the storm of 1898 called the remaining parts of the road a "highway." Massachusetts Board of Harbor and Land Commissioners, *Plan of New Mouth of North River, Scituate: Opened by Storm of November 1898*, [map, July 1899], URI http://hdl.handle.net/2452/48567, from *Public Document No. 11, Annual Report of the Board of Harbor and Land Commissioners for the year 1899* (Boston: Wright & Potter, 1900), see 48–49, https://www.digitalcommonwealth.org/search/commonwealth-oai:ww72bf51k, http://archives.lib.state.ma.us/handle/2452/48567, and https://books.google.com/books?id=2nQTAAAAYAAJ&source=gbs_navlinks_s.

33 "Plan of Scituate and North River, in reference to Bridge … from Papers of Act June 19, 1801." [Bridge over North River, Plymouth Co.], surveyor's name not given, 200 rods to an inch, Massachusetts State Archives, No. 1586 "Maps and Plans," SC1/series 50, Third Series Maps, v. 25, p. 21.

34 See Philbrick, *Mayflower* (2007); Robert Macfarlane, *The Old Ways: A Journey on Foot* (New York: Penguin Books, 2013), ch. 5; Lyle Nyberg, *Summer Suffragists: Woman Suffrage Activists in Scituate, Massachusetts* (Scituate: by author, 2020), 155 (1876, Smith family).

35 John Galluzzo, *The North River: Scenic Waterway of the South Shore* (Charleston, SC: The History Press, 2008); "Scituate man to paddle 72-miles in a canoe for fundraiser," *Scituate Mariner*, June 7, 2012 (source of quote), https://scituate.wickedlocal.com/article/20120607/NEWS/306079795; Caleb Estabrooks, "Tackling the Wampanoag Paddle," NSRWA website, July 2, 2019, https://www.nsrwa.org/tackling-the-wampanoag-paddle/; Randall Elgin, "Solo kayaker travels ancient Wampanoag Canoe Passage," [New Bedford] *Standard-Times*, July 5, 2005, A6, updated January 13, 2011, https://www.southcoasttoday.com/article/20050705/news/307059982.

36 See also Robbie Ethridge, "Navigating the Mississippian World: Infrastructure in the Sixteenth-Century Native South," in Gregory A. Waselkov and Marvin T. Smith, eds, *Forging Southeastern Identities: Social Archaeology, Ethnohistory, and Folklore of the Mississippian to Early Historic South* (Tuscaloosa: University of Alabama Press, 2017), ch. 4, 62 at 71 and elsewhere, https://www.google.com/books/edition/Forging_Southeastern_Identities/na0hDgAAQBAJ?hl=en&gbpv=0&kptab=overview.; Theodor de Bry, "Native Americans Making Canoes," engraving, 1590, courtesy of the John Carter Brown Library at Brown University, https://artsandculture.google.com/asset/native-americans-making-canoes-theodor-de-bry/_QEuIx96k9pypQ?hl=en.

37 *Historical Markers Erected by Massachusetts Bay Colony Tercentenary Commission* (1930), https://archive.org/details/historicalmarker00mass; Russell C. Bixby, "Roadside Marker Inventory Massachusetts Bay Colony- Tercentenary Commission Markers (MBC-TC) 1630 - 1930," presentation, November 1, 2011, https://www.historyarchives.org/rbixby/BasicMBC-TC-Presentation-toRecorderNovember12011.pdf; Scituate Historical Commission minutes, various; Ruth Thompson, "Scituate Third Cliff re-dedication ceremony marks history," *Scituate Mariner*, November 15, 2016; Bulrush Studios, "Restoration of Scituate's Tercentenary Marker on Third Cliff, October 29, 2016," video (fascinating), https://www.youtube.com/watch?v=8Nqyn3zx8ug.

38 Bangs, *Seventeenth-Century Town Records*, vol. 1, 11.

39 Deane, *History of Scituate*, 9–10.

40 Samuel Eliot Morison, *The Maritime History of Massachusetts 1783–1860* (Boston: Houghton Mifflin Company, 1921, fourth printing, 1961), 2 (source of quote); Vinal, *Salt Haying in the North River Valley*, 27.

41 Michael Gowell, "Piscataqua Gundalows," 2001, https://www.gundalow.org/gundalows-in-history/.

42 Bailey, *Historical Map*; Bangs, *Seventeenth-Century Town Records*, vol. 1, 12.

43 A. Robbins and S. A. Turner, surveyors, *Map of Scituate, Mass.* [map], 1 inch = 100 rods (Boston: Pendleton's Lithography, 1831), Harvard Map Collection, Digital Maps,

http://vc.lib.harvard.edu/vc/deliver/~maps/MATWN_3764_S322_1831_R6, also on file at Massachusetts State Archives, 1830 series maps, v. 11, p. 2, no. 2095.

[44] Deane, *History of Scituate*, 9–10, 360–363; Bailey, *Historical Map*; Bangs, *Seventeenth-Century Town Records,* vol. 1, 14, 228 (map of original settlement showing Turner's property in town, not his farm). I have not traced ownership of properties back to colonial times in detail.

[45] A property transfer was recorded on February 20, 1634, of "Twenty-six acres of upland on the southwest corner of Third Cliff to Humphrey Turner … the marsh and swamp to the west." Bangs, *Seventeenth-Century Town Records*, vol. 1, 76 (item 67), see also 11–12 ("neither opposed …"), 79, 80, 83, 233–235. A later writer who appears to have been a descendant of Turner wrote that the Native Americans "gave him a large tract of cleared land, part of their own cornfields, as a token of their love and gratitude." Torrey, *Home! or the Pilgrims' Faith Revived*, 15. See discussion earlier in this book on the Josias Wampatuck deed of 1653.

[46] Deane, *History of Scituate*, 9–10.

[47] Bangs, *Seventeenth-Century Town Records*, vol. 1, 18.

[48] Deane, *History of Scituate*, 360, and see 9–10.

[49] Mary L. F. Power, "Turner Family Notes," typewritten genealogical notes, c. 1942 (see page 71), 74, in three-ring white binder labeled "929.2 TURNER Turner," SHS. These notes by Mary Power (1862–1947) were prepared from the 1920s up to about 1942; they were transcribed in more readable form in 1988, identifying the author, by the Friends of the Scituate Archives; these are in a three-ring white binder, entitled "Turner Family Genealogy," labeled "929.2 TURNER Power," SHS. Where possible, citations are given to both binders. The equivalent to page 71 of "Turner Family Notes" is pages 110–111 in "Turner Family Genealogy." The equivalent to page 74 is unknown.

[50] DAR, *Old Scituate*, 28.

[51] Power, "Turner Family Notes," 2, "Turner Family Genealogy," 6.

[52] Galluzzo, *The North River*, 74 (Boston Sand and Gravel Company started removal of vast amounts of Colman Hills in 1914, lasting until large fire in 1963).

[53] Tax valuation lists; Deane, *History of Scituate*, 363; Jacob Turner, *Genealogy of the Descendants of Humphrey Turner with Family Records, in Two Parts* (Boston: David Turner, Jr., 1852) (author describes the work as "complex and multifarious"), copies in Turner Family file, SHS, and online at https://archive.org/details/genealogyofdesce1852thur; volumes on file, SHS, including a three-volume computer listing of Turner descendants.

[54] Power, "Turner Family Genealogy," 9; Deane, *History of Scituate*, 362 (for example, description of part of 80-acre parcel passing from Humphrey Turner's son John to his descendant Elisha, whose daughter Lydia Turner married Samuel Adams Turner).

[55] Power, "Turner Family Notes," 45 (#98 James Turner), 62 (#133 Nathaniel Turner), 64 (#135 James Turner), "Turner Family Genealogy," 70 (#98 James Turner), 101 (#133 Nathaniel Turner), 103 (#135 James Turner); Jarvis M. Freymann, "Turner Family," notes and excellent chart showing this line of descendancy, in Turner Family file, SHS.

[56] Power, "Turner Family Notes," 62 (#133 Nathaniel Turner), "Turner Family Genealogy," 101 (source of quote); Briggs, *Shipbuilding on North River,* 128, https://archive.org/details/historyofshipbui00brigg. A deed from James to his son Nathaniel in 1792 conveyed half an acre of this property "on which the said Nathaniel Turner the Third has lately erected a new Dwelling House." James Turner to Nathaniel Turner 3d, June 23, 1792, PCRD, book 82, page 67. The Assessor's Database once said this was built in 1665, which seems incorrect. See Lyle Nyberg, "Nathaniel Turner Farmhouse," 141 Driftway, SCI.1239, MACRIS.

[57] Power, "Turner Family Notes," unnumbered page, handwritten entry for Sally James Turner born 1792 under #98 James Turner in generation V; *Biographical Review*, 383 (entry for "Augustus Cole"). The *Biographical Review* says Sallie J. (Turner) Cole (not "Sally") was a daughter of Nathaniel Turner (not James Turner), but I follow Power's notes.

[58] Nathaniel Turner Jr. to James Turner and Samuel Humphrey Turner, deed, April 3, 1804, PCRD, book 227, page 43.

[59] 1831 Map.

[60] Turner, *Genealogy of Humphrey Turner*, App. A, 50; Freymann, "Turner Family."

[61] Power, "Turner Family Notes," 72 (#149.ii. Samuel Humphrey Turner), "Turner Family Genealogy," 112; *Proceedings of the Most Worshipful Grand Lodge of Ancient Free and Accepted Masons of the Commonwealth of Massachusetts* (Boston: Press of Rockwell & Churchill, 1876), Quarterly Communication, June 14, 1876, 28, https://books.google.com/books?id=pz4wAQAAMAAJ&source=gbs_navlinks_s.

[62] *Directory of Cohasset, Scituate, Marshfield, Duxbury and Norwell* (Quincy, MA: J. H. Hogan Co., 1894), 152, on file, SHS, and online, https://archive.org/details/directoryhistory00quin.

[63] Harold Howard, compiler, *Towns of Scituate and Marshfield Massachusetts Directory 1918: Containing an Alphabetical List of the Inhabitants, a Summer Resident Directory, Street Directory and Classified Business Directory; a List of Town Officials and Churches, Diagrams of Boston Theatres and Census of Massachusetts* (Boston: Harold Howard, 1918), 60, on file, SHS ("1918 Directory"); "What Is A Market Garden? Definition And Meaning," Market Business News website, http://marketbusinessnews.com/financial-glossary/market-garden/; "market garden," Dictionary.com website (term first recorded in1805-1815), http://www.dictionary.com/browse/market--gardening; "market gardener," Google Books Ngram Viewer (use of term peaked about 1911); John Simpson, "What has the OED become?" Nordiska Studier i Leksikografi 11, 2012, 59–60 (term originated in 1811), https://tidsskrift.dk/nsil/article/download/19131/16764.

[64] Benjamin T. Turner, Samuel H. Turner, and Mary E. Poole to William W. Waterman, May 16, 1895, PCRD, book 697, page 29 (multiple parcels, including "land with the buildings thereon" and "Old Abbey"); William W. Waterman to Boston Sand and Gravel Company, August 31, 1927, PCRD, book 1537, page 409 (8 acres plus Old Abbey Field [2 acres]); J. H. Hogan *1894 Directory*, 152; Nyberg, "Nathaniel Turner Farmhouse" (141 Driftway); *1895 VL*, 78; *1926 VL*, 101 (two houses).

[65] Donald L. Jacobus, *Descendants of Robert Waterman of Marshfield, Massachusetts*, vol. 1 (New Haven, CT: Edgar F. Waterman, 1942, reprinted by Higginson Book Company, Salem, MA), 604–605 (source of quote); Turner family file, SHS. Charles H. Waterman started a steamboat service in 1915. See unidentified newspaper clipping, "Charles H. Waterman Dies at his Scituate Residence," obituary, presumably 1939, in Waterman Family file, SHS.

[66] Lyle Nyberg, "Old Abbey Field and Pasture," 0 New Kent Street, Form H — Parks and Landscapes, SCI.957, MACRIS; Waterman-Vines family archives, SHS.

[67] C. O. Boutelle, et al., *Coast charts no. 9 & 10, Massachusetts Bay with the coast from Cape Ann to Cape Cod* (Washington, DC: United States Coast Survey, 1872, 1877, corrected 1885), map, scale 1:80,000, Lionel Pincus and Princess Firyal Map Division, The New York Public Library, New York Public Library Digital Collections, http://digitalcollections.nypl.org/items/568cb7d0-527c-0134-bc1b-00505686a51c; *Town of Scituate* [map], scale 1 inch = 1700 feet, in J. E. Judson, *Topographical Atlas of Surveys: Plymouth County together with the town of Cohasset, Norfolk County, Massachusetts* (Springfield, MA: L. J. Richards & Co., 1903), plate 31, including insets for Village of Scituate, North Scituate Beach, etc. ("1903 map"), State Library of Massachusetts, Massachusetts Real Estate Atlas Digitization Project, URI http://hdl.handle.net/2452/206055, http://www.mass.gov/anf/research-and-tech/oversight-agencies/lib/massachusetts-real-estate-atlases.html, and https://www.flickr.com/photos/mastatelibrary/9466953246/in/album-72157634981171273/ (also available from the Plymouth County Registry of Deeds website); Harrison L. House, Surveyor, *Plan of Land in Scituate, Mass., Surveyed for Scituate Country Club* (Oct. 1919), 1 inch = 100 feet, PCRD, plan book 3, serial no. 3080, page 50; Nyberg, "Old Abbey Field and Pasture," 0 New Kent Street, MACRIS; author's experience and discussion later in text on Rivermoor.

[68] Marking, probably with input from Richard Vines, on back of copy of photo, SHS.

[69] "Daniel A. Vines," 1920 US Census [database on-line], Scituate, Plymouth, MA, roll T625_627, sheet 10A, Enumeration District 143; *1918 Directory*, 59 (Vines, misspelled as Vine), 60 (Waterman); Harold Howard, compiler, *Towns of Scituate and Marshfield Massachusetts Directory 1926: Containing Alphabetical List of Inhabitants and a Street Directory Classified Business Directory; a list of Town Officials; Churches, Schools, Teachers, Societies, Associations, Clubs, Institutions and Summer Resident Directory* (Boston: Harold Howard, 1926), 77 (Vines), SHS ("*1926 Directory*").

[70] *Annual Report of the Officers of the Town of Scituate for the Year Ending December 31, 1927*, "Report of Town Clerk-Marriages," 131.

[71] William W. Waterman to Boston Sand and Gravel Company, August 31, 1927, PCRD, book 1537, page 409 (8 acres plus Old Abbey Field [2 acres]); *1928 VL*, Nonresidents, 13 (for Boston Sand and Gravel Company); Margaret Cole Bonney, "Under the Hills," SHS Newsletter, vol. 3, issue 7, February 1999, 2-3, https://scituatehistoricalsociety.squarespace.com/s/1999-Newsletters.pdf.

[72] "Daniel A. Vines," 1930 US Census [database on-line], Scituate, Plymouth, MA, roll T626, sheet 10A, Enumeration District 12-99, HeritageQuest; "Lottie S. Waterman," 1930 US Census [database on-line], Scituate, Plymouth, MA, roll T626, sheet 13B, Enumeration District 12-99, HeritageQuest.

[73] "Report of Selectmen, 1933," *Annual Report of the Officers and Committees of the Town of Scituate for the Year Ending December 31, 1933*, 10.

[74] Boston Sand and Gravel Company to Daniel A. & Susie G. Vines, December 30, 1944, PCRD, book 1878, page 371 (8 acres, with reference to plan book 6, page 825); Daniel A. & Susie G. Vines to Raymond C. & Marian F. Hafey, July 13, 1950, PCRD, book 2105, page 117 (8 acres); Raymond C. & Marian F. Hafey to

Eunice E. Burnham, January 8, 1952, PCRD, book 2187, page 314 (8 acres); Eunice Burnham to Richard W. & Audrie P. Burton, June 9, 1954, PCRD, book 2348, page 300 (8 acres).

[75] Nyberg, "Nathaniel Turner Farmhouse," 141 Driftway, SCI.1239, MACRIS, with continuation sheets.

[76] Jacobus, *Descendants of Robert Waterman*, 604-605; Waterman Family file, including "Waterman" two-page genealogy listing, SHS; SHS Newsletter, vol. 3, issue 9, April 1999, 6, https://scituatehistoricalsociety.squarespace.com/s/1999-Newsletters.pdf; "William 'Bill' Vines," obituary, November 27, 2003, *The Hartford Courant* as published in Legacy.com, http://www.legacy.com/obituaries/hartfordcourant/obituary.aspx?pid=1637565; "Elizabeth Vines," obituary, September 12, 2006, *Quincy (MA) Patriot Ledger* as published in Legacy.com, http://www.legacy.com/obituaries/southofboston-ledger/obituary.aspx?n=elizabeth-vines&pid=19200682; Sisters of Divine Providence, Kingston, MA, website, https://cdpsisters.org/locations/kingston; "Richard W. Vines," obituary, April 20, 2017, *Boston Globe* as published in Legacy.com, http://www.legacy.com/obituaries/bostonglobe/obituary.aspx?page=lifestory&pid=185138486; SHS Bulletin, June 1960 (Fred T. Waterman's death), https://static1.squarespace.com/static/51214249e4b0dce195c484bb/t/5862b3b315d5dbc399371fd2/1482863544169/1960+Newsletters.pdf. A family gravestone is in Union Cemetery, per author's visit 10/2/2017: William Wade Waterman, his wife Lottie Scott Torrey, Frederick T. Waterman, and Grace W. Vines.

[77] Power, "Turner Family Notes," 63-64 (#135 James Turner), "Turner Family Genealogy," 103; Deane, *History of Scituate*, 363.

[78] Deane, *History of Scituate*, 360.

[79] Power, "Turner Family Notes," 63–64 (#135 James Turner), "Turner Family Genealogy," 103; Ruth Turner to Michael Welch, deed, January 26, 1836, PCRD, book 188, page 20 (including about 40 acres of land with dwelling house and barn).

[80] "To Explore Oldest Farming Acres In Scituate," *South Shore Mirror*, June 22, 1972, Farming file, SHS (source of quote).

[81] *1918 Directory*, 60; "Coleman Hills, Scituate, Mass.," postcard, c. 1907-1915, postmarked 1921, SHS, Twomey/Jacobson collection; unknown photographer, Welch Farm photo, early 1900s, SHS; later discussion in text about William Waterman's sale of land to the Scituate Country Club in 1919.

[82] Deane, *History of Scituate*, 4 (guzzle at North River); DAR, *Old Scituate*, 241-242 (guzzle created at Musquashcut Pond by storm of 1851); Town of Scituate Conservation Commission meeting minutes, October 26, 2016, 2, https://www.scituatema.gov/sites/scituatema/files/minutes/october_26_2016_0.pdf, and January 4, 2017, 2, https://www.scituatema.gov/sites/scituatema/files/minutes/january_4_2017.pdf (guzzle near 23 Sunset Drive).

[83] Deane, *History of Scituate*, 23.

[84] Stilgoe, *Alongshore*, 90; DAR, *Old Scituate*, 118, 120.

[85] DAR, *Old Scituate*, 239.

[86] John R. Stilgoe, *Alongshore* (New Haven: Yale University Press, 1994), chapter 3 ("Guzzle"), 88 (source of quotes) and 87–90.

[87] "Tide Power in Colonial Boston," The West End Museum website, https://thewestendmuseum.org/tide-power-in-colonial-boston/.

[88] Chas. Turner, *A Plan of the Town of Scituate, in the County of Plymouth, taken in Conformity to Resolve of the General Court, which passed June the 26th 1794*, map, 200 rods to an inch, 1795, Massachusetts State Archives, No. 1242 "Maps and Plans," copy on file, SHS; record of Scituate Town Meeting, November 1, 1802, vol. C-8B, 59 ½, Town Archives.

[89] An Act to Authorize Jesse Dunbar and Others, Owners of the Mill at Scituate Harbour, in the County of Plymouth, to Erect Dams Across Mill Creek, and Maine Creek, So Called, At Said Harbour, 1802 Mass. Acts 113 (approved March 7, 1803), and An Act in Addition to, and for Repealing the Second Section of an Act Entitled "An Act to Authorize Jesse Dunbar and Others, Owners of the Mill at Scituate Harbour, in the County of Plymouth, to Erect Dams Across Mill Creek, and Maine Creek, So Called, At Said Harbour," 1803 Mass. Acts 70 (approved January 30, 1804), https://books.google.com/books?id=hVVNAQAAMAAJ&source=gbs_navlinks_s.; Deane, *History of Scituate*, 18; unknown author, untitled, hand-drawn map of "new dam proposed" site, undated but probably 1801, later labeled "Jessee Dunbar, Esq. [Harbor] 700.2 Map 3" with hand-drawn affixed sheet showing present streets aligned with elements of the map, marked "E B. Bonney 1951," map file cabinet, SHS; DAR, *Old Scituate*, 118, 120; Barbara Murphy, *Irish Mossers and Scituate Harbour Village* (n.p., 1980), 55-56. Thanks to Robert Jackman for furnishing copies of the 1801 and 1795 maps in emails of March 11 and March 15, 2018. The 1795 map is discussed in more detail in John R. Stilgoe, *Landscape and Images* (Charlottesville, VA: University of Virginia

Press, 2005), 60-61, at end of chapter "Jack-o'-lanterns to Surveyors: The Secularization of Landscape Boundaries," https://books.google.com/books?id=OFFQBgAAQBAJ&source=gbs_navlinks_s. A "Road to Mill" is shown running east from Front Street on "Plan of Scituate Harbor and Village," in Briggs, *Shipbuilding on North River* (1889), 368–369, 421 (map key). The location is now covered by the large parking lot at Cole Parkway.

[90] DAR, *Old Scituate*, 118, 120, 220 (Tilden-Prouty tide mill); 1831 map; *Town of Scituate Mass.*, in *Atlas of Plymouth County, Massachusetts* [map], 1 inch = 135 rods (Boston: Geo. H. Walker & Co., 1879), hereinafter "1879 Map," page 33 (and see 36, Village of Scituate Harbor, detail), State Library of Massachusetts, Massachusetts Real Estate Atlas Digitization Project, URI http://hdl.handle.net/2452/205573, http://www.mass.gov/anf/research-and-tech/oversight-agencies/lib/massachusetts-real-estate-atlases.html (for detailed view), and https://www.flickr.com/photos/mastatelibrary/8881938110/in/album-72157633790765207/) (also available from the Plymouth County Registry of Deeds website); Murphy, *Irish Mossers*, 55-56 (mill and mill dam).

[91] 1879 map; Murphy, *The Coming of Age*, 78 (bridge authorized 1866); author's observations.

[92] George W. Brown and Annie E. Brown to Charles V. Stenbeck, deed, July 17, 1903, PCRD book 866, page 23. The deed also conveyed property adjacent to the mill wharf.

[93] Postcards on file in SHS, A-N and O-W boxes, including "The River and Town, SCITUATE, Mass." (also online at https://commons.wikimedia.org/wiki/Category:Scituate,_Massachusetts), "Old Mill Dam at Scituate, Mass." (Chas. N. Frye, Pub.) (similar to "Old Stone Wharf" postcard, and "Waterfront from Bridge, Scituate, Mass." (postmarked 1915); double-wide postcard in Russell Fish files, SHS, published by W. P. Gannett, North Scituate, Mass., with handwritten note "Back of Welches from marsh in back."

[94] US *House Journal*, 20th Cong., 1st sess., May 5, 1828, 680 (petition of Scituate, Marshfield, Pembroke, and Hanover), https://memory.loc.gov/ammem/amlaw/lwss.html; US *House Journal*, 20th Cong., 2d sess., December 8, 1828, 31 (petition referred to Committee of Commerce), https://memory.loc.gov/ammem/amlaw/lwss.html; US *House Journal*, 22d Cong., 1st sess., December 21, 1831, 79 (petition referred to Committee on Internal Improvement), https://memory.loc.gov/ammem/amlaw/lwss.html.

[95] H.R. Doc. 142, 20th Cong., 2d Sess. (March 3, 1829), 22, https://babel.hathitrust.org/cgi/pt?id=uc1.b3983170;view=1up;seq=356.

[96] Deane, *History of Scituate*, 23.

[97] See United States Congressional serial set 192, US *House Journal*, 21st Cong., 1st sess., 79, and same at serial set 195, H.R. Doc. 2, 21st Cong., 1st Sess. (report of Secretary of War, November 30, 1829), 77, https://babel.hathitrust.org/cgi/pt?id=uc1.b3983174;view=1up;seq=14. That document contains the report of the Army's Chief Engineer, which says at 77 (emphasis added):

> Of the surveys enumerated under this head as in progress at the time of my last Annual Report, *all have been completed, and were reported to Congress last year*, except the survey of the Wabash river, and the examination of sites for an armory on the Western waters, on which a report will be made this Winter.

Report of the Chief Engineer to Hon. John H. Eaton, Secretary of War, November 18, 1829, starting at 68. At 79 is "Part III. Surveys Under Special Acts and Resolutions of Congress," which includes Item 3 at 78, saying "Survey of North river, between Scituate and Marshfield, Massachusetts, to ascertain the expediency of removing obstructions at the mouth of the same, and to make an estimate of cost." Table A at 88–89 says $171.25 was spent of the $180 in funds appropriated for 1829 for "Survey of North river, below Scituate and Marshfield, to ascertain the expediency of removing obstructions to the mouth of the same, Massachusetts."

[98] United States Congressional serial set 206, Brevet Lt. Col. John Anderson to Brig. Gen. C. Gratiot, "Report on the Survey of North River, Massachusetts," February 1830, H.R. Doc. 16, 21st Cong., 2d Sess. (December 23, 1830), https://babel.hathitrust.org/cgi/pt?id=uc1.b3983188;view=1up;seq=791.

[99] Anderson, "Report on the Survey," 2; Des Barres, *A Chart of Massachusetts Bay* (shifting sands).

[100] Anderson, "Report on the Survey."

[101] US *House Journal*, 32d Cong., 1st sess., February 24, 1852, 381 (citizens and ten senators of Massachusetts), https://memory.loc.gov/ammem/amlaw/lwss.html; US *House Journal*, 32d Cong., 1st sess., March 5, 1852, 432, https://memory.loc.gov/ammem/amlaw/lwss.html; US *House Journal*, 32d Cong., 1st sess., April 8, 1852, 569, https://memory.loc.gov/ammem/amlaw/lwss.html; US *House Journal*, 33d Cong., 1st sess., January 16, 1854, 222–223 (resolution directing Secretary of War to communicate to the House the report of the survey ordered by the last Congress), https://memory.loc.gov/ammem/amlaw/lwss.html.

[102] Act of August 30, 1852, "An Act making Appropriations for the Improvement of certain Harbors and Rivers," 32d Cong., 1st sess., ch. 104, 56, at 57, 10 Stat. 56, http://www.loc.gov/law/help/statutes-at-large/32nd-congress/session-1/c32s1ch104.pdf.

[103] Letter from Secretary of War Jefferson Davis, January 20, 1854, "A report of a survey of Scituate harbor and North river," H.R. Doc. 31, 33d Cong., 1st Sess. (hereinafter *1854 Report of Survey of Scituate Harbor and North River*), https://archive.org/details/unitedstatescon338offigoog (starting at page 583 of 624), and https://books.google.com/books?id=DXZHAQAAIAAJ&source=gbs_navlinks_s. The 1854 report is cited in Jane K. Thompson, *First Cliff, Scituate, 1630-2013: History of a New England Coastal Neighborhood* (Baltimore, MD: Otter Bay Books, 2013), 4, note 15.

[104] *1854 Report of Survey of Scituate Harbor and North River*; "Little, Edward Preble," in Biographical Directory of the United States Congress online, http://bioguide.congress.gov/scripts/biodisplay.pl?index=L000350;

[105] "Military Appointments and Confirmations," *New York Times*, August 7, 1861 (listing Henry P. Andrews), https://www.nytimes.com/1861/08/07/archives/military-appointments-and-confirmations.html; Henry Porter Andrews, *The Descendants of John Porter of Windsor, Conn. 1635-9*, vol. 2 (Saratoga Springs: G. W. Ball, printer, 1893), 752, https://books.google.com/books?id=UptIAAAAMAAJ&source=gbs_navlinks_s; J. G. Barnard, *Memoir of Joseph Gilbert Totten, 1788-1864* (1866), including 84-87 (Minot's Light), http://www.nasonline.org/publications/biographical-memoirs/memoir-pdfs/totten-j-g-1.pdf; "Brigadier General Joseph Gilbert Totten," Commanders of the Corps of Engineers website of Army Corps of Engineers, http://www.usace.army.mil/About/History/Commanders/; "John G. Barnard," in George W. Cullum, *George W. Cullum's Register of Officers and Graduates of the United States Military Academy*, vol. 1 (third ed., 1891), 530, http://penelope.uchicago.edu/Thayer/E/Gazetteer/Places/America/United_States/Army/USMA/Cullums_Register/708*.html; "John Barnard," [incorporator of National Academy of Sciences], National Academy of Sciences website, http://www.nasonline.org/member-directory/deceased-members/20000655.html; *Catalogue of Military, Naval, and Scientific Books published by D. Van Nostrand* (New York: D. Van Nostrand, 1869), 10 (listing background of Gen. Barnard), https://books.google.com/books?id=wdkOAAAAYAAJ&source=gbs_navlinks_s. As to Gen. J. G. Barnard's role in the Scituate survey, see *The United States Army and Navy Journal and Gazette of the Regular and Volunteer Forces*, vol. 16 (New York: Army and Navy Journal, Inc., May 24, 1879), 748, http://books.google.com/books?id=Pvk-AQAAMAAJ&printsec=frontcover#v=onepage&q&f=false. His photo by Matthew Brady was formerly at Old Pictures website, http://www.old-picture.com/mathew-brady-studio/General-Barnard-G-J.htm, available at https://web.archive.org/web/20131128233111/http://www.old-picture.com/mathew-brady-studio/General-Barnard-G-J.htm.

[106] DAR, *Old Scituate*, 242, 218; "Storm's Ravages at Scituate," *Boston Globe*, November 29, 1898, 7.

[107] Stilgoe, *Alongshore*, 90.

[108] FEMA Mapping MapsOnline, website for Town of Scituate, https://www.mapsonline.net/scituatema/fema.html.

[109] Angeline M. Cole to Alfredo Gomes and Alice T. Gomes, deed, August 31, 1945, PCRD, book 1890, page 422 (four acres of "land in said Scituate, called Pitcock Field and Pitcock Swamp"); Christine Fontes and Eva A. Fontes to Alfredo Gomes and Alice T. Gomes, deed, November 23, 1945, PCRD, book 1894, page 391 (nine acres, evidently southwest of the four-acre parcel).

[110] Henry J. Cole to Angeline M. Cole, deed, January 18, 1916, PCRD, book 1240, page 1 ("undivided half interest in the field land called 'Pitcock,' formerly called 'Pitcock Pasture' situate on Westerly side of Kent St."); 1906 VL printed after page 128 in *Annual Report of the Town Officers of the Town of Scituate for the Year Ending December 31, 1906*, 24; William Marsh, *The Pidcock Family History* (n.p., 2d ed., c. 1988-1992), 2d-3d pages, http://pidcockfamily.org/wp-content/uploads/2014/08/pidcockhistory-2nd-edition.pdf; Ebenezer W. Peirce, *Peirce's Colonial Lists: Civil, Military and Professional Lists of Plymouth and Rhode Island Colonies, Comprising Colonial, County and Town Officers, Clergymen, Physicians and Lawyers. With Extracts from Colonial Laws Defining Their Duties. 1621–1700* (Boston: A. Williams & Company, 1880), 58 (George Pitcock listed as a surveyor of highways in Scituate in 1657), https://books.google.com/books?id=C4hBAAAAYAAJ&source=gbs_navlinks_s; Bangs, *Seventeenth-Century Town Records*, vol. 1, 70-73, and many other references to George Pitcock in volumes 1 and 3.

[111] Conversation with Kim Dias, granddaughter of Alfredo and Alice Gomes, August 31, 2017; Town of Scituate, 1968 aerial photograph [interpositive] CGL-124, 1" = 100', Town Archives, copied by author April 12, 2017.

[112] "Archdiocese plans housing project," *The Anchor* (Fall River, MA), August 7, 1980, vol. 34, no. 22, 10, https://issuu.com/the_anchor/docs/08.07.80; Alfredo Gomes to Planning Office for Urban Affairs, Inc., deed, August 11, 1980, PCRD, book 4865, page 56; Assessor's Database. Although North River Road goes through it, the assessor's database lists this as 152 Kent Street, having 11 acres (Parcel 60-3-4).

[113] Conversation with Brittany Lawrence, August 22, 2017; conversation with Kim Dias, August 31, 2017; "Alfred Gomes — Garden, August 30, 1987," Gomes family VHS videotape, courtesy of Gomes family.

[114] Harrison L. House, "Houselots, on Rufus Clapp Farm of Scituate Harbor Mass. Dated June 20th 1903," plan, scale 1 inch=50 feet, PCRD, plan book 2, page 194; Jane Atherton, "Scituate's Famous Bulrush Farm Closes Barn Doors," *South Shore News*, 7, April 9, 1959, Farming file, SHS; Bonney, *My Scituate*, 9 (Bonney also wrote a book about growing up at Brushy Hill, *Brushy Hill Scituate*, published in 1989); "Scituate of Yesteryear," photo with caption (source of quote).

[115] Nancy Mehegan, "Family farmer, 77, tills the past," *Patriot Ledger*, clipping (Prouty) in Farming file, SHS.

[116] DAR, *Old Scituate*, 224; Cap'n Bill, "Old Scituate Heritage," *South Shore Mirror*, January 19, 1961, 17.

[117] *South Shore News*, July 20, 1961, Farming file, SHS; "To Explore Oldest Farming Acres In Scituate," *South Shore Mirror*, June 22, 1972, Farming file, SHS; *Scituate Mirror*, ad, August 15, 1974, 8; Scituate Planning Board meeting minutes, January 9, 2014, 7, www.scituatema.gov/sites/scituatema/files/minutes/minutes-file/2-13-14_meeting_minutes.pdf; realtor ads for Ava's Lane and Lauren Lane; "Tilden, Nathaniel J." post on Genealogy Data website, posted 2000 and prior, http://hoocher.com/Brian-s_Pages/dat153.html.; "Tilden, Thomas House," 147 Tilden Road, SCI.130, MACRIS (the house's number is now 143 Tilden Road); "Appleton Farms," Trustees of Reservations website, http://www.thetrustees.org/places-to-visit/northeast/appleton-farms.html ("Appleton Farms is one of the oldest continuously operating farms in the country, established and maintained by nine generations of the Appleton family); Joseph E. Garland, *The North Shore: A Social History of Summers Among the Noteworthy, Fashionable, Rich, Eccentric and Ordinary on Boston's Gold Coast, 1823–1929* (Beverly, MA: Commonwealth Editions, 2003), 201 (Appleton Farms founded in 1638). See also Nathaniel Tilden, "Farming Scituate Marsh Lands," *Scituate Mirror*, 12, May 8, 1975, Farming file, SHS; Todd Heth, "The Last Farmer: Scituate man, 75, not ready to quit yet [after farming 25 acres on Country Way since 1946]," *Quincy (MA) Patriot Ledger*, August 3, 1993, Farming file, SHS; Michael Grey, "Scituate, Mass. Tilden Farm History," posted December 6, 2005, https://www.genealogy.com/forum/surnames/topics/tilden/258/.

[118] Conversation with Ron and Cindy Simon, April 20, 2019; website of Simons Greenhouse and Farmstand (R & C Farms), http://www.randcfarms-simons.com/; conversation with Stephen Litchfield, May 10, 2019. See "Citizens Discuss Water Plans," *Scituate Herald*, September 16, 1932, 1 (water supply from wells at Webster farm at Greenbush); George H. Pollard to Stephen C. and Laura M. Webster, deed, June 2, 1924, PCRD, book 1463, page 267 (21 acres on north side of Main Street, over to Cross Street, plus 10 acres of marsh, with right of first refusal to purchase adjoining 60 acres formerly owned by Samuel Hatch and known as the Thompson land); Edward F. Hatch to Stephen C. and Laura M. Webster, deed, September 22, 1928, PCRD, book 1573, page 7 (one acre of land "called the Hammett Field").

[119] "Hyland Hill Farm," SEMAP website [Antonio Andrade], https://guide.farmfreshri.org/food/farm.php?farm=3350, and sign at farm stand. See Deane, *History of Scituate*, 129, 291, 401 (Jonathan Jackson, whose descendant Jonathan Jackson married Mehitabel Hyland in 1757).

[120] Author visit to Mann Farmhouse and Museum, with tour by Bill Krusell, May 20, 2018.

[121] Author visit to Mann Farmhouse and Museum, with tour by Bill Krusell, May 20, 2018; image from Planet Jr. catalog (Philadelphia: S. L. Allen & Co., Washington, DC: G. Edward Shultz, 1915), 6, https://archive.org/details/planetjrshultzss1915schu/page/n1/mode/2up.

[122] Lucy Otis to Caleb W. Prouty, deed, June 17, 1841, PCRD, book 206, page 12 ("about one third of an acre of land owned in common with my sister Lydia James, known or called the abbey place"), recorded December 28, 1842; Elisha and Lydia James to Caleb W. Prouty, deed, March 15, 1843, PCRD, book 227, page 123 ("the Abbey Place"), recorded December 7, 1847; Eliza D. Torrey to Samuel H. Turner, deed, July 21, 1883, PCRD, book 493, page 215 ("Old Abbey pasture" comprising seven acres); Daniel B. Hallett to James H. Bouve, deed, September 22, 1870, PCRD, book 367, page 103 ("Old Abby Meadow"). The *1895 VL*, 78 (for owner William W. Waterman), includes "Old Abbey [Field]," 2 acres, and "Abbey Pasture," 8 acres. For current acreage of the pasture, see discussion in text below.

[123] 1831 Map; Bailey, *Historical Map*.

[124] *Boston Daily Advertiser*, December 12, 1874, quoted in Margaret Cole Bonney, *Scituate's Sands of Time* (n.p., 1988), 9; Charles C. Lincoln for John Bamber, Town Engineer, "Abbey=The Old," in "Topology of Landmarks (Scituate), Book 1, A-E," (1950–1951), three-ring binder, 974.482 Lincoln, SHS (source of quote). See detail of unidentified plan, probably by Plymouth County surveyor, reflecting 1961 planned widening of Driftway with New Street (later New Kent Street), identifying lilacs, privet hedge, two cedars, one cherry tree, and two apple trees at 141 Driftway, a copy of which is included in the historical building documentation form. Nyberg, "Nathaniel Turner Farmhouse," 141 Driftway, SCI.1239, MACRIS.

[125] Caleb W. Prouty seems to have aggregated the property from 1841 until selling it as a seven-acre parcel in 1860. Lucy Otis to Caleb W. Prouty, deed, June 17, 1841, PCRD, book 206, page 12, Elisha and Lydia James to Caleb W. Prouty, deed, March 15, 1843, PCRD, book 227, page 123; Caleb William Prouty to Ziba C. Small, et

al, deed, January 1, 1860, PCRD, book 299, page 77. The latter describes the property as being on Kent Street bounded on the north by land of Caleb Prouty, on the west by said Kent Street, on the south by Water Street [the Driftway] and on the east by land of Samuel H. Turner and Augustus Cole. The description is curious; if it said east by Kent Street, it would clearly describe the Old Abbey parcel. Perhaps the description is wrong, or Kent Street was relocated (unlikely), or this was not an Old Abbey parcel.

[126] Lucy Otis to Caleb W. Prouty, deed, June 17, 1841, PCRD, book 206, page 12; C. O. Boutelle, et al., *Coast charts no. 9 & 10, Massachusetts Bay with the coast from Cape Ann to Cape Cod* (Washington, DC: United States Coast Survey, 1872, 1877, corrected 1885), map, scale 1:80,000, Lionel Pincus and Princess Firyal Map Division, The New York Public Library, New York Public Library Digital Collections, https://digitalcollections.nypl.org/items/7ceb35f0-745d-0134-acfa-00505686a51c.

[127] John H. Young to Samuel H. Turner, deed, December 3, 1859, PCRD, book 690, page 468, not recorded until May 3, 1895 (opaque description of property containing about eight acres "including at the easterly part about two acres more or less of field land divided from the rest of the granted premises by a fence" [Abbey Field?]); Eliza D. Torrey to Samuel H. Turner, deed, July 21, 1883, PCRD, book 493, page 215 ("Old Abbey pasture" comprising seven acres). The *1861 VL* has no mention of "Abbey" for Samuel H. Turner. The *1866 VL* includes the Old Abbey [field] for Samuel H. Turner. The *1880 VL*, 63 (for Samuel H. Turner), includes Old Abbey field, 2 acres, but no Abbey pasture, suggesting that the pasture was later obtained by the 1883 deed from Eliza Torrey. The *1890 VL*, 69 (for Samuel H. Turner), includes "Old Abby" [Field], two acres, and "Abby Pasture," eight acres.

[128] Benjamin T. Turner to William W. Waterman, deed, May 16, 1895, PCRD, book 697, page 29 (10 parcels).

[129] William W. Waterman to Burleigh N. Crockett, deed, September 3, 1900, PCRD, book 808, page 113 (evidently including Old Abbey pasture); Burleigh N. Crockett to Consumers Sand Company, deed, January 12, 1901, PCRD, book 827, page 389.

[130] Internet search for "consumers sand company;" Kenneth J. Schoon, "Sand Mining in and around Indiana Dunes National Lakeshore," June 2015, formerly available at National Park Service website, https://www.nps.gov/rlc/greatlakes/sand-mining-in-indiana-dunes.htm; Matthew Hall, "6 things you need to know about sand mining," Mining Technology website, posted May 7, 2020, https://www.mining-technology.com/features/six-things-sand-mining/.

[131] Consumers Sand Company to Boston Sand and Gravel Company, deed, February 12, 1914, PCRD, book 1169, page 369; Cronon, *Changes in the Land*, 156.

[132] Boston Sand and Gravel website, http://www.bostonsand.com/; Margaret Cole Bonney, "Under the Hills," SHS Newsletter, vol. 3, issue 7, February 1999, 2–3 (source of quote), https://scituatehistoricalsociety.squarespace.com/s/1999-Newsletters.pdf. Views of the company's operations are on a number of postcards, including "Boston Sand & Gravel, Scituate, Mass.," https://www.mindat.org/loc-204249.html, and http://www.widowswalkgolf.com/-course-environment. A later president of the company in the 1950s and 1960s lived in Scituate, according to "Dean M. Boylan," obituary, published in the *Boston Globe* from July 25 to July 26, 2012, http://www.legacy.com/obituaries/bostonglobe/obituary.aspx?pid=158734043. An interesting profile of the company is in an article by Mike Ross, "Boston Sand and Gravel and the northbound train," January 3, 2016, *Boston Globe*, https://www.bostonglobe.com/ideas/2016/01/03/boston-sand-and-gravel-and-northbound-train/9oCgrxOSKNMuMnwIZMAveM/story.html.

[133] "Coleman Hills, Scituate, Mass.," postcard, c. 1907–1915, postmarked 1921, SHS, Twomey/Jacobson collection; Jonathan Morin Olly, "Imagining the Old Coast: History, Heritage, and Tourism in New England, 1865–2012" (PhD diss., Brown University, May 2013), 80 n. 114, Brown University Digital Repository, https://repository.library.brown.edu/studio/item/bdr:320535/.

[134] Harrison L. House, Surveyor, *Plan of Land in Scituate, Mass., Surveyed for Scituate Country Club* (Oct. 1919), 1 inch = 100 feet, PCRD, plan book 3, serial no. 3080, page 50; Nyberg, "Old Abbey Field and Pasture," 0 New Kent Street, MACRIS.

[135] William W. Waterman to Boston Sand and Gravel Company, deed, September 16, 1927, PCRD, book 1537, page 409 (two-acre Old Abbey field and eight acres essentially comprising the Nathaniel Turner farmhouse and lot with later address of 141 Driftway). The *1928 VL*, Nonresidents, 14, lists "Old Abby Field" at the end of property owned by Boston Sand and Gravel Company.

[136] "Famous South Shore Landmark Destroyed: Coleman Heights Hotel at Greenbush Was Burned to the Ground the Night of July 9, 1918," unidentified newspaper clipping from about 1938, probably *Scituate Herald*, with caption "(From our files of July 12, 1918)," Scituate Miscellany file, SHS; John Galluzzo, "Yesterdays: Scituate faces Hingham's 'Fearless Five,'" *Scituate Mariner*, March 3, 2016; "Widow's Walk Golf Course Rises on Historic Ground — Part II," SHS Newsletter, vol. 1, issue 6, January 1997, 4, citing Margaret Cole Bonney, *My*

Scituate (n.p., 1988), http://scituatehistoricalsociety.org/s/1997-Newsletters.pdf. Galluzzo and Bonney say the fire occurred June 25, but the newspaper clipping is a near-contemporaneous account on July 9. The hotel building does not show up on the *1919 VL* for property of the Boston Sand and Gravel Company.

[137] *1928 VL*, Nonresidents, 13-14. The largest single amount, 130 acres, was for some of the lots of the Colman Heights development of the late 1800s that never took off.

[138] Harrison L. House, *Town of Scituate Mass* [Assessor's maps], May 1928, with handwritten annotations, 1 inch = 100 feet, Sheet 60, Town Archives. The parcel north of the Old Abbey was extensively mined by the Boston Sand and Gravel Company, and the Old Abbey site was included in the company's operations. Nyberg, "Old Abbey Field and Pasture," 0 New Kent Street, MACRIS.

[139] L. Vernon Briggs, *History and Genealogy of the Briggs family, 1254-1937*, vol. 2 (Boston: Charles E. Goodspeed & Co., 1938), 409, https://babel.hathitrust.org/cgi/pt?id=wu.89062857503, and https://hdl.handle.net/2027/wu.89062857503; Nancy Burns, "Heyday of Boston Sand & Gravel," *Scituate Mariner*, November 1, 1979, clipping in "Businesses — Pre-1980" file, SHS; 1935 and 1940 USGS maps, Scituate quadrangle, scale 1:24,000 and 1:31,680, respectively; W. Ray Freden, "The Back Roads From Seaview Part 4," A History of Seaview & Marshfield, MA, blog, posted November 21, 2018, http://wrayfreden.com/.

[140] For example, see "Boston Sand & Gravel Co., Scituate, Mass.," postcard at bottom of page on Widow's Walk golf course website, http://www.widowswalkgolf.com/-course-environment.

[141] Burns, "Heyday of Boston Sand & Gravel," *Scituate Mariner*.

[142] Galluzzo, *The North River*, 74; Kezia Bacon, "Nature (Human and otherwise): Six walking trails with surprising histories," *Scituate Mariner*, March 3, 2021, https://www.wickedlocal.com/story/mariner/2021/03/03/six-walking-trails-with-surprising-histories/6839786002/; "Driftway Conservation Park," NSRWA website, https://www.nsrwa.org/listing/driftway-conservation-park/. See Joseph Carty, "Boston Sand and Gravel plant," photo, 1939 (conveyor loading barges), University of Massachusetts Boston, Joseph P. Healey Library, https://openarchives.umb.edu/digital/collection/p15774coll6/id/8766.

[143] Galluzzo, *The North River*, 74; Kezia Bacon, "Nature (Human and otherwis."

[144] *Town of Scituate Streets and Ways 2010* [compilation] (n.p., March 5, 2010), 3-ring binder, SHS.

[145] Boston Sand and Gravel Company to Town of Scituate, order of taking, August 12, 1975, PCRD, book 4091, page 726, referring to plan of August 1, 1975; Boston Sand and Gravel Company to Town of Scituate, deed, August 14, 1975, PCRD, book 4091, page 733; Loring H. Jacobs Co. for Town of Scituate, *Compiled Plan of Land in the Town of Scituate, Massachusetts, Located at Driftway and Stockbridge Road*, plan, 1" = 200', August 1, 1975, PCRD, plan book 18, page 594; see *1895 VL*, 78 (for William W. Waterman, eight acres).

[146] Report of the Department of Public Works, *Annual Report of the Town Officers and Committees of Scituate for the year ending December 31, 1974* (n.p., n.d.), 119–121 (with photo of "Stockbridge dump" and discussion of need for solid waste transfer facility); Wallace, Floyd, Ellenzweig, Moore, Inc., "Coastal Zone Study, Phase II, Scituate, Massachusetts: Coastal Characteristics and Analysis of Critical Issues," prepared for the Scituate Planning Board (September 1976), discussion and photo between 132 and 143, copy on file in archives of Third Cliff-Rivermoor Improvement Association ("TCRIA"), courtesy of Adria Gallagher; conversation with Mat Brown, July 23, 2017; Jarvis M. Freymann, "Widow's Walk Golf Course Rises on Historic Ground (Part I)," SHS Newsletter, vol. 1, issue 5 (December 1996), 6 (with two views or photos of Eaton's Hotel on page 7), http://scituatehistoricalsociety.org/newsletter-archive-04/

[147] *1993 Scituate Town Report*, 77, Annual Town Meeting, March 3, 1993, Article 29.

[148] Town of Scituate to Scituate Housing Authority, deed, June 13, 1995, PCRD, book 13695, page 343 (Parcel 3).

[149] *1995 Scituate Town Report*, 200 (deed from Town to Scituate Housing Authority has been finalized). Affordable housing is explained in Ruth Thompson, "Scituate affordable housing projects in the works," *Scituate Mariner* website, posted May 23, 2015, http://scituate.wickedlocal.com/article/20150523/news/150529171.

[150] CPA Projects Database, Community Preservation Coalition, http://www.communitypreservation.org/projects/report (search for Scituate, category Housing) (approved 2007-03-03). See "Parcel 3 Feasibility Study," Morse Engineering Company, Inc., website, http://www.morsecoinc.com/?portfolio=parcel-3-feasibility-study.

[151] Karen Sunnarborg, consultant, *Town of Scituate Housing Production Plan*, December 2008, draft/final 2-20-09, https://www.scituatema.gov/sites/scituatema/files/file/file/final_scituate_housing_production_plan.pdf.

[152] "Project Overview," c. 2013, McKenzie Engineering Group website, http://mckeng.com/portfolio-item/scituate-housing-authority/.

[153] Ruth Thompson, "Scituate opens discussions on affordable housing off Kent Street: Housing Authority looking to neighbors on plan of affordable units," *Scituate Mariner* website, posted May 7, 2014, http://scituate.wickedlocal.com/article/20140507/News/140506952.

[154] Richard Bochenek and Richard Dennis, Scituate Community Preservation Committee Funding Request Form, application for proposed "Cedar Hollow" project at intersection of Old Kent and the Driftway, October 28, 2014, http://www.scituatecpc.org/docs/applications/DriftwayLand_ThirdCliffResidents_RichardBochenek_Richard Dennis_2014.pdf.

[155] Bochenek and Dennis, CPC Funding Request, 2014.

[156] Bochenek and Dennis, CPC Funding Request, 2014.

[157] Karen Sunnarborg, *Town of Scituate Housing Production Plan* (January 2015), 44, from Scituate Housing Authority website, https://www.scituatema.gov/housing-authority (as "Scituate's Housing Plan Study").

[158] "Senior Center Site Feasibility Study," Town of Scituate email to residents, June 21, 2017: "The Scituate Senior Center Site Feasibility Study presented to the Board of Selectmen on June 20, 2017, is posted on the Town of Scituate website for your review. The consultant will be presenting this study to the Council on Aging (COA) Board at their next scheduled meeting and the COA will then hold a public meeting to gain input and answer questions you may have."

[159] The presentation was by Joel Bargmann, Bargmann Hendrie + Archetype, Inc., based in part on a study by the Center for Social and Demographic Research on Aging of the University of Massachusetts Boston, commissioned by Town of Scituate Council on Aging, "Aging in Scituate: An Assessment of Services and Programs for Our Community." The presentation is online at https://www.scituatema.gov/sites/scituatema/files/pages/senior_center_site_study_presentation_6-20-2017.pdf. It has a topographic description and results of geotechnical engineering reports on all four sites. It says "Sub-Surface Soil Contamination" was tbd for all sites. It says the Old Abbey site ("New Kent Street" site) "contains glacial till rendering site construction during winter wet season undesirable" and an Environmental Impact Statement and Conservation Commission approval would be required.

[160] Ruth Thompson, "Scituate senior center site selected," *Scituate Mariner* website, posted October 27, 2017, http://scituate.wickedlocal.com/news/20171027/scituate-senior-center-site-selected.

[161] Lyle Nyberg, former Gates School, 327 First Parish Road, SCI.1251, MACRIS; Ruth Thompson, "Ribbon-cutting ceremony held for new Scituate Senior Center," *Scituate Mariner*, posted May 17, 2021, https://www.wickedlocal.com/story/scituate-mariner/2021/05/17/scituate-senior-center-officially-opens/5096185001/.

[162] Lyle Nyberg, "Old Abbey Field and Pasture," 0 New Kent Street, SCI.957, MACRIS; author's observations.

[163] Greg Derr, "Rows to Hoe," *Quincy (MA) Patriot Ledger*, July 20, 2012, copy in Farming file, SHS.

[164] MACRIS Maps, http://maps.mhc-macris.net/ (under MassGIS Layers, select Prime Farmland, showing site as "farmland of statewide importance"); "Farmland Protection Policy Act," USDA NRCS website, https://www.nrcs.usda.gov/wps/portal/nrcs/main/national/landuse/fppa/; "Important Farmland Soil Map Units in Massachusetts," NESoil website (not official), http://nesoil.com/important.html; "Prime Farmland Soil Data Layer," page 15, in "Community Farmland Connections" guide by New Entry Sustainable Farming Project, 2010-2014, https://nesfp.org/sites/default/files/resources/new_entry_gis_mapping_guide.pdf.

[165] *1836 VL* (East Ward, for Michael Welch), 97; *1835 VL* (East Ward, for Ruth Turner, widow, evidently widow of James Turner who had equivalent property amounts in 1831), 92; *1831 VL* (East Company, for James Turner, evidently spouse of Ruth Turner), 179; "Early Families of Scituate," article with bibliography and map at bottom of page, SHS website, http://scituatehistoricalsociety.org/early-scituate-families/; Mrs. Frances Johnson (a descendant of Michael Welch) reminiscences in Late Summer 1988 newsletter of TCRIA, courtesy of Gail Ledwig and Skip DeBrusk, hereinafter "Johnson manuscript."

[166] This 19 acres was not included on the *1835 VL* for Ruth Turner, the prior owner, and she had no livestock, which Michael Welch had. Michael Welch may have acquired additional property at this time, since the 1836 deed from Ruth Turner mentions only 40 acres. Ruth Turner to Michael Welch, deed, January 26, 1836, PCRD, book 188, page 20 (including about 40 acres of land with dwelling house and barn).

[167] E. Parker Welch to William H. Welch, deed, July 5, 1901, PCRD, book 1260, page 460; E. Parker Welch to Minnie L. Welch, deed, July 5, 1901, PCRD, book 1172, page 384.

[168] Ruth Turner to Michael Welch, deed, January 26, 1836, PCRD, book 188, page 20 (including about 40 acres of land with dwelling house and barn); *Biographical Review,* 398 (158 acres); Valuation lists, including *1892 VL* (E. Parker Welch about 68 acres and Michael Welch about 102 acres). Michael Welch died in 1892, and property for his estate was carried on tax valuation lists until after 1897.

[169] *Biographical Review,* 383 ("Augustus Cole"). James Cole is mentioned as early as 1677 in town records. Bangs, *Seventeenth-Century Town Records,* vol. 3, 183.

[170] 1879 Map; 1831 Map. The house is also indicated on a coastal map from 1866 and a similar one from 1877, along with several houses at the end of the Driftway, and one house at or near the southern point of Third Cliff. C. O. Boutelle, et al, and US Coast Survey, *Coast Charts No. 10 & 11, Boston Bay and approaches,* scale 1:80,000 (1866), Norman B. Leventhal Map Center, https://collections.leventhalmap.org/search/commonwealth:3f463363n; US Coast Survey [Carlile Pollock Patterson, Supt. of the Survey of the Coast of the US, et al], *Coast Chart No. 109, Boston Bay and Approaches. - Coast Charts 109 & 110, Massachusetts Bay with the Coast from Cape Ann to Cape Cod,* (indep. issue, 1877), https://commons.wikimedia.org/wiki/File:1877_U.S._Coast_Survey_Map_or_Chart_of_Boston_Bay_and_Harbor_-_Geographicus_-_BostonBay-uscs-1877.jpg.

[171] Power, "Turner Family Notes," 64 (#135 James Turner), "Turner Family Genealogy," 103. As discussed elsewhere, the statement that Michael Welch was the Steward is probably inaccurate. The *Biographical Review,* 398, says only that he was employed at the Marine Hospital.

[172] *1821 VL,* unnumbered page in Harbour Company section in middle; *1825 VL; 1831 VL,* 179 in East Company section at end; *1836 VL,* 97 in East Ward section (Michael Welch).

[173] Nathaniel Turner Jr. to James Turner and Samuel Humphrey Turner, deed, April 3, 1804, PCRD, book 227, page 43. This might indicate passage for farming purposes, but suggests that James Turner had a dwelling there.

[174] 1840 US Census; 1879 Map; conversation with descendant Michael W. [Welch] Johnson, October 17, 2017.

[175] "Geo. F. Welch Laid At Rest," obituary, *Scituate Herald,* June 5, 1931, 1, copy in Welch Company file and in *Scituate Herald* issues, SHS (hereinafter "George F. Welch obituary") (says Michael Welch was chief steward); Early Vital Records of Massachusetts website, http://ma-vitalrecords.org/MA/Plymouth/Scituate/Images/Scituate_B405.shtml; "AMEDD/NCO Enlisted Soldier History," U.S. Army Medical Department, Office of Medical History, https://history.amedd.army.mil/corps/nco/historynco.html; "E. Parker Welch" and "George F. Welch," *Biographical Review,* 398–401 (E. Parker Welch, with illustration of him, saying only that Michael Welch was *employed* at the US Marine Hospital, without giving a title), and 557 (George Welch); William H. Eaton, "Welch" article dated September 26, 2005, in Welch Company file, SHS.

[176] Power, "Turner Family Notes," 72 (the name Edmond is typed over), "Turner Family Genealogy," 103.

[177] "Parker, Willard," in *The National Cyclopaedia of American Biography,* vol. 9 (New York: James T. White & Company, 1907), 337 [with portrait], https://books.google.com/books?id=7m9GAQAAMAAJ&source=gbs_navlinks_s. See also "Willard Parker, M. D., LL. D. [1800–1884]," obituary [May 3, 1884], in George F. Shrady, ed., *The Medical Record,* vol. 25 (New York: William Wood & Company, 1884), 492–493, https://books.google.com/books?id=l5FMAQAAMAAJ&source=gbs_navlinks_s; "Extracts from Letters from Dr. Willard Parker, of New York, to Dr. Edward Jarvis, of Dorchester, 1828-1881" in George B. Shattuck, M. D., ed., *The Boston Medical and Surgical Journal,* vol. 116 (Boston: Cupples and Hurd, 1887), 342-343 [April 7, 1887], https://books.google.com/books?id=7q81AQAAMAAJ&source=gbs_navlinks_s.

[178] *Vital Records of Scituate Massachusetts to the Year 1850, vol. I — Births* (Boston: New England Historic Genealogical Society, 1909), 405 (Edmond Parker Welch born Nov. 5, 1833)), https://archive.org/details/vitalrecordsofsc01newe.

[179] *Statements of the Origin, Regulations and Expenses of the United States Marine Hospital at Chelsea, for the Relief of Sick and Disabled Seamen in the Port of Boston and Charlestown, Massachusetts* (Boston: printed by Benjamin True, 1834), 5, https://books.google.com/books?id=oTwFAAAAYAAJ&source=gbs_navlinks_s; "Turner, Charles, Jr., (1760–1839)," online Biographical Directory of the United States Congress, http://bioguide.congress.gov/scripts/biodisplay.pl?index=T000416 (appointed steward of hospital, impliedly after 1823); "Extract from the Journal of Charles Turner, Jr., Esq.," in *Proceedings of the Massachusetts Historical Society,* vol. 17 (Boston: Massachusetts Historical Society, 1880), 206–216 at 207 (in proceedings of October 1879), Stable URL: http://www.jstor.org/stable/25079550. See also Turner, *Genealogy of Humphrey Turner,* App. J, 53 (served 14 years as steward). But see Helen Tilden Wild, "Galen James," Medford Historical Society Papers, vol. 11, ch.12 [read before the Medford Historical Society, April 4, 1908] (Galen James married daughter of Hon. Charles Turner Jr. in 1817 when she was living with her family at the Marine Hospital in Chelsea), Perseus Digital Library, http://www.perseus.tufts.edu/hopper/text?doc=Perseus:text:2005.05.0011:chapter=13&highlightauth=turner%2Ccharles#match1. Deane's *History of Scituate,* 361, says Turner was "now" [1831] the Master of that hospital. No sources have been found to indicate the hospital had a Master, and Statements of the Origin mentions only:

Steward (or Steward and Overseer), principal nurse, nurses reporting to the principal nurse, Orderly Men, Surgeon, Physician, Director (probably same as Steward), and Patient (or Hospital Pupil or Seaman).

[180] "Extract from the Journal of Charles Turner," 207.

[181] *Biographical Review*, 398-401; Deane, *History of Scituate*, 361. The US Marine Hospital began in 1804 in Charlestown, moved to Chelsea in 1827, and was replaced by the Chelsea Naval Hospital in 1836. John W. Trask, "The United States Marine Hospital, Port of Boston: Massachusetts's Oldest Hospital," *New England Journal of Medicine* 221 (October 12, 1939), 549-556, doi: 10.1056/NEJM193910122211501. See also Gautham Rao, "Sailors' Health and National Wealth: Marine hospitals in the early republic," article on Common-place website (with image of Chelsea Marine Hospital from 1834), October 2008, http://www.common-place-archives.org/vol-09/no-01/rao/; "Chelsea Naval Hospital and Magazine," in Stephen P. Carlson, *Charlestown Navy Yard Historic Resource Study*, App. A, Chronology (Boston: National Park Service, 2010), 1082–1083, https://archive.org/details/charlestownnavyy00carl. An 1857 plan shows the site as it was being redeveloped. L.H. Bradford & Co, and United States Marine Hospital at Boston, "Plan of the U.S. Marine Hospital estate Chelsea, Mass." (S.l: s.n, 1857), Norman B. Leventhal Map & Education Center at Boston Public Library, https://collections.leventhalmap.org/search/commonwealth:1257bb993.

[182] Deane, *History of Scituate*, 20-21. The scene is depicted in a later, detailed map, O. H. Tittmann, H. L. Whiting, et al, US Coast Survey, *Sketch of North River, Mass.*, [map], scale 1:40,000 (n.p., 1870), Digital Commons at Salem State University, http://digitalcommons.salemstate.edu/maps_massachusetts/4/.

[183] Murphy, *Irish Mossers*, 1, 3–4, 10, 21, 156; Emily Toomey, "The Most Irish Town in America Was Built on Seaweed," *Smithsonian Magazine*, July 22, 2019, https://www.smithsonianmag.com/innovation/most-irish-town-america-built-seaweed-180972701/.

[184] DAR, *Old Scituate*, 203 (quote); Murphy, *Irish Mossers*, 1. The descriptions of the Ephraim Young house appear to match the Dunbar, David House, 38 Greenfield Lane, SCI.103, MACRIS. A house appears there on maps as early as the 1831 map. The house was built about 1750, and still exists.

[185] Murphy, *Irish Mossers*, 1, 3–4, 10, 21, 156; Barbara Murphy, *The Coming of Age*, 92 (quoting or paraphrasing obituary of Daniel Ward in *South Shore Herald*, January 14, 1881); Michael Welch to Daniel Ward, deed, December 7, 1850, PCRD, book 244, page 198. Grantor and grantee indexes at PCRD for 1802–1859 show no transactions by O'Brien. The first appearance of Daniel Ward in the town's tax valuation lists seems to be in 1849, when he was assessed a tax of $1.27 on real estate. *1849 VL*, South Ward.

[186] Murphy, *Irish Mossers*, 1, 3–4, 10, 21, 156; tax valuation lists for various years (Welch family).

[187] [Moses Foster Sweetser, ed,] *New England: A Handbook for Travellers* (Boston: James R. Osgood and Company, 1873), 49, https://archive.org/details/newenglandhandbo00swee_0. Scituate is also called "a quaint old seaport with a summer hotel and good bathing (on Peggotty Beach)" in another travel guide, from 1877 (earlier editions back to 1870 may exist). *Appletons' Hand-book of American Summer Resorts with Principal Routes of Travel* (New York: D. Appleton and Co., 1877), 152, https://catalog.hathitrust.org/Record/100327478.

[188] *Thirteenth Exhibition of the Massachusetts Charitable Mechanic Association, Boston, September and October, 1878* (Boston: Alfred Mudge & Son, Printers, 1878), 44 (after 215 pages of the 12th exhibition) ("Moss Gatherers, Peggotty Beach, Scituate"), https://books.google.com/books?id=_AwAAAAAMAAJ&source=gbs_navlinks_s; and Frank Henry Shapleigh, *Peggoty Beach at Scituate [1879]*, WorthPoint.com website, http://www.worthpoint.com/worthopedia/peggoty-beach-scituate-frank-henry-shapleigh (painting sold February 18, 2006).

[189] Will Irwin, *Scituate: 1636–1936*, 31 (illustration), 35-37; Bonney, *Scituate's Sands of Time*, 7; Scituate Historical Society, *Scituate*, Images of America series (Charleston, SC: Arcadia Publishing, 2000), 30.

[190] Kristi Funderburk, "Did Dickens inspire Peggotty Beach's name?" *Scituate Mariner* website, July 14, 2016, updated July 16, 2016, http://scituate.wickedlocal.com/news/20160716/did-dickens-inspire-peggotty-beachs-name. A search of the WPA card index of town records found no early references to Peggotty Beach.

[191] Murphy, *Irish Mossers*, 3 (quoted in text); Murphy, *The Coming of Age*, 92 (quoting or paraphrasing obituary of Daniel Ward in *South Shore Herald*, January 14, 1881); Assessor's Database; discussion in text.

[192] Daniel Ward to E. Parker Welch, deed, November 19, 1859, PCRD, book 310, page 256 [recorded June 10, 1862]. The *1853 VL*, 71, and *1859 VL*, 125-126, both show Daniel Ward still owning a ½ acre lot and building on Third Cliff, almost certainly Bleak House. The double house was later sometimes called "Twin House," on the northern end of Third Cliff. See, for example, *1896 VL*, 114 (Daniel Ward [Jr.] sold house, house lot, shed, and moss house to George F. Welch), *1904 VL*, 81, and *1905 VL*, 86. The 1903 map marks the house as owned by E. P. Welch. George Welch still owned the house in 1916. John Galluzzo, "Yesterdays: 100 Years Ago in Scituate: October 1916," *Scituate Mariner*, A9, October 13, 2016.

[193] Current town records state that the house now at 6 Dickens Row was built in 1930. Assessor's Database. However, Murphy, *Irish Mossers*, 3, contains a photo of the house from the early 1900s and states that it was still "standing today [1980] but considerably altered, although it still shows having once been a double house." Also, a historical essay from about 1985 by a fifth-grade student said that the house still existed and was called the Alden House. Jamie Pickwick, "The First Irish Mosser," in *Scituate's Heritage: The People Who Made it Strong*, (n.p., c. 1985), 35. A wide house labeled "Alden" that appears to be a double house is shown on a 1921 plot plan. Harrison L. House, C. E., *Plan of Land at North End of Third Cliff, Scituate, Mass., 1921*, 1 inch = 40 feet, PCRD, plan book 3, serial no. 3129, page 89, sheet 1 of 2 (road labeled "Passageway 18 ft. wide" is Dickens Row). The Assessor's Database indicates that in 1985 there was demolition and new construction at 6 Dickens Row, and files in the Town Archives confirm that the prior house was razed. Building permit and demolition permit information are on file in Building Department and Town Archives (permits 85-312 and 85-313, June 24, 1985).

[194] DAR, *Old Scituate*, 249 (quoted), and see generally 245–261; Constance Lindner, "In small shipwreck treasures, vast new horizons," *Boston Globe*, August 23, 2009, http://archive.boston.com/news/local/articles/2009/08/23/from_a_scituate_shipwrecks_treasures_students_gain_vast_new_horizons/.

[195] Murphy, *Irish Mossers*, 3–5, 156–157, with photo of the "Big House" as it appeared in 1980; Thompson, *First Cliff, Scituate*, 44, 46, 207–208, 239–242; Murphy, *The Coming of Age*, 92. The *1859 VL*, 125-126, shows Daniel Ward still owning a ½-acre lot and building on Third Cliff, and additional buildings, with no mention of a *house* on First Cliff. However, his total tax jumped from $3.49 in 1849, to $10.82 in 1854, to $12.64 in 1859, which presumably included the Big House on First Cliff. Salvage work ("plundering wrecks") is discussed in Samuel Eliot Morison, *The Maritime History of Massachusetts 1783–1860* (Boston: Houghton Mifflin Company, 1921, fourth printing, 1961), 149–150. The house was sold in the autumn of 2021, with the property listing mentioning the salvaged staircase. Redfin property listing, August 31, 2021, https://www.redfin.com/MA/Scituate/6-Roberts-Dr-02066/home/16435524.

[196] Murphy, *Irish Mossers*, 3–5, 156–157; Thompson, *First Cliff, Scituate*, 44, 46, 207–208, 239–242; Murphy, *The Coming of Age*, 92.

[197] Murphy, *Irish Mossers*, 21, 156; "Carrageenans," on "The Seaweed Site: information on marine algae," http://www.seaweed.ie/uses_general/carrageenans.php; John Galluzzo, "How the Irish rebuilt Scituate," *Scituate Mariner* website, posted August 2, 2016, http://scituate.wickedlocal.com/news/20160802/how-irish-rebuilt-scituate. From a historical perspective, mossing is a relatively recent practice. See "A short history — aquaculture — Origins," European Union website, https://ec.europa.eu/fisheries/cfp/aquaculture/aquaculture_methods/history_en.

[198] Murphy, *Irish Mossers*, 3–4, 10, 21, 36; DAR, *Old Scituate*, 229-230; Lyle Nyberg, "Daniel Ward house," 6 Roberts Drive, SCI.1237, MACRIS; "William Ward House," 154 Edward Foster Road, SCI.73, MACRIS; Veronica Worthington, "Seaweed Pudding," Edible Cape Cod website, posted May 12, 2014, http://ediblecapecod.ediblecommunities.com/recipes/seaweed-pudding; Robert M. Downie, "Block Island Blancmange," Quahog.org website, reprinting article from *Block Island Summer Times*, Fall 2006, http://www.quahog.org/factsfolklore/index.php?id=154; "Along the South Shore," *Harper's New Monthly Magazine*, vol. 57, no. 337 (New York, Harper & Brothers, Publishers, June 1878), 1–14 at 8, https://books.google.com/books?id=lEtOAQAAMAAJ&source=gbs_navlinks_s. A news report said, "The industry mostly ended in town during the summer of 1997, when the equipment used by the consumer purchasing Irish moss broke down and was not repaired." Jessica Foster, "Scituate's seaweed sea change," *Scituate Mariner*, February 1, 2018, page B10.

[199] "Kelp Vs. Seaweed," SFGate website, http://healthyeating.sfgate.com/kelp-vs-seaweed-10040.html; "Irish Moss (Chondrus crispus)," Maine Coast Sea Vegetables website, http://www.seaveg.com/shop/index.php?main_page=index&cPath=25; Evelyn Roehl, "Irish Moss" and "Kelp" in *Whole Food Facts: The Complete Reference Guide* (Rochester, VT: Inner Traditions International / Healing Arts Press, 1996, originally published 1988), 174, https://books.google.com/books?id=H8lwmA52ltIC&source=gbs_navlinks_s. "Carrageen," in Daniel C. Gilman, Harry T. Peck, Frank M. Colby, eds., *The New International Encyclopædia*, vol. 4 (New York: Dodd, Mead and Company, 1909), 256, https://books.google.com/books?id=giQVAAAAYAAJ&source=gbs_navlinks_s; "Carrageenan," Wikipedia, https://en.wikipedia.org/wiki/Carrageenan.

[200] "Ireland: Carrageen Moss Blancmange," on European Cuisines website, http://www.europeancuisines.com/Ireland-Irish-Carrageen-Carragheen-Carrageenan-Carragheenan-Moss-Blancmange-Pudding-Dessert-Recipe; "Carrageenans," on "The Seaweed Site: information on marine algae," http://www.seaweed.ie/uses_general/carrageenans.php; Sue Scheible, "South Shore Wonders: Maritime &

Irish Mossing Museum in Scituate," *Quincy (MA) Patriot Ledger* website, posted August 11, 2017, updated August 12, 2017, http://www.patriotledger.com/news/20170811/south-shore-wonders-maritime--irish-mossing-muscum-in-scituate; exhibits at Maritime & Irish Mossing Museum, Scituate; Susan Hand Shetterly, *Seaweed Chronicles: A World at the Water's Edge* (Chapel Hill, NC: Algonquin Books of Chapel Hill, 2018), 76-82.

[201] Amanda Fiegl/Abigail Tucker, "Eating Irish Moss," September 28, 2010, *Smithsonian Magazine*, https://www.smithsonianmag.com/arts-culture/eating-irish-moss-100792221/.

[202] A. Howard Clark, "The Fisheries of Massachusetts," in George Brown Goode, *The Fisheries and Fishery Industries of the United States* (Washington, DC: US Commission of Fish and Fisheries, 1887), Section II, Part III, G.70 and G.71 ("The Fisheries of Scituate and Duxbury"), 214, 219–220, https://www.google.com/books/edition/The_Fisheries_and_Fishery_Industries_of/zk85AQAAIAAJ?hl=en; Murphy, *Irish Mossers*, 21. Augustus Cole is listed in the *1886 VL* (printed in Town Report), 27, with a house valued at a respectable $1,400, plus barn, buildings, 19 acres "great field" ($2,265), and over 25 acres of salt marsh. He could be the "A. Cole" whose house is indicated on the north side of the Driftway next to Colman Hills on the 1879 map, and he is described (with image) in the 1897 *Biographical Review*, 383.

[203] Clark, "The Fisheries of Massachusetts," 214 (headquarters, extent), 219-220.

[204] Paul McCarthy, "Town of Scituate Massachusetts, Historical Map & Street Directory" (n.p., 1976), author's collection.

[205] Jane Walsh, "The most Irish town in America is named using US census data," IrishCentral website, November 25, 2015, http://www.irishcentral.com/news/the-most-irish-town-in-america-is-named-133427563-237789381.html; US Census Bureau, "Selected Social Characteristics in the United States: 2010 American Community Survey 1-Year Estimates," US Census Bureau American FactFinder website, http://factfinder.census.gov/faces/tableservices/jsf/pages/productview.xhtml?pid=ACS_10_1YR_DP02&prodType=table [the website has been decommissioned, and the author has since been unable to find equivalent data tables on the Census Bureau website]. Scituate's neighboring town of Marshfield has two census tracts — Marshfield Hills and Ocean Bluff-Brant Rock — that have a higher percentage of Irish ancestry than Scituate. Gerry Tuoti, "Where are the most Irish towns in Massachusetts?" *Marshfield Mariner*, March 13, 2017, https://marshfield.wickedlocal.com/news/20170313/where-are-most-irish-towns-in-massachusetts. Elaura Rifkin, "Massachusetts' Real Irish Bragging Rights," *National Geographic* website, March 15, 2012 (dealing with the "Irish Riviera"), https://www.nationalgeographic.com/travel/intelligent-travel/2012/03/15/massachusetts-real-irish-bragging-rights/.

[206] Assessor's hand-drawn plot plans, about 1930–1935, by street, Town Archives; author's analysis in 2017 of Assessor's Database.

[207] Author's knowledge; Rumania (Meyer Bloomfield); China (Chalkley); Japan (Yatsuhashi Harumichi); Germany (Herman Shaneck); Wales (Thomas J. Edwards); France (Pierre Laneres); Mayflower: Marian Holt, Walter O'Neil, J. Colby Bassett.

[208] Various properties listed in MACRIS, including 20 Town Way (SCI.132), 138 Gilson Road (SCI.101), and other houses listed in a search in MACRIS for the Rivermoor area, and searches at Zillow.com; Assessor's Database; Murphy, *Irish Mossers*, 22 (James Quinn and John Curran), 108-109 (Capt. Stanley); J. H. Hogan *1894 Directory*, 143 (Festus Nee), and entries for Currans, who were all listed as mossers; Martin Curran to John Welch, deed (for what was later called the Stephen Joyce House, 138 Gilson Road), January 9, 1882, PCRD, book 475, page 459. 137 Gilson Road was built in 1750, according to the Assessor's Database, but the current owner states it was built in 1857 in a "barn-raising" collective effort by local Irish residents, based on her historical discussions with long-time residents, including Catherine "Kate" (Welch) Loughlin (1884-1973). Linda Barnhart, interview by author, May 1, 2016.

The MACRIS database consists of historical documentation forms mostly generated locally, mostly from local agencies and organizations such as the Scituate Historical Society. The Society has many files on historical sites recorded in MACRIS. The historical documentation forms and the Assessor's Database sometimes differ as to when a house was built. The Assessor's Database appears to enter 1900 as a default date for older properties. Based on various title searches for properties on Bassin Lane, the author has no reason to doubt the correctness of the 1900 date for houses at 3, 6, 9, and 15 Bassin Lane. A house at 15 Bassin Lane shows up on a plan by E. T. Child, *Plan of Property of Mrs. Lachlan Wallace, Third Cliff, Scituate, Mass.*, scale 1" = 16', Dec. 20, 1900, PCRD, plan book 11, page 408. Some of the houses on Bassin Lane, particularly 15 Bassin Lane, have been extensively altered.

The author is unable to confirm when many of the houses in the north end of Third Cliff were built. However, historical maps (discussed in the text) reflect early houses, and some of the names attached to them can be confirmed. For example, J. Curran and M. Curran marked on the 1879 Map correspond to John Curran (and three other Currans) living on "Third Cliff" and his brother Martin Curran (and three other Currans) living on

Kent Street (near Third Cliff), as listed in "Directory and History of Scituate, Mass." in J. H. Hogan *1894 Directory*. The Directory lists all the Currans as mossers. It was Martin Curran who sold the cottage at 138 Gilson Road to John Welch in 1882. Martin Curran to John Welch, deed, January 9, 1882, PCRD, book 475, page 459. As another example, the 1879 Map also shows the "V. Nee" cottage. It is listed in MACRIS as "Foley, D. - Withem, Harold House," 34 Driftway, SCI.1152 (range 1900). The Assessor's Database lists it as having been built in 1920, even though the cottage has a plaque outside saying "The Nee Cottage, built by Festus Nee, 1872," and it is mentioned in E. Parker Welch to George F. Welch, deed, August 27, 1902, PCRD, book 864, page 108. Festus Nee is listed in the J. H. Hogan *1894 Directory*, 143, as a mosser with home on Third Cliff. For these and other houses, tax valuation lists may indicate when they were built.

[209] "Captain Frederick Stanley," *Biographical Review*, 558 (house built 1873); "Stanley, Capt. Fredrick H. House," 14 Bassin Lane, SCI.3, MACRIS; conversation with Elizabeth Foster, May 15, 2019; "Crew of Eight Safe," *Boston Globe*, February 14, 1894, 1; "Vessel Piled Up — Her Crew Saved," *Boston Globe*, January 31, 1909, 1, 12; "Two Life-Savers Retire," *Boston Globe*, March 23, 1915, 13.

[210] 1905 postcard of Stanley House, https://commons.wikimedia.org/wiki/File:The_Stanley_House,_Scituate,_MA.jpg; *Scituate Historical Society Newsletter*, vol. 3, issue 6 (January 1999), 3, online at the Society's website; E. G. Perry, *A Trip Around Cape Cod: The South Shore and Historical Plymouth* (Boston: E. G. Perry, 1898), 253 (ad), https://catalog.hathitrust.org/Record/100493805.

[211] 1831 Map.

[212] Henry R. Walling, *Map of the County of Plymouth* [map], 1 inch = 240 rods (Boston: D. R. Smith & Co., 1857), hereinafter "1857 Map," Library of Congress, Geography and Map Division, https://www.loc.gov/item/2012592354/.

[213] Murphy, *Irish Mossers*, 22, citing the 1870 US census.

[214] Walling & Gray, *Official Topographical Atlas of Massachusetts: from Astronomical, Trigonometrical and Various Local Surveys* [map], 1 inch = 2 ½ miles (1:158400) (Boston: Stedman, Brown & Lyon, 1871), 32, State Library of Massachusetts, Massachusetts Real Estate Atlas Digitization Project, URI http://hdl.handle.net/2452/205981,http://www.mass.gov/anf/research-and-tech/oversight-agencies/lib/massachusetts-real-estate-atlases.html (for detailed view) and https://www.flickr.com/photos/mastatelibrary/9452223882/in/album-72157634952207573/.

[215] Murphy, *Irish Mossers*, 22, lists 89 names of mossers based on the 1870 US census, which does not show addresses and is not listed geographically.

[216] Of the 89 names in *Irish Mossers*, 22, about 10–14 lived on First Cliff, according to Thompson, *First Cliff, Scituate*, 6 (note 22). But only about 7 lived on First Cliff, according to the 1879 map: Ward (6 names), McDonald (1). About 20 lived on Third Cliff, by my count, based largely on the 1879 map: Butterly (3 names), Hoar, Sullivan, Wherity, Graham, Fallon (2), O'Neil (3), Quinn, Regan, Donohue, Mitchell, Curran (2), Whearty (2).

[217] *Atlas of Plymouth County, Massachusetts* (Boston: Geo. H. Walker & Co., 1879), Business Notices section at back, under "Scituate," State Library of Massachusetts, Massachusetts Real Estate Atlas Digitization Project, http://www.mass.gov/anf/research-and-tech/oversight-agencies/lib/massachusetts-real-estate-atlases.html (for detailed view) and https://www.flickr.com/photos/mastatelibrary/8881812782/in/album-72157633790765207/.

[218] Murphy, *The Coming of Age*, 151 (street names); Town of Scituate, Selectmen's Records 1871-1896, Town Archives, item 1535, pages 73–74, April 13, April 21, 1877 (Selectmen approve road from Kent Street to northwest corner of cliff); "Watering Place Notes," *Sunday Herald* newspaper clipping [probably *Boston Sunday Herald*], June 17, 1877, from EC Manson/Edith Manson Freeman scrapbook, copy in "Hotels, Inns" file, SHS; Martin Curran to John Welch, deed, January 9, 1882, PCRD, book 475, page 459; WPA card file, Town Archives, under "Welch-Michael," summarizing documents S-101, page 124, March 12, 1889, and S-101, page 125, March 30, 1889 (town way from Water Street to Highland Street), documents recorded at Town of Scituate, Selectmen's Records 1871-1896, Town Archives, item 1535, pages 124-126, March 12, March 25, April 1, 1889 (26 foot wide way); Town of Scituate, Town Records [incl. Town Meeting Minutes], vol. 11, 1882-1906, 17-19, February 20, 1897 (town way from Water Street to Highland Street laid out based on petition); Town Records [incl. Town Meeting Minutes], vol. 11, 1882-1906, 41-45, County Commissioners consideration and approval of town way from Water Street to Highland Street, May 1, 1900 (40 foot wide way). The Commissioners awarded compensation for taking of land for the town way to E. Parker Welch, Mary Welch (no relation to E. Parker Welch), Jane O'Neil, Bridget Quinn, and Bridget Mitchell. The town's annual report for 1900 records expenditures for a new road on Third Cliff. *Annual Report of the Town Officers of the Town of Scituate for the Year Ending December 31, 1900*, 7 (Town Meeting, March 5, 1900, voted to indefinitely postpone

Article 35 "in regard to building a new road on Third Cliff"), and 37 ($1,500 appropriation nearly all spent for new road on Third Cliff). No doubt, this activity to finish Gilson Road was connected with the subdivision plan filed by the Scituate Beach Land Association, discussed below in the text.

[219]Murphy, *Irish Mossers*, 22. Mosser residency is supported by Town of Scituate, "Repairs on Third Cliff Road," *Annual Report of the Selectmen, Assessors, and Overseers of the Poor of the Town of Scituate for the Financial Year ending Feb. 1, 1883* (Plymouth: Avery & Doten, 1883), 19 et seq. This lists persons paid for the repair work, the largest amount going to "E. P. Welch & Son" and other amounts to about 45 persons, most of whom seem to have been mossers, including four Currans and three O'Neals.

[220] Metageologist, "The west of Ireland: a geological journey," Metageologist blog, posted January 23, 2013, http://all-geo.org/metageologist/2013/01/western-ireland-geology/ ("It turns out that the Atlantic connection is more than poetic. For the best bits of its geological history, the north west of Ireland was part of the continent of Laurentia, now mostly found on the other side of the Ocean."); "Ireland and Plate Tectonics," Ask About Ireland website, http://www.askaboutireland.ie/reading-room/environment-geography/physical-landscape/Irelands-physical-landsca/the-formation-of-the-phys/ireland-and-plate-tectoni/; "Ireland — where Europe and North America meet," Ingenious Ireland website, http://www.ingeniousirelandonline.ie/en/stories/st0003.xml?page=4; Geoff Manaugh and Nicola Twilley, "What Did the Continents Look Like Millions of Years Ago? An artist-geologist renders the history of the Earth with maps," *The Atlantic* website, https://www.theatlantic.com/technology/archive/2013/09/what-did-the-continents-look-like-millions-of-years-ago/279892/, in which geologist Ronald Blakey says:

> By, say, 250 million years ago, most of the continents were together. Then, when they started to split apart in the Triassic and Jurassic—especially in the Triassic and Cretaceous—the split occurred in such a way that what had been part of North America was actually captured, if you will, by Europe and taken over to become the British Isles.
>
> Scotland and at least the northern half of Ireland were captured and began to drift with Europe. On the other hand, North America picked up Florida—which used to be part of Gondwana—and so forth.

Similarly, England was connected to what became New England. Dicus, *Window Seat*, 31.

[221] "George H. Nee," US Army Center of Military History website, http://www.history.army.mil/moh/index.html (listings based on 1979 US Senate report), and http://www.history.army.mil/moh/warspain.html#NEE; Medal of Honor Historical Society of the United States website, http://www.mohhsus.com/medal-of-honor; John "J-Cat" Griffith, "George H. Nee," Find A Grave website entry, https://www.findagrave.com/cgi-bin/fg.cgi?page=gr&GRid=6841020; Valerie Vitali to David Ball, SHS, letter, March 19, 1996, black binder in house files, Exhibit L, SHS; David Corbin, "Scituate Commentary: Celebration of the cannon," *Scituate Mariner* website posted November 20, 2009, http://scituate.wickedlocal.com/x1682928531/SCITUATE-COMMENTARY-Celebration-of-the-cannon. George H. Nee is listed as a summer resident on Town Way in *1926 Directory*, 105.

[222] E. Parker Welch et ux to John Curran, deed, April 9, 1863, PCRD, book 317, pages 42–43 (describing triangular land at Water Street as it turned south, where it was called "the Highway leading to the Beach;" Daniel Noonan release of rights in new Dwelling House and buildings built by him and John Curran, April 9, 1863, PCRD, book 317, page 43; John Curran et ux to John Flaherty, deed, March 25, 1884, PCRD, book 505, page 278; 1903 map.

[223] Martin Curran to John Curran [brother], deed, April 1, 1882, PCRD, book 478, page 230; Trisha, "John Curran," Find A Grave website entry, http://www.findagrave.com/cgi-bin/fg.cgi?page=gr&GRid=103145078 (John Curran, 1829-1901, with copy of will leaving property to children Mary and Charles); Mary F. O'Connor to Charles P. Curran [brother], deed, March 25, 1915, PCRD, book 1214, page 30; Joseph J. Curran [son of Charles P. Curran] to George Vollmer, deed, August 21, 1951, PCRD, book 2163, page 102; unknown, genealogy chart in "Jack Curran Surfman" file of David Ball, SHS. Town records support a date of construction for 137 Gilson perhaps as late as 1866, although the records do not specify where the property is. The *1859 VL* includes no Currans. The *1866 VL*, approximately 16th page, lists Martin Curran with no house and instead his brother John Curran was shown as owning a house and ½ acre of house lots. The *1875 VL*, approximately 14th page, shows Martin Curran owning a house, barn, and ½ acre house lot, with no listing for John Curran. In any event, this is one of the two or three oldest houses on Third Cliff.

[224] *Biographical Review*, 398-401; George F. Welch obituary; Thompson, *First Cliff, Scituate*, 20–21, 25, 236–239.

[225] George F. Welch obituary; "Anable, Anthony House, or Bayside - Meeting House Inn," 1984, 12 Meeting House Lane, SCI.115, MACRIS (1984 submission).

[226] *1850 VL*, 51; *1859 VL*; *1873 VL*, Dr. Ruth Bailey answers to TCRIA questionnaire about 1988 in Association's archives.

[227] *1869 VL,* 63 ("½ House" and "New Barn"); *1870 VL,* 64; *1871 VL,* 65 ("2 Houses"); *1883 VL,* 76; *1886 VL,* 77 ("2 Cliff Houses"); *1897 VL,* 78 ("Bijou" and "Parker").

[228] "In Scituate Cottages. Hosts of People Summering at a Quiet South Shore Resort." *Boston Globe,* August 9, 1891, 13; "Scituate," *Boston Globe,* July 15, 1900, 22.

[229] 1880 US Census, Schedule 1-Inhabitants, Scituate, Plymouth County, Massachusetts, page 5, dwelling 53, family 58, line 50, Michael Welch household; digital images, HeritageQuest, citing NARA microfilm publication T9, roll not identified.

[230] George F. Welch obituary; *Biographical Review,* 557 (and see 565); *1943 Town of Scituate Annual Report,* 33 (death of Hattie Welch); William H. Eaton, "Welch" article dated September 26, 2005, in Welch Company file, SHS; Assessor's card for 28 Otis Place, Fiscal Year 2009 (year built 1740). George Welch's Otis Place residence was likely the oldest house on a street of old houses, according to author's analysis of assessor's records. It appears on the 1903 map by Judson, adjacent to E. Parker Welch's residence on Allen Place, and steps away from the Welch Company location. The Otis Place residence is covered in the "Otis Place" file, SHS. The historical residence was demolished in 2015, although there still were pictures of it on Google Maps/Street View (from July 2015) as of May 2017, and on page 136 of Duncan Bates Todd, *The Fourteenth Lot* (Scituate: by author, 2004).

[231] 1918 Directory, 109–110.

[232] *The Plymouth County Directory and Historical Register of the Old Colony* (Middleboro, MA: Stillman B. Pratt & Co., 1867), 160, https://archive.org/details/plymouthcountydi00prat_0; Mrs. George F. Welch, *History of Methodist Episcopal Church, Scituate, Mass., 1825–1925* (n.p., printed by kind permission of the Daughters of the American Revolution, Scituate, Mass.).

[233] Welch Company file, SHS; E. Parker Welch to George F. Welch, deeds, February 27, 1891, PCRD, book 611, pages 436, 437, 438; "Welch, George F. Coal and Lumber Company Store," 162 Front Street, SCI.1073, MACRIS, including continuation sheet; Johnson manuscript. The company started as "E. Parker Welch and Son" and later became the "George F. Welch Company." See E. Parker Welch to George F. Welch, deed, February 27, 1891, PCRD, book 611, page 438 (purchases from 1865 on).

[234] Briggs, *Shipbuilding on North River,* 391 (last ship 1864), 257–258; Turk Tracey & Larry Architects, LLC, *Community-Wide Preliminary Survey, Scituate, Massachusetts* (n.p., Town of Scituate, December 12, 2002), 6, Scituate Planning Board, portions online on Scituate Historical Commission website; John J. Galluzzo, *True To Our Roots: The Legacy of Alonzo W. Perry* (Virginia Beach, VA: Donning Co. Publishers, 2011), 10–15; Scituate Historical Society, *Scituate,* Then & Now series (Charleston, SC: Arcadia Publishing, 2002), 15; David T. Dixon, "Two Scituates: Development and Division in a Summer Resort 1870–1900," paper for University of Massachusetts at Boston, History 600: Historical Research and Methods, May 10, 2001, 7–8, 16–19, 30, SHS, and furnished by email to author, June 6, 2017. The fishing industry in neighboring Cohasset had a slower decline, from a peak year of 1851 until the close of its fisheries in 1885. Edwin Victor Bigelow, *A Narrative History of the Town of Cohasset, Massachusetts* (Cohasset: Committee on Town History, 1898), 425.

[235] 1854 Report of Survey of Scituate Harbor and North River, 10.

[236] *Annual Report of the Chief of Engineers, United States Army, to the Secretary of War, for the Year 1888, Part I* [of four] (Washington: Government Printing Office, 1888), 50th Cong., 2d sess., H. Rep. Ex. Doc. 1, pt. 2, vol. 2, 458–461, https://archive.org/stream/bub_gb_S5oAAAAAMAAJ#page/n3/mode/2up.

[237] Welch Company file, SHS.

[238] Welch Company file, SHS; E. Parker Welch to George F. Welch, deeds, February 27, 1891, PCRD, book 611, pages 436, 437, 438; William H. Eaton, "Welch" article dated September 26, 2005, in Welch Company file, SHS, citing the J. H. Hogan *1894 Directory;* "A Saga of the Welch Company by 'The Yankee'" article in Welch Company file, SHS; "New England Notes" and "With the Corporations," *New York Lumber Trade Journal,* (New York: New York Lumber Trade Journal Inc.), November 1, 1914, I:37, https://books.google.com/books?id=J_4xAQAAMAAJ&source=gbs_navlinks_s; Johnson manuscript.

[239] Tax valuation lists, 1892–1903, and author analysis of the lists, particularly "Store Building" valued at $4,000 in *1898 VL,* 79. The building still exists, albeit with a plaque saying "1876" and without its third story. The third story was destroyed by fire in 1959. See articles in Welch Company file, SHS. The 1897 *Biographical Review* says the main store was 55' x 85' and three stories, but a recent Google Maps satellite view shows that the current building (without the restaurant to the north and gift shop to the south) is more like 75'x 100-135' which suggests it was built (or replaced) after 1897.

[240] "A Saga of the Welch Company by 'The Yankee'" on page 3 of article [likely by William H. Eaton] in Welch Company file, SHS. Tax valuation lists partially support this description of a storm in 1893. A "Counting Room & Shed" valued at $1,675 in 1892 no longer appeared on the tax rolls in 1893, replaced by a "Store & Shed"

valued at $2,700. But one wonders if the historian meant the big storm of 1898, not 1893. The town report for 1893 records no town payments to people for fighting (or "watching") fires, but the one for 1898 does.

241 *Annual Report of the Town Officers of the Town of Scituate for the Year Ending December 31ˢᵗ, 1893* (Plymouth: Avery & Doten, book and job printers, 1894), 26–27 (miscellaneous expenses); *Annual Report of the Town Officers of the Town of Scituate for the Year Ending December 31, 1894* (Plymouth: Avery & Doten, book and job printers, 1895), 28 (fire apparatus at the harbor); *Annual Report of the Town Officers of the Town of Scituate for the Year Ending December 31, 1898*, 22–25 (miscellaneous expenses), 35–36 (expenses of storm); *Annual Report of the Town Officers of the Town of Scituate for the Year Ending December 30, 1899*, 16-19 (miscellaneous expenses including a few for the Welch and other fires). Thanks to Robert Jackman for pointing out these fire-related expenses.

242 Harrison L. House, *Wharf Properties of George F. Welch, Located in Scituate, Mass., 1919, corrected to April 1923, Scale 1 inch = 40 feet*, PCRD, plan book 3, page 504; 1903 map, subplan Plate 31 for Village of Scituate; various trade journals, and Russell Fish papers, courtesy of Sue Logan, on file in SHS.

243 Welch Company file, SHS.

244 Welch Company file, SHS; unidentified newspaper clipping (source of quote), c. 1941, Russell Fish papers.

245 Welch Company website, http://www.welchcompany.com/.

246 WPA card file, Town Archives, under "Welch-George F.," summarizing numerous documents, including S-102, page 3, March 8, 1897; S-102, page 35, March 22, 1901, and S-103, page 3, April 8, 1905, C-21, page 26, April 11, 1908; S-104, page 66, April 26, 1913.

247 Town of Scituate, *Selectmen's Records 1871–1896*, Town Archives, item 1535, page 87, March 3, 1880 (E. P. Welch one of those appointed Weigher of Coal & Hay); WPA card file, Town Archives, under "Welch, E. Parker," summarizing numerous documents, including *Town Records* S-103, page 20, March 5, 1906; C-12, page 47, March 2, 1908; C-16, page 181, March 24, 1911; C-17, page 19, February 3, 1912; *Annual Report of the Officers of the Town of Scituate for the Year Ending December 31, 1911*, 7; Thompson, *First Cliff, Scituate*, 238.

248 *Biographical Review*, 401; Harvard University, *Quinquennial Catalogue of the Officers and Graduates of Harvard University* (Cambridge: Harvard University, 1890), 180, 434, https://books.google.com/books?id=LuMTAAAAIAAJ&source=gbs_navlinks_s; Thompson, *First Cliff, Scituate*, 25, 39, 236-239.

249 "Walbach, George G. House," 30 Circuit Avenue, SCI.1238, MACRIS. Both properties are listed on the 1903 map and both are shown on the 1926 Sanborn map, sheet 13, upper right. On that map, the house now at 30 Circuit Avenue is shown inside the circle leading from the Private Way off Edward Foster Road. That house is also shown on a 1922 plan. Harrison L. House, *Plan of House Lots on the First Cliff, Scituate, Mass. 1922*, PCRD, plan book 3, page 506. The Assessor's Database lists the date of construction as 1930, but Jane K. Thompson's book, the *Biographical Review*, and the house's appearance strongly suggest a date of about 1888, the year George Walbach married Mary Welch.

250 Edgar B. Herwick III, "How Shacks for the Shipwrecked Spawned Mass. General Hospital" (first Scituate hut was at Humarock-Fourth Cliff), WGBH website, posted February 28, 2014, https://news.wgbh.org/post/how-shacks-shipwrecked-spawned-mass-general-hospital. According to the Humane Society's website, "The first hut was placed at Scituate Beach in 1787." This was a mile south of Fourth Cliff, according to M. A. DeWolfe Howe, *The Humane Society of the Commonwealth of Massachusetts: An Historical Review, 1785–1916* (Boston: The Humane Society, printed by The Riverside Press, Cambridge, 1918), 57-59, https://catalog.hathitrust.org/Record/001581969; DAR, *Old Scituate*, 244 (first hut in Scituate was on Fourth Cliff). See also, Scituate Historical Society, *Scituate*, Images of America series (Charleston, SC: Arcadia Publishing, 2000), 41 (first Scituate hut was at base of Third Cliff); Scituate Historical Society, *Scituate*, Then & Now series, 28 (first Scituate hut was at base of Third Cliff); Robert F. Bennett, *Sand Pounders* (Washington, DC: US Coast Guard, 1988), 25 (first Scituate hut was on Fourth Cliff).

251 DAR, *Old Scituate*, 253–255 (E. Parker Welch assisted in rescues); *Biographical Review*, 398-401; Humane Society of the Commonwealth of Massachusetts, *Annual Report, 1885* (Boston: Nathan Sawyer & Son, 1886), 22, https://babel.hathitrust.org/cgi/pt?id=mdp.39015033932628;view=1up;seq=5; Humane Society of the Commonwealth of Massachusetts, *Report:1899 and 1900* (Boston: Nathan Sawyer & Son, 1900), 28–29, 40–41, 124 (life-saving stations 29 & 30 at Third Cliff), https://books.google.com/books?id=bEYDAAAAMAAJ&source=gbs_navlinks_s; William Murphy letter to Mr. Edward Rowe Snow, January 14, 1978, SHS (mentioning Henry Welch's assistance and discussing stranding of steamer *Devonian* on Third Cliff in 1906); "The Devonian Floated," *Lewiston* [ME] *Evening Journal*, February 16, 1906, p. 7, col. 2, https://news.google.com/newspapers?nid=1913&dat=19060215&id=yNUgAAAAIBAJ&sjid=9GoFAAAAIBAJ&pg=1112,738393&hl=en.

252 DAR, *Old Scituate*, 253. George F. Welch joined the Masons in 1896, and a copy of his Masonic membership card is on Ancestry.com. A Masonic emblem is on his gravestone, per author's visit to Union Cemetery October 2, 2017.

253 See discussion below in text of the Clarence Miller family, including daughter Harriet Miller's memories of the lifesaving station at Third Cliff. The Society continued to maintain lifeboats and lifeboat stations along the Massachusetts coast through the 1930s, according to the Society's website http://www.masslifesavingawards.com/history/; F. M. Thorn, Superintendent, US Coast and Geodetic Survey, *Atlantic Local Coast Pilot: Sub-divisions 6-7. Cape Ann to Monomoy* (Washington, DC: Government Printing Office, 1888), 13, https://books.google.com/books?id=HM1AAQAAMAAJ&source=gbs_navlinks_s; Humane Society of the Commonwealth of Massachusetts, *Annual Report, 1885* (Boston: Nathan Sawyer & Son, 1886), 22, https://babel.hathitrust.org/cgi/pt?id=mdp.39015033932628;view=1up;seq=5; Humane Society of the Commonwealth of Massachusetts, *Report:1899 and 1900* (Boston: Nathan Sawyer & Son, 1900), 28-29, 40-41, 124 (life-saving stations 29 & 30 at Third Cliff), https://books.google.com/books?id=bEYDAAAAMAAJ&source=gbs_navlinks_s; The Humane Society of the Commonwealth of Massachusetts, *Biennial Report, 1907 and 1908* (Boston: Nathan Sawyer & Son, Printers, 1908), 15, https://babel.hathitrust.org/cgi/pt?id=mdp.39015033932644;view=1up;seq=3, permanent link to book, http://hdl.handle.net/2027/mdp.39015033932644 (life-saving station 30 at Third Cliff, combining life boat and Hunt gun).

254 Dennis R. Means, "A Heavy Sea Running: The Formation of the U.S. Life-Saving Service, 1846–1878," in *Prologue Magazine* (National Archives), Winter 1987, vol. 19, No. 4, 223–243, http://www.archives.gov/publications/prologue/1987/winter/us-life-saving-service-1.html; website of Hull Lifesaving Museum, http://www.lifesavingmuseum.org/exhibitsandcollections.html; Judson, 1903 map (showing site of "Mass. Humane Soc." station on Third Cliff and other locations). The establishment of a lifesaving station at Third Cliff was credited to George Lunt (1803–1885), who had retired to Scituate in 1877. Lawrence S. Mayo, "Lunt, George" in Dumas Malone, ed., *Dictionary of American Biography*, vol. 11 (New York: Charles Scribner's Sons, 1933), 507-508, https://archive.org/details/dictionaryofamer11amer: "He became interested in the improvement of Scituate harbor, and it is said that the work done on it by the federal government in the eighties and likewise the establishment of a life-saving station at the Third Cliff are attributable largely to his efforts and influence."

255 Edward Rowe Snow, "Thomas Flynn's Story," clipping, probably from *Patriot Ledger*, 1958 (source of quotes from Flynn); "Six Saved From Sea at Scituate," *Boston Globe*, March 6, 1917, 1 & 11; "Loss of American Vessels Reported During Fiscal Year 1917," in *Merchant Vessels of the United States* (Washington, DC: US Department of Commerce, Bureau of Navigation, 1918), 424, https://books.google.com/books?id=xP7rYdejc4wC&source=gbs_navlinks_s.

256 *Biographical Review*, 398–401 (E. Parker Welch born 1833); J. H. Hogan *1894 Directory*, 145 (mosser); Elizabeth Nilsson, Executive Director, Humane Society of Massachusetts, email, July 7, 2016; Howe, *The Humane Society*, 382-385; *Annual Report of the Officers & Committees of the Town of Scituate for the Year Ending December 31, 1937*, 182 (Christopher O'Neil death January 19, 1937); *1935 Town of Scituate Annual Report*, 116 (Jane O'Neil death December 1, 1935, age 84 years, 1 month, which differs from US Census records saying she was born about 1867); "Stranded Devonian Floated Undamaged: Big Steamship Lies Over Night Off Quarantine Station: Ashore 15 Hours in Dangerous Position off Third Cliff at Scituate," *Boston Daily [Globe]*, February 16, 1906, 1; Murphy, *Irish Mossers*, 45 (mosser in 1870 US census), 148-152 (reprinting Devonian articles in *Boston Globe*, February 16, 1906); "Effected Many Spectacular Rescues in Shipwrecks — He and Crew Risked Lives," Christopher O'Neil obituary clipping from unknown newspaper in possession of Ray Zucker, January 20, [1937] (source of quote); Humane Society of the Commonwealth of Massachusetts to Frank Fallon, deed, September 24, 1936, PCRD, book 1714, page 527, per Registry (PCRD) website, search for "Humane." Christopher O'Neil lived on Gilson Road, Third Cliff, according to (a) Judson's 1903 map, and (b) Assessor's hand-drawn plot plans, by street, about 1930–35, Town Archives.

257 Mary F. Supple to Christopher O'Neil, Jr., deed, September 25, 1919, PCRD, book 1338, page 503. Christopher sold the property in 1928. Christopher O'Neil, Jr., to Ray C. Johnson, deed, June 25, 1928, PCRD, book 1557, page 142. The *1926 Directory*, 67, lists Christopher, Jr., as a fisherman, living on Crescent Avenue on Second Cliff with his wife Mary.

258 Christopher O'Neil obituary, clipping from unidentified newspaper, January 20 [1937?], courtesy of Ray Zucker; 1930 and 1940 US Census; Ray Zucker email, June 23, 2017.

259 1930 US Census, Population Schedule, Scituate, Plymouth County, Massachusetts, District 99, sheet 9B, Third Cliff, dwelling 236, family number 238, lines 78-83, digital images, HeritageQuest, citing NARA microfilm publication T626, 2,667 rolls, roll not identified; "The Alden Line: Famous lovers left a huge

progeny," *LIFE* magazine, vol. 25, No. 22, November 29, 1948, 131 (with accompanying photo), https://books.google.com/books?id=tUoEAAAAMBAJ; conversation with Jerry Pallotta, July 21, 2016; conversation with Joby Norton, August 2, 2016; Registrars of Scituate, *Street List of Residents Twenty Years of Age and Over in the Town of Scituate as of January 1, 1956* (Boston: printed by Spaulding-Moss Co., 1956), SHS.

[260] Jack Farley, interview by author, November 18, 2016; John L. Sullivan, video interview with neighbors (left to right) Alice Gallagher, Polly Bowers, Dr. John Bowers, and Jack Farley, October 24, 2001 ("Sullivan interview"), in possession of John L. Sullivan. With Sullivan's permission, digital copies are in TCRIA archives, and with author, and on author's YouTube channel, https://www.youtube.com/channel/UCaIOjxJxV1cq3bx9XfxI-oQ.

[261] *Town Records, C-20*, unnumbered and undated page; Will Irwin, "Togo, Mayor of Scituate: A True Dog Story, Illustrations by Henry J. Soulen," *The American Magazine*, vol. 78, no. 2, August 1914 (New York: Phillips Pub. Co., 1914), 11–16 & 83–86, https://books.google.com/books?id=9Vg_AQAAMAAJ&source=gbs_navlinks_s.

[262] Conversation with Ray Zucker, May 26, 2017.

[263] *Osgood's New England*, 49.

[264] *Appletons' Hand-book of American Summer Resorts with Principal Routes of Travel* (New York: D. Appleton and Co., 1877), 152, https://catalog.hathitrust.org/Record/100327478. See also Bushrod Washington James, Aleksandr Ivanovich Voeïkov, *American Resorts: With Notes Upon Their Climate* (Philadelphia: F. A. Davis, 1889), 33, https://books.google.com/books?id=1i4wAAAAYAAJ&source=gbs_navlinks_s.

[265] "Watering Place Notes," *Sunday Herald* newspaper clipping [probably *Boston Sunday Herald*], June 17, 1877, from EC Manson/Edith Manson Freeman scrapbook, copy in "Hotels, Inns" file, SHS.

[266] "Along the South Shore," *Harper's New Monthly Magazine*, vol. 57, no. 337 (New York, Harper & Brothers, Publishers, June 1878), 1–14 at 8–11, https://books.google.com/books?id=IEtOAQAAMAAJ&source=gbs_navlinks_s.

[267] Hager & Handy, *History of the Old Colony Railroad*, 345.

[268] Letter from Joseph H. Turner, 1885 or 1886, to *The Carroll Record* (Carrollton, MO), reprinted in *South Shore News*, August 11, 1971, 24, Turner Family file, SHS.

[269] Perry, *A Trip Around Cape Cod*, 186-192, 252-253 (ads), https://catalog.hathitrust.org/Record/100493805.

[270] For example, Abigail Adams Homans (1879–1974) (likely photographer), "Kelper on Peggotty Beach," etc., Adams-Homans family photographs, Photo. Coll. 41 (XT), vol. 1, photographs 74, 75, 79, 80 and 82, August 29, 1891, Massachusetts Historical Society Photo Archives. See also photo of Peggotty Beach: unknown photographer, "Drying Irish moss, Scituate, Mass., C-835" (on reverse), file copy of Philadelphia Commercial Museum, Photographic Views Massachusetts, Roxbury-Worcester, Photo. Coll. 10, Massachusetts Historical Society Photo Archives.

[271] "The Seaweeds of the United States," *National Geographic Magazine*, vol. 16 (Washington, DC: National Geographic Society, May 1905), 244–245, photos from Hugh M. Smith, Bureau of Fisheries, https://books.google.com/books?id=vw8OAQAAIAAJ&source=gbs_navlinks_s. The same magazine describes gathering kelp and creating kombu in Japan in an article "The Fisheries of Japan" (starting at 201, see 211–215). A description of "Moss Fishing" is found in a September 10, 1885 letter from Joseph H. Turner to *The Carroll Record* (Carrollton, MO), reprinted in *South Shore News*, August 18, 1971, 36, Turner Family file, SHS.

[272] Dixon, "Two Scituates," 21–24, 36, and supporting "Table: Number of Scituate Non-resident Dwelling Owners as a Percentage of Number of Registered Voters [1869-1899]."

[273] "Scituate," *Boston Globe*, August 5, 1900.

[274] Thomas Engellenner, Fred Curtis, and William W. Seifert, eds., "The Boston South Shore Area: Some Problems and Conflicts" (n.p.: MIT National Sea Grant Program, Sea Grant Project 04-6-158-44007, 1977), 6, Coastal Zone Information Center, NOAA website, https://repository.library.noaa.gov/view/noaa/9634.

[275] MHC Reconnaissance Survey Town Report: Norwell, 1.

[276] Tolles, *Summer by the Seaside*, xvi, ch. 1 "Introduction," 89; O'Connell, *Becoming Cape Cod*, 47–49.

[277] Tolles, *Summer by the Seaside*, 38 (quoted). "Privatization" of space is Tolles's term. See also Lucy Carsen, "The Making of America's Great Northeast Summer Resorts," luxurydefined website by Christie's International Real Estate, posted June 27, 2019, https://www.christiesrealestate.com/blog/the-making-of-americas-great-northeast-summer-resorts/.

[278] "Summer Excursion Routes" (Philadelphia: Pennsylvania Railroad Co., 1884), 17 ("The summer colony will find most hospitable quarters at the Logan House" in Altoona, Pennsylvania), https://books.google.com/books?id=JwkIAAAAQAAJ&source=gbs_navlinks_s; "Table Gossip," *Boston Daily Globe*, August 21, 1887, 13 ("summer colony at Kennebunkport"); "By Sea and Mountain: Newport, R. I.," *Form: The Monthly Magazine of Society*, 39 (New York: Form Publishing Co., November 1898),

https://books.google.com/books?id=K5JEAQAAMAAJ&source=gbs_navlinks_s; "summer colony," Google Books Ngram Viewer; Slautterback, *Always Delightfully Cool*; Thomas Farragher, "A Connecticut home fit for Hollywood royalty," *Boston Globe*, March 29, 2017, Metro section, and with revised title, March 30, 2017, B1; Alison Arnold, "The Glades a tradition with the Adams family," *Boston Globe*, August 6, 1978, 61; Jane Anderson, "Offshore getaways, onshore hideaways," *Boston Globe*, June 16, 1977, B13. The *Boston Globe*, for example, used "summer colony" 42 times a year in 1900–1901, but this declined to two a year in 2012–2016.

279 *Merriam Webster's Collegiate Dictionary* (Springfield, MA: Merriam-Webster, Inc., 10th ed. 1993) (source of quote); Lyle Nyberg, "100 years ago: Locals spent the summer in Scituate," *Daily Times Chronicle*, April 18, 2017. Winchester residents discussed or mentioned in this book include families of Clarence Miller, Arthur Rogers, Howard Guild, Charles B. Stretch, and (of course) Thomas Lawson.

280 Many early Roman colonies were new foundations requiring construction of the walls, public buildings, and (later) houses. "Colonia" on Livius.org website, created in 2003, updated in 2017, http://www.livius.org/articles/concept/colonia/. Rivermoor did not have walls, or even gates as in today's gated communities.

281 *Merriam Webster's Collegiate Dictionary*.

282 National Weather Service, NOAA Online Weather Data, using Boston, "monthly summarized data," mean average temperatures for summer months in selected groups of three years (1891–93, 1901–03, 1914–16, 2014–16), showing temperature trends rather than daily highs, http://w2.weather.gov/climate/xmacis.php?wfo=box; Willis Carrier website, http://www.willliscarrier.com/about.php; Will Oremus, "A History of Air Conditioning," *Slate* magazine, posted July 15, 2013, originally published 2011, http://www.slate.com/articles/arts/culturebox/2011/07/a_history_of_air_conditioning.html.

283 Katie Redefer, "Revere Beach marks 125 years as the nation's first," *Boston Globe*, July 14, 2021, B3; "Revere Beach Reservation Historic District," National Park Service website, https://www.nps.gov/places/revere-beach-reservation-historic-district.htm.

284 Clifton Johnson, *Highways and Byways of New England, including the states of Massachusetts, New Hampshire, Rhode Island, Connecticut, Vermont and Maine* (New York: The Macmillan Company, 1915), 31, 83, 276–77 ("swim"), https://archive.org/details/highwaysbyways00john; O'Connell, *Becoming Cape Cod*, 32-33 and cover illustrations; Stilgoe, *Alongshore*, chapter 11 ("Bikinis"); unknown photographer, unnamed photos of children at beach (author's copy designation IMG_1001 and IMG_1064, for example), c. 1912, in "1900–1916," Woodworth family photograph album. Album is 10 in. by 12 in., with photos mostly 3 ¼ in. by 3 ¼ in., in possession of A. Vernon Woodworth III, who kindly allowed the author to photograph and scan the album; Vernon Woodworth, emails, July 7, 2016, and September 24, 2021.

285 O'Connell, *Becoming Cape Cod*, 32–33 and cover illustrations; Stilgoe, *Alongshore*, chapter 11 ("Bikinis"); "1900–1916," Woodworth family photograph album.

286 Rebecca M. Rogers, "Resort Architecture at Nahant 1815–1850," *Old Time New England*, vol. 65, no. 237 (Summer/Fall 1974), 20, Historic New England website, http://www.historicnewengland.org/preservation/your-older-or-historic-home/articles/pdf220.pdf; Lynn Chamber of Commerce website, http://lynnareachamber.com/town-of-nahant/; see Massachusetts Historical Commission, *MHC Reconnaissance Survey Town Report: Nahant* (Boston: Massachusetts Historical Commission, 1985), 11, https://www.sec.state.ma.us/mhc/mhcpdf/townreports/Essex/nah.pdf. These town reports are online at https://www.sec.state.ma.us/mhc/mhchpp/TownSurveyRpts.htm. See also Garland, *The North Shore*, 5–10 (first summer cottage on North Shore opened in 1820 in Nahant, and Nahant Hotel, first resort hotel, opened in 1823).

287 Massachusetts Historical Commission, *MHC Reconnaissance Survey Town Report: Oak Bluffs* (Boston: Massachusetts Historical Commission, 1984), 1–2, 8–9, http://www.sec.state.ma.us/mhc/mhcpdf/townreports/Cape/oak.pdf; "History of the Campground," Martha's Vineyard Campmeeting Association (MVCMA) website, http://www.mvcma.org/history.html. The MVCMA is a National Historic Landmark and was founded by the Methodists. The camp meeting movement started with tents. For another example of a camp community, also Methodist in origin, starting in 1872, see "Rehoboth Beach History," Rehoboth Beach, Delaware, website, http://www.rehoboth.com/community/town-history/34-rehoboth-beach-early-history.html.

288 O'Connell, *Becoming Cape Cod*, 13–16, 20.

289 In Hingham, 43 acres were subdivided for a resort hotel (Rose Standish House) and surrounding cottages, "Samuel Downer," Hingham Public Library website, formerly at https://hinghampubliclibrary.omeka.net/exhibits/show/legendary-locals/arts-entertainment/samuel-downer; Massachusetts Historical Commission, *MHC Reconnaissance Survey Town Report: Hingham* (Boston: Massachusetts Historical Commission, 1979), 9, https://www.sec.state.ma.us/mhc/mhcpdf/townreports/Eastern/hin.pdf;

see Slautterback, *Always Delightfully Cool*, 1879 Map, 34, 44. The rise (1870-1871) and fall (1896) of "Downersville," the Rose Standish House, and Melville Garden (with its bowling and shooting alleys, billiard tables, flying horses, menagerie, bear pit, and other attractions) are described in Lorena Laing Hart and Francis Russell Hart, *Not All Is Changed: A Life History of Hingham* (Hingham: Hingham Historical Commission, 1993), 164–168, 238–239. Even with such attractions gone, Crow Point remained a well-to-do summer colony through at least the 1930s, with golf, yachting, and tennis. Hart and Hart, *Not All Is Changed*, 346. The era of large resort hotels in Hingham began in 1832. Tolles, *Summer by the Seaside*, 63–67.

[290] Massachusetts Historical Commission, *MHC Reconnaissance Survey Town Report: Salisbury* (Boston: Massachusetts Historical Commission, 1985, updated 1997), 13–18, https://www.sec.state.ma.us/mhc/mhcpdf/townreports/Essex/sls.pdf; Dixon, "Two Scituates," 2-3, citing Betsy H. Woodman, "Salisbury Beach, 1638–1913: A Place to Gather," Essex Institute Historical Collections, vol. 124, no. 1 (1988), 38–74.

[291] Massachusetts Historical Commission, *MHC Reconnaissance Survey Town Report: Hull* (Boston: Massachusetts Historical Commission, 1979), 4–6, https://www.sec.state.ma.us/mhc/mhcpdf/townreports/Eastern/hul.pdf. The 1879 Map shows a thriving shore colony on its maps, 41-42, and on its large and splendid illustration by R. P. Mallory, "Nantasket Beach. View from Sagamore Hill," 40A, 41A. In 1905, Paragon Park came to Nantasket — a huge amusement park with carousel and roller coaster. Hart and Hart, *Not All Is Changed*, 254–255. Paragon Park is mentioned and pictured in a glowing review of Hull in "Chas. M. Rockwood, "Gateway of Boston Harbor," *New England Magazine: An Illustrated Monthly*, vol. 42, no. 6 (Boston: New England Magazine Co., August 1910), 693, https://books.google.com/books?id=Krs4AQAAMAAJ&source=gbs_navlinks_s. The era of large resort hotels in Hull and Nantasket began in 1848. Tolles, *Summer by the Seaside*, 63–67.

[292] "About World's End," website of The Trustees of Reservations, http://www.thetrustees.org/places-to-visit/south-shore/worlds-end.html. World's End is a peninsula with a "country park" begun in 1880 by having many trees planted and adding curving roads designed by Frederick Law Olmsted. Hart and Hart, *Not All Is Changed*, 216. After the threatened subdivision was averted in 1890, other development possibilities arose in 1967, including its use as a home for the United Nations; The Trustees of Reservations finally arranged for its purchase and preservation. Hart and Hart, *Not All Is Changed*, 406.

[293] Massachusetts Historical Commission, *MHC Reconnaissance Survey Town Report: Revere* (Boston: Massachusetts Historical Commission, 1981), 7, https://www.sec.state.ma.us/mhc/mhcpdf/townreports/Boston/rev.pdf; Kristin Toussaint, "This day 120 years ago, Revere opened as the nation's first public beach," July 12, 2016, *Boston Globe* website, https://www.boston.com/culture/history/2016/07/12/day-120-years-ago-revere-opened-nations-first-public-beach; "Revere Beach Reservation Historic District," US Department of the Interior, National Park Service, website, https://www.nps.gov/nr/travel/massachusetts_conservation/revere_beach_reservation.html. The 1875 opening of the Narrow Gauge railway from Boston had an explosive impact on Revere Beach, and eventually Winthrop, according to Garland, *The North Shore*, 152–162.

[294] Massachusetts Historical Commission, *MHC Reconnaissance Survey Town Report: Cohasset* (Boston: Massachusetts Historical Commission, 1979), 6, https://www.sec.state.ma.us/mhc/mhcpdf/townreports/Eastern/coh.pdf.

[295] Kathryn Grover, "Automobile-Age Tourism in Eastham, 1900–1960: A Context Statement," August 2005, prepared for the Eastham Historic Properties Survey Project, 23-24, and Larson Fisher Associates, "Town of Eastham Historic Properties Survey Project Final Report," August 15, 2005, Eastham's website, http://www.eastham-ma.gov/Public_Documents/EasthamMA_webdocs/HistoricResoureSurveys/Eastham%20Survey/.

[296] "Taxed to the Limit," *Boston Globe*, July 7, 1901, 1.

[297] D. N. Tower, Surveyor, *Plan of the Collier Field, North Scituate Beach*, scale 50 ft. to an inch, September 1891, PCRD, plan book 1, page 103, sheet 6 of 7.

[298] Bonney, *Scituate's Sands of Time*, 30 (source of quote), and see discussion at 30–31, and 77–79.

[299] *Boston Herald*, June 23, 1893, as quoted in Dixon, "Two Scituates," 36. For an excellent article showing the past of Minot (North Scituate Beach) with period postcards, see Kelly Anne Clinton, "Beach association looks to pass Minot Beach ownership to town of Scituate," *Scituate Mariner* website, posted October 20, 2011, http://www.wickedlocal.com/article/20111020/NEWS/310209823.

[300] McCallum & Young, *Cliff Hotel*, particularly 14 ("bluff" in ads from Summers era, 1914–1942); D. N. Tower, Surveyor, *Plan of the Collier Field, North Scituate Beach*, scale 50 ft. to an inch, September 1891, PCRD, plan book 1, page 103, sheet 6 of 7 ("bluff"); *1896 VL* (printed, in 1877 Town Report), 210–211 (Mary R. Cushing of Cohasset owning unfinished hotel valued at $5,000, many cottages, and new houses); various deeds, including Alice D. Place to Sarah J. Rich, deed, October 13, 1899, PCRD, book 784, page 525 (property on Collier

Avenue with right to use path to the beach, and "with a right to place a bath house not exceeding six feet square on the beach under said bluff."

301 The Scituate Beach Land Association Declaration of Trust, January 9, 1900, PCRD, book 799, pages 237–243; Articles of Agreement between H. A. Poole, et al, and Loyal Barton, et al, trustees of Scituate Beach Land Association, January 9, 1900, PCRD, book 799, page 236; L. Burton, *Plan No. 2 of Sea Shore Lots Owned by the Scituate Beach Land Association Located in Scituate, Mass.* [Gilson Road], 50 feet per inch, January 1, 1900, PCRD, plan book 1, page 215, sheet 4 of 4; Harrison L. House, C. E., *Plan No. 1 of Sea Shore Lots Owned by the Scituate Beach Land Association, August 13, 1902*, 1 inch = 100 feet, PCRD, plan book 2, page 62, last sheet.

302 L. Burton, *Plan No. 2 of Sea Shore Lots*; various searches by author for Scituate Beach Land Association and George Welch at PCRD website and onsite grantor-grantee indexes.

303 J. H. Hogan *1894 Directory*, 134; *1901 VL*, 28; Fred Freitas, email, August 28, 2018 (account by Frederick Stanley, keeper of Fourth Cliff station); *Annual Report of the Operations of the United States Life-Saving Service for the Fiscal Year Ending June 30, 1884* (Washington: Government Printing Office, 1885), https://books.google.com/books?id=wHgDAAAAYAAJ&source=gbs_navlinks_s.

304 Lyle Nyberg, Joseph Flynn house, 72 Gilson Road, SCI.1180, MACRIS; *1918 Directory*; E. Parker Welch to Joseph Flynn, deed, January 16, 1901, PCRD, book 814, page 442, and correcting deed, April 2, 1901, PCRD, book 818, page 329; L. Burton, *Plan No. 2 of Sea Shore Lots Owned by the Scituate Beach Land Association Located in Scituate, Mass.* [Gilson Road], 50 feet per inch, January 1, 1900, PCRD, plan book 1, page 215, sheet 4 of 4; John Curran et ux to John Flaherty, deed, March 25, 1884, PCRD, book 505, page 278 ("highway leading to the beach or sea"); *1901 VL*, 28 (new house valued at $1,500); 1910 US Census, Scituate, Plymouth, Massachusetts; Roll: T624_613; Page: 5A; Enumeration District: 1245; FHL microfilm: 1374626, Ancestry.com, 1910 United States Federal Census [database on-line]. Lehi, UT, USA; Elmer G. Allan, Commissioner [appointed to partition real estate owned by the late Joseph Flynn] to John J. Hughes and Alice T. Hughes, deed, December 18, 1944, PCRD, book 1879, page 168.

305 E. Parker Welch to Joseph Flynn, deed, January 16, 1901, PCRD, book 814, page 442, and correcting deed, April 2, 1901, PCRD, book 818, page 329 (including "a right to take water for home use from the spring on the westerly side of said land in common with others"). See also separate discussions of "the falls" on the Cliff, and later town water and sewer connections.

306 Judson, 1903 map, plates 31 and 32 (inset); Dixon, "Two Scituates," 31, 37; "Scituate: Shore's Manifold Attractions Draw Large Numbers," *Boston Globe*, July 30, 1905, 10. The Barker Farm Beach development shown on the 1903 map encompassed the Scituate Beach Land Association's subdivision around Hatherly Road and, further east, a large parcel that became the subject of a later subdivision plan for Barker Farm, George H. Wetherbee Jr., *Sea Shore Lots at Barker Farm, Scituate, Mass., Owned by Otis Barker*, scale on map, April 1911, PCRD, plan book 1, page 783.

307 DAR, *Old Scituate*, 96.

308 Deane, *History of Scituate*, 150.

309 WPA card file, Town Archives, under "Third Cliff Road Committee," summarizing document in Vol. C-9, pages 177–178, April 1, 1833, and same document in Town of Scituate Records.

310 Torrey, Home! or the Pilgrims' Faith Revived, 15.

311 1854 Report of a Survey of Scituate Harbor and North River, 8.

312 Wilkins, "Historical Sketch," *North Scituate Beach*, third page of the Wilkins sketch; Murphy, *The Coming of Age*, 149–150 (street names).

313 E. Parker Welch et ux to John Curran, deed, April 9, 1863, PCRD, book 317, pages 42–43.

314 George F. Welch to Sarah E. Young, deed, December 15, 1905, recorded November 7, 1923, PCRD, book 42518, page 359.

315 Agnes L. Coffin to John R. Coffin, deed, May 26, 1931, PCRD, book 1614, page 84.

316 "How the Sea Eats Away Third Cliff, Scituate." *Boston Globe*, January 23, 1910, SM12.

317 Linda Barnhart, interview by author, May 1, 2016; TCRIA, Inc., "The Heritage of Third Cliff," in Third Cliff-Rivermoor Newsletter (Summer 1986), 3, courtesy of Gail Ledwig, containing reminiscences of resident Sabina Welch, who was born in the house at 138 Gilson Road in 1885, and later lived there and owned the property; Sabina was of a different Welch family from the Michael E. Parker-George F. Welch family. "Stephen Joyce House," 138 Gilson Road, SCI.101, MACRIS. A deed of property in the Bassin Lane area at the north end of the cliff refers to Falls. Thomas Flynn to Annie W. Wallace, deed, September 25, 1900, PCRD, book 806, page 360 ("thence easterly by the sea to a stake and land of Freeman Coffin at the Falls"). A later deed, probably also in the Bassin Lane area, conveys a lot of 11,232 square feet "commencing at the southeast corner on the brow of the Third Cliff or Falls adjoining land now owned by Margaret Stanley and running along the brow of the Cliff." George F. Welch to William N. Ambler, deed, December 24, 1918, PCRD, book 1312, page

553. The stories of washerwomen perhaps involve waterfalls at the south end of the cliff. Deeds of property at what is now 137 Gilson Road describe the property as bounded "Easterly by the Falls" (1882), or "easterly by the Cliff or Falls" (1915), and a deed of property a bit further south, at the east end of the Driftway, refers to "the Falls, so called." Martin Curran to John Curran [brother], deed, April 1, 1882, PCRD, book 478, page 230; Mary F. O'Connor to Charles P. Curran [brother], deed, March 25, 1915, PCRD, book 1214, page 30; John M. Corcoran, Trustee of the Bailey Realty Trust, to Ruth B. [Bailey] Gammon, deed, June 27, 1968, PCRD, book 3451, page 243 (Parcel 3). The waterfalls may have included the watercourse shown running west to east and exiting down the cliff to the ocean on the 1906 Rivermoor plan. References to "Falls" most likely meant waterfalls rather than rock falls, an uncommon usage. There are no waterfalls today.

318 Krusell and Bates, *Marshfield*, 6 (map), 144 (map), 150; Galluzzo, *The North River*, 83–88, 112; *1854 Report of a Survey of Scituate Harbor and North River*; Warren Upham, "The Structure of Drumlins," Proceedings of the Boston Society of Natural History, vol. 24 (Boston: printed for the Society, 1890) [presented April 17, 1889], 228–242, at 231 (source of quote), https://books.google.com/books?id=qnpGAQAAMAAJ&source=gbs_navlinks_s;

319 Briggs, *Shipbuilding on North River* (1889), 198 (source of quote).

320 Deane, *History of Scituate*, 114.

321 John Curran et ux to John Flaherty, deed, March 25, 1884, PCRD, book 505, page 278; E. Parker Welch to John Curran deed, April 9, 1863. The earlier deed says "Said sale is made on the condition that said Grantee his heirs and Assigns shall make all the partition fence on the south and west sides and maintain the same forever. And said Grantor reserves from the Sale all rights of the Beach or the sea-shore opposite said granted land however the same may hereafter be moved by the inroads of the sea on or over said granted land." Similar language appeared in the later deed. The stone wall ("partition fence") between the 3 Driftway and 9 Collier Road properties still existed as of mid-2018.

322 Telephone conversation with Charles "Chick" Fagan, a Clapp descendant, May 1, 2018.

323 Murphy, *Irish Mossers*, 145–147; *Harbor and Land Commissioners, Plan of New Mouth*. The *1906 VL* entry for George Welch's "Lamprey House Lot" (later 16 Collier Road) includes the notation "abandoned front," perhaps indicating the erosion or destruction of land next to the ocean.

324 Jack Farley, interview by author, November 18, 2016. John Flynn and William Flynn are listed (along with other Flynns) on Gilson Road or Third Cliff in a 1937 listing of residents, and their ages indicate they were born in 1884–1885. Assessors of Scituate, *List of Persons Twenty Years of Age and Older Residing in Town of Scituate on January 1, 1937* (Scituate: The Satuit Press, 1937), SHS.

325 The otherwise admirable 1903 map by Judson shows the new mouth of the North River, but it has a fault that is relevant to assessing the damage inflicted by the 1898 storm. The angle at which Water Street traverses the cliff and intersects with Gilson Road is inaccurate. If used as a basis for comparing later maps, it suggests that the whole part of the cliff south of Water Street (all of Rivermoor) was shifted sideways to the west. In fact, there was no such shift, as is clear by comparing later maps, such as USGS maps, with a pre-storm 1893 USGS map (and an 1888 map on which it was based). US Geological Survey, *Massachusetts, Duxbury Sheet [Quadrangle]* [map], 1:62,500 (Washington DC: USGS, 1893), USGS Store, http://ngmdb.usgs.gov/maps/TopoView/viewer/#13/42.1590/-70.7217 (click on "62,000," then center of map, then "8 maps," then 1893 map, any edition before 1918, when the new mouth was finally shown). The 1903 map correctly has the southern end of Third Cliff pointing south, rather than southwest as shown on prior coastal survey maps. For example, see C. O. Boutelle, et al., *Coast charts no. 9 & 10, Massachusetts Bay with the coast from Cape Ann to Cape Cod* (Washington, DC: United States Coast Survey, 1872, 1877, corrected 1885), map, scale 1:80,000, Lionel Pincus and Princess Firyal Map Division, The New York Public Library, New York Public Library Digital Collections, http://digitalcollections.nypl.org/items/568cb7d0-527c-0134-bc1b-00505686a51c.

326 Michael Carlowicz, "Coastline Change," NASA Earth Observatory website, posted June 12, 1984, updated through August 2020, http://earthobservatory.nasa.gov/Features/WorldOfChange/cape_cod.php. See also Rob L. Evans, "Rising Sea Levels and Moving Shorelines: New tools and techniques show promise for better predictions and decisions about coastline change," *Oceanus Magazine*, vol. 43, no. 1 (Woods Hole, MA: Woods Hole Oceanographic Institution, November 2004), published online at http://www.whoi.edu/oceanus/feature/rising-sea-levels-and-moving-shorelines; "Beach Basics" excerpts from Orrin H. Pilkey, Tracy Monegan Rice, and William J. Neal, *How to Read a North Carolina Beach* (Chapel Hill: University of North Carolina Press, 2004), at Coastal Care website of Santa Aguila Foundation, http://coastalcare.org/educate/beach-basics/.

327 One report estimated the spit moved 300 feet west. Wallace, "Coastal Zone Study, Phase II," 59. This seems grossly understated. Based on the 1879 Map, the 300-foot erosion of the *cliff* mentioned in the text, and current

Google maps, the author estimates the southern tip of the spit has moved more than 3,000 feet west of its location before the storm of 1898. See author's paper "Notes on a Photo Showing Beach That Connected Third and Fourth Cliffs," SHS. See also Dicus, *Window Seat*, 33.

[328] For example, an early photo (in the possession of Nancy Howell) shows a house on the east (ocean) side of Collier Road at Cliff Avenue about 1909. No later maps show this house, and today the plot is too small, the cliff is too close, for a house.

[329] 1854 Report of Survey of Scituate Harbor and North River, 8.

[330] WPA card file, Town Archives, under "Third Cliff," summarizing document S-106, page 115, January 31, 1924, a document that is in a portion of the Selectmen's Records that is missing from the Town Archives.

[331] Third Cliff-Rivermoor Association newsletter, Autumn 1984, in Association's archives, said:

> An unofficial measurement has been taken concerning the erosion of the edge of the Cliff. The last recorded measurement was taken from the corner of the Festus Nee House on the Driftway in 1879. The same measurement was taken last week indicating that the Cliff has eroded 300 feet (approximately) during the time elapsed. This study was part of individual research being conducted by a naturalist who makes her home on Third Cliff and who spends her time enjoying and studying the beauties of our Cliff and Beach.

[332] "Third Cliff, Showing Steps, Scituate, Mass.," postcard, early 1900s, back labeled "E. Feola, Printer, Scituate," SHS (Hobson collection?). The beach at the northern end of Third Cliff seems to have been at least 30 feet wide, according to Harrison L. House, C. E., *Plan of Land at North End of Third Cliff, Scituate, Mass., 1921*, 1 inch = 40 feet, PCRD, plan book 3, serial no. 3129, page 69; Robert Jackman email to author, January 18, 2016. In addition, an early photo of the beach connecting Third and Fourth Cliffs before the storm of 1898 shows a beach going along and around the south end of the cliff (photo courtesy of Historical Research Associates). The fronting beach appears in several postcards, some of which are copied elsewhere in this book.

[333] *Acts and Resolves of the General Court of Massachusetts, 1906* (Boston: Wright & Potter Printing Co., State Printers, 1906), ch. 496 and ch. 536, https://archive.org/details/actsresolvespass1906mass, mentioned in Murphy, *The Coming of Age*, 104; Wallace, "Coastal Zone Study, Phase II," 59, and App. E "Massachusetts Division of Waterways, Foreshore Protection Projects, Town of Scituate (Partial Listing, 1921-1971);" Jim O'Connell, "Shoreline Change: Coastal Landform Management Dilemma," in Tracey I. Crago and Sheri D. DeRosa, eds., "Coastal Landform Management in Massachusetts: Proceedings of a Workshop held at the Woods Hole Oceanographic Institution, Woods Hole, MA USA October 9–10, 1997," Woods Hole Oceanog. Inst. Tech. Rept., WHOI-98-16 or WHOI Sea Grant Report WHOI-W-97-001 (Woods Hole, MA, 1998), 15, 21-22, https://www.whoi.edu/fileserver.do?id=74625&pt=2&p=88900; WPA card file, Town Archives, under "Third Cliff," summarizing document C-12, page 494, March 10, 1919, and same document, recording Special Town Meeting approval of Article 3, and *Annual Report of the Officers of the Town of Scituate for the Year Ending December 31, 1919*, 84 (Town Meeting approved Article 3 appropriating $1,500 for breakwater at Third Cliff, although it is not clear that it was spent); *Annual Report of the Officers and Committees of the Town of Scituate for the Year Ending December 31, 1931*, at "Report of Selectmen," 10. In the 1930s, and perhaps more generally, shorefront landowners were required to sign a consent (with limited release of liability) for the government's construction of a seawall or other type of shore protection, as shown by what appears to be a standard typed form signed by Harriet H. Miller, Trustee [owner of lots 206 and 207 and the way between them, along with "the house that Harriet built"], October 10, 1933, Town Archives. An early-1900s postcard shows a boardwalk or possibly forms for pouring a cement seawall around the southern end of Third Cliff, near the house at the end of Michael Avenue. "Fourth Cliff and North River Cut, Scituate, Mass. Copyright W. N. Seaver," courtesy of Paul Bowers.

[334] "Third Cliff, Scituate, Mass.," aerial photo postcard, photo by Almac Studio, Marshfield, MA, published by Community Press, Inc., SHS (Hobson collection?); Goldberg-Zoino & Associates, Inc., "Investigation of Third Cliff, Scituate, Massachusetts," report, prepared for Board of Selectmen, Scituate, Massachusetts, File No. 1361 (April 1975), figure 1361-1 (showing end of old seawall at northern end of Third Cliff), Town Archives.

[335] See *Murphy v. Conway*, 20 LCR 26a, MISC 06-317624 (Trial Court, Land Court Department, Plymouth County, 2012), Massachusetts Cases website, at "Evolution of Third Cliff" section, http://masscases.com/cases/land/20/20lcr26.html.

[336] See Google Earth Timelapse for an approximation.

[337] Lori, "See the Photos from the King Tides, Oct. 17–19, 2016!" NSRWA website, posted October 13, 2016, https://www.nsrwa.org/help-us-document-king-tide-oct-17-19-2016/, and linked photos at https://mycoast.org/reports/29685.

[338] *North and South Rivers Guide*; Vinal, *Salt Haying in the North River Valley*, 6–8, 16, 25–26; Murphy, *The Coming of Age*, 49 (source of quote); Thomas Buford Meteyard, *Scituate, North River*, c. 1894, in *Scenes from Vagabondia*, 62

(for example); Harrison L. House, *Town of Scituate Mass* [Assessor's maps], May 1938 with various revisions, latest March 2015, 1 inch = 1,000 feet, Sheet 64, July 17, 1922, 1 inch = 100 feet, on display at Scituate Town Hall. The 1922 version of sheet 64 is on file in Town Archives. The current version of the map, at least for sheet 64 (which covers Rivermoor), is essentially the same as the 1922 version (lot numbers, lot locations, street locations, and geographical features including cliff edges), but with added house footprints, parcel IDs, and street numbers. As to mosquito control on Cape Cod from the late 1920s to the 1990s, see McConnell, *Becoming Cape Cod*, 51–52.

[339] Galluzzo, *The North River*, 67–71, with photo of boundary ditch on 69; author review of various aerial photos, and author review of Google Maps/Satellite Views, October 7, 2016; The Great Marsh website of the Great Marsh Coalition, https://greatmarshcoalition.org/.

[340] Author's observations; E. K. Soper and C. C. Osbon, Bulletin 728, "The Occurrence and Uses of Peat in the United States," (Washington, DC: US Department of the Interior, US Geological Survey, 1922). Peatland is both a sink and a source (if disturbed) of carbon dioxide that contributes to global warming. William Booth, "Serious about climate change? Get serious about peat." *Washington Post*, November 10, 2021, https://www.washingtonpost.com/world/2021/11/10/cop26-peat-carbon/; Chris Mooney, "An enormous missing contribution to global warming may have been right under our feet," *Washington Post*, June 4, 2021, https://www.washingtonpost.com/climate-environment/2021/06/04/an-enormous-missing-contribution-global-warming-may-have-been-right-under-our-feet/.

[341] Author trek on Rivermoor beach with Paul Bowers, September 17, 2016; 1879 Map; photo of beach connecting Third and Fourth Cliffs before 1898, courtesy of Historical Research Associates; DAR, *Old Scituate*, 242–243; House, *Town of Scituate Mass* [Assessor's maps], Sheet 64. For a description of a different landscape in Scotland of rocks and peat, not next to the ocean, see Robert Macfarlane, *The Old Ways: A Journey on Foot* (New York: Penguin Books, 2013),"Peat" chapter starting at 139.

[342] "Shorebirds: What Are They? Why Collect Them?," RJG Antiques website, http://www.rjgantiques.com/Learn_Shorebirds.aspx; Cronon, *Changes in the Land*, 23, 31, 100; John M. Levinson, Somers G. Headley, *Shorebirds: The Birds, the Hunters, the Decoys* (Centreville, MD: Tidewater Publishers/Schiffer Publishing, 1991), 29-31, https://books.google.com/books?id=mZG-315AlxEC&source=gbs_navlinks_s; McConnell, *Becoming Cape Cod*, 4–5 (Webster and others), 40 (Chatham in the 1860s); Gurdon Trumbull, *Names and Portraits of Birds which Interest Gunners, with Descriptions in Language Understood of the People* (New York: Harper & Brothers, 1888), https://archive.org/details/namesportraitsof00trum (targets of the gunners); Murphy, *Tourists' Guide to Down the Harbor*, 31 (coot shooting at Cohasset coast), 36 (hunting "sea fowl" at Brant Rock in Marshfield).

[343] Perry, *A Trip Around Cape Cod,* 195 (source of quote).

[344] Vinal, *Salt Haying in the North River Valley,* 24–25. See images in Dorothy Clapp Langley, compiler, *Clapp: Record of Clapp Family of Greenbush, Mass. 1866–1986* (Portland, ME: Fit to Print, 1987), 29–30, Scituate Town Library.

[345] Bonney, *My Scituate*, 40.

[346] 1903 map, sub plan, plate 32.

[347] Clifton Johnson, *Highways and Byways of New England*, 186.

[348] Levinson & Headley, *Shorebirds: The Birds, the Hunters, the Decoys*, 32.

[349] *Cohasset Cottager*, 1, column 6, October 27, 1883, https://archive.org/stream/10271883CohassetCottager_ppml/10_27_1883%20Cohasset%20Cottager#page/n0/mode/2up/search/scituate.

[350] Galluzzo, *The North River*, 83–85; Joseph Foster Merritt, *Old Time Anecdotes of the North River and the South Shore* (Rockland, MA: Rockland Standard Publishing Company, 1928), 18, photograph after 18, 72, https://catalog.hathitrust.org/Record/010027973; Lysander Salmon Richards, *History of Marshfield* (Plymouth: The Memorial Press, 1901), 212–214, https://archive.org/details/historymarshfie01richgoog; "Storm's Ravages at Scituate," *Boston Globe*, November 29, 1898, 7.

[351] Dwelley and Simmons, *History of Hanover*, 275 (game laws and Massachusetts law of 1906 protecting songbirds and insectivorous birds). Market-hunting for waterfowl was outlawed early in the 1900s, notably by the Weeks-McLean Act of 1913. Nelson Bryant, "Outdoors; Decoys Bring High Prices," *New York Times*, May 18, 1986, http://www.nytimes.com/1986/05/18/sports/outdoors-decoys-bring-high-prices.html; Hillary, "Centennial Milestone," blog post (excerpt from *Sanctuary* magazine), posted March 14, 2013, and reply, http://blogs.massaudubon.org/yourgreatoutdoors/2013/03/. The federal Migratory Bird Hunting Stamp Act, effective in 1934, required annual Duck Stamps in addition to state licenses to hunt ducks, geese, swans or brant. Proceeds from the stamps have been used to purchase waterfowl refuges, making this one of the most

successful conservation programs. "History of the Federal Duck Stamp," US Fish & Wildlife Service website, https://www.fws.gov/birds/get-involved/duck-stamp/history-of-the-federal-duck-stamp.php.

[352] Hayes Robbins, "An Old Town by the Sea," *New England Magazine* (Boston: America Co., April 1904), vol. 30, no. 2 [in collected issues, March-August, 1904], 167–174, at 167 and 172 (source of quote), https://archive.org/details/newenglandmagaziv30bost; Trumbull, *Names and Portraits of Birds which Interest Gunners*. Hunting for shorebirds in season (in this case, July 15 to August 1) is described in Walter Drew, "Shore Bird Shooting," *The Sportsman's Magazine*, vol. 1, no. 1, October 1896 (New York: The Sportsman's Magazine Co., 1896), 2–13, https://books.google.com/books?id=308QAAAAYAAJ&source=gbs_navlinks_s; see also "Shore Bird Shooting" chapter in Richard D. Ware, *In the Woods and On the Shore* (Boston: L. C. Page & Co., 1908), 69–105, https://books.google.com/books?id=swcIAwAAQBAJ&source=gbs_navlinks_s; Galluzzo, *The North River*, 77 (hotel catering to shorebird hunters in spring and fall).

[353] Ball, *To the Point*, 30, with 1912 photo and recipe for coot stew.

[354] Jones, "The Rise of a Coastal Leisure Destination"; Krusell and Bates, *Marshfield*, 55 (coot hunting and recipe for coot stew); Grover, "Automobile-Age Tourism in Eastham," 7-9.

[355] Nicholas Kilmer, ed., "Thomas Buford Meteyard Paintings and Watercolors," Exhibition Catalog (New York: Berry-Hill Galleries, Inc., 1989), 60 (*Fisher Huts, Summer, Scituate*, c. 1893, showing six huts), 63 (*Hummerock, Scituate*, c. 1900-06, showing about six huts). *Scenes from Vagabondia: Thomas Buford Meteyard & Dawson Dawson-Watson From Giverny to Scituate, 1890–1910*, Exhibition Catalog (Cambridge, MA: Pierre Menard Gallery, 2009), has Meteyard's wonderful abstract views of the cliffs and the connecting beach between Third Cliff and Fourth Cliff without huts: 17 (*Third and Fourth Cliffs, Scituate*, 1893), 58 (*Marshes*, 1893–1894), 78 (*Scituate, Red and Green, The Dunes*, c. 1894). The catalog also has Meteyard's views of what appears to be the connecting beach with various quantities of huts: 69 (*Winter on the Marsh*, 1894, three huts), 74 (*Fishers' Huts, Summer, Scituate*, c. 1894, seven huts), 75 (*Mossers' Huts*, c. 1894, eight huts), 76 (*The Marsh, Scituate*, c. 1894, perhaps twenty huts). See also Libby Bischof, "Testudo: A Forgotten New England Artists' Retreat," *Nineteenth Century* 30, 2 (2010), 21–29; David B. Dearinger, "Thomas Buford Meteyard (1865–1928): Travels through Impressionism" (Boston: Boston Athenaeum 2017), exhibition catalog.

[356] Paula Buckley letter to Mrs. Polly Bowers, probably 1986. The letter said that 50 Collier (where she summered for many years) "had been originally a fishing/hunting shack & was probably built (the back part) about 1900." The "Cedar Camp" cottage at 77 Collier, discussed below, is another possible example of a hunting shack.

[357] *1910 VL*, 134 (prior valuation lists did not break out this cottage or its lot); House, *Town of Scituate Mass*, Sheet 64 (street addresses); J. H. Hogan *1894 Directory*, 322-323; Phyllis Haskell (granddaughter of Charles W. Thomas) to author, letter, June 11, 2019; Massachusetts Secretary of State "Search for Citations to Vital Record (1841 - 1910)" website; various US census records; author's review of deeds recorded at Plymouth County Registry of Deeds, including George F. Welch to Charles W. Thomas and Alpheus W. Thomas, deed, August 3, 1908, PCRD, book 1034, page 493, and Charles W. Thomas and Alpheus W. Thomas to Rachel W. Cartland, deed, August 2, 1937, PCRD, book 1728, page 521; author's review of Assessor's Database and US census records for the Thomases; *Scituate Herald*, July 10, 1931, 7 ("Mr. and Mrs. Alpheus Thomas spent the holiday week-end at their cottage at Rivermoor").

[358] 1918 Sanborn map, sheet 8; author's observations and review of Assessor's Database; "Cedar Camp," 77 Collier Road, SCI.1131, MACRIS (including author's continuation sheets). The second smallest cottage on Third Cliff seems to be the historical Stephen Joyce House at 138 Gilson Road (760 square feet), discussed elsewhere in the text, based on the author's review of Assessor's Database. The North River marshes were known for their cedar trees. Bangs, *Seventeenth-Century Town Records*, vol. 1, 13.

[359] Maria Ellis (Baker) Thomas (born 1859), diary entry for late November or early December 1898, courtesy of Phyllis Haskell, copy on file with author.

[360] Haskell letter; Phyllis Haskell emails, June 17 & 18, 2019; *Scituate Herald*, September 13, 1935, 6 ("Charles Thomas loaned many of his stuffed game birds to local Sportsman's clubs for exhibition purposes at Brockton Fair"); Robert Knox, "Hingham folk artist carved a place in duck decoy history," *Boston Globe*, September 18, 2014, https://www.bostonglobe.com/metro/regionals/south/2014/09/17/hingham-folk-artist-joe-lincoln-carved-place-duck-decoy-history/9pmbuNC2Y2CnBLooMCnAFM/story.html.; Maryellen Dever, "Carving Out A Place in a South Shore," *South Shore Magazine*, posted about 2015, https://www.thesouthshoremagazine.com/1240/folk-art-tradition/.

[361] Carol E. & John N. Mesheau, *Ridge Hill, Norwell, Massachusetts, and the World Around It, 1600–1955* (Norwell: Holly Acres Publications, 1997), 343-345, incl. n. 28 (source of quote), SHS; Phyllis Haskell email, March 1, 2021 (noting that the photo on page 344 identified as Clem with his mounted birds is really Charles). Deeds

and plans on file in PCRD indicate the later shop was at 34 High Street, just off Washington Street, and not far south of Queen Anne's Corner.

362 Valerie Vitali, telephone interview by author, September 4, 2016; see also Valerie Vitali, president, Third Cliff-Rivermoor Association to Scituate Board of Health, May 16, 1988, and Valerie Vitali, "Commentary," *Scituate Mariner*, c. 1989, both in Association's archives.

363 *Forty-First Annual Report of the Receipts and Expenditures of the Town of Norwell and Reports of Its Several Official Boards and Officers, for the Year 1890* (Boston: Town of Norwell, 1891), 39, https://books.google.com/books?id=FDsb3iGREqIC&source=gbs_navlinks_s; *Fifty-First Annual Report of the Town Officers of the Town of Norwell for the Year Ending Dec. 31, 1900* (Rockland: Free Press Publishing Co., 1901), 7, 10, 26, https://archive.org/details/townofnorwellann1900unse/page/n2; *Journal of the Thirty-Ninth National Encampment of the Grand Army of the Republic, Denver, Colorado, September 7th and 8th, 1905* (Boston: n.p., 1905), 26, https://books.google.com/books?id=WqH1bHilKDMC&source=gbs_navlinks_s; *Acts and Resolves Passed by the General Court of Massachusetts in the Year 1892* (Boston: Secretary of the Commonwealth, 1892), chapter 151, page 139, https://books.google.com/books?id=3VZNAQAAMAAJ&source=gbs_navlinks_s.

364 C. C. Lynch, "STILL AT LARGE. 'Jack, the Wild Man,' Causes a Scare. Norwell Citizens Keep Their Doors Barred. Sentries Posted on the Lone Highways. Possible Solution of the Town's Mystery. Missing Farm Laborer May be the Man." *Boston Globe*, September 9, 1891, 4, copied in Loren Coleman, *Monsters of Massachusetts: Mysterious Creatures in the Bay State* (Mechanicsburg, PA: Stackpole Books, 2013), 71, https://books.google.com/books?id=xZxxAAAAQBAJ&source=gbs_navlinks_s, and "Valley Swamp Monster" post by Loren Coleman, June 27, 2010, on CryptoZooNews website, http://www.cryptozoonews.com/vllyswmon/; *Boston Globe*, September 9, 1891, 2 (extra edition). The 1879 map, page 32, and the 1903 map, plate 17, both show Alpheus Thomas on Washington Street just east of Queen Anne's Corners, and E. B. Damon on Grove Street, just east of Prospect Street (where today there are four-way stop signs). The 1903 map shows the Valley Swamp just west of E. B. Damon's house and farm, where the "Wild Man" was spotted.

365 See, generally, tax valuation lists, 1903 map, and author searches for Scituate Beach Land Association at PCRD.

366 Water Street was renamed the Driftway, its original name, in 1915, per Charles Lincoln, "Streets of Scituate" (compiled 1950), SHS. The Stephen Joyce house of the 1870s was on property conveyed to Martin Curran, who conveyed it to John Welch in 1882, and it stayed in that Welch family (unrelated to the Michael Welch family), including Sabina Welch, for several generations up to 1990. SHS file on 138 Gilson Road and deeds referenced therein; Martin Curran to John Welch, deed, January 9, 1882, PCRD, book 475, page 459; Assessor's Database.

367 E. Parker Welch to William H. Welch, deed, July 5, 1901, PCRD, book 1260, page 460; E. Parker Welch to Minnie L. Welch, deed, July 5, 1901, PCRD, book 1172, page 384.

368 E. Parker Welch to George F. Welch, deed, August 27, 1902, PCRD, book 864, page 108; Johnson manuscript; *1918 Directory*, 60.

369 The town's annual report for 1904 records in detail the town way (Collier) laid out at the Third Cliff. *Annual Report of the Town Officers of the Town of Scituate for the Year Ending December 31, 1904*, 80–83 (Selectmen determination December 22, 1904). The Town Meeting of March 6, 1905, accepted the layout of the road and appropriated $1,500 to build it. *Annual Report of the Town Officers of the Town of Scituate for the Year Ending December 31, 1905*, 72 (Article 23). See also "Alteration. Collier Road. Third Cliff." entry February 23, 1924, *Town Records, C-17* [vol. 28], 240–241 (making upper end of Collier Road, laid out in 1905, a uniform width of 35 feet), and "Collier Road and Moorland Road from Lincoln Avenue to Lincoln Ave." entry February 23, 1924, *Town Records, C-17* [vol. 28], 243–245 (accepting "all portions of Collier Road and Moorland Road not accepted by the Town of Scituate in the years 1905 and 1921"), Town Archives.

370 See Marc A. Weiss, *The Rise of the Community Builders: The American Real Estate Industry and Urban Land Planning* (Washington, DC: Beard Books, 1987, 2002 reprint), 6-7, 17, https://books.google.com/books?id=ZXjddnZYyLYC&source=gbs_navlinks_s.

371 Frank S. Alger [publisher], "People I Have Known in Scituate," *Marshfield Mail*, August 28, 1936, 3, Marshfield Historical Society, Newspapers and Clippings Box 2, reference 2008.0112; "In Memoriam" section at front of *Annual Report of the Town Officers and Committees of the Town of Scituate for the Year Ending December 31, 1939*.

372 Ripley Hitchcock, "Summer Home: The Organization of Summer Communities," *The Outing Magazine*, vol. 52 (New York: The Outing Publishing Co., 1908), 498, https://books.google.com/books?id=06g2AQAAIAAJ&source=gbs_navlinks_s.

[373] Town of Scituate, "A List of Taxable Polls and Estates in the Town of Scituate for the Year 1906," 114-115, bound at the end of *Annual Report of the Town Officers of the Town of Scituate for the Year Ending December 31, 1906*. The *1906 VL* has about 1,100 entries for resident taxpayers and 600 for nonresident taxpayers.

[374] Stephen Litchfield, Surveyor, *Plan of Rivermoor, 3rd Cliff Scituate Mass, Owned by George F. Welch* (April 1, 1906), 1 inch = 50 feet, PCRD, plan book 1, serial no. 1548, page 560 ("1906 plan"). The plan's lot numbers are still used in the Assessor's current map, so the plan is a key document to convert lot numbers to street addresses, and was so used by the author. House, *Town of Scituate Mass* [Assessor's maps], Sheet 64.

[375] 1906 plan.

[376] There was no lot number for the large triangular area east of Collier Road between Water Street and Parker Avenue, which E. Parker Welch had sold in 1863. E. Parker Welch et ux to John Curran, deed, April 9, 1863, PCRD, book 317, pages 42-43. Nor was there a lot number for the large quadrilateral area (showing two houses) on the inner part of the block on Water Street between Moorland Road and Collier Road. E. Parker Welch had sold that property to his older brother in 1902. E. Parker Welch to Charles P. Welch, deed, August 25, 1902, PCRD, book 996, page 325. The deed described the property as about ¾ acre having two small cottages "known as the Welch & McNelley." The property lines were straightened in 1912 to correspond with the linear 1906 plan. Charles P. Welch to George F. Welch, deed, and George F. Welch to Charles P. Welch, deed, both of January 1, 1912, PCRD, book 1110, pages 286 & 287. Charles Welch sold the property in 1917. Charles P. Welch to Clinton L. Newell, deed, September 1, 1917, PCRD, book 1292, page 106. The property was shown on the 1918 Sanborn map with two structures, the one on the left (west) being called "The Maplewood." Oddly, neither the 1918 Sanborn map nor the 1939 Sanborn map showed the straightened lines.

[377] 1906 plan.

[378] 1903 map ("Mass. Humane Society"); 1906 plan; George F. Welch to Humane Society of the Commonwealth of Massachusetts, deed, January 7, 1910, PCRD, book 1040, page 551. By 1918, the station was moved to or established at lot 208, as shown on the Sanborn maps. George Welch had already sold lot 41 (18 Collier) in 1905 and a house may have been on that site as early as 1900. According to construction dates in the Assessor's Database, other houses were at the later-numbered 2, 9, 33, 39 Collier (1899, per valuation lists), and 50 Collier. Most or all of these were owned by the Welches. These were at the northern end of Rivermoor, and the very southern point of Rivermoor was not developed until 1909 or so. In addition, the Welches had already built houses on Collier at number 11 (Bijou, 1871), 14 (Parker, 1871), and 16 (Lamphrey/Lamprey/Eastview, c. 1900), which were not shown on the 1906 plan.

[379] It was speculated that the house now at 10 Cliff Avenue was originally a stable or blacksmith and was the structure shown on the 1857 Map as being owned by M. Welch. "Cliff Avenue" file, about 1984, at the SHS and corresponding MACRIS file, 10 Cliff Ave., SCI.38. However, this seems inaccurate since the structure on the 1857 Map was on the south side of Water Street (Driftway) and not that close to what became Cliff Avenue. The house at 10 Cliff was built after 1911 and before 1915. George F. Welch to Henry H. Eames, deed, December 21, 1911, PCRD, book 1107, page 429 (lot 43); *1915 VL*, 111 (bungalow, lot 43). The 1911 deed says "The Grantor reserves for himself, his heirs or assigns the privilege of removing the building in the northeasterly corner of the lot within three months of the date hereof." This was the small structure shown on the 1906 plan, straddling property lines, and evidently it was removed because it is not listed on the later valuation list. Some residents have said that the neighborhood long ago had a farrier (a craftsman who trims and shoes horses' hooves), and an old forge in the basement of 10 Cliff, and indeed that basement has a massive brick fireplace, according to author's visit, courtesy of current owners, September 10, 2016.

[380] Entries for Sarah E. Young, in *1905 VL*, 131, and *1906 VL*, 134; discussions in text about 33 Collier (built in 1908), Cedar Camp cottage (77 Collier), Bijou, and Parker. The barns were likely on the west side of what appears to be Moorland, near the marsh and not far from the Welch farmhouse, in a photo from about 1912. Unknown photographer, unnamed photo (author's copy designation IMG_0984), c. 1912, in "1900–1916," Woodworth family photograph album.

[381] 1903 map.

[382] See Cathy Newman, "Whose Moors Are They?" *National Geographic*, May 2017, 84. In selecting the term, George Welch could not know that its use would wane. Today, its usage is less than a third of its usage in 1906. "moor," Google Books Ngram Viewer. Perhaps this reflects a decline in the amount of moorland, or in its importance to people.

[383] Charles Dickens, *A Christmas Carol* (London: Chapman & Hall, 1843), in Stave Three: The Second of the Three Spirits, https://www.gutenberg.org/files/46/46-h/46-h.htm; "Taxed to the Limit; … Scituate's Busy Day," *Boston Globe*, July 7, 1901, 23 (Moor's cottage on Third Cliff)).

[384] For example, see "moor," William Douglas Parish, William Francis Shaw, *A Dictionary of the Kentish Dialect and Provincialisms in Use in the County of Kent, Issue 54* (London: Trübner & Co. for English Dialect Society, 1887),

104 ("Swampy and wet pieces of ground"),
https://books.google.com/books?id=ecyZm0LAXG0C&source=gbs_navlinks_s.

385 Nancy S. Seasholes, *Gaining Ground: A History of Landmaking in Boston* (Cambridge, MA: MIT Press, 2003), 172n100 (alphabetical). Arthur D. Gilman (1821–1882) gets credit for developing the street plan and street names for Back Bay. "Arthur Delavan Gilman," Back Bay Houses: Genealogies of Back Bay Houses, website, https://backbayhouses.org/arthur-delavan-gilman/; Stephen Puleo, *A City So Grand: The Rise of an American Metropolis, Boston 1850-1900* (Boston: Beacon Press, 2010), ch. 4.

386 Seasholes, *Gaining Ground*, 210 (fig. 8.1), 218 (fig. 8.6), and 215–220; "What is a Fen?" US Department of Agriculture, Forest Service, website, https://www.fs.fed.us/wildflowers/beauty/California_Fens/what.shtml; "fen," Online Etymology Dictionary, http://www.etymonline.com/index.php; Henry Wadsworth Longfellow, opening lines of "The Slave in the Dismal Swamp," from *Poems on Slavery* (Cambridge, MA: John Owen, 1842), 18 ("In dark fens of the Dismal Swamp / The hunted Negro lay; …"), https://archive.org/details/poemsonslavery00long.

387 *1915 Directory*, 59 (Burns).

388 Seasholes, *Gaining Ground*, 229.

389 Bainbridge Bunting, *Houses of Boston's Back Bay: An Architectural History, 1840–1917* (Cambridge, MA: Belknap Press of Harvard University, 1967), 5–6.

390 "moor," *Webster's New Collegiate Dictionary* (Springfield, MA: G. & C. Merriam Co., 1956); "moor," Online Etymology Dictionary, http://www.etymonline.com/index.php; "moor," Eugene Ehrlich, et al., *Oxford American Dictionary* (New York: Oxford University Press, 1980); "moor," C. T. Onions, ed., *The Oxford Dictionary of English Etymology* (Oxford: Clarendon Press, 1966, reprinted 1978); "moor" in Walter W. Skeat, *A Concise Etymological Dictionary of the English Language* (New York: Harper & Brothers, 4th ed., 1893), https://catalog.hathitrust.org/Record/000115918. Other words, like peat, have similar dark connotations. Booth, "Serious about climate change? Get serious about peat." *Washington Post*, November 10, 2021: "Moor, bog, fen, mire, flush, swamp, slough. Peatlands have gotten a bum rap. They're inhospitable, useless. Too wet to plow, too dry to fish, the old farmers say."

391 Daniel Pool, *What Jane Austen Ate and Charles Dickens Knew: From Fox Hunting to Whist – the Facts of Daily Life in Nineteenth-Century England* (New York: Touchstone/Simon and Schuster, Inc., 1994), 161, https://books.google.com/books?id=HKj8jUM630EC&source=gbs_navlinks_s.

392 Tom Leach, "Sea Change: The Wychmere Seashore Cottages," on Threeharbors.com website, http://www.threeharbors.com/Wychmere%20Cottages/wychsyndicate.html (delightfully documented history of cottage development in Harwich, MA).

393 *Boston Evening Transcript*, June 20, 1906, p. 10, col. 5, Google news, https://news.google.com/newspapers?nid=2249&dat=19060620&id=4Y0-AAAAIBAJ&sjid=y1kMAAAAIBAJ&pg=3208,3068534&hl=en. It is not clear which house was offered for rent. The Bijou at 11 Collier, the Parker at 14 Collier, and the Lamprey at 16 Collier, were all mentioned in the *1905 VL*. Only the Lamprey (built 1900) could be considered "new," based on the author's research (see Appendix A), and it was already there by 1901. *Boston Globe*, July 7, 1901, 23. Perhaps it was the Marguerite, which might have been constructed before the 1908 date that this author could verify.

394 Rogers, "Resort Architecture at Nahant," 11–31. Calling a porch a "piazza" is more common in Britain than in America, and *loggia* is the proper term in Italy, according to a useful guide to architectural styles. Virginia Savage McAlester, *A Field Guide to American Houses: The Definitive Guide to Identifying and Understanding America's Domestic Architecture* (New York: Alfred A. Knopf, 2013), 54-55 [2015 paperback edition preview at https://books.google.com/books?id=fjbaCwAAQBAJ&source=gbs_navlinks_s]. In Italy, a *piazza* is an open space surrounded by buildings, like a public square. "Piazza," Designing Buildings Wiki, last edited June 13, 2021, https://www.designingbuildings.co.uk/wiki/Piazza.

395 McAlester, *Field Guide to American Houses*, 409. These could also be considered American four-square in style for the basic house without the added wraparound porches.

396 "Cliff Avenue" file and photo donated in spring 2021, SHS; James L. Garvin, *A Building History of Northern New England* (Hanover, NH: University Press of New England, 2001), 133–134, preview at https://books.google.com/books?id=oC4zG5aR4rwC&source=gbs_navlinks_s; Scituate Historical Society's postcard collections (postcard labeled "Copyright W.N. Seaver," probably from 1915–1919), copied elsewhere in this book. The Scituate Historical Society has an old photo of the house, copied in chapter 13 in the Haumans discussion.

397 Author's observations and photos; author's analysis of tax valuation records indicating house ages.

398 Laurel Fritz and Meghan Elliott, "More Than Square," STRUCTURE magazine, May 2016 (C3 Ink, publisher, for National Council of Structural Engineers Associations, ASCE's Structural Engineering Institute,

and the Council of American Structural Engineers), STRUCTURE magazine website, http://www.structuremag.org/?p=9872.; Larry Millett, *AIA Guide to the Twin Cities* (St. Paul, MN: Minnesota Historical Society Press, 2007), 299; Garvin, *A Building History*, 47–48.

399 Valerie Vitali, telephone interview by author, September 4, 2016; Johnson manuscript; staircase examples from author's tours by owners of homes at 7 Lincoln in May 2016 and 18 Michael in August 2017, for examples.

400 John Leeke, "Behind the Scenes with Beadboard," *Old House Journal* online, posted 2006, updated September 3, 2021, https://www.oldhouseonline.com/interiors-and-decor/behind-the-scenes-with-beadboard/; "Ask the Editors: Beauty and the Bead," *Old-House Interiors*, Vol VI, No. 4 (Gloucester, MA: Gloucester Publishers, June/July 2000), 98, https://books.google.com/books?id=7jAEAAAAMBAJ&source=gbs_navlinks_s; examples from author's tours by owners of homes at 7 Lincoln and 74 Collier in 2016, and 3 Driftway.

401 Scituate Water Company and other rolled files (plans), c. 1891–1900, accessed December 2015, SHS; Bonney, My Scituate, 3; 1903 map; *Scituate: Right of Way and Track Map, Old Colony R.R. Co., operated by The New York New Haven and Hartford R.R., from Braintree to Kingston* [map], 1 [inch] = 100 feet (Boston: New York, New Haven and Hartford R.R. Co., June 30, 1915), Archives & Special Collections at the Thomas J. Dodd Research Center, New York, New Haven and Hartford Railroad Valuation Maps - Massachusetts Railroad Valuation Maps Collection, University of Connecticut, Connecticut Digital Archive, http://archives.lib.uconn.edu/islandora/object/20002%3A860099623; Scituate Historical Society, *Scituate*, Then & Now series, 46. The plans on file at SHS include: (a) E. Worthington, Jr., Civil Engineer, *Scituate Harbor Water Works. Scituate, Mass. Pipe Lines shown in red. Scale 300 feet per inch. September 26, 1891* (pipes running out to near the end of Sand Hills, another line along Brook Street to north of Sand Hills, a line for part of Kent Street, and a line out Willow Street but not all the way out to Beaver Dam springs), (b) *Scituate Water Company, August 4, 1900, Scale 700 Feet per inch, To Accompany Proposal Dated August 4, 1900*, no author given (pipes and/or pumping stations in North Scituate Beach area, way out Willow Street to what is now Country Way, and nothing in the Egypt area where the standpipe and Lawson Tower was built), and (c) what seems a less ambitious but probably final plan, E. Worthington, Jr., & Co., Engineers, *Scituate Water Works, Scituate, Mass., Piping Plan for Scituate Harbor, Scale - 500 ft. per inch*, undated but probably 1900 (Willow Street from the standpipe in Scituate Center near Town Hall and the High School into the harbor, along Front Street, and then out Brook Street, part of Central Street [First Parish Road], and part of Union Street [Stockbridge Road], over to what is now Meeting House Lane).

402 Lyle Nyberg, "Beaver Dam Spring Bottle," April 13, 2018, memo on file, SHS.

403 *Boston Globe*, May 1, 1904, 28. A detailed history of Scituate's water supply is in James E. Glinski, *Old Oaken Buckets: Scituate and its Water Supply* (Scituate: Scituate Historical Society, 2020).

404 1908 Sanborn map, sheet 1; Alger, "People I Have Known in Scituate" (Joseph Ward's fish market).

405 *Marshfield Mail*, March 11, 1910, 1, Marshfield Historical Society, Newspapers and Clippings Box 2, reference 2008.0112. The Franklin Publishing Company published this paper as well as the *Scituate Herald, Cohasset Cottager, Norwell News,* and other papers.

406 Russell Fish papers.

407 "Scituate. Old Town Attracts many Tourists to Its Beauty Places," *Boston Globe*, July 31, 1910, 25.

408 *Marshfield Mail*, March 11, 1910.

409 Annual Report of the Adjutant General of the Commonwealth of Massachusetts for the Year Ending December 31, 1907, Public Document No. 7, 135, in Public Documents of Massachusetts, vol. 10 (Boston: Secretary of Massachusetts, 1908), https://books.google.com/books?id=Edc2AQAAMAAJ&source=gbs_navlinks_s; J. Harry Hartley, "Cavalry In Camp at Scituate," *Boston Globe*, August 21, 1907, 3.

410 Mary Hathaway (Smith) Hall reported: "[a group of friends] & I drove to 3rd cliff & saw troop A, at dress parade and sword drill, cavalry exercises &c." Mary H. Smith to Roy Hall (probably son), copy of letter, postmarked September 4, 1900, Hall family file, SHS.

411 1910 US Census, Schedule 1-Inhabitants, Scituate, Plymouth County, Massachusetts, pages 9 and 10 of 22 (original sheet numbers 5A and 5B), digital images, HeritageQuest, citing NARA microfilm publication T624, 1,178 rolls, roll not identified. An interesting history of lobster fishing in Canada says its origins were in Massachusetts, and "The original wooden lath [lobster] trap is said to have originated in Cape Cod in 1810." "History of Lobster Fishing and Processing," The American Lobster website, http://www.parl.ns.ca/lobster/history.htm.

412 Linda Barnhart, interview by author, May 1, 2016; unknown former neighbor across the street from Sabina Welch, March 27, 2019; *Annual Report of the Town Officers of the Town of Scituate for the Year Ending December 31, 1896* ("Scituate Light," printers, 1897), 45 (John Welch, accidental drowning, age 56); 1900 US Census,

Schedule 1-Inhabitants, Scituate, Plymouth County, Massachusetts, roll 675, page 6B, Enumeration District 1147, FHL microfilm 1240675, digital images, HeritageQuest.

413 *1911 VL*, 85; *1915 Directory*, 60–61; Valerie Vitali, telephone interview by author, September 4, 2016; TCRIA, Inc., "The Heritage of Third Cliff," in Third Cliff-Rivermoor Newsletter (Summer 1986), 3; telephone conversation with Elizabeth Davey, June 5, 2018 (rented larger house on Gilson Road from Sabina Welch); discussion with Kathy Brown (relative of Sabina Welch), March 16, 2017 (bedrooms).

414 *Annual Report of the Town Officers of the Town of Scituate for the Year Ending December 31, 1895* (Plymouth: Avery & Doten, printers, 1896), 42 (Sabine Welch born May 24, 1895); Linda Barnhart, interview by author, May 1, 2016; Valerie Vitali, telephone interview by author, September 4, 2016; TCRIA, Inc., "The Heritage of Third Cliff," in Third Cliff-Rivermoor Newsletter (Summer 1986), 3; Claire McDonough, "Sabina Welch remembers …," *Scituate Mariner*, undated copy, about 1980 (after May 24), 1 (or 2) and 3 (source of quotes in text).

415 McDonough, "Sabina Welch remembers …" (source of quotes in text); 1926 Sanborn map (location of church); Kathy Brown (relative of Sabina Welch) discussions with author, March 16 and May 10, 2017 (R. H. Stearns store and pension); *Marshfield Mail*, August 28, 1936, 4 (Sabina and Delia Welch spent three weeks' vacation from R. H. Stearns with their mother on Gilson Road), Marshfield Historical Society, Newspapers and Clippings Box 2, reference 2008.0112.

416 Kathy Brown (relative of Sabina Welch) discussions with author, March 16 and May 10, 2017 (R. H. Stearns store and pension).

417 Dina & Frank Crowley, September 11, 2012, letter to Neil F. Duggan, Building Commissioner, Zoning Enforcement Officer, Scituate, MA, Re: 138 Gilson Road (sign), copy in realtor marketing records viewed November 13, 2016; *1926 Directory*, 78, 121. The sign was displayed in the house when it was on the market.

418 Dina & Frank Crowley, September 11, 2012, letter to Neil F. Duggan; Stephen Litchfield, photographs of medal, attached to his email to author, January 4, 2017. The medal's recipient, Martin Quinn, is in one of the pictures on display in the Irish Mossing and Maritime Museum, Scituate, owned and operated by the Scituate Historical Society.

419 "Martin Quinn," 1900 US Census, Scituate, MA, roll 675, page 6B; Howe, *The Humane Society, 1785-1916*, 335, 382-383. Thanks to Frank Crowley and his mother Elaine Crowley for loaning the medal to photograph.

420 Mariquita Gill, *Coastal Scene* (c. 1899), offered for sale and sold by Skinner auctioneers, website, http://www.skinnerinc.com/auctions/2779B/lots/466; [Alice] Beckington, ["Crest of Third Cliff"] [photograph], labeled "Plate III. A photograph from nature in which the attractions are most fortunately balanced," in "The Elements of Beauty: V. Balance" [editorial] in Henry Turner Bailey, ed., *The School Arts Book*, vol. 11 (Boston, MA: The School Arts Publishing Co., September 1911–June 1912), 529–539, at 536–537, https://books.google.com/books?id=5ZY3AQAAMAAJ&source=gbs_navlinks_s. The editor of the publication, Henry Turner Bailey, was a noted resident of Scituate. A solitary house at the top of the cliff also appears in an undated photograph/postcard "The Third Cliff, Scituate, Mass." in the postcard collection and Lester Hobson collection at the Scituate Historical Society, and in Thomas Hall, *Shipwrecks of Massachusetts Bay* (Charleston, SC: History Press, 2012), 113.

421 Frederick Damon photo, view looking south to Third Cliff, Scituate Historical Society, a copy of which appears in Murphy, *Irish Mossers*, 3; SHS postcard collections, including "The Third Cliff, Scituate, Mass.," postcard similar to Damon photo, published by Souther-Mears Co., Boston.

422 Linda Barnhart, interview by author, May 1, 2016; Valerie Vitali, telephone interview by author, September 4, 2016 (noting that some of the apple trees are still there); Bill Giniewicz, interview by author, March 6, 2016.

423 1903 map; Charles Lincoln, "Streets of Scituate" (compiled 1950), SHS (Water Street was discontinued at Greenbush in 1911); Galluzzo, *The North River*, 74 (Boston Sand and Gravel Company started removal of vast amounts of Colman Hills in 1914, lasting until large fire in 1963); 1926 Sanborn map, sheet 1; aerial photographs, scale 500' to an inch, c. 1954–1961, Town Archives. The Boston Sand and Gravel Company's acquisitions of land in Scituate began in February 1914. Henry T. Cole, Angeline M. Cole and Clarence T. Cole to Boston Sand and Gravel Company, deed, February 14, 2014, PCRD, book 1168, page 570.

424 Town of Scituate, 1968 aerial photograph [interpositive] CGL-124, 1" = 100', Town Archives.

425 "Helen Bailey" and "Sarah L. Seaverns," Ancestry.com and The Church of Jesus Christ of Latter-day Saints. 1880 United States Federal Census [database on-line]. Lehi, UT, USA:. Original data: Tenth Census of the United States, 1880 (NARA microfilm publication T9, 1,454 rolls), records of the Bureau of the Census, Record Group 29. National Archives, Washington, D.C., enumeration district 551, sheet 13A; Jotham W. Bailey and Helen M. Bailey to Henry A. Seaverns, deed, May 17, 1884, PCRD, book 509, page 126; *1894 J. H. Hogan Directory*, 126 (Willard L. Bailey); presentation by Robert Jackman in class, May 9, 2018 (Jotham and Willard Bailey). See Helen M. Bailey of Scituate to Frederic T. Bailey, July 22, 1899, release, PCRD, book 779, page 556.

[426] E. Parker Welch to Helen M. Bailey, deed, October 25, 1900, PCRD, book 814, page 69; Mark J. Flaherty to Helen M. Bailey of Scituate, widow, deed, June 6, 1904, PCRD, book 880, page 460; postcard postmarked July 23, 1909, SHS postcard collections, Twomey/Jacobson collection.

[427] Edward S. Bailey and Willard L. Bailey (Ruth's father) [heirs of Helen M. Bailey] to H. Miriam Agnew, deed, September 30, 1920, PCRD, book 1373, page 323, recorded February 16, 1921; Edward S. Bailey and H. Miriam Agnew [heirs of Helen M. Bailey] to Willard L. Bailey (Ruth's father), deed, February 15, 1921, PCRD, book 1373, page 322; Caroline A. Bailey (Ruth's mother) to Lucy E. Smith, deed, December 10, 1934, PCRD, book 1680, page 229; Lucy E. Smith to Caroline A. Bailey and Ruth Bailey, deed, December 10, 1934, PCRD, book 1680, page 229; 1992 *Scituate Town Report*, 85, report of Ruth Bailey's death listing her parents as Willard L. and Caroline Bailey.

[428] E. Parker Welch to Catherine Nee, deed, December 20, 1900, PCRD, book 814, page 215; Francis Mulkern by mortgagee South Scituate Savings Bank to Catherine Nee, foreclosure deed, December 20, 1900, PCRD, book 817, page 264; John Nee and Catherine Nee to South Scituate Savings Bank, mortgage, December 20, 1900, PCRD, book 816, page 96.

[429] Scituate Beach Land Association to James J. Covington, deed, August 5, 1908, PCRD, book 1005, page 131; *1909 VL*, 106; James J. Connington to John Stephen Gill, deed, September 9, 1921, PCRD, book 1397, page 383 (land "together with the Buildings and improvements thereon"); "Correspondence. Local Unions. Boston," *The American Photo Engraver*, vol. 2, no. 7, June 1910, 171–172; "The Boston Strike," *The American Photo Engraver*, vol. 2, no. 10, September 1910, 245–247; "Injurious Effects of Chinese White, Metal, Platinum, Chromates and Cyanides Used in the Making of Photo-Engravings," *The American Photo Engraver*, vol. 3, no. 7, July 1911, 201–203; "Correspondence. Local Unions. Boston," *The American Photo Engraver*, vol. 3, no. 7, July 1911, 221 (source of quote); all *American Photo Engraver* articles in vol. 2–3 (Chicago: International Photo Engravers' Union of North America), https://books.google.com/books?id=ISIMAAAAYAAJ&source=gbs_navlinks_s.

[430] "Globe Employees Fete 'Father' Gill," *Boston Globe*, July 17, 1922, 9. Note the foot-racing photos from the Woodworth family photo album, one of which is copied in chapter 13.

[431] *Boston Sunday Globe Magazine*, August 5, 1923, 80 (magazine page 2).

[432] John S. Gill to Mildred Luciano, deed, January 24, 1927, PCRD, book 1519, page 385; Assessor hand-drawn plot plans, by street, about 1930–35, Town Archives (showing house there); *The South Shore Social Register and Who's Who on Cape Cod* (Boston: Davis Pub. Co., 1938), 122; Daniel F. Appleton, surveyor, *Plan of Land in Scituate, Mass.*, scale 40 feet to an inch, June 1939, PCRD, plan book 6, page 97 (showing empty lot).

[433] Chas W. Restarick, "Real Estate Transactions," *Boston Globe*, August 8, 1909, 16.

[434] Scituate Beach Land Association to Catherine Nee, deed, September 9, 1909, PCRD, book 1045, page 15 (lot 5); Scituate Beach Land Association to Catherine Nee, deed, September 18, 1909, PCRD, book 1045, page 18 (lot 4); Scituate Beach Land Association to Catherine Nee, deed, October 20, 1911, PCRD, book 1107, page 36 (lot 6); Scituate Beach Land Association to Catherine Nee, undated, deed, notarized July 21, 1912, PCRD, book 1123, page 553 (lot 7); Appleton, *Plan of Land*, 1939; *1912 VL*, 54, showing Catherine Nee owning lots 4, 5, 6, 7, with "Lower House" on lower lot, Barn on upper lot, Moss house on lot 4, "Upper House" on lot 5, and "House uncompleted 1912" on lot 6.

[435] Author's synthesis of individual property title searches at PCRD, various tax valuation lists, and Harold Howard directories; "Scituate," *Boston Globe*, August 5, 1900. The *1906 VL* has George F. Watson owning a house, stable, and lots 21–22. The *1912 VL*, 120, has Sarah H. Scott of Worcester owning a house ("Watson"), a stable, and lot 22 on Third Cliff. The *1910 VL*, 110, has Olive Gore owning a house at lot 25, Plan 2, Third Cliff, and the *1915 Directory*, 64, lists her husband Harry W. Gore at "Seaholme" on Third Cliff, also at 8 Beacon in Boston; the same directory, 59, lists C. E. Brier as owning a house on Third Cliff. Harold Howard, *Resident and Business Directory of Scituate and Marshfield Massachusetts* (Harold Howard, 1915), Businesses file, SHS ("*1915 Directory*"),

[436] *1912 VL*, 120, entry for nonresident Scituate Beach Land Company; *1920 VL*, entry for nonresident South Shore Land and Building Trust.

[437] Henry A. Litchfield, *Survey for George F. Welch, Scituate, Mass., December 19th, 1918, Scale 20 ft. to an inch*, PCRD, plan book 3, page 67.

[438] Finding Aid, Yatsuhashi Harumichi Family Papers, Freer Gallery of Art and Arthur M. Sackler Gallery Archives, Smithsonian Institution, Washington, D.C., gift of James Arthur Marinaccio, 1994, https://sirismm.si.edu/siris/yatsuhashi.html; Annie P. Foster to Harumichi Yatsuhashi, deed, February 16, 1931, PCRD, book 1608, page 474; Edward J. Ball to Harumichi Yatsuhashi, deed, February 27, 1931, PCRD, book 1608, page 475; *1938 South Shore Social Register*, 124; Sumiko Yatsuhashi to Borbon Realty Trust, deed, September 10, 1984, PCRD, book 5782, page 236; Assessor's Database, for FY 2019.

[439] George F. Welch to Antoinette Pray, deed, September 16, 1901, PCRD, book 830, page 15; *1902 VL*, 109; Antoinette Pray of Norwell to Marion E. Brown, wife of Capen Brown of Boston, deed, November 11, 1920, PCRD, book 1369, page 490; 1903 map ("A. Pray"); Assessor's Database; *1921 VL*, entry for nonresident Marion E. Brown; *Boston Globe*, July 30, 1922, 19; DAR, *Old Scituate*, 118–120; search for Marion Brown, Scituate properties, on PCRD website; *1938 South Shore Social Register*, 121.

[440] 1903 map ("E. P. Welch"); *1897-1903 Valuation Lists*, for George F. Welch ("D. Ward" house and shed, and "Bleak House," on Third Cliff); *1919 VL*, 100 (William N. Ambler, including "House Trotwood" and barn); William N. Ambler to William E. McCoy, deed, April 23, 1919, PCRD, book 1316, page 531 (deed for land with buildings thereon, being lot B on plan "Survey for George F. Welch, Scituate, Mass., drawn by Henry A. Litchfield dated December 18, 1918"); William E. McCoy to Bessie W. McCoy, deed, July 11, 1919, PCRD, book 1330, page 445; *1920 VL*, 140 (Bessie W. McCoy with house "Trostwood"); Bessie W. McCoy by Executrix to Helen C. Dwyer, deed, February 15, 1963, PCRD, book 3005, page 387; Bessie W. McCoy by Guardian to Jeffrey Daly and Ronda M. Daly, deed, September 9, 2002, PCRD, book 22855, page 3; Assessor's Database.

[441] *1901 VL*, 110, entry for H. G. Shanack [sic]; *1906 VL*, entry for Herman G. Shanock [sic]; 1903 map ("H. G. Shaneck"); George F. Welch to Herman G. Shaneck, deed, October 22, 1900, PCRD, book 808, page 319; *1915* and *1918 Directories*; Ernest S. Woodaman, ed., *Directory of Directors in the City of Boston and Vicinity* (Boston: Ernest S. Woodaman, 1911), 323, https://books.google.com/books?id=_YIpAAAAYAAJ&source=gbs_navlinks_s; *Acts and Resolves Passed by the General Court of Massachusetts in the Year 1880* (Boston: Commonwealth of Massachusetts, 1880), 305 (changes of names), https://books.google.com/books?id=tUcSAAAAYAAJ&source=gbs_navlinks_s.

[442] George F. Welch to Herman G. Shaneck, deed, October 22, 1900, PCRD, book 808, page 319.

[443] See Murphy *Irish Mossers,* 3 (photo), which shows the double house next to the Shaneck house, and a practically bare Third Cliff at the turn of the century.

[444] Herman G. Shaneck to William H. Harney, deed, March 8, 1919, PCRD, book 1318, page 373; *1921 VL*, entry for Charles E. Holt, with house ("Shannock"); Assessor's Database.

[445] *Murphy v. Conway*; George H. Wetherbee Jr., Civil Engineer, *Plan of Land in Scituate, Mass., Belonging to George F. Welch & Thomas F. McManus (April 1911)*, 1 inch = 40 feet, PCRD, plan book 1, page 666 (Eagles Nest); *1916 VL*, 88 ("House Marion" only); *1917 VL*, 96 (both Marion and Edith); *1918 VL*, 94 (Marion and Edith, followed by "House at end of Porter Road"); *1919 VL*, 93 (Marion and Edith only); *1920 VL*, 95 (both Marion and Edith, first time listed on Porter Road).

[446] John Galluzzo, "Galluzzo: Scituate Gets a Steamboat," *Scituate Mariner*, posted May 25, 2015, http://scituate.wickedlocal.com/article/20150525/NEWS/150528446; George F. Welch obituary. Interestingly, George Welch was not one of those listed as a builder or contractor in a 1915 business directory. Rather, he was listed along with five others under "Real Estate." *1915 Directory*, 77, 79, 98.

[447] *Rivermoor, Scituate, Mass.* [photograph] (n.p., c. 1910) (photo title written on photo in white, "1910" written in pencil on photo mat), in possession of Nancy Howell, current owner of the property on which "Indian Knoll" stood, and same photo as postcard in the postcard collection of the SHS, marked on the back as "Pub. By C. W. Frye, Scituate, Mass. Series 147" with postmark of 1910. The boulder in the photo is likely the one shown between lots 168 and 169 on the 1906 plan, which is still there. The house has a gambrel roof with a full-width shed dormer and wraparound porches. The roof was typical of the Dutch Colonial subtype of Colonial Revival houses from 1895 to the 1930s. McAlester, *Field Guide to American Houses*, 410-411, 424-425. The house is listed as "House 1911" in the *1912 VL* and as "Indian Knoll" by the time of its listing in the *1917 VL*. The house was named "Indian Knoll" by 1912, when it was rented for the summer by Mr. & Mrs. Arthur V. (Margaret Kennard) Woodworth and Mrs. Charles Warren Kennard [Margaret's mother]. *Social Register, Summer, 1912*, 558. Based on the Woodworth family photograph album, it appears they rented Indian Knoll starting in 1912. "1900–1916," Woodworth family photograph album. Margaret Woodworth purchased the property in 1919, as discussed later in the text. The current owner, whose family has owned the property since 1949, said she was told that Native Americans liked the site because the sun both rose and set over water; arrowheads were found on the site. Nancy Howell, email to author March 2, 2016, and interviews by author March 3 and May 11, 2016. See also author's paper on file, SHS, "Notes on the Woodworth Family Photo Album '1900-1916,' Scituate, MA," September 28, 2016, revised October 4, 2016.

[448] William Smith, "Colonia," in *A Dictionary of Greek and Roman Antiquities* (London: John Murray, 1875), 315-320, as excerpted in Bill Thayer, "Colonia" on LacusCurtius website, http://penelope.uchicago.edu/Thayer/E/Roman/Texts/secondary/SMIGRA*/Colonia.html.

[449] McAlester, *Field Guide to American Houses*, 87–88 (planned), 78 (Riverside).

[450] Author interview with residents, including owners of 7 Lincoln (built 1911), and 74 Collier (1912).

[451] TCRIA, Inc., "The Heritage of Third Cliff," in *Third Cliff-Rivermoor Newsletter* (Summer 1986), 3, courtesy of Gail Ledwig. The approximate years and quantities of houses built in Rivermoor and Third Cliff are in Appendix B.

[452] Tax valuation lists for various years, including 1907, 87, 1909, 94–95, Town Archives; "Scituate," *Boston Globe*, July 15, 1900, 22 ("Mr and Mrs Lamphrey of Marshfield Hills have a cottage at Third Cliff"); "Taxed to the Limit; … Scituate's Busy Day," *Boston Globe*, July 7, 1901, 23 (Mr. & Mrs. E. W. Haskell staying at the Lamprey); discussion later in text (Trotwood at 4 Dickens Row). The J. H. Hogan *1894 Directory* does not list Lamphreys in Marshfield, and the US census for 1900, 1910, and 1920 list Lamphreys in Boston and Medford, but not Marshfield.

[453] George F. Welch to Sarah E. Young, deed, December 15, 1905, recorded November 7, 1923, PCRD, book 1451, page 359 (saying "Only reserving the beach as the land may wash away by the action of the sea."), and separate note citing tax valuation list listings for Young. Note the delay in recording. Later deeds reference the Welch to Young deed, such as Norman F. & Grace N. Coolbroth to Finton J. & Marie L. Mohyde, deed, July 1, 1961, recorded July 6, 1961, PCRD, book 2863, page 268.

[454] The house appears on a postcard postmarked August 1908, SHS postcard collections, album LSS #2. This book uses that year of 1908 as the earliest verifiable date of construction, although it is possible it was built earlier. See "Scituate's Busy Day," *Boston Globe*, July 7, 1901, 23 (Killians and Dowds "are at the Marguerite"). The house first appears on the tax records in the *1909 VL*, 94–95, as owned by George F. Welch, on "House Lot East Side #1." The *1910 VL*, 88, lists a house at lot #1, Rivermoor. This corresponds to a lot on the 1906 plan of Rivermoor at the corner of the Driftway (then called Water Street) and Collier Road. The *1911 VL*, 87, lists this as a house at the corner of "Water & front" (meaning the front of the cliff) at lot #1, Rivermoor. Later valuation lists call this house "Marguerite." A different postcard showing the house is postmarked July 23, 1909, SHS postcard collections, Twomey/Jacobson/ collection. The note on the back includes, "This gives you an idea of the height of the cliff. I have put a little X over our house; just the back shows. Marion." (Could this have been Marion Welch?) The little X is not over The Marguerite.

[455] Bill Giniewicz (a past owner of The Marguerite), interview by author, March 6, 2016, including his account of the recollections of Dr. Ruth Bailey (1904–1992), who lived across from The Marguerite at 8 Driftway. George Welch had two daughters. Marion married a Scituate doctor, T. [Thomas] Branch Alexander, on October 15, 1907. Edith married Julius Zinn in 1915, but the marriage did not last, since she was living with her parents in 1918, and she married William James of Scituate in 1921. *1918 Directory*, 26, 60, 62a; Town of Scituate, *Annual Report of the Town Officers of the Town of Scituate for the Year Ending December 31, 1907*, 104; Town of Scituate, *Annual Report of the Officers of the Town of Scituate for the year Ending December 31, 1915*, 98; *1926 Directory*, 56. The Marguerite was mentioned as a summer rental in a 1909 newspaper article. "Scituate," *Boston Globe*, July 4, 1909, 24, so the house was built by then. George Welch retained ownership of the property until selling it in 1918. George F. Welch to Helen V. Low, deed, March 29, 1918, PCRD, book 1302, page 165. The *1912 VL*, 128, lists property owned by George's older brother Charles P. Welch on Third Cliff: two houses with their lots, lots 1 and 2; these are not the same as lot 1 (the site of The Marguerite) and lot 2 on the 1906 Rivermoor plan; the only property Charles Welch owned was the unnumbered parcel on that plan, west of Collier Road.

[456] "Dr. Michael W. Johnson," obituary, *Scituate Mariner*, October 7, 2021, 9A. The house at 29 First Parish Road is known (in part) as the Dr. Thomas B. Alexander house, SCI.77, MACRIS. The MACRIS cover sheet says the house was built in 1814 (same date in Assessor's Database), with architect(s) E. Parker Welsh and Son. The accompanying detailed MACRIS form, from 1984, more accurately says the house was a cape built in the 1700s, with major alterations including by E. Parker Welch & Son in 1907 (colonial style second story added). The year 1907 is when George Welch's daughter Marion married Dr. Alexander. Just after their marriage on October 15, E. Parker Welch deeded the house to his granddaughter Marion Collier Alexander on November 15, 1907. This is according to the first page of a 1912 mortgage, Marion Collier Alexander and Thomas Branch Alexander to Rockland Cooperative Bank, mortgage, April 23, 1912, PCRD, book 1119, page 174. Dr. Alexander was the school physician, according to the *1918 Directory*. Dr. & Mrs. Alexander had two daughters, Harriet and Frances (who married Dr. Harald Johnson). The detailed MACRIS report says the house was the residence of Dr. & Mrs. Harald N. [Frances M.] Johnson. The later owner, Dr. Michael W. Johnson, was a doctor, the son of Dr. & Mrs. [Frances] Johnson, grandson of Dr. & Mrs. [Marion] Alexander, and a great-grandson of George & Hattie [Harriet] Welch. That makes three successive generations of doctors, not counting Michael Welch's service as chief steward at the Chelsea Marine Hospital and Michael's wife Sarah's service as chief nurse there.

[457] McAlester, *Field Guide to American Houses*, 146, 409–410, 416–417, 555; author's knowledge.

[458] According to one neighbor, George Welch built houses on one street per year. Valerie Vitali, telephone interview by author, September 4, 2016.

[459] Author's review of deeds at PCRD, including George F. Welch to Chauncy W. Chamberlain, deed, July 9, 1909, PCRD, book 1027, page 425 (lot 162, 78 Moorland, at the southern point of Rivermoor. For 78 Moorland, it is assumed the house was built in 1909, and a house appears there on Sanborn maps of 1918, 1926, and 1939. The Assessor's Database lists it as built in 1890, but it does not seem to appear in tax valuation lists of the late 1800s for the Welches, who would have owned it. For 77 and 79 Collier, see George F. Welch to Charles W. Thomas and Alpheus W. Thomas, deed, August 3, 1908, PCRD, book 1034, page 493, and George F. Welch to Ernest L. Loring, deed, May 2, 1910, PCRD, book 1054, page 122.

[460] 1908 and 1909 Valuation Lists. See Appendix B.

[461] Lyle Nyberg, historical building inventory forms (Form B) for 6, 10, 14, 18, and 22 Michael Avenue, December 2016, filed in MACRIS, and references cited therein.

[462] *1911 VL* (where it is listed as ½ built as of the spring) and *1912 VL*.

[463] "Nearby Summer Resorts Fast Filling With Rest Seekers," Boston Globe, June 19, 1910, 14; *Social Register, Summer, 1911: Contains the Summer Addresses of Residents of New York, Washington, Philadelphia, Chicago, Boston, …, vol. 25, no. 58* (New York: Social Register Association, June, 1911), 533, https://books.google.com/books?id=SJJIAAAAYAAJ&source=gbs_navlinks_s. The phone number, 67-3, is the same as listed in later Social Registers.

[464] *Social Register, Summer, 1912*, 550; *Social Register, Summer, 1913: Contains the Summer Addresses of Residents of New York, Washington, Philadelphia, Chicago, Boston, …, vol. 27, no. 63* (New York: Social Register Association, June, 1913), 568, https://books.google.com/books?id=ffZBAQAAMAAJ&source=gbs_navlinks_s.

[465] Maurice Gerstein, ed., *Medical Directory of Greater Boston 1915-1916, Fifth Edition* (Boston: Boston Medical Publishing Company, 1916), 127, 488, 527, https://archive.org/details/medicaldirectory00gers; Arthur M. Greenwood and Theodore K. Lawless, "Hemangiosarcoma of the Skin," *Arch Derm Syphilol.* 1922;6(1):10-20. doi:10.1001/archderm.1922.02360010013003.

[466] "Rivermoor Colony, Third Cliff, Scituate, Mass." postcard, Scituate, Historical Society.

[467] "Rivermoor Colony, Third Cliff, Scituate, Mass." postcard, Scituate, Historical Society.

[468] Assessor's Database; *1905 VL*; House, *Town of Scituate Mass*, Sheet 64 (street addresses); author's review of deeds recorded at Plymouth County Registry of Deeds; conversation with owner July 30, 2021.

[469] Unknown photographer, view of the point of Rivermoor, c. 1912, in "1900–1916," Woodworth family photograph album (author's copy designation IMG_0986).

[470] George F. Welch to Margaret C. Colgate, deed, August 3, 1908, PCRD, book 996, page 482.

[471] *1909 VL*, 106.

[472] US Census for 1900, Boston Ward 25, Suffolk County, MA; Roll: 688; Page: 16A; Enumeration District: 1542; FHL microfilm: 1240688, [database online]. Provo, UT, USA: Ancestry.com Operations Inc, 2004. Original data: United States of America, Bureau of the Census. Twelfth Census of the United States, 1900. Washington, D.C.: National Archives and Records Administration, 1900. T623, 1854 rolls, roll not specified, HeritageQuest.

[473] George F. Welch to Susan L. Hunt, deed, August 31, 1908, PCRD, book 1004, page 519.

[474] *1909 VL*, 115 (lot 74); *1910 VL*, 113 (lot 73 and house, Susan Hunt listed on Linden Street, Allston).

[475] 1926 Sanborn map; *1918 Directory*, 79; *Manual of the Public Schools of the City of Boston* (Boston: Rockwell and Churchill, City Printers, 1896), 49, https://archive.org/details/manualofpublicsc1896bost.

[476] "Gurney, Thomas W. — Colgate, Margaret House," RCK.129, MACRIS; Robert E. Moody, ed., *Bostonia: The Boston University Alumni Magazine*, vol. 7, no. 2 (Boston: Boston University, November 1933), 22, https://open.bu.edu/bitstream/handle/2144/19438/Bostonia1933v7n2_web.pdf; *Journal of the House of Representatives of the United States, 63d Congress, 2d Session*, vol. 63, issue 2 (Washington, DC: Government Printing Office, 1913), 725 (July 1, 1914: "By Mr. Mitchell: Petition of A. Gertrude Dudley, Margaret C. Colgate and others, of Rockland, Mass., urging woman-suffrage legislation; to the Committee on the Judiciary."), https://books.google.com/books?id=g01RAQAAMAAJ&source=gbs_navlinks_s.

[477] Margaret C. Colgate to Albert E. Lynch, deed, July 20, 1928, PCRD, book 1556, page 386; Susan L. Hunt to Elmer G. Phinney and Bessie F. Phinney, deed, August 17, 1928, PCRD, book 1558, page 327.

[478] "Scituate," *Boston Globe*, July 4, 1909, 24.

[479] The *1912 VL* entries for George Welch (p. 80) list "Tichnor" at "Tichnor Court" but the title information is opaque. For "Hazlemere" (1909), see Lyle Nyberg, "Hazlemere," 95 Hatherly Road, SCI.1236, MACRIS.

[480] "Scituate," *Boston Globe*, July 15, 1900, 22 (naming renters for "Parker cottage" and "The Bijou", and saying "Mr and Mrs Lamphrey of Marshfield Hills have a cottage at Third Cliff"); Lyle Nyberg, "Hazlemere," 95 Hatherly Road, SCI.1236, MACRIS; 1918 and 1926 Sanborn maps (house names and lot numbers) and House, *Town of Scituate Mass*, Sheet 64 (street addresses and lot numbers); E. Parker Welch and Mark J. Flaherty to

George F. Welch, deed, July 1, 1905, PCRD, book 918, page 535 ("Lamprey Property"), and George F. Welch to Ernest A. James, deed, June 8, 1916, PCRD, book 1244, page 512 ("The Lamphrey Collier Rd. Lot 40").

[481] For a list of house names in Rivermoor, see Appendix A. They first appeared in the *1897 VL*, 78 ("Bijou" and "Parker") under E. Parker Welch's name, then in scribbled notes in the *1905 VL*, 86 (Bijou, Parker, Lamprey) under George Welch's name, and they began to be formally listed in the *1906 VL*, 87. The location of Bijou was at today's 11 Collier. In the *1906 VL*, the Lamprey and Parker house lots were noted as "West side" and Bijou as "East side," and this almost certainly meant which side of Collier Road the property was on, suggesting Bijou was at 11 Collier, as confirmed by later valuation lists showing it on lot 222 on the east side of Collier.

The 1918 and 1926 Sanborn maps include names for about 20 of the 60 or so houses in Rivermoor. About another 30 named houses can be located using tax valuation lists after 1914 under listings for George Welch. Apart from Rivermoor, tax valuation lists often refer only to "3rd Cliff," without a lot number. Sometimes they refer to "Plan 2" with a lot number that can be traced to the 1900 Gilson Road Plan of the Scituate Beach Land Company. In either case, house names are rarely stated. No names there appear on the 1926 Sanborn map. Names can be located by (1) performing a title search for each property to determine its owners in particular years, then (2) checking all owners' names in the particular valuation lists to see if a house (or just a lot) is listed and whether its name is listed. The author followed this process for more than 10 properties that appeared to be old on Gilson and other Third Cliff roads. This is the source of house names (if any) for those properties.

[482] "Scituate," *Boston Globe*, August 21, 1910. As to the "Viola" location, see discussion in text about Helen M. Bailey's ownership dating to 1900 and Dr. Ruth Bailey's later ownership.

[483] Early examples include private mailing cards with an image of the owner's summer estate, such as those featuring Sunnycroft, postmarked as early as 1905. To date cards that are undated, or for which their postmarks are not present or are illegible, Jonathan Olly explains:

> The age of a postcard is determined as follows: the "undivided back" postcards of 1901-1907 have no vertical line on the reverse of the card. The back is meant only for the address. The "divided back" era from 1907-1915 has a vertical line down the middle of the backside of the card, allowing one half for the address, the other for a message. The "white border" era from 1915-1930 has a white border around the image on the front of the card, as well as the now standard divided back.

Jonathan Morin Olly, "Imagining the Old Coast: History, Heritage, and Tourism in New England, 1865-2012" (PhD diss., Brown University, May 2013), 80 n. 114, Brown University Digital Repository, https://repository.library.brown.edu/studio/item/bdr:320535/, citing Beverly H. Kallgren, "Postcards," in Burt Feintuch and David H. Watters, eds., *The Encyclopedia of New England: The Culture and History of an American Region* (New Haven, CT.: Yale University Press, 2005), 1491; "Postcard History" in Smithsonian Archives, http://siarchives.si.edu/history/exhibits/postcard/postcard-history; Todd Ellison; "Tips for determining when a U.S. postcard was published," website of Center of Southwest Studies, Fort Lewis College, last revised August 7, 2006, https://www.fortlewis.edu/finding_aids/images/M194/PostcardDating.htm.

[484] See "Timeline of Color Photography," Photographic Resource Center at Boston University, website, https://www.bu.edu/prc/GODOWSKY/timeline.htm.

[485] Postcard collections, SHS; author's postcard collection (postmarks ranging from 1906 to about 1923); *The South Shore Blue Book, Containing Lists of the Summer Residents of the Principal Resorts Along the South Shore including Hull, Nantasket, Jerusalem Road, Cottage City, Falmouth, Marshfield, Duxbury, Scituate, Woods Hole, Cohasset, Etc.* (Boston: Boston Suburban Book Co., 1906), 32 (A. A. Seaverns), 38 (Frye), 40 (Litchfield), 42 (Damon), Scituate Town Library; 1910 US Census (Edna A. Litchfield, postmaster, born about 1867). Frederick North Damon (1870-1907, per 1907 Town Report) attended dental school in Baltimore and received a degree as Doctor of Dental Surgery in 1894, but then turned to photography. F. J. S. Gorgas, M.D., D.D.S., Richard Grady, M.D., D.D.S., eds, *The American Journal of Dental Science*, vol. 27, third series (Baltimore: Snowden & Cowman, 1894), 570, https://books.google.com/books?id=OyTSAAAAMAAJ&source=gbs_navlinks_s; Scituate Historical Society, *Scituate*, Images of America series (Charleston, SC: Arcadia Publishing, 2000), 15. In the 1906 Blue Book, Dr. F. N. Damon was listed as living at "Woodbine" cottage in Sand Hills, with a winter address at 38 Woodbine, Roxbury, the same as Mr. & Mrs. C. A. Damon. There was an Anthony Feola listed in the 1915 Directory in Scituate as a photographer (not a postmaster), and his wife Eliza died in 1909, so perhaps she was the publisher E. Feola. See Nyberg, 18 Wampatuck Avenue, SCI.1249, MACRIS (including copy of photo postcard of house published by E. Feola, Scituate, MA).

[486] Postcard collections, SHS; author's postcard collection; postcard images courtesy of Gail Ledwig (red convertible and others). Publishing information is sometimes lacking. "Rivermoor Colony, Third Cliff," is marked "Copyright W.N. Seaver," and some other postcards are marked "Chas. W. Frye, Pub." The

Twomey/Jacobson collection acquired by the Society has at least 16 different postcards of Rivermoor, and more of Third Cliff and cliff-top houses.

487 *1909 VL*, 106.

488 "Rivermoor, Scituate, Mass." postcard, courtesy of Gail Ledwig.

489 For example, see Rivermoor photo, courtesy of Nancy Howell, and Frederick Damon picture postcard of "The Pyramid" in Egypt, the latter copied in SHS Newsletters, vol. 7, issue 9 (April 2003), 8, and vol. 7, issue 10 (May 2003), 8, http://scituatehistoricalsociety.org/newsletter-archive-04/.

490 "Alteration. Collier Road. Third Cliff." entry February 23, 1924, *Town Records, C-17* [vol. 28], 240-241, (making upper end of Collier Road, laid out in 1905, a uniform width of 35 feet), and "Collier Road and Moorland Road from Lincoln Avenue to Lincoln Ave." entry February 23, 1924, *Town Records, C-17* [vol. 28], 243-245 (accepting "all portions of Collier Road and Moorland Road not accepted by the Town of Scituate in the years 1905 and 1921"), *Town Records, C-17* [vol. 28], 249 (Parker Avenue, accepted 1925, as recorded in book marked 1735, location 10 [16?]-3-2 and "Selectmen, Street Layout Descriptions, Series #20, 1925-1929"), in Town Archives; *Town of Scituate Streets and Ways 2010*; Charles Lincoln, "Streets of Scituate" (handwritten notes compiled 1950), SHS; "Michael Avenue" in WPA card index, Town Archives. Because Lincoln's notes refer to specific town meeting votes, they are used in the text instead of the 2010 compilation, as follows: Cliff in 1929 instead of 1939, Lincoln in 1921 instead of 1931. Michael Avenue was formerly known as Meadow Road, Meadow Lane, or Rivermoor Road, according to Murphy, *The Coming of Age*, 151. However, Lincoln's notes state that the town meeting voted in 1924 to indefinitely postpone changing Michael Avenue to Rivermoor Road, and in 1928 to indefinitely postpone changing Michael Avenue to Meadow Road. See *Annual Report of the Officers of the Town of Scituate for the Year Ending December 31, 1924*, 62 (Article 26), 67 (Article 67), and 68 (Article 69); "Michael Avenue" in WPA card index, Town Archives (including entries for March 1, 1926, and March 7, 1927: "Name not to be changed"). See discussion in text about George Welch's 1924 petition to change the name of Michael Avenue, named for his grandfather.

491 Rebecca Onion, "A Telephone Map of the United States Shows Where You Could Call Using Ma Bell in 1910," The Vault (Slate's history blog), posted March 16, 2015, https://slate.com/human-interest/2015/03/history-of-the-american-telephone-system-map-of-bell-coverage-in-1910.html.

492 Southern Massachusetts Telephone Company confirmation of pole locations, filed with town, November 12, 1912, *Town Records, C-17* [vol. 28], 36–41, Town Archives (listing about 40 separate authorizations by selectmen from 1898 to 1912); examples include authorizations to New England Telephone and Telegraph Company of Massachusetts in *Town Records, C-16*, 21 (1898) and 34 (1899). These required the telephone wires to be not less than 20 feet above the ground. Some authorizations were for joint or identical locations of poles, poles that would handle electrical power wires as well as telephone wires. *Town Records, C-20*, 25 (1927-New England Telephone and Telegraph Company of Massachusetts and The Electric Light and Power Company of Abington and Rockland, all wires to be not less than 18 feet above ground). Such utility poles have electrical power wires at their uppermost part, with telephone wires at their lowermost part. Joshua, "7 Interesting Facts About Utility Poles That Dot The American Landscape And Line U.S. Highways & Byways," The Fun Times Guide website, https://travel.thefuntimesguide.com/utility-poles/; California Public Utilities Commission, "A Natural History of the Wooden Utility Pole (July 2017)," formerly at http://www.cpuc.ca.gov/ppd_work/.

493 Murphy, *Irish Mossers*, 57 (photo of "Wm. P. Richardson" store from 1890); *Cohasset Cottager*, 4, column 3, ad, June 30, 1883, https://archive.org/stream/06301883CohassetCottager_ppml/06_30_1883%20Cohasset%20Cottager#page/n3/mode/2up/search/scituate; J. H. Hogan *1894 Directory*, 147 (William P. Richardson pharmacist on Front Street).

494 Item 33, "W. H. Richardson (Store)" on the 1903 map (inset for Scituate Village); "Drugs" store shown on the 1908 Sanborn map, sheet 1 ("S. Shore Av." is really Beal Place); "Drugs" store shown on 1918 Sanborn map, sheet 3.

495 Jarvis Freymann, *Scituate's Educational Heritage 1630–1990* (Scituate Historical Society, 1990), 176; Free Public Library Commission of Massachusetts, *Report of the Free Public Library Commission of Massachusetts*, vol. 9 (Boston: Wright & Potter Printing Co., State Printers, 1899), 324, https://books.google.com/books?id=QKs9AAAAYAAJ&source=gbs_navlinks_s; P.Y.O.C. Social Library Association to William P. Richardson, deed, March 11, 1893, PCRD, book 644, page 450; ad for Richardson's Pharmacy, undated, with W. P. R. legend, clipping in "Businesses — Pre-1980" file, SHS.

496 A drug store and telegraph office appears on Front Street as item 33 on *Plan of Scituate Harbor and Village*, in Briggs, *Shipbuilding on North River*, 368-369, 421 (map key), published in 1889, and the ad appears in the J. H. Hogan *1894 Directory*, 96.

497 *South Shore Herald*, Scituate, August 24, 1860, clipping in "Businesses — Pre-1980" file, SHS

[498] "Telephone and Multiple Telegraph," essay about the Alexander Graham Bell Family Papers at the Library of Congress, Library of Congress website, https://www.loc.gov/collections/alexander-graham-bell-papers/articles-and-essays/telephone-and-multiple-telegraph/.

[499] *Annual Report of the Town Officers of the Town of Scituate for the Year Ending December 30, 1899*, 16–17 (miscellaneous expenses).

[500] *Official Directory, July 1901* (Boston: New England Telephone and Telegraph Company, 1901), 640, https://archive.org/stream/officialdirector19011newe#page/n5/mode/2up.

[501] *Town Records*, C-17, 36–41.

[502] *The South Shore Blue Book* (1906) (unnumbered pages, two-page ad toward the end, for The Southern Massachusetts Telephone Co.).

[503] "Capitol Hill's Telephonic Revolution," US House of Representatives "History, Art & Archives" website, https://history.house.gov/Exhibitions-and-Publications/Electronic-Technology/Telephone/.

[504] Bill Eaton, "Daisy Carpenter Recalls Early Days of Telephone," unidentified news clipping (probably from *Quincy (MA) Patriot Ledger*, and evidently from the 1960s based on the references in the clipping), "Telephones" file, SHS. Perhaps the Coveney Block included what became of the Richardson's drug store, and perhaps the Coveney Block once was at 76 Front Street. See Catherine J. Coveney, Lessor, and Satuit Bar & Grille, Inc., July 14, 1965, Notice of Lease, PCRD, book 3223, page 654. It was later replaced and just south of this location is the Jack Conway realty office (80 Front Street), next to the Coastal Heritage Bank (72 Front Street); just north is the CVS drug store. The Gates clothing store had a location at 97 Front Street in Scituate Harbor, now occupied by The Galley restaurant. Paul McCarthy, "Town of Scituate Massachusetts, Historical Map & Street Directory" (n.p., 1976), author's collection.

[505] *Town Records*, C-17, 36–41.

[506] *Town Records, C-17*, 36-41 (November 13, 1906).

[507] Virtual Museum, on Telecommunications History Group website, http://www.telcomhistory.org/vm/histories.shtml; Rebecca Onion, "A Telephone Map of the United States Shows Where You Could Call Using Ma Bell in 1910," the Vault history blog on Slate website, http://www.slate.com/blogs/the_vault/2015/03/16/history_of_the_american_telephone_system_map_of_bell_coverage_in_1910.html; "Telephone Service" in WPA card index, Town Archives, including entries for minutes of selectmen's meetings June 26, 1909, October 2, 1909, March 12, 1910, and March 22, 1910. The 1910 map shows a branch to Brockton but no lines to Scituate.

[508] *Town Records, C-17*, 100 (record of selectmen's meeting, May 29, 1914).

[509] *Social Register, Summer, 1911*, 533; *Social Register, Summer, 1912*, 550.

[510] Murphy, *The Coming of Age*, 105; "Scituate High School," 327 First Parish Road, SCI.1251, MACRIS.

[511] Margaret Cole Bonney, *Brushy Hill Scituate* (n.p., 1989), 59; John Galluzzo, "Yesterdays: Scituate faces Hingham's 'Fearless Five,'" *Scituate Mariner*, March 3, 2016. H. M. Macdonald is listed in the 1918 New England Telephone directory with residence on Allen Place, and Harry M. Macdonald is listed in the *1918 Directory*, 46 (wife Mabel P.) as druggist, Front Street, home, Allen Place; William P. Richardson is listed, 53, as being in the insurance business.

[512] Murphy, *The Coming of Age*, 111.

[513] Bonney, *Scituate's Sands of Time*, 14; 1910 US Census (Edna F. Litchfield, operator, telephone exchange, born about 1888).

[514] *1915 Directory*, 33 (Daisy L. Graves), *1918 Directory*, 38 (Daisy L. Graves), 50 (company). The 1900 US census says Daisy was born in October 1883.

[515] New England Telephone and Telegraph Company, *Telephone Directory, Summer Issue, 1918, Brockton District*, 99-103, courtesy of Sally Rossi-Ormon (directory covers 25 towns); *1918 VL* (total residences listed at end).

[516] *Telephone Directory, 1918*, 99–103.

[517] *Telephone Directory, 1918*, 99, 135.

[518] Cronon, *Changes in the Land*, 156; *1911 VL*, 87; *Plan of Rivermoor* (1906); unknown photographer, various photographs, c. 1912, in "1900–1916," Woodworth family photograph album (author's copy designation IMG_0984, 0987, 0990, and 1014); Cronon, *Changes in the Land*, 119–120. William H. Welch was listed as a market gardener in the *1915 Directory*, 92.

[519] *Boston Globe*, August 10, 1909.

[520] Garvin, *A Building History*, 130; Robert Schweitzer and Michael W. R. Davis, *America's Favorite Homes: Mail-order Catalogues as a Guide to Popular Early 20th-Century Houses* (Detroit: Wayne State University Press, 1990), 63–64, 90, https://books.google.com/books?id=rKoLHrcwe2MC&source=gbs_navlinks_s; Burnham Kelly, *The Prefabrication of Houses* (Cambridge, MA, and New York: Technology Press of MIT and John Wiley and Sons, Inc., 1951), 11, www.survivorlibrary.com/library/the_prefabrication_of_houses_1951.pdf; Ralph Hammann,

"Prefabrication" in R. Stephen Sennott, ed., *Encyclopedia of Twentieth Century Architecture, Vol. 3 P-Z* (New York: Fitzroy Dearborn, 2004), 1060, preview, https://books.google.com/books?id=O9jeQtQ5CKgC&source=gbs_navlinks_s; Frank Smith, "Hodgson," in *The Genealogical History of Dover, Massachusetts* (Dover: Historical and Natural History Society, 1917), 145; Richard Hart Vara, "Hodgson Houses," in *Dover Days Gone By* (Dover: Dover Historical Society, 2010), 198–199; Paul H. Tedesco, *Dover*, Images of America series (Charleston, SC: Arcadia Publishing, Inc., 2000), 44–46; James C. Massey and Shirley Maxwell, "Pre-Cut Houses," in *Old-House Journal*, November-December 1990, vol. 18, no. 6 (Brooklyn: Old House Journal Corp., 1990), 36, https://books.google.com/books?id=eQiKBlvwrHcC&source=gbs_navlinks_s; James B. Tedesco and Paul H. Tedesco, "Hodgson, Ernest Franklin," *American National Biography Online*, October 2008 update, http://www.anb.org/articles/10/10-02293.html; Judith G. Stetson, "Mail Order Houses," *Spritsail*, vol. 18, no. 2 (summer 2004), 2-25 (use of Hodgson and other prefabs at the Marine Biological Laboratory, Woods Hole, Cape Cod), http://woodsholemuseum.org/oldpages/sprtsl/v18n2-MailOrder.pdf. One authority says that Sears, as well as Pacific Ready-Cut Homes, sold kit houses starting in 1908. Jon Gorey, "When Sears sold the American dream," *Boston Sunday Globe*, July 30, 2017, H1; Rosemary Thornton, "Richard Nixon's Childhood Home in Yorba Linda, California," posted April 15, 2016, and "Is That Really a Sears Kit Home? Nine Easy Ways to Tell," posted May 21, 2011, on Sears Modern Homes former website, http://www.searshomes.org/index.php/2016/04/15/richard-nixons-childhood-home-in-yorba-linda-california/ (and other posts on that website); "What Is a Sears Modern Home?" in Sears Archives website, http://www.searsarchives.com/homes/; "Collection Historical Note," Rosemary Thornton Papers, 1914-2005, Special Collections and University Archives, Old Dominion University, https://www.lib.odu.edu/archon/?p=collections/findingaid&id=58&q=&rootcontentid=34881; see Rebecca Hunter, Historical Architectural Research website, http://www.kithouse.org/. These contained pre-cut lumber, whereas Hodgson cottages and houses contained pre-manufactured panels that could be assembled quickly. Examples of large ads for Hodgson Portable Houses include *The House Beautiful*, vol. 49, February 1921, 147, and April 1921, 347 (New York: The House Beautiful Publishing Co., Inc., 1921), https://catalog.hathitrust.org/Record/000640136, and https://books.google.com/books?id=NbQ7AQAAMAAJ&source=gbs_navlinks_s. Joseph Bailey of Scituate and Boston was a pioneer of portable houses, shipping them out to California in the 1860s. "55 Commonwealth," Back Bay Houses website, https://backbayhouses.org/55-commonwealth/.

[521] "Hodgson Camp Houses," sales booklet (30 pages) (n.p., E. F. Hodgson Co., 1933), https://archive.org/details/HodgsonCampHouses; "Hodgson Prefabricated Houses," sales booklet (49 pages) (n.p., E. F. Hodgson Co., 1937), 22 (Troy), https://archive.org/details/E.F.HodgsonCo.

[522] *Clark's Boston Blue Book for 1920: The Elite Private Address and Club Directory and Ladies' Visiting List, Containing Names of over Twenty-two Thousand Residents from Selected Districts in Boston, Brookline, Cambridge and Newton* (Boston: Sampson & Murdock Company, 1919), 26, https://babel.hathitrust.org/cgi/pt?id=hvd.hn4hnr;view=1up;seq=5, permanent link https://hdl.handle.net/2027/hvd.hn4hnr.

[523] "Hodgson Camp Houses," 20 (source of quote) and other pages.

[524] "Hodgson Camp Houses," 20 and other pages; "Hodgson Houses," sales booklet (64 pages) (n.p., E. F. Hodgson Co., 1933), 3–5 and other pages, https://archive.org/details/HodgsonHouses; "Hodgson Portable Houses," sales booklet (50 pages) (E. F. Hodgson Co., 1908), on former Hodgson Houses website, http://hodgsonhouses.net/Catalogs.htm; Paul H. Tedesco and James B. Tedesco, former Hodgson Houses website, http://hodgsonhouses.net/index.html. McAlester's chapter on manufactured houses starts about 1930 and does not mention Hodgson. McAlester's appendix notes that prefabricated houses were sold by mail order retailers like Montgomery Ward and Sears Roebuck, and later by Macy's department store. McAlester, *Field Guide to American Houses*, 149, 766.

[525] George F. Welch to Florence S. Hodgson, deed, June 10, 1909, PCRD, book 1024, page 388.

[526] Florence S. Hodgson to Emily Eaton Brown, deed, May 2, 1912, PCRD, book 1115, page 529 ("this conveyance includes the house and all other buildings now standing or being up the lot [180] above described"); Ernest F. Hodgson to Emily Eaton Brown, deed, June 12, 1920, PCRD, book 1357, page 484 (conveying any interests he might have had); *1921 VL*, 147 (listing for Artho L. Schofield with house "Hodgson" and lot 180 Rivermoor); *1910 VL*, 112 (Florence Hodgson, "House (Portable)" valued at $600); *1913 VL*, 94 (Emily Eaton Brown, house valued at $600).

[527] Assessor's Database; *1923 VL*, c. 147 (Artho L. Schofield, house "Hodgson" valued at $800); *1924 VL*, 174 (Artho L. Schofield, house "Hodgson" valued at $1,500); *1925 VL*, 181 (Artho L. Schofield, house "Hodgson"

valued at $1,500 and garage valued at $175); *1942 VL,* 69 (Marion Mason O'Shea, house valued at $1,250); Sanborn maps.

[528] "Hodgson Houses," 29; discussion in text below, including Appendix C.

[529] "Hodgson Houses;" *1932 VL,* 30 (Clarence Miller, Maidstone, $5,000), and 113 (Margaret Woodworth, Indian Knoll, $5,500).

[530] Most notes are omitted in this summary, but are available in the *Summer Suffragists* book.

[531] "In Memoriam: Meyer Bloomfield, February 11, 1878 – March 12, 1938," *Occupations: The Vocational Guidance Journal* (now *Journal of Counseling & Development*), vol. 16, no. 7 (Blackwell Publishing Ltd, April 1938), 666, 694–695, online by John Wiley & Sons, Ltd, doi:10.1002/j.2164-5892.1938.tb00354.x.

[532] "In Memoriam," *Occupations*; Sanford M. Jacoby, *Employing Bureaucracy: Managers, Unions, and the Transformation of Work in the 20th Century* (Mahwah, NJ: Lawrence Erlbaum Associates Publishers, 2004, revised ed.), 55–56, https://books.google.com/books?id=xCt6AgAAQBAJ&source=gbs_navlinks_s. An excellent survey of Meyer Bloomfield's work is in Mark L. Savickas, "Meyer Bloomfield: Organizer of the Vocational Guidance Movement (1907–1917)," *The Career Development Quarterly*, March 2009, vol. 57, no. 3, 259–273, text available online.

[533] Savickas, "Meyer Bloomfield: Organizer," 260-261.

[534] "Scituate Betterment Club Has Done Wonderful Job," *Scituate Herald*, September 3, 1937, 1, at 7, col. 3.

[535] Palmer Coates website, http://palmercoates.com/.

[536] "Josiah Colby Bassett," *Boston Globe*, March 8, 1940, 19; *Quinquennial Catalogue of the Officers and Graduates of Harvard University, 1636-1915* (Cambridge: Harvard University Press, 1915), 532, 741, https://books.google.com/books/about/Quinquennial_Catalogue_of_the_Officers_a.html?id=JiNOAAAAMAAJ; "J.C. Bassett, Lawyer Dies," *Boston Herald*, March 8, 1940, copied in "Josiah Colby Bassett," in Bassett Family Association Database, http://www.bassettbranches.org/tng/getperson.php?personID=I14680&tree=1A. Bassett likely appears in his law school class photo, with some 125 people, at Charles Warren, *History of the Harvard Law School and of Early Legal Conditions in America, Volume III. Illustrated* (New York: Lewis Publishing Company, 1908), after 272 (photo), 274 (listing), https://archive.org/details/historyofharvard03warruoft. The Harvard Law School building is pictured about 1901 in a photo by Detroit Publishing Company, copied by Library of Congress, https://www.loc.gov/item/2016794227/.

[537] "Norman L. Bassett," Wikipedia article, https://en.wikipedia.org/wiki/Norman_L._Bassett; "George Kemble Bassett," Bassett Family Association Database, http://www.bassettbranches.org/tng/getperson.php?personID=I14682&tree=1A; "Gardner Colby," Wikipedia article, https://en.wikipedia.org/wiki/Gardner_Colby; email from Jim Merrick, Colby College Libraries, August 5, 2021.

[538] *Boston Globe*, June 20, 1915, 17; *1918 Directory*, 66; *Social Register, Summer 1920* (New York: Social Register Association, 1920), 497, https://babel.hathitrust.org/cgi/pt?id=wu.89058297177;view=1up;seq=1, permanent link, https://hdl.handle.net/2027/wu.89058297177.

[539] *1938 South Shore Social Register*, 132; "Hermon Holt Jr., Ex-Law Partner," obituary, *Boston Globe*, January 8, 1968, 30; *Quinquennial Catalogue - Harvard 1915*, 744; *The Mayflower Descendant, A Quarterly Magazine of Pilgrim Genealogy and History*, vol. 28 (Boston: Massachusetts Society of Mayflower Descendants, 1930, Heritage Books reprint 1996), 189, preview, https://books.google.com/books?id=hod04FbhUHsC&source=gbs_navlinks_s; Elizabeth McCarthy to Marian W. Holt, deed, October 29, 1930, PCRD, book 1603, page 413 (Cliff Avenue, lot 48); Marian W. and Hermon Holt Jr. to Pierre Laneres, deed, December 5, 1930, PCRD, book 1605, page 322 (eastern half of lot 48); Hermon Holt Jr. to Catherine W. Spaulding, deed, September 12, 1940, PCRD, book 1795, page 149 (lots 61, 62, 50, 49, 31 and 32); Marian W. and Hermon Holt Jr. to Catherine W. Spaulding, deed, September 12, 1940, PCRD, book 1795, page 150 (western half of lot 48). Holt likely appears in his law school class photo, with some 125 people, at Warren, *History of the Harvard Law School*, after 284 (photo), 326 (listing).

[540] "Furlong, Charles Wellington, 1874–1967," Dartmouth Library Archives & Manuscripts, https://archives-manuscripts.dartmouth.edu/agents/people/1341; and "Charles Furlong papers," Dartmouth Library Archives & Manuscripts, https://archives-manuscripts.dartmouth.edu/repositories/2/resources/1141; "Charles Wellington Furlong papers, 1896–1967," finding aid, University of Oregon Libraries, Archives West, http://archiveswest.orbiscascade.org/ark:/80444/xv23562; "Charles Wellington Furlong," Smithsonian American Art Museum, https://americanart.si.edu/artist/charles-wellington-furlong-1704; Charles Wellington Furlong, "Tribal Distribution and Settlements of the Fuegians, Comprising Nomenclature, Etymology, Philology, and Populations." *Geographical Review* vol. 3, no. 3 (March 1917), 169–87 (map on 177), https://doi.org/10.2307/207659; "Third Cliff," *Scituate Herald*, August 21, 1936, 4, col. 4; "Col Furlong of

Boston Ends Latest Adventure in Africa: Returns to London After Covering 7000 Miles, Bagging Elephants and Lions, and Finding Lone Survivor of Livingstone Party," *Boston Globe*, July 2, 1930, 12 (source of quote). Furlong's papers were not reviewed for this book.

541 George W. Boland and Robert A. Young, executors of will of James Young, to Charles W. Furlong of Scituate, deed, May 13, 1931, PCRD, book 1611, page 532; Charles W. Furlong of Old Oaken Bucket Road, Scituate, to Norman F. Coolbroth and Grace N. Coolbroth of 84 Ellison Park, Waltham, deed, July 21, 1942, PCRD, book 1832, page 271 (two parcels on Collier Road including strip of land next to lot 42 [10 Cliff]); note in chapter 20 about Coolbroth house.

542 "Col. C. W. Furlong Home From Lecture Trip," *Scituate Herald*, March 28, 1941, 4; *1944 VL*, 110; "House of Eight Gables," 304 Old Oaken Bucket Rd, SCI.121, MACRIS.

543 Furlong papers, University of Oregon; "Henry T. Bailey papers, 1880–1931," finding aid, University of Oregon Libraries, Archives West, http://archiveswest.orbiscascade.org/ark:/80444/xv767546.

544 "Col. Furlong At Norwell Tells Real History," *Scituate Herald*, August 13, 1937, 2; Mat Brown, Bob Gallagher, and Carol Miles, *Legendary Locals of Scituate, Massachusetts* (Charleston, SC: Legendary Locals/Arcadia Publishing, 2013), 12 (with photo); *Journal of American Folk-lore*, Volume XXVII (Lancaster, PA: American Folk-Lore Society, 1914), 438 (Newton; member in 1914), https://books.google.com/books?id=6DOdAAAAMAAJ&source=gbs_navlinks_s.

545 *Scituate, 1636–1936*, with booklet's credits on last page; "Report of Tercentenary Executive Committee," *Annual Report of the Officers & Committees of the Town of Scituate for the Year Ending December 31, 1936*, 367 at 370, https://archive.org/details/annualreportofto1934scit/page/370/mode/2up.

546 "Scituate," *Boston Globe*, June 21, 1914, 6 (quote).

547 John R. Stilgoe, *What is Landscape?* (Cambridge, MA: MIT Press, 2015), 116-119, 217; "Kingscote," The Preservation Society of Newport County website, http://www.newportmansions.org/explore/kingscote (one of Newport's earliest "cottages" built in 1839); Visit New England website, http://www.visitri.com/state/mansions/.

548 Assessor's Database; US Census Bureau, "Median and Average Square Feet of Floor Area in New Single-Family Houses Completed by Location" (1973 figures are the earliest on this chart, and the earliest available from the Census Bureau), https://www.census.gov/const/C25Ann/sftotalmedavgsqft.pdf; US Census Bureau, "2015 Characteristics of New Housing," "Median and Average Square Feet" table, 345, entire set of tables at https://www.census.gov/construction/chars/; and see US Census Bureau, "Highlights of Annual 2015 Characteristics of New Housing," https://www.census.gov/construction/chars/highlights.html. One study has calculated average house sizes back to 1920, when a new single-family house averaged 1,048 square feet. Evan Comen, "The Size of a Home the Year You Were Born," 24/7 Wall St. website, posted May 25, 2016, http://247wallst.com/special-report/2016/05/25/the-size-of-a-home-the-year-you-were-born/. The estimated average house size in 1900 was less than 1,000 square feet. NAHB Research Center, Inc., "Review of Structural Materials and Methods for Home Building in the United States: 1900 to 2000" (Washington, DC: US Department of Housing and Urban Development, Office of Policy Development and Research, 2001), 2, www.huduser.gov/portal/Publications/PDF/review.pdf. The term "cottage" appears to have returned to its original meaning as a small house by the 1930s, when cottage colonies and motels with separate structures appeared on Cape Cod and other places. O'Connell, *Becoming Cape Cod*, 54–56.

549 John Galluzzo, "How the Irish rebuilt Scituate," *Scituate Mariner* website, posted August 2, 2016, http://scituate.wickedlocal.com/news/20160802/how-irish-rebuilt-scituate.

550 "Scituate," *Boston Globe*, June 21, 1914, 6. The Mayo was later assigned number 18 Lincoln.

551 "W. H. Mayo, Brookline, Bequeathed $50,000," *Boston Globe*, September 21, 1927, 2; "Three Teachers Guests," *Boston Globe*, January 26, 1908, 7. See "Coming Out Party for Miss Mayo and Miss Rankin," *Boston Globe*, November 21, 1928, 4; "Mayo, William F. Co.," Summer St. listing, 1916 *Boston Directory*, 1380.

552 "Scituate," *Boston Globe*, June 21, 1914, 6; "Scituate," *Boston Globe*, June 27, 1915, 4; "Scituate; New Residences Constructed for Growing Summer Colony," *Boston Globe*, June 1, 1911, 18. Mitton cottage was built on lots 29 and 52, the equivalent of 12 Moorland, according to *1912 VL*, 80. It was demolished about 2015.

553 *The Lawyers' List* (New York: Hubert R. Brown, 1913), 114, https://books.google.com/books?id=7y4UAAAAIAAJ&source=gbs_navlinks_s; *The Lawyers' List* (New York: Hubert R. Brown, 1920), 128, https://archive.org/details/lawyerslist05browgoog; "Arthur G. Mitton, Prominent Attorney Here, in 69th Year," *Boston Globe*, May 20, 1952, 20. He represented Jordan Marsh in *In re Hanover Trust Co.*, 135 N.E. 166 (Massachusetts Supreme Judicial Court, April 21, 1922), https://books.google.com/books?id=sPcKAAAAYAAJ&source=gbs_navlinks_s.

554 Edward J. Mitton listing, 1880 US Census, Population Schedule 1, Cambridge, Middlesex County, Massachusetts, E.D. 435, page 15, lines 5–9, digital images, HeritageQuest; Edward J. Mitton listing, 1900 US

Census, Population Schedule 1, Brookline Town, Norfolk County, Massachusetts, E.D. 1019, sheet 21, lines 20-25, digital images, HeritageQuest.

[555] BAK, "Jordan Marsh," The Department Store Museum blog, posted October 2011, http://www.thedepartmentstoremuseum.org/2010/09/jordan-marsh-company-boston.html; "Edward R. Mitton, 77, was president of Jordan Marsh," *Boston Globe*, June 26, 1973, 39, and "Newton services today for Edward R. Mitton," *Boston Globe*, June 27, 1973, 39; Anthony M. Sammarco, *Jordan Marsh: New England's Largest Store* (Charleston, SC: History Press, 2017), 147-149 and other pages.

[556] Anderson, *Summer Estates*, 11, 21; "Grasshead," 45 Little's Point Road (1882, demolished), SWA.122, MACRIS; Garland, *The North Shore*, 278–279.

[557] *1917 VL*, for example (still spelled as "Mitten"); George F. Welch to Lillian M. Greene, deed, September 11, 1919, PCRD, book 1332, page 18; Paul Bowers, email to author, September 19, 2016.

[558] "Scituate," *Boston Globe*, July 4, 1909, 24; *Boston Globe*, June 20, 1915, 17; *Boston Globe*, June 27, 1915, 4; *1930 VL, A-L*, 67, listing for Hazel Eichorn as owner of a "House (Leonard)" at this location. The house, at 22 Collier, has since been demolished.

[559] "Scituate," *Boston Globe*, June 27, 1915, 4, compared to "Scituate," *Boston Globe*, June 21, 1914, 6.

[560] Assessor hand-drawn plot plans, by street, about 1930-35, Town Archives (containing street addresses). Numbering of houses was not completed until 1936, under a federal project, according to Murphy, *The Coming of Age*, 129. The *Boston Globe* did not include house names in "Scituate," *Boston Globe*, July 26, 1931, 1. The 1939 Sanborn map (Rivermoor section) did not include house names.

[561] Author's observations. See Anderson, *Summer Estates*, 43-45, 128-129 (Swampscott). Cottage locations can be found using 1918 and 1926 Sanborn maps (showing house names) and the current assessor's map, House, *Town of Scituate Mass*, Sheet 64 (street addresses overlaid on lot numbers from the 1906 Rivermoor Plan). Of the 22 cottages listed in the 1914 news article, 9 appear on the 1918 Sanborn map, and locations for most of the others can be identified using early tax valuation lists. Most current Third Cliff homeowners are unaware of these historical names, which are listed in Appendix A.

[562] The practice of having house signs, or "quarterboards," was discussed in an article by Jon Gorey, "Household Names," *Boston Sunday Globe*, September 3, 2017, H1, available at http://realestate.boston.com/uncategorized/2017/08/31/should-you-name-your-house/. The article quotes Paul McCarthy, then co-owner of Nantucket Carving and Folk Art. McCarthy was a woodcarving and quarterboard fixture in Scituate in the 1970s and later, and now works in Nantucket. https://www.paulmccarthywoodcarving.com/; "Paul McCarthy Woodcarving," Nantucket Online, https://www.nantucketonline.com/paul-mccarthy-woodcarving/. Now the tradition in Scituate is carried on by Paul Kukstis, Kukstis Woodcarving, http://www.kukstis.com/. Kristi Funderburk, "MEET THE ARTIST: Kukstis carves career for himself in Scituate," *Scituate Mariner* website, posted November 28, 2014, http://scituate.wickedlocal.com/article/20141128/news/141127631; Ruth Thompson, "Scituate woodcarver Paul Kukstis carves out his passion," *Scituate Mariner* website, posted December 20, 2012, http://www.wickedlocal.com/x1783185592/Scituate-woodcarver-Carving-out-his-passion. Partly because of these woodcarvers, naming cottages continues to be popular throughout Scituate. Kerriann Kelleher, "What's in a name? Cottage names define Scituate neighborhood," *Quincy (MA) Patriot Ledger*, website, posted June 29, 2016, updated July 8, 2016, http://www.patriotledger.com/news/20160629/whats-in-name-cottage-names-define-scituate-neighborhood.

[563] *From Boston to Plymouth: A series of views of historical places enroute to Pilgrim Land in commemoration of the ter-centenary celebration* (n.p., 1921), no page number, SHS; 1918 VL, 93; Harrison L. House, *Wharf Properties of George F. Welch, Located in Scituate, Mass., 1919, corrected to April 1923, Scale 1 inch = 40 feet*, PCRD, plan book 3, page 504.

[564] "Sand and Gravel Brevities," *Rock Products and Building Materials*, vol. 17, issue 3 (Chicago: Francis Publishing Company, December 7, 1915), 28, https://books.google.com/books?id=jd9QAAAAYAAJ&source=gbs_navlinks_s.

[565] Town water came from a private water company for years. See 1926 Sanborn map, sheet 1; Glinski, *Old Oaken Buckets*. The 1931 Town Report said the town purchased the Scituate Water Company and it included maps showing that water ran to parts of Third Cliff: Water Street to Collier Road and part of Moorland Road, with short branches to the eastern side of Parker Avenue and the western side of Cliff Avenue, and longer branches covering Michael and Lincoln Avenues. Proposed future extensions included the remainder of Moorland Road. *1931 Town Report*, "Report of Selectmen," 11–12, and "Report of Water Department," plates A & B, 180–181; 1918 Sanborn map, sheet 1 (below medallion) (average consumption). The Sanborn insurance company was interested in towns' water supplies in case of fire.

[566] *1915 Directory*, 14; *1918 Directory*, 16; daughter of Clarence C. Miller [Harriet M. "Teddy" Ellis (1920–2009)], "12 Parker Ave.," unpublished letter, about 2000, in possession of John L. Sullivan.

567 John Galluzzo, "Yesterdays: Ladies Aid Society hosts mock trial," *Quincy (MA) Patriot Ledger* website, posted August 31, 2015, http://www.patriotledger.com/article/20150831/NEWS/150839939 (mentions Rivermoor post office in August 1915); *1915 Directory*, 14, 31 (Miss Beatrice A. Flaherty, "confectionery and postmistress"); 1918 Sanborn map; *1918 Directory*, 16, 36. Several Flaherty residences appear at Collier and Water on the 1903 map, and the post office was possibly in one of the structures built in 1863, as noted elsewhere about the John Curran house, including chapter 4 on Early Houses. See Daniel Noonan release of rights in new Dwelling House and buildings built by him and John Curran, April 9, 1863, PCRD, book 317, page 43. An undated photograph/postcard "Cottages and Post Office, Third Cliff, Scituate, Mass." in the Lester Hobson collection at the SHS seems to show the post office at that location.
568 *1926 Directory*, 50 ("Fallon Frank F. (Ellen H.) genl mdse The Driftway, h do, R"); *1930 VL*; *1938 South Shore Social Register*, 131 ("Mrs. Frank Fallon"). The post office moved between 1918 and 1926 to a structure near the northeast corner of the Driftway (Water Street) and Gilson Road (the later name for Highland in this area, also called County Road or County Highway), and it was run by the Fallon family. *1926 Directory*, 32; 1918 Sanborn map (showing shed at corner of the Highland-Water [Gilson-Driftway] intersection with house just to its east); 1926 Sanborn map (showing post office at second structure east of the Highland-Water intersection). A "John Fallone" is shown as owning a house there on the 1903 map. The 1926 directory lists the Rivermoor post office on the Driftway, with postmaster Frank F. Fallon.
569 "Third Cliff Postoffice at Scituate Destroyed," *Boston Globe*, November 14, 1935, 12. By 1939, a new structure appeared as the post office with an adjoining structure (probably the store); *Scituate, Plymouth County, Massachusetts* [map], 1 inch = 100 feet (New York: Sanborn Map Company, August 1939), sheet 14, State Library of Massachusetts, Special Collections, film box 709, reel 37; Third Cliff-Rivermoor Improvement Association minutes of meeting, August 26, 1949, in Association's archives; Paula Buckley letter to Mrs. Polly Bowers, probably 1986.
570 George F. Welch to Charles W. Frye, deed, April 24, 1909, PCRD, book 1028, page 208; 1918 Sanborn map, sheet 8; *1915 Directory*, 32; *1918 Directory*, 37.
571 1918 Sanborn map; *1918 Directory*, 46 (listing for Goon S. Loy, laundry and home at Front Street, corner of Brook Street), 47 (listing for Meadowbrook Laundry on Brook Street), and 108 (listing both). It was reported that the Meadowbrook Laundry was founded and owned by James W. Turner (born 1874, developer of area around Turner Avenue and Wampatuck Avenue), and the building burned and was not replaced by him. Power, "Turner Family Notes," 71, "Turner Family Genealogy," 111–112; see "Rain Caused Heavy Damage in Scituate," *Boston Globe*, July 11, 1921, 2 (fire). The laundry legacy continued at the corner of Front and Brook. Corson's Town Cleaners and Scituate Cleaners were located there, according to Scituate Historical Society, *Scituate*, Then & Now series, 18. Also, "Scituate Cleansers" appears in a photo of the building at this corner, south of where Maria's Submarine Shop is now, in a photo by William Wigmanich from evidently the early 1970s, filed in Town Archives, location 19-1-3.
572 Unknown photographer, "1900–1916," Woodworth family photograph album (several photos about 1913-1916 showing tennis court with "Indian Knoll" cottage in background behind tennis players, child playing croquet, and footraces on Rivermoor beach); John ("Jack") H. Spurr, letter to author, May 15, 2016 (croquet). A tennis court is probably the white area near the center in "Rivermoor, Scituate, Mass.," postcard, postmarked 1917, courtesy of Gail Ledwig. On close examination, it appears to show a fence on the west end of the court, which was on vacant lots on the south side of Michael Avenue.
573 *Omaha [NE] Bee*, May 19, 1915, 11 (largest item in classified ads, under "For Rent"), http://nebnewspapers.unl.edu/lccn/sn99021999/1915-05-19/ed-1/seq-11.pdf. The ad also appeared in the *Pittsburgh Gazette Times*, April 1, 1915, 14, https://news.google.com/newspapers?nid=1126&dat=19150401&id=bf5QAAAAIBAJ&sjid=HGYDAAAAIBAJ&pg=4686,4105310&hl=en, and the *Boston Evening Transcript*, April 7, 1915, Part 3, page 8, https://news.google.com/newspapers?nid=2249&dat=19150407&id=3CcnAAAAIBAJ&sjid=ggMGAAAAIBAJ&pg=4777,1440896&hl=en.
574 The "Manufactured for the Trade" chapter in Brown, *Inventing New England*, 105-134, argues that Nantucket promoted, even largely invented, its quaintness to attract nostalgic tourism.
575 Russell Fish files, SHS.
576 Molly Watson, "The Enduring History of the Glenwood Stove," Edible Communities website, posted April 10, 2017, https://www.ediblecommunities.com/home/the-enduring-history-of-the-glenwood-stove/.
577 Aron, *Working At Play*, 61–63; *Boston Globe*, June 23, 1914, 15; *Boston Globe*, May 8, 1915, 15; *Boston Globe*, April 17, 1918, 13; examples of 8-9 room houses at 10 and 12 Parker Avenue in Scituate in Assessor's Database as of the end of 2016. For an interesting list (which I have not fact-checked) of what things were like in 1915, see Lyn, "Here's Looking at You: The Year was 1915," [Hillsboro, IL] *Journal-News* website, posted January 12,

298

2015, http://www.thejournal-news.net/opinion/commentary/here-s-looking-at-you-the-year-was/article_565162d6-99f9-11e4-8ff9-bf9e0d2432b5.html?mode=story.

[578] O'Connell, *Becoming Cape Cod*, 20.

[579] Eleanor Early, *And This is Cape Cod!* (Boston: Houghton Mifflin Co., 1936), 179-180, as quoted in O'Connell, *Becoming Cape Cod*, 49, note 8.

[580] O'Connell, *Becoming Cape Cod*, 49-50, 51 (illustration). According to O'Connell, Oyster Harbors in 2003 had over a hundred homes; Rivermoor today has about a hundred homes.

[581] *Boston Globe*, June 20, 1915, 17.

[582] Boston Globe, June 27, 1915, 4; 1915 Directory.

[583] Author's calculations based on 15 houses mentioned that were in Rivermoor (all but "Sunshine," location unknown), excluding sequential rentals of same house ("Russell" and "Moorfield"), out of 37 houses built by then (some of which may have already been rented or sold). All five houses on Michael were rented.

[584] John Galluzzo, "Yesterdays: Scituate faces Hingham's 'Fearless Five,'" *Scituate Mariner*, March 8, 2016; *Cambridge Chronicle*, September 20, 1913, 15 (Trott), https://cambridge.dlconsulting.com/cgi-bin/cambridge?a=d&d=Chronicle19130920-01.2.115.

[585] John Galluzzo, "Yesterdays: Scituate faces Hingham's 'Fearless Five,'" *Scituate Mariner*, March 8, 2016; Eric White, "In Memory of Fathers," Boston Society of Architects/AIA website, posted June 15, 2016, https://www.architects.org/news/memory-fathers; Robert M. Fogelson, *Downtown: Its Rise and Fall, 1880-1950* (New Haven: Yale University Press, 2001), 139-140, preview, https://books.google.com/books?id=6X-WCewsP-AC&source=gbs_navlinks_s; "Blackall, Clarence Howard" in Albert Nelson Marquis, ed., *Who's Who in America, vol. 7, 1912–1913* (Chicago: A. N. Marquis & Company, 1912), 181, https://books.google.com/books?id=v4MGW6mbi0QC&source=gbs_navlinks_s.

[586] *Social Register, Summer 1920* (New York: Social Register Association, 1920), https://babel.hathitrust.org/cgi/pt?id=wu.89058297177;view=1up;seq=1, permanent link, https://hdl.handle.net/2027/wu.89058297177.

[587] Turk Tracey & Larry Architects, LLC, *Scituate Historical & Cultural Resources Survey of Egypt and Minot/North Scituate Beach* (n.p., Town of Scituate, June 18, 2004), 16 (North Scituate Beach a "good representative example" recommended for National Register District), and Turk Tracey & Larry Architects, LLC, *Scituate Historical & Cultural Resources Survey of Scituate* (n.p., Town of Scituate, December 20, 2007), 14 (all three cliffs are representative examples, but only First Cliff recommended for evaluation for potential National Register District), both on file at Scituate Historical Commission and on its website, http://www.scituatema.gov/historical-commission/pages/historical-surveys.

[588] 1908, 1918, 1926 Sanborn maps.

[589] Email from Jim Boynton, November 26, 2018; Turk Tracey *2004 Survey*, 2; 1926 Sanborn map; Massachusetts Historical Commission, *MHC Reconnaissance Survey Town Report: Scituate* (Boston: Massachusetts Historical Commission, 1981), 2 (upper income North Scituate Beach "representing the only instance of clustering relatively 'high style' late 19th century residential structures in the town" except for a few estates elsewhere), 12, https://www.sec.state.ma.us/mhc/mhcpdf/townreports/SE-Mass/sci.pdf; 1903 map; Wilkins, "Historical Sketch," *North Scituate Beach*; "Continuity and Change - North Scituate" (quotes from the Secretary's Report of the North Scituate Beach Improvement Association for 1906–07), SHS website, http://scituatehistoricalsociety.org/continuity-and-change-in-north-scituate.

[590] *Annual Report of the Town Officers of the Town of Scituate for the Year Ending December 30, 1899*, 27 ("Building Sewer at North Scituate Beach"); 1908 Sanborn map, sheet 2, upper right ("Independent Electric Plant" next to laundry); Hatherly Country Club website, https://www.hatherlycc.com/club/scripts/library/view_document.asp?NS=PUBLIC&DN=HISTORY; *United States Golf Association Year Book 1921* (n.p., 1921), 104, https://books.google.com/books?id=5jUQAAAAYAAJ&source=gbs_navlinks_s (Hatherly Country Club founders 1912).

[591] MHC, *MHC Reconnaissance Survey Scituate*, 12 (Seaside Chapel designed by Henry Turner Bailey built 1894), 11 (summer chapels built at North Scituate Beach 1903 and Sand Hills 1913); "Seaside Chapel, North Scituate Beach" and "Roman Catholic Church" in DAR, *Old Scituate*, 208–209 (chapel built 1894), 207; Wilkins, "Historical Sketch," *North Scituate Beach*, 28th unnumbered page in sketch (chapel built 1896); 1903 map, List of Owners Names in North Scituate Beach, items 189-190 (R. C. Church); *1906 VL*, 135. The earliest tax reference found for the Seaside Chapel was in the *1897 VL*, 114, which lists it as a Baptist Chapel off Beach Street (now Gannett Road), valued at $1,250. The chapel is pictured in a postcard from about 1915–1923, published by J. K. Gannett, Jr., of Minot, MA, untitled and not postmarked, a photocopy of which is in "Churches-Seaside Chapel" file in the SHS; its appearance matches an illustration of a program in the same file

for a preaching service at the chapel featuring a talk by Henry Turner Bailey. The Seaside Chapel property was sold in 1939 after a determination it was no longer used for religious purposes. George M. Amerige, James A. Armstrong, and C. E. Vernon Jensen, trustees, to Claire A. Stiles, deed, September 2, 1939, PCRD, book 1775, page 548. The chapel was converted into a house at what is now 14 Ocean Avenue and it does not look like a chapel. The house was later the summer home of Boston mayor James Michael Curley and family.

[592] Wilkins, "Historical Sketch," *North Scituate Beach*, 29th to 30th unnumbered pages in sketch.

[593] DAR, *Old Scituate*, 242 (1898 damage at North Scituate's Rocky Beach, also Sand Hills); "New Residences Constructed for Growing Summer Colony," *Boston Globe*, June 18, 1911, 18.

[594] "1900–1916," Woodworth family photograph album; *Social Register, Summer, 1911*, 541 (listed in North Scituate); Lyle Nyberg, "Place Cottage," 17 Collier Avenue, SCI.1242, MACRIS; *Social Register, Summer, 1912*, 558 (listed at "Indian Knoll"); *1918 Directory* (listing for Woodworths); George F. Welch to Margaret K. Woodworth, deed, October 9, 1919, PCRD, book 1332, page 410. Margaret Woodworth's father, Charles Kennard, previously had the family summering in Blue Hill, Maine. "Table Gossip," *Boston Globe*, May 17, 1885, 12: "Mr. Charles W. Kennard and family of Chestnut street went last week to their summer house at Blue Hill." This appears to be Blue Hill, Maine (not the Blue Hills of greater Boston), which was an early summer colony. "The History of Blue Hill," Blue Hill Historical Society website, https://bluehillhistory.org/history/. Margaret Woodworth sold the property in 1933. Margaret K. Woodworth to Marie G. Newell, deed, February 13, 1933, PCRD, book 1642, page 139 (all personal property included except, "1 baby's crib, mattress and pillow; 1 single iron bed; 2 bicycles; personal articles of clothing, books and family photographs.")

[595] Porter E. Sargent, *A Handbook of New England* (Boston: Porter E. Sargent, 1916), 527–530, https://books.google.com/books?id=z0AAAAAAYAAJ&source=gbs_navlinks_s.

[596] Bonney, *My Scituate*, 2; interviews with current residents, including John L. Sullivan, January 20, 2016.

[597] Geo., "Hatfield's Colors," *A Postcard from Canton* website, posted March 17, 2013, http://cantonhistory.blogspot.com/2013/03/hatfields-colors.html. This site has a detailed biography of Hatfield, with a photo captioned "Joseph Hatfield at Third Cliff, Scituate, Mass. 1918 (Courtesy of the Canton Historical Society.)"

[598] "1915 primary drew 376 voters in Scituate," WickedLocal.com website, posted October 23, 2015, http://scituate.wickedlocal.com/article/20151023/NEWS/151028531/?Start=1; *1918 Directory*, 81; *1926 Directory*, 101; "Scituate," *Boston Globe*, July 4, 1909, 24. Josephine Lewis is buried in Scituate's Union Cemetery.

[599] *Scituate Cliffs*, Plenty of Paintings website, http://www.plentyofpaintings.com/Mariquita-Gill/Scituate-Cliffs-oil-painting.html; *Marsh Landscape* (c. 1905), Heritage Auctions website, https://fineart.ha.com/itm/fine-art-painting-american/modern-1900-1949-/mariquita-gill-american-1861-1915-marsh-landscape-circa-1905oil-on-canvas15-x-22-inches-381-x-559-cm-signe/a/5174-70069.s?ic3=ViewItem-Auction-Archive-ThisAuction-120115; "Lucy Littell, 1882," Brookline Historical Society website, http://www.brooklinehistoricalsociety.org/archives/listPhotos.asp?mainList=archives&subList=MarnieWilliams; Acts and Resolves Passed by the General Court of Massachusetts in 1899 (Boston: Secretary of the Commonwealth, Wright & Potter Printing Co., State Printers, 1899), 641 (Changes of Names: November 14, 1898, from Mariquita Gill Cobb to Mariquita Sherriff Gill, Scituate), https://books.google.com/books?id=e2YSAAAAYAAJ&source=gbs_navlinks_s.

[600] SHS files on artists reviewed by author; Nicholas Kilmer, "Why the Nude Person?" in *Mystery Readers Journal*, vol. 21, no. 2 (Berkeley, CA: Mystery Readers International, Summer 2005), http://mysteryreaders.org/journal-index/art-mysteries-ii/; Nicholas Kilmer, "Thomas Buford Meteyard: A Biography," in Nicholas Kilmer, ed., *Thomas Buford Meteyard Paintings and Watercolors*, exhibition catalog (New York: Berry-Hill Galleries, Inc., 1989); "'The Bawdy House Set' A 19th Century Art Colony at Scituate, Massachusetts, 1889–1910," 19thCenturyArtColony.org website http://www.19thcenturyartcolony.org/; "Scituate," *Boston Globe*, July 4, 1909, 24; "Meteyard, Thomas Buford" in Albert Nelson Marquis, ed., *Who's Who in America, vol. 7, 1912–1913* (Chicago: A. N. Marquis & Company, 1912), 1435, https://books.google.com/books?id=v4MGW6mbi0QC&source=gbs_navlinks_s.

[601] "Beckington, Alice" in Marquis, *Who's Who 1912–1913*, 140; email from Purr Whalley, March 26, 2018, and various emails since then from Alex Gow of Bow, NH, who has the watercolor.

[602] Nicholas Kilmer and David Noonan, Jr., "The Scituate Connection," in *Scenes from Vagabondia*, 23; Shannon Aaron, "Notes on a Vagabond Life," in *Scenes from Vagabondia*, 106; Dawson Dawson-Watson Catalogue Raisonné Project, www.dawsondawson-watson.org.

[603] "Lysander Salmon Richards," Find A Grave website, https://www.findagrave.com/memorial/147583130/lysander-salmon-richards; conversation with Dottie Melcher, Marshfield Historical Society, May 7, 2017; 1903 map, plate 27 ("L. S. Richards"); "Bawdy House," 19thCenturyArtColony.org website; Marshfield Historical Society website,

http://www.marshfieldhistoricalsociety.com/our-collections; "Fanny Otis Bartlett Richards," Chevy Chase Historical Society website, http://chevychasehistory.org/node/279/; Cynthia Hagar Krusell, *Plymouth Colony to Plymouth County: The Land, the Church, the People 1680–1690* (Marshfield: Pondside Publishing, 2010), 48, preview, https://books.google.com/books?id=DyRKAgAAQBAJ&source=gbs_navlinks_s. Based on the 1903 map, the Richards house was probably at about 230 Spring Street; the house there now was built in 1926 with 3 ½ acres of land. See Marshfield Assessor Maps, part 1, sheet D19, parcel 01-08, https://www.marshfield-ma.gov/assessors. See also *Cohasset Cottager*, October 20, 1883, 4, col. 1 ("Miss Eleanor Richards has left town to spend the winter months with friends in Washington, D. C."), https://archive.org/stream/10201883CohassetCottager_ppml/10_20_1883%20Cohasset%20Cottager#page/n3/search/richards.

[604] SHS files on artists reviewed by author; Krusell and Bates, *Marshfield*, 151 (illustration caption); *1918 Directory*; "Antique Golf Painting 'Rare' Sears Gallagher Watercolor …. Rare" eBay listing by "antiquenut81" ended June 16, 2015, http://www.ebay.com/itm/ANTIQUE-GOLF-PAINTING-RARE-SEARS-GALLAGHER-WATERCOLOR-RARE-/261925236991; "5 American Watercolorists: Sears Gallagher, Hayley Lever, Dodge Macknight, John Whorf, and Annie Gooding Sykes," MutualArt website, https://www.mutualart.com/Exhibition/5-American-Watercolorists--Sears-Gallagh/4976298E307191F2; Sears Gallagher's watercolor "Third Cliff, Scituate, Massachusetts" was on Spanierman Gallery website, http://www.spanierman.com/5-American-Watercolorists/Third-Cliff,-Scituate,-Massachusetts/8/1/, but website is now inactive, and may be viewed at https://web.archive.org/web/20080902024321/http://www.spanierman.com/.

[605] SHS files on artists reviewed by author (including names of artists listed in the *Scituate Herald*, September 4, 1936), interviews of local residents by author, and *Harold Howard Directories* from 1918, 1926, and 1938; "Scituate," *Boston Globe*, July 4, 1909, 24; *1915 Directory*, 73 ("Artists"); "Miss Elizabeth R. Scott," [obituary], *Boston Globe*, October 7, 1928, 1; Frank Nason listing, 1940 US Census, Population Schedule, Scituate, Plymouth County, Massachusetts, Greenbush, S.D. 15, E.D. 12-68, sheet 1B, line 76, digital images, HeritageQuest, citing NARA microfilm publication T627, roll not identified; 1930 US census for Joyce Bloomfield, New York City; Lincoln Bloomfield, Jr., email, June 18, 2017; "Joyce MacCorquodale," *The Gazette* [Colorado Springs, CO], January 20, 2008, Legacy.com website, http://www.legacy.com/obituaries/gazette/obituary.aspx?n=joyce-maccorquodale&pid=101572141. Both Nason and Bloomfield had paintings in a 1936 art exhibit, one of the town's tercentenary events. "Third Cliff," *Scituate Herald*, September 4, 1936, 4.

[606] Clarence E. and Frances Brier are listed in the *1926 Directory*, 41, as having a home on Highland (today's Greenfield Lane), served by the Rivermoor post office, even though they owned property on Gilson Road. They were from Chestnut Hill in Boston. She is listed as an artist in A. J. Philpott, "Women 18 to 55 in Cinderella Contest: Emergency Fund Total is Now $2,082,427.60," *Boston Globe*, February 8, 1935, 1 & 29. A portrait of her by John Hilliard is pictured and featured in A. J. Philpott, "Contemporary Paintings and Sculptures Now on Exhibition at Boston Art Club," *Boston Globe*, May 6, 1935, 4. Mr. & Mrs. Brier are listed on Highland, Third Cliff, in *1938 South Shore Social Register*, 121.

[607] Telephone conversation with Elizabeth Davey, June 5, 2018; "Artist Biography" website, http://www.seawyxstudios.com/artistbio.html, no longer active, but see https://web.archive.org/web/20190311002441/http://www.seawyxstudios.com/artistbio.html.

[608] Teresa R. Tobin to Claudia M. [sic] Edgell, deed, July 10, 1961, PCRD, book 2864, page 442 (Gilson Road property, sold in 1971); John L. Sullivan, Jr., to Stephen M. Edgell and Claudia Kelty Edgell, Husband and Wife, deed, October 14, 1968, PCRD, book 3489, page 558 (9 Collier Road property); John D. Clemson, "The Henry Z. Cobb House, 8 Sheffield West, Winchester, Massachusetts," prepared October 22, 2008, at John Clemson website, http://clemsonpreservation.com/pdf/8SheffieldWest.pdf; conversation with Pete Hanlon, March 13, 2016 (dog shows).

[609] Brown, et al, *Legendary Locals of Scituate, Massachusetts*, 118; Jon T. Duane to William A. Sexton, deed, March 26, 1980, PCRD, book 4810, page 417; William A. Sexton to Jon T. Duane and Elizabeth A. Duane, November 3, 1986; "SCTV Scituate Thursday Talks Bill Sexton (Cartoonist)," video of local cable broadcast, October 15, 2012, https://archive.org/details/SCTV_Scituate_Thursday_Talks_Bill_Sexton_Cartoonist and https://www.youtube.com/watch?v=YQZcPd0aSdomore.

[610] 1900 US Census, Charles E. Holt and Doris Holt, Somerville, MA; 1900 US Census, Hauman, Revere, Suffolk, Massachusetts; Page: 22; Enumeration District: 1576; Ancestry.com [database on-line], Provo, UT, USA; Bureau of the Census. Twelfth Census of the United States, 1900, Washington, D.C., National Archives and Records Administration, 1900. T623, 1854 rolls; *1915 Directory*, 65 (Holt, Third Cliff); *The South Shore Blue Book* (1906), 38 (Mr. & Mrs. C. E. Holt, Trottwood Cottage, W. Somerville); "Scituate," *Boston Globe*, July 4,

1909; *1915 Directory*, 65 (Holt owning house on Third Cliff); *1918 Directory*, 78 (Holt, Third Cliff); William H. Harney to Charles E. Holt, deed, October 25, 1920, PCRD, book 1360, page 417 (Shannock property at northern end of Third Cliff); *1926 Directory*, 98 (Holt owning house on Dickens Row); various deeds, including Charles Edward Holt, Second, to Doris Caroline Hauman, deed, March 10, 1954, conveying three parcels on northern end of Third Cliff, PCRD, book 2357, page 457; 1920 US Census, Lexington, Middlesex County, Massachusetts, District 0170, 12 Oakland Street, dwelling 68, family 89, sheet 4B, lines 59–62, digital images, HeritageQuest, citing NARA microfilm publication T625, 2,076 rolls, roll not identified, Record Group 29 (Charles & Caroline Holt at 12 Oakland with daughter Doris and son Charles Jr.).

[611] "Future Read from Hand Imprints," *Boston Globe*, June 23, 1909, 9 (with photo of Hauman); 1930 US Census, Lexington, Middlesex County, Massachusetts, District 256, 10 Oakland Street, dwelling 28, family 31, sheet 170-2A, lines 34–36, digital images, HeritageQuest, citing NARA microfilm publication T626, 2,667 rolls, roll not identified (George & Doris Hauman at 10 Oakland); "George and Doris Hauman Papers" in de Grummond Children's Literature Collection, The University of Southern Mississippi, http://www.lib.usm.edu/legacy/degrum/public_html/html/research/findaids/DG0430.html; Scituate Historical Society, *Scituate*, Images of America series (Charleston, SC: Arcadia Publishing, 2000), 30; "History of LACS," Arts and Crafts Society of Lexington, formerly at http://www.lacsma.org/About/HistoryofLACS/1960-1984/tabid/416/Default.aspx (George Hauman designed lunette for the society).

[612] George and Doris Hauman, *Happy Harbor: A Seashore Story* (New York: Macmillan, 1938); Watty Piper, *The Little Engine That Could* (New York: Platt & Munk, 1954); J. J. Sedelmaier, "Watty Piper's 1930 'The Little Engine That Could,'" *Print* website article (comparing illustrations in 1930 edition with those of 1954 edition), posted September 10, 2012, http://www.printmag.com/obsessions/watty-pipers-1930-the-little-engine-that-could/.

[613] Dave Kindy, "The illustrator who did: 'The Little Engine That Could' was just another book for Doris Hauman," *South Shore Mirror*, November 1, 1979, clipping in file "Art & Artists — Hauman, Doris," SHS.

[614] Obituary clippings in file "Art & Artists — Hauman, Doris," SHS; "Doris Hauman, 87: Illustrated Children's Books," *Boston Globe*, August 21, 1984, *Boston Globe* Archives online.

[615] Bernard Mackenzie, along with Phyllis J. Ketter, Alfred Montanari, Matt Brown, Sandra Higgins, "Scituate Historical Society Calendar 2000: Featuring Sketches of Front Street, Second and Third Cliff Circa 1915" (Scituate: Scituate Historical Society, [1999]), courtesy of Sandy Higgins (calendar contains historical notes on each panel, and notes on the provenance of scroll, in possession of Sandy Higgins). Capt. Stanley was born about 1845 according to the 1910 US Census. He lived on Third Cliff and was keeper of the US Life Saving Service station on Fourth Cliff. "Stanley, Capt. Fredrick House," 14 Bassin Lane, SCI.3, MACRIS; Murphy, *Irish Mossers*, 108–109.

[616] "Fain," Dictionary of the Scots Language, Scottish National Dictionary (1700-), http://www.dsl.ac.uk/entry/snd/fain_adj1_v.

[617] Tom Eames scroll; E. Parker Welch to Thomas Graham, deed, January 7, 1871, PCRD, book 373, page 32 (equivalent of 24 Town Way); Mary E. Graham, et al to Mary Graham, deed, November 13, 1907, PCRD book 980, page 463; *1920 VL*, 34 (Mary E. Graham heirs, also Richard Graham); discussion of Shaneck in text; Harney to Holt deed cited above; Assessor's Database; conversation with Kirk Hauman, June 30, 2018.

[618] George F. Welch to Henry H. Eames of Somerville, deed, September 27, 1906, PCRD, book 94, page 28 (lot 211); *1907 VL*, 102 (with note: "New house 1908 $700"); George F. Welch to Henry H. Eames, deed, December 21, 1911, PCRD, book 1107, page 429 (lot 43); *1912 VL*, 97 (Rivermoor house lot 11 crossed out and 43 penciled in), but *1913 VL*, 103, still has lot 211, so *1914 VL*, 104, is the first to list a "bungalo" on lot 43; *1918 Directory*, 73 (Henry H. & Cora B. Eames, home in Somerville); George F. Welch to Cora B. Eames, deed, August 5, 1919, PCRD, book 1328, page 437 (lot 44, adjacent to lot 43, "land with the buildings thereon"); Cora B. Eames, widow, to William Dudley Swain and Mabel F. Swain, deed, May 4, 1937, PCRD, book 1726, page 173 (lots 43 and 44).

[619] 1920 US Census, Eames, Somerville Ward 7, Middlesex, Massachusetts; Roll: T625_718; Pages: 5A & 5B; Enumeration District: 455, Ancestry.com [database on-line], Original data: Fourteenth Census of the United States, 1920 (NARA microfilm publication T625, 2076 rolls). Records of the Bureau of the Census, Record Group 29, National Archives, Washington, D.C.; 1930 US Census, Thomas Eames & wife Marjorie, Somerville, Middlesex, Massachusetts; Page: 15B; Enumeration District: 0453, Ancestry.com [database on-line], Bureau of the Census, Fifteenth Census of the United States, 1930, Washington, D.C., National Archives and Records Administration, T626, 2,667 rolls; 1930 US Census, Thomas Eames & wife Marjorie, Arlington, Middlesex, Massachusetts; Roll: m-t0627-01601; Page: 17B; Enumeration District: 9-26, Ancestry.com [database on-line], Bureau of the Census, Sixteenth Census of the United States, 1940, Washington, D.C.:

National Archives and Records Administration, 1940, T627, 4,643 rolls. See Thomas H. Eames, "Vision and Learning," *Optometry and Vision Science*, vol. 36, issue 4 (April 1959), 215-219, https://journals.lww.com/optvissci/Citation/1959/04000/VISION_AND_LEARNING__.7.aspx; Thomas H. Eames, "Correspondence between Visual Acuity, Refractive Error, and the Speed of Visual Perception," *Br J Ophthalmol.*, 1953 May; 37(5): 312–313, https://www.ncbi.nlm.nih.gov/pmc/articles/PMC1324106/; Thomas H. Eames, "Visual Handicaps to Reading," *The Journal of Education* 141, no. 3 (1959): 1–35. http://www.jstor.org/stable/42800036.; "Dr. T. H. Eames, Eye Specialist," obituary, *Boston Globe*, June 12, 1975, 57. It appears from internet searches that Thomas Eames was a ham radio enthusiast, and was also interested in shipwrecks near Scituate (*Etrusco* and the Steamer *Portland*). See "A Cumulative Index for *Steamboat Bill* and *PowerShips* from 1940 to 2011" (East Providence, RI: Steamship Historical Society of America, 2010), www.sshsa.org/media/January2012SBandPSIndex.pdf or http://www.sshsa.org/media/PowerShips/SB_and_PS_Index.pdf. It is not known whether or how Thomas Eames knew George Hauman before George married Doris in 1924.

620 "Thomas J. Edwards Dead in Melrose," *Boston Globe*, March 21, 1928, 3. The house was probably built after 1912, when a deed to Thomas J. Edwards said:

> the grantee or his heirs or assigns shall not erect a building or any part of a building or projections thereon within thirty-eight feet of said Cliff Ave., except that a piazza not more than one story high may be built not nearer than thirty feet to said Cliff Ave.; that this dwelling house and garage shall cost not less than Two Thousand Dollars; that no swine or fowl shall be kept on the premises and that no objectionable out-buildings shall be erected thereon.

George F. Welch to Thomas J. Edwards, deed, August 1, 1912, PCRD, book 1127, page 353 (lots 46 and 47); Thomas J. Edwards to William F. Seale, deed, April 1, 1918, PCRD, book 1303, page 186. The house appears on the 1918 Sanborn map, unnamed, and it was named "Edwards" in the *1921 VL*. Owners from 1994 to 2016 kept a chicken coop on the premises.

621Website of Nancy Sargent Howell, http://www.nancyhowellstudio.com/; South Shore Art Center website (Valerie Vitali); "Take an Art Walk," *Scituate Mariner* website (Joanne Papandrea), posted April 30, 2015, http://scituate.wickedlocal.com/article/20150430/NEWS/150439410, and obituary, https://www.mcnamara-sparrell.com/obituary/Joanne-Papandrea. Sue Dreamer, who grew up on the Driftway, is also an artist and illustrator. TCRIA, Inc., "The Heritage of Third Cliff," in Third Cliff-Rivermoor Newsletter (Summer 1986), 6; Amazon searches for "Sue Dreamer."

622 Paul Bowers, interview by author, May 21, 2016, for example; Edward Rowe Snow, *True Tales of Pirates and Their Gold* (New York: Dodd, Mead & Co., 1953, 2d printing 1954); Edward Rowe Snow, "Scituate Treasure" in "Sea and Shore Gleanings" column, *Boston Traveler*, January 14, 1937 (copy courtesy of David Ball, SHS); Headsman, "1820: William Holmes, Edward Rosewaine, and Thomas Warrington, pirates," Executed Today website, posted June 15, 2017, http://www.executedtoday.com/2017/06/15/1820-william-holmes-edward-rosewaine-and-thomas-warrington-pirates/; *United States v. Holmes, et al.*, 5 Wheat. 412 (US Sup. Ct., 1820). A report of the trial of Holmes and his mates is online. "The Trial of William Holmes, Thomas Warrington, and Edward Rosewain on an Indictment for Murder on the High Seas" (Boston: Joseph C. Spear, 1820), http://lcweb2.loc.gov/service/lawlib/law0001/2010/201000238009947/201000238009947.pdf.

623 Edward Rowe Snow's "traveling museum" of artifacts had placards such as this: "SKELETON OF SO-CALLED THIRD CLIFF PIRATE, WILLIAM HOLMES, WHO WAS HANGED IN BOSTON ON JUNE 15, 1820 AFTER BURYING TREASURE AT THIRD CLIFF, SCITUATE. THE BODY OF HOLMES WAS LATER USED FOR DISSECTION BY DR. J. W. WEBSTER, WHO WAS LATER HANGED HIMSELF FOR THE MURDER OF DR. PARKMAN." Olly, "Imagining the Old Coast," 295 and n. 422, citing Edward Rowe Snow Collection, Box 37, Folder 16, Howard Gottlieb Research Center, Boston University.

624 "Mann Historical Museum Treasure," *Scituate Historical Society Bulletin*, vol. 33, no. 1, June 28, 1980, 4-5, SHS website; Barbara Fitzgerald, "Scituate historians still wonder about more hidden treasure," *Quincy (MA) Patriot Ledger*, November 23, 1989 (copy courtesy of David Ball, along with other documentation of old coins found); David Ball, interview by author, August 1, 2016).

625 1918 Sanborn map; McAlester, *Field Guide to American Houses*, 67 (auto sales skyrocketed after 1918 and by 1929 four out of five families owned an auto). This marked Scituate's possible transition from a "railroad suburb" to an "early automobile suburb," using the terminology of McAlester, *Field Guide to American Houses*, 64-67. Still, Dr. Ruth Bailey recalled that in the 1920s and 1930s, Mr. Doherty used to drive a horse-drawn "bus" about town, from the railroad station to the cliffs, according to her answers to the questionnaire of Third Cliff-Rivermoor Improvement Association, about 1988, in Association's archives. This was a century after the introduction of "omnibuses" for public transportation. McAlester, *Field Guide to American Houses*, 61.

[626] *The Automobile Blue Book 1915*, vol. 2 (Chicago and New York: The Automobile Blue Book Publishing Company, 1915) (published with "the exclusive official endorsement of the American Automobile Association"), 305 (map), 389–392 (Route 263), 392–394 (Route 264), https://books.google.com/books?id=ins1AQAAMAAJ&source=gbs_navlinks_s. The *Automobile Blue Book* did not seem to say how long it took to drive these routes, although in some towns in New Hampshire, it cautioned against speed traps where the speed limit was 12 miles per hour. *Automobile Blue Book 1915*, 331, 955. Speed limits in Massachusetts were "'reasonable and proper', 8 miles on curves, crossings, etc., 15 miles in thickly settled sections; elsewhere, 20 miles." *Automobile Blue Book 1915*, 1271.

[627] Sargent, *A Handbook of New England*, "Key Map of New England," cover (first page of scan), 527–530. The same route (following the shore from Nantasket to Plymouth) appears in "Ford Trails" in *Ford Pictorial* (Detroit: Ford Motor Company, August 1925), Dezo's Garage, https://www.xr793.com/ford-1920-1929.

[628] "More Praise from Mitchell Owner," *Boston Globe*, October 29, 1916, 54; John Galluzzo, "Yesterdays: 100 Years Ago in Scituate: October 1916," *Scituate Mariner*, A9, October 13, 2016 (noting trip); *Marshfield Mail*, March 11, 1910, Marshfield Historical Society, Newspapers and Clippings Box 2, reference 2008.0112. A good illustration of the Mitchell Little Six is the company's ad in *Automobile Topics*, vol. 32, January 3, 1914 (New York: E. E. Schwarzkopf, 1914), 639, https://books.google.com/books?id=hetZAAAAYAAJ&source=gbs_navlinks_s. A new Mitchell Little Six (with a six-cylinder engine) cost $1,895, almost as much as a new house in Rivermoor. Dr. Alexander's personal property was never valued by the town at more than $800 during 1915 to 1918, and in 1918, his auto was valued at $500. Evidently, such are the depredations of depreciation. He had no valuation for real property during this time. The couple lived on Central Street (later named First Parish Road) in a property that his wife Marion's family had provided her.

[629] According to the *1918 VL*, 93, George Welch had $10,750 of "Furniture in 43 Houses," many of which houses were in Rivermoor, for an average of $250 per house. This was a significant amount compared to a typical house valuation of $2,000 and lot of $225 (or $325 for a double lot).

[630] George F. Welch to Helen V. Low, deed, March 29, 1918, PCRD, book 1302, page 165, for the property that became 3 Driftway. A slightly different version of this language appeared in George F. Welch to Clarence C. Miller, deed, July 17, 1919, PCRD, book 1327, page 268:

> Said premises are conveyed subject to the following restrictions namely: That no building shall be erected on the said premises costing less than $1000.00; that said building or buildings shall set back from the street upon which they front at least 30 feet; that no fowl or swine shall be kept upon the premises.

In a separate conveyance with similar language, "no building" in the first restriction was qualified by the words "other than a garage" in George F. Welch to Clarence C. Miller, deed, December 1, 1919, PCRD, book 1341, page 485. In denying swine a place in Rivermoor, George Welch may have been influenced by his brother Henry's keeping of two hogs on his Third Cliff farm. See, for example, *1904 VL*, 81, and *1903 VL*, 77.

[631] McAlester, *Field Guide to American Houses*, 87-91. The Massachusetts Zoning Enabling Act was passed in the early 1920s. Massachusetts Department of Housing and Community Development, *The Zoning Act: Massachusetts General Laws, Chapter 40A* (Boston: Commonwealth of Massachusetts, 2016), introductory pages.

[632] Wilkins, "Historical Sketch," *North Scituate Beach*.

[633] "Big Day for Scituate: Town to Welcome Home 162 Soldiers and Sailors of the World War," *Rockland* [MA] *Standard*, July 3, 1919, 5; Murphy, *The Coming of Age*, 115–119, with copy of program of events of the 1919 event on 119; Patrick Browne, "Civil War Monuments of the South Shore, Part Two," Historical Digression blog, posted September 12, 2015, https://historicaldigression.com/2015/09/page/2/, and sources cited. For a first-hand account of the July 4 celebration at Dreamwold, see "George Hyland's Diary, July 1919," The Beehive blog, Massachusetts Historical Society, posted July 3, 2019, http://www.masshist.org/beehiveblog/2019/07/george-hylands-diary-july-1919/.

[634] "Rockland Liquor Dealers are Sitting Tight," *Rockland* [MA] *Standard*, July 10, 1919, 1.

[635] Author's analysis of George F. Welch deeds listed in grantor indexes in Plymouth County Registry of Deeds shows that from 1915 to 1921 only two or four deeds were issued each year for Rivermoor properties, except for 1919, when 24 deeds were issued. Most of the 1919 deeds were in the second half of the year, after the town's valuation lists, and they conveyed 111 of the 222 lots in Rivermoor.

[636] "Rockland People Lose Property: Much Damage Done To Shore Cottages All Along The Coast—Worst Storm Since 1898," *Rockland* [MA] *Standard*, November 13, 1919, 1. George Welch, perhaps weary from all the sales activity, left in December to winter in Florida with his daughter. "Scituate," *Scituate Herald*, December 19, 1919, page 4.

637 Scituate Country Club website, http://www.scituatecc.com/club/scripts/section/section.asp?GRP=14337&NS=PG; William W. Waterman Agreement with Clarence C. Miller, et al, to sell land, September 5, 1919, PCRD, book 1331, page 593; William Henry Welch Agreement with Clarence C. Miller, et al, to sell land, September 5, 1919, PCRD, book 1331, page 595; Harrison L. House, Surveyor, *Plan of Land in Scituate, Mass., Surveyed for Scituate Country Club* (Oct. 1919), 1 inch = 100 feet, PCRD, plan book 3, serial no. 3080, page 50; William H. Welch to Scituate Country Club, deed, November 14, 1919, PCRD, book 1341, page 274; William W. Waterman to Scituate Country Club, deed, November 14, 1919, PCRD, book 1341, page 279.

638 Alexander W. Williams, *A Social History of the Greater Boston Clubs* (Barre, MA: Barre Publishers, 1970), 52-56, and see 140-141 ("the country club or the yacht club became the nucleus of a new summer colony" in the 1880s); Garland, *The North Shore*, 228–229, 233-234; Hatherly Country Club website.

639 Mark A. Hewitt, *The Architect & the American Country House, 1890–1940* (New Haven: Yale University Press, 1990), 10–11.

640 Williams, A Social History of the Greater Boston Clubs, 56.

641 *United States Golf Association Year Book 1921* (n.p., 1921), 124, https://books.google.com/books?id=5jUQAAAAYAAJ&source=gbs_navlinks_s; *1918 Directory*, 76, 83, 89; *1926 Directory*, 94 (Gates), 104 (Miller); Plymouth County Registry of Deeds information discussed in text and in above notes. As of 1923, Henry H. Wilder was a member of The Country Club in Brookline, and took leadership roles in the US Golf Association, Green Committee of the United States Golf Association, *Bulletin of the Green Section of the U.S. Golf Association*, vol. 3, no. 12 (Washington, DC, December 15, 1923), 304, https://books.google.com/books?id=Qfs2AQAAMAAJ&source=gbs_navlinks_s. See S. Harold Greene obituary, *Hartford Courant*, November 21, 1937, 27.

642 William W. Waterman Agreement with Clarence C. Miller, S. Harold Greene, and Henry H. Wilder, "acting as committee for a prospective golf or country club," August 30, 1919, PCRD, book 1331, page 593, and William H. Welch Agreement with Clarence C. Miller, S. Harold Greene, and Henry H. Wilder, "acting as committee for a prospective golf or country club," August 30, 1919, PCRD, book 1331, page 595. The club's original 60 acres appear to have grown to 70 acres, including a cranberry lot, by 1927, when the property was valued by the town at $18,300 (less than the consideration set forth in the original deeds). Town of Scituate, *Town of Scituate Valuation List 1927 (Supplement to Town Report of 1927)*, 202. The acreage was reduced to 58, according to the *1929 VL*, 82, but with the same $18,300 total property valuation, including $8,000 for "House (Welch)" and $150 for a stable. William Wade Waterman (June 1, 1866–November 17, 1928) is buried in Scituate's Union Cemetery.

643 William H. Welch to Scituate Country Club, deed, November 14, 1919, PCRD, book 1341, page 274; William W. Waterman to Scituate Country Club, deed, November 14, 1919, PCRD, book 1341, page 279; author's analysis of other deeds.

644 Lyle Nyberg, "Turner-Welch Farmhouse, Scituate Country Club," 91 Driftway, SCI.1232, MACRIS, and references cited therein.

645 Will Irwin, "The Story of Scituate," in *Scituate, 1636–1936*, 6; "New Golf Course on Scituate Land: Tennis Also, and Farmhouse for Clubhouse for Scituate Country Club," *Scituate Herald*, September 5, 1919; "Scituate Country Club House Nearly Completed," *Hull Beacon*, May 21, 1920, page 1, microfilm, Town of Hull Library.

646 "Scituate," *Boston Globe*, July 9, 1922, 14; D. J. McGuiness, "Ouimet Around in 75 Strokes," *Boston Globe*, July 28, 1923, 8; Michael Whitmer, "Francis Ouimet win recalled, 100 years later," *Boston Globe* website, posted August 13, 2013, https://www.bostonglobe.com/sports/2013/08/12/remembering-francis-ouimet-years-later/vR0HL1rmGBxVNTDRh51WzH/story.html; "Scituate," *Boston Globe*, August 2, 1926, A5; Charles River Country Club website.

647 Betty McKenzie [probable, based on attribution in later booklets], Scituate Country Club description, probably for booklet, before 1982, SHS. Clarence E. and Frances Brier had a home on Highland (today's Greenfield Lane), and as noted above in the discussion of an artists' colony, they were from Chestnut Hill in Boston. "Miss Edwards Bride of Russell T. Hatch," *Boston Globe*, April 17, 1921, 18, and "Scituate," *Boston Globe*, July 4, 1926, B3. Pearly E. Barbour later had a cottage on Second Cliff. "Scituate," *Boston Globe*, July 16, 1933, A14.

648 Hilda Stenbeck, "Scituate Country Club History to add to details of Scituate Herald paper of Sept. 5, 1919," June 21, 1990, SHS. Hilda Stenbeck was a member of the club since at least 1931, according to other papers on file in SHS. She was a local historian and Town Archivist.

649 "Scituate," *Boston Globe*, July 4, 1926, B3. At least Brier, Greene, and Nason were members of the Scituate Country Club. Stretch and Nason later became full-year residents of Rivermoor. See 1937 assessor's list of persons, cited below, and *1938 South Shore Social Register*, 123–124.

650 "Scituate," *Boston Globe*, July 22, 1928, B6. At least Brier and Miller were members of the Scituate Country Club. Cullen was listed on Parker Avenue in 1938. *1938 South Shore Social*, 132.

651 "Scituate," *Boston Globe*, July 14, 1929, A21.

652 "Bonnie Doon Wins Whippet Club Race," *Boston Globe*, August 12, 1929, 7; "Scituate Golfers Prove Right to Title By Starring in South Shore Field Day," *Herald* [Scituate?], August 25, c. 1930 [based on age of 15-year-old Arthur Rogers, son of dentist Dr. Arthur V. Rogers of Parker Avenue, and 1937 *Winchester Star* articles on the precocious golfer], Third Cliff-Rivermoor Association archives; various newspaper clippings, SHS.

653 Author's analysis of dates houses were built according to early tax valuation lists, and George F. Welch deeds listed in grantor indexes in PCRD.

654 Author's analysis of dates houses were built according to early tax valuation lists, and George F. Welch deeds listed in grantor indexes in PCRD. Howard R. Guild is listed in the *1915 Directory*, 64, as a renter on Collier Road, and in the *1918 Directory*, 77, as an owner on Collier Road. He and his wife are listed at Collier Road, with winter residence in West Roxbury, in *1938 South Shore Social Register*, 122. William N. Ambler is shown as a Boston property owner, including at "Index to Deeds: 4 Arlington," Back Bay Houses website, https://backbayhouses.org/index-to-deeds-4-arlington/.

655 Author's analysis of George F. Welch deeds listed in grantor indexes in Plymouth County Registry of Deeds; 1918 and 1926 Sanborn maps; Assessor's Database; US Department of the Interior, National Park Service, "Lancaster Mills [Clinton, MA]," National Register of Historic Places Registration Form, signed December 22, 2009 (details on S. Harold Greene background), MACRIS file CLI.136 "Lancaster Mills - Mill #1 - Weaving Mill," (click on NR button); George F. Welch to Lillian M. Greene, deed, September 11, 1919, PCRD, book 1332, page 18.

656 Author's analysis of George F. Welch deeds listed in grantor indexes in Plymouth County Registry of Deeds; 1918 and 1926 Sanborn maps; Assessor's Database; Howard Redwood Guild, *Ancestry of Calvin Guild, Margaret Taft, James Humphreys and Rebecca Covell Martin, 1620-1890* (Salem, MA: Salem Press, 1891) (details on Howard Guild background), https://www.familysearch.org/library/books/records/item/457472-redirection; *Annual Report of the Trustees, Museum of Fine Arts, Boston, Forty-Third Annual Report for the Year 1918* (Boston: T. O. Metcalf Co., 1919), vol. 43–49, various pages, https://books.google.com/books?id=66QZAAAAYAAJ&source=gbs_navlinks_s.

657 Author's analysis of George F. Welch deeds listed in grantor indexes in Plymouth County Registry of Deeds; 1918 and 1926 Sanborn maps; Assessor's Database; Albert Nelson Marquis, ed., "Woodworth, Arthur Vernon," *Who's Who in New England* (Chicago: A. N. Marquis & Co., 2d ed., 1916), 1182, https://books.google.com/books?id=5jk1AAAAIAAJ&source=gbs_navlinks_s; Arthur Vernon Woodworth Papers, Harvard Business School Archives, Baker Library (Arch GA 95), https://hollisarchives.lib.harvard.edu/repositories/11/resources/452.

658 Massachusetts Secretary of State "Search for Citations to Vital Record (1841 - 1910)" website; "Margaret Woodworth," *Boston Globe*, November 18, 1954, 44 (obituary); *Annual Register of the Alumnae Association of Smith College with Report for 1906* (n.p.: Alumnae Association of Smith College, 1906), 58, https://archive.org/details/annualregisterof00smit/page/n5/mode/2up.

659 1930 US Census, Woodworth, Mount Vernon Street, Boston, MA, ward 5, block 21, enumeration district 12-598, supervisor's district 12, sheet 5A (April 7, 1930)(children's ages at last birthday listed as 25, 23, 18, 15)(home value listed as $30,000); *Harvard College Class of 1891 Secretary's Report Number V* (1911), 128-129 (in freshman crew photo), 258, https://books.google.com/books?id=NdwmAAAAYAAJ&source=gbs_navlinks_s; Margaret K. Woodworth to Marie G. Newell, deed, February 13, 1933, PCRD, book 1642, page 139 (source of quote). The 1925 *Boston Directory* listed Arthur V. Woodworth at 97 Mount Vernon Street, and presumably his family continued there in the new building built in 1926-1927. 97-99 Mount Vernon St, BOS.14969, MACRIS.

660 By 1927, William N. Ambler no longer owned any lots in Rivermoor, although he owned property elsewhere in Scituate valued at a then-formidable $35,750. *1927 VL*, 108.

661 Brown, *Inventing New England*, 82–85. Brown's chapter "Cottage Heaven" chronicles the transformation of the Oak Bluffs area of Martha's Vineyard from Methodist camp meeting grounds to secular cottage cities and a model for later northeastern shore resorts.

662 Conversation with Ray Zucker, May 26, 2017.

663 Dixon, "Two Scituates," 39.

664 "Clarence C. Miller, Insurance Man, Dead; Headed Life Underwriters of Boston; Resident of Winchester 23 Years — Funeral Friday," [obituary with photograph], *Boston Globe*, September 20, 1928, 15; *Winchester Star*, July 19, 1918, 4, and August 9, 1918, 3, https://archive.org/details/WinStar_070518_092718; Nyberg, "Locals spent the summer in Scituate;" discussion in text above; 1920 and 1930 US census data for the Miller family:

1920 US Census, Winchester, Middlesex County, Massachusetts, District 0531, 10 Lagrange Street, dwelling 52, family 53, digital images, HeritageQuest, citing NARA microfilm publication T625, 2,076 rolls, roll not identified; 1930 US Census, Winchester, Middlesex County, Massachusetts, District 0538, 10 Lagrange Street, dwelling 306, family 338, digital images, HeritageQuest, citing NARA microfilm publication T626, 2,667 rolls, roll not identified.

[665] Daughter of Clarence C. Miller [Harriet M. "Teddy" Ellis (1920-2009)], "12 Parker Ave.," unpublished letter, about 2000, in possession of John L. Sullivan. Despite the letter's title, the family lived at 10 Michael Avenue, based on *1926 Directory*, 104, author's observations, 1918 and 1926 Sanborn maps, and *1927 VL*, 180. The house was built in 1915 according to the Assessor's Database, but was actually built in 1909, according to the *1910 VL*. The 1918 Sanborn map and the *1927 VL* both call the house "Maidstone." The house is pictured, middle of three houses, on a postcard entitled "Michael Ave., Rivermoor, Scituate, Mass." labeled "Chas. W. Frye, Pub." with no postmark, SHS postcard collections (Twomey/Jacobson, also Album LSS #2). Harriet's letter is a source for quotations or descriptions later in this book. Family information in this paragraph is based on the following sources, in roughly chronological order: John W. Leonard, ed., *Woman's Who's Who of America: A Biographical Dictionary of Contemporary Women of the United States and Canada 1914–1915* (New York: The American Commonwealth Co., 1914), 563, https://books.google.com/books?id=aHUEAAAAYAAJ&source=gbs_navlinks_s; "Clarence C. Miller: Now in Charge of Penn Mutual's Boston Agency," *The Insurance Press*, December 25, 1918, p. 4, col. 3, in *The Insurance Press*, vol. 47 (New York: The Insurance Press, 1918), https://books.google.com/books?id=uUBJAAAAYAAJ&source=gbs_navlinks_s; Thomas W. Herringshaw, *The American Elite and Sociologist Blue Book* (Chicago: American Blue Book Publishers, 1922), 356, https://books.google.com/books?id=iKs6AQAAIAAJ&source=gbs_navlinks_s; "C. C. Miller is Stricken," *The Standard*, July 15, 1922, in *The Standard*, vol. 91 (Boston: The Standard Publishing Co., 1922), 113, https://books.google.com/books?id=z_EgAQAAMAAJ&source=gbs_navlinks_s; *The Insurance Field — (Life Edition)*, July 21, 1922, 22, in *The Insurance Field — (Life Edition)*, vol. 45-46 (Louisville, KY: The Insurance Field Company, 1922), https://books.google.com/books?id=mUA1AQAAMAAJ&source=gbs_navlinks_s; "Clarence C. Miller Improving," *The Standard*, July 22, 1922, in *The Standard*, vol. 91 (Boston: The Standard Publishing Co., 1922), 148, https://books.google.com/books?id=7Q4-AQAAMAAJ&source=gbs_navlinks_s.

[666] Miller/Ellis, "12 Parker Ave." (source of quote); Plymouth County Registry of Deeds search by author (17 lots purchased in 1919, part of 1 lot purchased in 1922, 2 lots sold in 1924), and search of PCRD website for "Clarence C. Miller" (5 sales of remaining lots by his estate from late 1937 to middle of 1939).

[667] Mary Kellogg, "The House That Harriet Built," *The House Beautiful*, September 1923, 234–235, 291–294; author's observations. The article has a plot plan, with photos and extensive discussion of the interior. The article's illustration of the cottage's exterior matches photos of 43 Collier Road in 2016. Assessor's Database (indicating house built 1925); Zillow website, http://www.zillow.com/homedetails/43-Collier-Rd-Scituate-MA-02066/57552581_zpid/. Clarence Miller's real estate holdings in Rivermoor were valued by 1927 at $17,900, equivalent to about four houses of the period. *1927 VL*, 180. After the Blizzard of 1978, Harriet's cottage was raised to avoid future flooding, according to a conversation with Kevin Lake, July 17, 2018.

[668] Miller/Ellis, "12 Parker Ave." (source of quote). See also Bonney, *My Scituate*, 3 (Scituate notorious for rum runners); Hart and Hart, *Not All Is Changed*, 300 ("For a time, the rumrunners hung safely off the Scituate coast, sending small boats ashore to load trucks, 'booze ships,' which then sped through Hingham").

[669] Miller/Ellis, "12 Parker Ave." Harriet described the car as a "beach wagon," a New England term for a station wagon used for trips to and from the beach, and she said it looked like a wooden box. This would make it an early "woody" or "woodie." An example is a "1925 Ford Beach Wagon" at the Owls Head Transportation Museum. The first beach wagon, mounted on a Model T Ford chassis, was introduced by a Beverly (MA) firm about 1918. Garland, *The North Shore*, 183. By 1929, Ford had become the dominant supplier of station wagons, which were a mark of prestige and status for the very wealthy. Richard Ratay, *Don't Make me Pull Over! An Informal History of the Family Road Trip* (New York: Scribner, 2018), 203–204.

The Scituate Yacht Club was formed in 1912 and was later called "elitist in nature" by the historian of the successor club formed in 1940. Oliver W. Woodburn, "The Scituate Harbor Yacht Club: A Perspective on Its Fiftieth Anniversary," [1990], http://shyc.net/files/pdfs/SHYC_History.pdf. The Scituate Yacht Club's first commodore (and presumably a founder) was W. Marriott Welch, a Scituate resident who was no relation to George F. Welch. He had a survey prepared in 1912 that evidently shows the site of the yacht club with an office along Jericho Road. Henry A. Litchfield, C.E., *Survey of W. Marriott Welch, Scituate, Mass., August 24, 1912, scale 20 ft. to an inch*, PCRD, plan book 1, page 905. His brother Hamilton Welch later researched and completed voluminous genealogical notebooks on file in SHS, including some on the several Welch families. See also "Scituate Yacht Club Is Now Formed," *Boston Globe*, March 30, 1913, 53; *1938 South Shore Social Register*, 22, 124.

[670] W. Ray Freden, "Prohibition & Rum Running in Humarock," A History of Seaview & Marshfield, MA, blog, posted February 28, 2011, http://wrayfreden.com.

[671] "Scituate Rum Runners' Haven; Liquor Going Through Town in Quantities," *Boston Globe*, January 26, 1923, 1; "Liquor of Rum Row Seized at Scituate; 82 Cases of Contraband Taken From Truck; Driver Fined, but Motorboat Crew Escapes," *Boston Globe*, May 8, 1924, 24; "500 Cases of Liquor Seized After Shots," *Boston Globe*, February 15, 1931, A24; "Customs Men Seize Craft Others Freed; Santa Rita Seen Near Site of Scituate Rum Haul," *Boston Globe*, January 9, 1932, 1 (source of quote).

[672] "Rum Seized at Summer Club of [Navy] Secty. Adams: Three Men Are Arrested; Two Escape," *Chicago Daily Tribune*, October 6, 1931, 15, Newspapers.com.

[673] "Bootleg liquor worth $45,000 was seized at the Third Cliff, Scituate, and a rum-runner tied up at the Customs House wharf being unloaded by federal agents. Scenes such as these are now practically unknown since the advent of licensed liquor," *Boston Herald*, October 18, 1936, 1 [presumed], copy courtesy of David Ball. The story was not reported in the *Boston Globe*.

[674] 1918 Sanborn map, including sheet 6 (Jericho Road dance hall); Ball, *To the Point*, 26 (Vinton's dance hall on Jericho Road, with 1910 photo); *1918 Directory*, 39 (listing for Walter Haynes as proprietor of Idle Hour); 1926 Sanborn map; Mill Wharf Cinemas website, http://www.sscinemas.com/mill-wharf-cinemas-scituate-ma.html; "Scituate's First Store," including Hilda Stenbeck corrections, and other items in "Businesses — Pre-1980" file, SHS (dancing above Frye's store); Selectmen's minutes, May 26, 1932 (approval of Sunday license for carmeled corn shop), Town Archives; "Stenbeck, Charles V. Ice Cream and Candy Shop," 116 Front Street, SCI.1071, MACRIS, built around 1890; postcard entitled "The 'Chanticleer' Scituate, Mass, C. V. Stenbeck, Prop," postmarked 1912, SHS postcard collection; Scituate Historical Society, *Scituate*, Then & Now series, 19; "I Remember Scituate by Daisy Thompson," SHS website, http://scituatehistoricalsociety.org/, under "Who and What" then under "Articles;" *1918 Directory*, 95; *1926 Directory*, 126 (Walter Haynes ran a bowling alley on Front Street). The Idle Hour Theatre, run by Walter Haynes, was on the second floor of the Richardson's pharmacy building. The Satuit Playhouse, run by Walter and Margaret Haynes as of 1926, was located about a block north of the Idle Hour Theatre, and was evidently rebuilt on the same site in 1937. "Scituate News — Roof is On," *Marshfield Mail*, July 2, 1937, 4, Marshfield Historical Society, Newspapers and Clippings Box 2, reference 2008.0112. This appears to have been later called the Scituate Harbor Playhouse, according to a poster for the late-1939 movie "Secret of Dr. Kildare." This also appears to be the site of the later Mill Wharf Cinemas at 1 Mill Wharf Plaza, in a building built in 2004, according to the Assessor's Database.

[675] *1938 South Shore Social Register*, 121 (source of quote); "Catherine J. O'Hara," obituary, *Boston Globe*, April 7, 1947, 13 (age 67, services at her home at 76 Front Street, leaving daughter Mrs. Joseph Coveney).

[676] Unattributed, undated photo, copy in possession of John L. Sullivan, probably furnished by Harriet Miller, who is likely in the photo, and, if so, the photo would be from the 1920s.

[677] Ben Zimmer, "Where did the Supreme Court get its 'parade of horribles'?: How an obscure Fourth of July custom from New England spawned a legal-world insult," *Boston Globe*, July 1, 2012 (quoted), https://www.bostonglobe.com/ideas/2012/06/30/where-did-supreme-court-get-its-parade-horribles/Y0jnIscamtgPEzO0PdtL9N/story.html. See also Bonney, *Scituate's Sands of Time*, 78: in the early 1900s, the Hatherly Playground Association in North Scituate "sponsored public celebration of July 4th with patriotic addresses, reading of the Declaration of Independence, and Antique and Horribles parade and culminating at night with a fireworks display;" Margaret Cole Bonney, *Brushy Hill Scituate* (n.p., 1989), 61 ("horribles" parades at Sand Hills); unknown photographer, "Lined up for our July Fourth "Horrible Parade" [Newells and Paines]," early 1900s, Photograph Album of the Newell Family of Newton, Massachusetts, Newton Free Library, http://ark.digitalcommonwealth.org/ark:/50959/9306t374w; Jennifer Levitz, "When Horribles Parades Are Too Horrible, Enter the Clipboards," *Wall Street Journal*, July 3, 2017, A1. Horribles parades or their Labor Day parade successors continue, at least in the Scituate-Marshfield area. James Kukstis, "Scituate Beach Association Labor Day parade enters 91st year," *Scituate Mariner*, August 24, 2017, posted on WickedLocal website August 23, 2017, http://scituate.wickedlocal.com/news/20170823/scituate-beach-association-labor-day-parade-enters-91st-year.

[678] Judith Smith diary entry, July 4, 1873, Judith Winsor Smith Papers, 1796–1945, Massachusetts Historical Society.

[679] For a more detailed examination of the lifeboat station's history, see Lyle Nyberg, "The Red Shed: The Massachusetts Humane Society on Third Cliff, Scituate," July 2016, unpublished monograph, on file, SHS. A 1978 news article reported "The old Third Cliff Life Saving Station was moved (probably by barge) to First Cliff, where it was used as a storage shed for sea moss. It was then moved across Edward Foster Road to become a part of Young's Boat Yard. It was damaged in the "Blizzard of '78", but has been repaired." William H. Muller, "North Scituate Beach lifesaving station has interesting history," *South Shore Mirror*, November 16,

1978, 24. If there is any truth to the statement, it would not describe the lifesaving station on Collier Road; it could have been the other one of two stations that once existed on Third Cliff.

680 "Clarence C. Miller" obituary in *Boston Globe*, September 20, 1928, 15; search for "Clarence C. Miller" (five sales by his estate from late 1937 to middle of 1939) on PCRD website.

681 The Humane Society of the Commonwealth of Massachusetts to Frank F. Fallon, deed, September 24, 1936, PCRD, book 1714, page 527 (lot 208); Nyberg, "The Red Shed;" Assessor's Database for 37 Collier Road.

682 Murphy, *The Coming of Age*, 111.

683 Murphy, *The Coming of Age*, 121.

684 "Mossing Buildings" in WPA card index, Town Archives, referencing Selectmen's meeting of April 20, 1928, recorded in *Selectmen's Records, 1926-1928*, 103, Town Archives (item 1539, location 16-3-3).

685 Annie E. Brown, et al, to Town of Scituate, Order of Taking, April 29, 1937, PCRD, book 1725, page 409; Henry A. Litchfield, Town Engineer, *Plan of Land at Peggotty Beach, Scituate Mass., February 16, 1937, scale: 40 feet to an inch*, PCRD, plan book 5, page 758; Town of Scituate, *Peggotty Beach Management Plan (draft)*, March 2008 or April 2009, prepared by LEC Environmental Consultants, Inc., 2, no longer on town website, available through Wayback Machine, https://web.archive.org/web/20130723110504/http://www.town.scituate.ma.us:80/peggotty/index.html. The concrete block "comfort stations" on Scituate's beaches were abused by teenagers, and were taken down in the late 1970s, according to remarks on January 17, 2018, by Anthony Antoniello, former Director, Scituate Department of Public Works. A postcard shows Peggotty Beach but seems inconclusive as to whether sheds existed when the photo was taken. "View of third cliff from second cliff, Scituate, Mass.," Tichnor Bros. Inc., Boston, Mass., c 1930-1945, Boston Public Library, Print Department, Digital Commonwealth, http://ark.digitalcommonwealth.org/ark:/50959/1z40kw93p.

686 Murphy, *Irish Mossers*, 36; "How Boston's South Shore Became the Irish Riviera," New England Historical Society website, http://www.newenglandhistoricalsociety.com/bostons-south-shore-became-irish-riviera/ ("Lucien Rousseau, the last commercial sea mosser, died in 1983"); Jack Hoey, "Harvesting Lifelong Lessons," Jackhoey's Blog, posted March 12, 2012, https://jackhoey.wordpress.com/2012/03/12/harvesting-lifelong-lessons/; Sue Scheible, "South Shore Wonders: Maritime & Irish Mossing Museum in Scituate," *Quincy (MA) Patriot Ledger* website, posted August 11, 2017, updated August 12, 2017, http://www.patriotledger.com/news/20170811/south-shore-wonders-maritime--irish-mossing-museum-in-scituate (Irish mossing ended July 1997).

687 Thomas Buford Meteyard, *Scituate Bay: The White Cliff*, c. 1894–1900, author's collection; Frederick Damon photo, view looking south to Third Cliff, SHS; Hauman, *Happy Harbor*, 17; Ryan, *Chasing the Alphabet*, 23-29, 111; conversation with Jerry Pallotta, July 21, 2016; conversation with Bob Chessia, September 28, 2017; email from Jerry Pallotta, September 17, 2018; Ball, *To the Point*, 2.

688 Conversations with Joby Norton, September 16, 2018, and June 27, 2021 (Irish moss and sea lettuce growing in waters at Third Cliff).

689 Conversations with Kathy Nyberg, July 2018, and Alma Pallotta, August 5, 2018.

690 Hauman, *Happy Harbor*, 42–44.

691 Assessor's Database; author's analysis.

692 Author's analysis of 1918 and 1919 tax valuation lists.

693 Summary data on last pages of tax valuation lists for 1900 to 1921. The *1920 VL* records 867 residents and 917 nonresidents.

694 The *1918 VL* lists the following: Thomas Lawson, $74,515 personal property plus $282,350 real property; George Welch, $11,050 personal property, $170,485 real property (about $59,000 of which, or 35%, was for Rivermoor properties). The *1919 VL* lists the following as top property owners: Thomas Lawson, $23,115 personal property, $282,400 real property; Glades Association together with Glades Club, $3,100 personal property, $183,600 real property; George Welch, $8,550 personal property, $136,400 real property.

695 Lyle Nyberg, "Seaside Summers in Scituate," presentation for Scituate Historical Society, July 16, 2018, video available from author's website. See, for example, George O. Allen, et al, Allen Associates Declaration of Trust, April 27, 1910, PCRD, book 1061, page 300 (shares); George H. Wetherbee Jr., *Sea Shore Lots at Barker Farm, Scituate, Mass., Owned by Otis Barker*, scale on map, April 1911, PCRD, plan book 1, page 783.

696 Author's analysis of tax valuation lists, newspaper reports, and Sanborn maps; summary data on last pages of tax valuation lists for 1906 to 1921.

697 *1918 Directory*, 97–98 (Bailey, Curtis, Damon, Hardwick, Hayward, Hobson, Lee, Litchfield, Longfellow, Merritt, Seaverns, Supple, and Vinton).

698 Author's analysis of *1918 VL* and *1921 VL*.

[699] Al, "100-Year Housing Price Index History," posted on Observations blog, June 11, 2011, last modified January 27, 2013, http://observationsandnotes.blogspot.com/2011/06/us-housing-prices-since-1900.html; Al, "What Would $10,000 in 19xx be Equivalent to Today?," posted on Observations blog, May 13, 2011, last modified March 9, 2013, http://observationsandnotes.blogspot.com/2011/05/what-10000-in-19xx-equal-today.html. Using that site's interactive inflation calculator reports inflation of 35% from 1918–1921. That period includes a recession and deflation from January 1920 to July 1921. J. R. Vernon, "The 1920-21 Deflation: The Role of Aggregate Supply," *Economic Inquiry* (Western Economic Association International, July 1991), vol. 29, issue 3, 29 (3): 572–580, doi:10.1111/j.1465-7295.1991.tb00847.x. See also, Stephen B. Reed, "One hundred years of price change: the Consumer Price Index and the American inflation experience," *Monthly Labor Review*, Bureau of Labor Statistics, U.S Department of Labor, April 2014, website, http://www.bls.gov/opub/mlr/2014/article/one-hundred-years-of-price-change-the-consumer-price-index-and-the-american-inflation-experience.htm.

[700] Al, "100 Years of Inflation-Adjusted Housing Price History," posted on Observations blog, July 23, 2011, last modified November 26, 2012, http://observationsandnotes.blogspot.com/2011/07/housing-prices-inflation-since-1900.html; Jason Kirby, "A chart to put the Canadian housing bubble in perspective," chart entitled "Real U.S. home prices (1890–2014)" (incorporating data from Robert J. Shiller), Maclean's website, posted March 13, 2014, http://www.macleans.ca/economy/realestateeconomy/a-canadian-housing-chart-that-puts-the-bubble-in-perspective/.

[701] Author's analysis of tax valuation lists. The town assessors valued total real estate in Scituate at $5,260,365 in 1918 and $6,765,680 in 1921 (both years as of April 1).

[702] Margaret Woodworth to George Welch, mortgage for lots 92-27 and more (17 total, Indian Knoll), c. October 9, 1919, PCRD, book 1332, page 411 ($8,000, 3 years, 6%). For Maidstone and other Michael Avenue properties: (1) Clarence Miller to Albert H. Houghton and Edward J. Ball, mortgage for lots 79-80 (Maidstone), June 26, 1919, PCRD, book 1326, page 412 ($3,800, 6% interest, payable quarterly), (2) Clarence Miller to George Welch, mortgage for lots 206, 207, 209, 210 (four), July 19, 1919, PCRD, book 1334, page 170 ($1,750, 3 years, 6%), (3) Clarence Miller to George Welch, mortgage for lots 106-112 (seven), July 22, 1919, PCRD, book 1327, page 269 ($2,500, 3 years, 6% payable semi-annually), and (4) Clarence Miller to George Welch, mortgage for lots 103, 105, 113, 114 (four), December 1, 1919, PCRD, book 1341, page 486 ($1,500, 3 years, 6%).

[703] McAlester, *Field Guide to American Houses*, 87-88; Adam Gordon, "The Creation of Homeownership," *Yale Law Journal* 115:186, 191, http://www.yalelawjournal.org/pdf/444_sxj226iq.pdf.

[704] Randal O'Toole, *American Nightmare: How Government Undermines the Dream of Homeownership* (Washington, DC: Cato Institute, 2012), 57, preview, https://books.google.com/books?id=D2ApWhVWSaUC&source=gbs_navlinks_s.

[705] Terence Palmer, "Borrower Experiences with Subprime Mortgage Loans in Gwinnett County, Georgia" (D.B.A. diss., Walden University, 2015), http://scholarworks.waldenu.edu/cgi/viewcontent.cgi?article=1327&context=dissertations; O'Toole, *American Nightmare*, 57 (Sears mortgages required 25% down payment).

[706] It also appears he was able to sell at prices below those charged by Sears; a 2,000-square foot house could cost as much as $4,000, and this was without labor, bricks, plumbing, electrical, furnaces, furniture, or the land. O'Toole, *American Nightmare*, 57; Sears Holdings Archives website, http://www.searsarchives.com/homes/, including links to images of homes for 1908–1914 and 1915–1920.

[707] *From Boston to Plymouth*, no page number.

[708] *1919 VL*, 100 (William N. Ambler, Twin Houses and Trotwood); George F. Welch obituary. In 1921, George's sister Mary, widow of George Walbach (a Harvard graduate and Boston attorney) sold her big estate on First Cliff to "an entrepreneur from Boston named William Ambler," who subdivided the property and sold off the lots over the next several years. Thompson, *First Cliff, Scituate*, 20, 62–64; "George G. Walbach," *Biographical Review*, 401; Mary Walbach to William Ambler, deed, October 1, 1921, PCRD, book 1397, page 431. William Ambler bought and re-sold George Welch lots in Rivermoor starting about 1919.

[709] *Boston Globe*, May 5, 1923, 5, col. 4 (source of quote); George F. Welch to Marshall C. Spring, deed, May 1, 1923, PCRD, book 1435, page 261 (and mortgage back to Welch at 263); House, *Wharf Properties of George F. Welch*, PCRD, plan book 3, page 504.

[710] In 1925, George F. Welch had a real estate office at 40 Court Street, Room 707, in Boston, and he resided at the Hotel Brunswick at Copley Square. *The Boston Directory for the year commencing July 1, 1925* (Boston: Sampson & Murdock, 1925), *Boston Streets: Mapping Directory Data* website, transcript edited by Digital Collections and Archives, Tufts University, http://bcd.lib.tufts.edu/view_text.jsp?urn=tufts:central:dca:UA069:UA069.005.DO.00005&chapter=d.1925.su

Welch. His name did not appear in the 1922 *Boston Directory*. According to a great-grandson, it was said that George Welch resided at the Canterbury Hotel in Boston. Conversation with Michael Johnson, September 30, 2016. That hotel, at 14 Charlesgate West, was just a few blocks from where Thomas Lawson lived, at 1 Charlesgate East. That is, until some time before 1923, when Lawson's fortunes had declined to the point where his 1 Charlesgate East property was demolished, and his Dreamwold estate in Scituate had to be sold; Lawson died in early 1925. "Charlesgate Hotel Ghost Stories & Haunted Folklore," Celebrate Boston website, http://www.celebrateboston.com/ghost/charlesgate-hotel-ghost.htm; "Overlooking the Fenway, Hotel Canterbury," postcard offered for sale at Cardcow.com, https://www.cardcow.com/309930/overlooking-fenway-hotel-canterbury-boston-massachusetts/; "534 Beacon (1 Charlesgate East)," Back Bay Houses website, https://backbayhouses.org/534-536-beacon/; Miles and Galluzzo, *Beauty, Strength, Speed*, 113. The manager (starting in 1911) and later owner of the Charlesgate Hotel in Boston, Herbert G. Summers, also operated the Cliff Hotel and cottages at North Scituate Beach starting in 1915. He had married in 1907 a woman from Scituate, Fanny Smith, whose parents ran the Mitchell House at North Scituate Beach. "Scituate," *Boston Globe*, July 26, 1931, A17; McCallum & Young, *Cliff Hotel*, 7; "Herbert G. Summers Dies In Florida," *Scituate Herald*, February 26, 1937, 1. He operated both the Charlesgate Hotel and the Cliff Hotel until his death. He became a civic leader in Scituate, elected as a selectman in 1921. Also, he was a Mason. McCallum & Young, *Cliff Hotel*, 7. In both respects, he and George Welch would have been well-acquainted with one another.

The George F. Welch Trust, with George F. Welch as one of three trustees, owned 362–366 Commonwealth Avenue, and 330 Dartmouth Street (at the corner of Beacon Street) in Boston's Back Bay. "362-366 Commonwealth" and "259 Beacon," Back Bay Houses website, http://backbayhouses.org/362-366-commonwealth/, and http://backbayhouses.org/259-beacon/. The trust also owned property on or near Huntington Avenue, on which taxes were owed. *City Record* (Boston: City of Boston, 1930), 1150, https://archive.org/details/cityrecord1930bost. Besides George Welch, one of the three trustees was Thomas B. Alexander, his son-in-law, a Scituate doctor who had married his daughter Marion. *Baker v. James*, 280 Mass. 43 (Superior Court, Suffolk County, 1932), Massachusetts Cases website, http://masscases.com/cases/sjc/280/280mass43.html. According to a great-grandson, it was said that George Welch was a leading property owner in Brookline, and later lost his fortune (like Thomas Lawson). Conversation with Michael Johnson, September 30, 2016. The author has not confirmed this.

[711] Conversation with Michael Johnson, George Welch descendant, October 11, 2017.

[712] For example, a 1922 deed references a plan entitled "Shore Acres, Egypt, Mass., lots for sale by E. Parker Welch, Esq., Scituate, Mass.," dated August 1896. George F. Welch and Angeline M. Cole to Henrietta Vinal, deed, May 11, 1922, PCRD, book 1422, page 302. Even after moving to Boston, George Welch continued to own property in Scituate, which was eventually sold off. For example, in 1927 George Welch owned property with Angelina M. Cole in Shore Acres, "an unpretentious cottage colony" according to the 1917 guidebook mentioned in the text. His interests in the more upscale Rivermoor were mostly sold before 1922, although his heirs continued to sell properties there in the late 1930s. *1927 VL*, 101, 219; author search of indexes in Plymouth County Registry of Deeds.

[713] George F. Welch obituary; *1931 Town Report*, Town Clerk: "Deaths Registered in Scituate in the Year 1931," 244 (cause of death: "Arterio-Sclerosis. Hypostatic Pneumonia"). A short obituary with photo is at "Funeral Rites Today for George F. Welch," *Boston Globe*, May 31, 1931, A20. His gravestone has a Masonic emblem, per author's visit to Union Cemetery, October 2, 2017.

[714] "George F. Welch" [obituary], *Rockland* [MA] *Standard*, June 4, 1931, 5.

[715] Scituate Historical Society, *Scituate*, Then & Now series, 15.

[716] Marshall C. Spring by mortgagee to Institution for Savings in Roxbury & Its Vicinity, foreclosure deed, December 5, 1933, PCRD, book 1653, page 178; Institution for Savings in Roxbury & Its Vicinity to The Welch Company, deed, June 1, 1939, PCRD, book 1769, page 18 (listing over seven parcels).

[717] Miriam Chesley, "gazing thru the past… Yesterday's Business… And Today's Too," *Scituate Mirror*, August 14, 1975, 7; Diana Schoberg, "Looking Back, Looking Ahead," *Quincy (MA) Patriot Ledger*, October 1-2, 2005; Gail Ledwig email to author, March 5, 2016; John ("Jack") H. Spurr, letter to author, May 15, 2016; Galluzzo, *True To Our Roots*, various; "A.W. Perry History," A.W. Perry, Inc., website, http://www.awperry.com/company-profile/#ourhistory; Louise J. Chambers to Nellie G. Perry, deed, July 2, 1946, PCRD, book 1920, page 359; Herbert G. Perry to Arthur P. and Meredith F. Wilcox [daughter of Herbert and Nell Perry], deed, September 11, 1969, PCRD, book 3547, page 680; 1918 Sanborn map. Herbert Perry's wife Nell bought the lots across Collier (lots 212-214) to preserve the ocean view from their home. S. Maxwell ("Sandy") Beal, telephone interview by author, June 27, 2016; Orel F. Martin to Nell G. Perry, deed, May 20, 1947, PCRD, book 1963, page 250.

311

[718] "Russell L. Fish, 79; Headed Scituate Company," *Boston Globe*, October 20, 1985, 101; Russell Fish papers; Welch Company file, SHS, including "Welch Co. for Sale," *Scituate Mariner*, November 18, 1982, and Julie A. Miller, "Just an 'average guy' with a seaside empire," *Quincy (MA) Patriot Ledger*, June 28, 1985, 10B; "No major changes planned at the Welch Company," *Scituate Mariner*, December 2, 1982, 5; Diana Schoberg, "Looking Back, Looking Ahead," *Quincy (MA) Patriot Ledger*, October 1-2, 2005.

[719] "Scituate," *Boston Globe*, July 16, 1922, 18.

[720] *Boston Globe*, July 30, 1922, 19.

[721] "Otway Hebron Chalkley," The Arnold and Moberly Family Genealogy on Webtrees website, http://www.myarnolds.com/individual.php?pid=I571&ged=Arnold.ged; "Otway Hebron Chalkley," obituary, *Courier-News* [Bridgewater, NJ], March 23, 1956, 14, https://www.newspapers.com/newspage/221310060/; search for "rachel riley" at "Search Vital Records (1841–1910)" website of Secretary of Massachusetts, , http://www.sec.state.ma.us/vitalrecordssearch/vitalrecordssearch.aspx.; Donna Albino, website on Mount Holyoke College history, formerly at http://home.mtholyoke.edu/~dalbino/letters/women/rriley.html; see also Webtrees: The Arnold and Moberly Family Genealogy website, http://www.myarnolds.com/family.php?famid=F12761&ged=Arnold.ged; Fred Kittler to author, January 29, 2017, email to author.

[722] *1918 Directory*, 87 (Harriet C. Riley on Third Cliff); *1926 Directory*, 110 (Harriet C. Riley on Highland, with Joseph C. Riley and Rebecca C. Riley [children of Harriet, and Rachel's siblings]; Florence E. Blackett to Joseph C. Riley, deed, May 5, 1922, PCRD, book 1411, page 159 (lot 34, where the cottage was located); *1923 VL*, 163 (house, garage, and lot 34); Edward C. Ramsdell to Joseph C. Riley, deed, August 15, 1923, BCRD, book 1444, page 279 (lot 33); Assessor's hand-drawn plot plans, by street, about 1930–35, Town Archives; "Notable Reunion Held in Scituate," *Scituate Herald*, September 29, 1950, 7; Joseph C. Riley to Seth Riley, deed, April 22, 1966, PCRD, book 3288, page 676; Assessor's Database.

[723] *1926 Directory*, 86 (Chalkley misspelled as "Chalkey"); *The Red and Black,* Commencement Issue, Sixth Month, 1936 (Locust Valley, NY: Friends Academy, 1936), 11, www.digifind-it.com/friendsacademy/DATA/yearbooks/1936.pdf; Friends Academy website, https://info.fa.org/; *The Briar Patch of Nineteen Forty* (Sweet Briar, 1940), 43, https://archive.org/details/briarpatch1940swee.

[724] Richard Kluger, *Ashes to Ashes: America's Hundred-Year Cigarette War, the Public Health, and the Unabashed Triumph of Philip Morris* (First Vintage Books Edition, 1997, originally published by Alfred A. Knopf, 1996, winning the 1997 Pulitzer Prize for General Non-Fiction), 101–102, https://books.google.com/books?id=dxI_us9Tq-QC&source=gbs_navlinks_s.

[725] *TIME*, vol. 32, no. 1, July 4, 1938, copy advertised at https://www.abebooks.com/Time-weekly-newsmagazine-Vol-XXXII-July/1015306416/bd.; The Center for Media and Democracy's Sourcewatch website, "Otway Hebron Chalkley," http://www.sourcewatch.org/index.php/Otway_Hebron_Chalkley, and "History of Philip Morris," http://www.sourcewatch.org/index.php/History_of_Philip_Morris, citing Anna M. Crewe and P. L. Crabtree, *Manufacturing Center Orientation Manual* (Philip Morris, August 1987), 3 (11th page), Philip Morris Records, https://www.industrydocumentslibrary.ucsf.edu/tobacco/docs/gldy0002; The Center for Media and Democracy's Sourcewatch website, "History of Philip Morris," citing Crewe and Crabtree, *Manufacturing Center Orientation Manual*, 3 (11th page),; "Philip Morris Companies Inc.," Reference for Business website, http://www.referenceforbusiness.com/history2/72/Philip-Morris-Companies-Inc.html.

[726] "Scituate," *Boston Globe*, February 20, 1924, 8; note at end of "Picture Postcards" section of "The Rivermoor Colony's Development" in chapter 11.

[727] US Geological Survey, *Massachusetts (Plymouth County), Scituate Quadrangle* [map], 1:24,000. 7.5 Minute Series (Washington DC: USGS, 1935), USGS Store, http://ngmdb.usgs.gov/maps/TopoView/viewer/#13/42.1590/-70.7217 (click on "24,000," then center of map, then "13 maps," then 1935 map). Largely in accord with the USGS map (except for the omission of Cliff Avenue and its houses) is the Rivermoor section of Bailey, *Historical Map*.

[728] Assessors of Scituate, *List of Persons Twenty Years of Age and Older Residing in Town of Scituate on January 1, 1937* (Scituate: The Satuit Press, 1937), SHS; 1939 Sanborn map. The 1937 assessor's list of persons is by last name, men first then women, with persons in four dwellings on Collier Road (Eichorn, Foster, MacKenzie, Mahon), two on Michael Avenue (Nason, Wilson), one on Lincoln Avenue (Stretch), and one on Brown Avenue (Heathcote).

[729] Charles M. Litchfield, "Report of the Chief of Police," Annual Report of the Officers of the Town of Scituate for the Year Ending December 31, 1929, 172–174.

[730] 1908 Sanborn map, 1 (Water Facilities note) (average daily consumption was 100,000 gallons in the winter and 225,000 in the summer; 1918 Sanborn map, 1 (200,000 in winter and 500,000 in summer); Bonney, *My Scituate*, 2; US Census Bureau, "Detailed Tables: Population of Counties, Incorporated Places, and Minor Civil

Divisions," in *Fourteenth Census of the United States, Taken in the Year 1920, Population 1920-Number and Distribution of Inhabitants*, vol. 1, table 51, p. 230 (population 2,534), http://www.census.gov/prod/www/decennial.html#y1920.

[731] *1918 Directory; 1926 Directory*; 1926 Sanborn map; analysis by author. The directories list summer residents and summer cottage streets. An asterisk indicated that the residents owned the cottage.

[732] *1926 Directory*; 1926 Sanborn map; June Jones, telephone interview by author, May 19, 2016 ("Midget" house on Michael Avenue built for a dentist); analysis by author, which includes various internet searches for Dr. Otho Schofield, Dr. Arthur V. Rogers (dentist on Parker Avenue), E. Frederick Cullen (Parker Avenue), Otway Chalkey (*Chalkley*, at Collier Road), Meyer Bloomfield, Guy B. McKinney, Arthur V. [Vernon] Woodworth and Toscha Seidel, all listed as summer residents in the directory. The 1926 directory lists Dr. Arthur V. Rogers (a dentist) as owning a house on Parker Avenue (which was at 10 Parker), even though the Johnson manuscript mentions him as being on "Dentist Avenue" (referring to Michael Avenue). See also "Second Cliff" handwritten note by unidentified woman who was a girl in 1910, in SHS files on the Cliffs ("2nd cliff was the tops of the cliff to live. 3rd cliff had Dentists. One street called Dentist's Alley.") By 1929, Dr. Arthur V. Rogers had become a permanent resident of Scituate, owning the historical Martin Hatch house off Greenfield Lane, also known as the Darius Harrub property of the mid-1700s on the offshoot of Greenfield Lane at 11 Elm Park. *Scituate, 1636–1936*, 45; "Harrub, Darius House," 11 Elm Pk, SCI.74, MACRIS.

[733] Selectmen's records, May 24, 1934, vol. S-110, page 13, referred to in "Michael Avenue" in WPA card index, Town Archives.

[734] "D. A. R. Meets At Rivermoor," *Marshfield Mail*, July 11, 1930, Marshfield Historical Society, Newspapers and Clippings Box 2, reference 2008.0112.

[735] *Marshfield Mail*, July 11, 1930, Marshfield Historical Society, Newspapers and Clippings Box 2, reference 2008.0112.

[736] *Marshfield Mail*, July 2, 1937, 4, Marshfield Historical Society, Newspapers and Clippings Box 2, reference 2008.0112.

[737] *Marshfield Mail*, August 28, 1936, 1, 4 (source of quote), Marshfield Historical Society, Newspapers and Clippings Box 2, reference 2008.0112

[738] *Scituate, 1636–1936*, 39–43 (program for the tercentenary celebration).

[739] "Miss Frances Perkins To Speak In Scituate: U. S. Secretary of Labor Will Give Address at Tercentenary Exercises at High School Auditorium," *Scituate Herald*, August 21, 1936, 1 (few times, former classmate); "Miss Perkins Coming to Scituate," *Scituate Herald*, August 28, 1936, 1; *Marshfield Mail*, August 28, 1936, 1, 4; "Address by Miss Perkins Arouses Enthusiasm; One of Principal Closing Events of Anniversary Week," *Scituate Herald*, September 11, 1936, 1, 8 (ancestry). For photos of Perkins, see Library of Congress photos at https://www.loc.gov/item/2004672052/ (1934) and https://www.loc.gov/resource/hec.41078/ (Harris & Ewing, 1936).

[740] *Marshfield Mail*, August 28, 1936, 4 (source of quote), Marshfield Historical Society, Newspapers and Clippings Box 2, reference 2008.0112.

[741] *1926 Directory* (Nasons listed as residents and summer residents, and Stretches listed as summer residents); *1937 Assessors' List of Persons*, 24 & 39 (Nason), 30 & 67 (Stretch), and 12 & 46 (Eichorn); list of presidents of Scituate Historical Society in Society's newsletter, June 2016, seventh page; Rev. Robert L. Weis, "Some of the Descendants of Ephraim Otis and Rachel (Hersey) Otis of Scituate, Massachusetts," July 1943, first page (dedications), SHS; Annie K. Sweet to Isabelle C. Nason, deed, May 19, 1922, PCRD, book 1413, page 198 (lots 83 & 84).

[742] *1926 Directory* (Nasons listed as residents and summer residents, and Stretches listed as summer residents); *1937 Assessors' List of Persons*, 24 & 39 (Nason), 30 & 67 (Stretch), and 12 & 46 (Eichorn); William N. Ambler to Ethel J. Stretch, deed, June 21, 1922, PCRD, book 1414, page 63 (lots 117 and 118, with house then called Mayo, later 18 Lincoln); Howard R. Guild to Ethel J. Stretch, deed, March 14, 1924, PCRD, book 1457, page 229 (lots 119 and 120); Gertrude H. Leonard to Hazel Eichorn, deed, April 25, 1927, PCRD, book 1529, page 362 (lots 72 and northerly half of 73); current assessor's map (to convert lot numbers to street addresses); *1930 VL, A-L*, nonresident section, 67, Hazel Eichorn of Boston owner of house (Leonard) and lots; "John Eichorn," *Fur News*, vol. 8, no. 5, November 2, 1908, in Volumes 7-8 (Somerville, NJ: A. R. Harding Publishing Company, 1908), 338, https://books.google.com/books?id=SUQAAAAAMAAJ&source=gbs_navlinks_s; "John Eichorn," *Fur Trade Review*, vol. 36, no. 3, October 1908 (New York: F. Stallknecht Corporation, 1908), 741 (source of quote), https://books.google.com/books?id=jak6AQAAMAAJ&source=gbs_navlinks_s. By 1938, it appears the Nasons had moved to 10 Driftway. *1938 South Shore Social Register*, 123. The Social Register's listing for "Rivermore" (which seemed to include other parts of Third Cliff) had 32 listings, with 17 of them showing winter residences.

[743] The author's review of grantees of deeds cited in these notes produced a total of 27 women and 20 men.

[744] Frank L. Nason, president, Scituate Country Club, to Harry Stenbeck, May 2, 1933, SHS.

[745] *Scituate Herald*, August 5, 1938, 5.

[746] US Coast Guard, *The Coast Guard At War: Beach Patrol* (Official History Series, vol. 27) (Washington, DC: US Coast Guard, 1945), 3, 5, 15, 41, 45, formerly at http://www.uscg.mil/history/articles/USCGatWar-BeachPatrol.pdf, and https://media.defense.gov/2017/Jul/02/2001772325/-1/-1/0/USCGATWAR-BEACHPATROL.PDF, formerly available from http://www.history.uscg.mil/Commemorations/World-War-II/igpage/2/.

[747] Paula Buckley letter to Mrs. Polly Bowers, probably 1986, with portions quoted in TCRIA newsletter "Cliff Notes," vol. 1, issue 4, July 2001 (source of quote in text), courtesy of Skip DeBrusk; Paul Bowers, interview by author, May 21, 2016 (recounting observations by resident John Buckley). Perhaps the foxhole was a mini-tower, covered, to protect the Coast Guard members from the elements, as shown in the photo in Dennis L. Noble, *The Beach Patrol and Corsair Fleet: The U.S. Coast Guard in World War II* (Washington, DC: US Coast Guard Historian's Office, 1992), second page, formerly at http://www.uscg.mil/history/articles/BeachPatrolCorsairFleet.pdf.

[748] A blimp (number K-11) from the South Weymouth Naval Air Station crashed in Scituate. US Navy, "Blimp Crashes at Scituate MA on evening of 31 July 43," photograph, http://ark.digitalcommonwealth.org/ark:/50959/fx71bn86d; photos at "K-11 Crash - July 31, 1943," and link to "ZP-11 Squadron Diary," in Air Ship Squadron page formerly at War Wings Art.com website, http://www.warwingsart.com/LTA/zp-11.html. The ZP-11 Squadron Diary, 11-12, briefly discusses the incident, in which nobody was hurt, http://www.warwingsart.com/LTA/ZP-11%20Squadron%20Diary.pdf.

[749] "Fourth Cliff Recreation Area: The History," website, http://fourthcliff.com/fourth%20cliff%20history.html. The history of the military on Fourth Cliff is summarized in Galluzzo, *The North River*, 79–81.

[750] Russell Fish papers.

[751] Russell Fish papers. Mr. Fish's election as president of the Northeastern Retail Lumbermens Association was reported in "Easing of Curbs on Building Urged: Lumbermen at Convention Ask Relaxation of Regulation X to Aid Defense Housing," *The New York Times*, February 1, 1951, 35 (with photo of Mr. Fish).

[752] Betty McKenzie, "Scituate Country Club," August 13, 1978, printed in 1996 booklet of the Scituate Country Club, SHS.

[753] "Dr. T. B. Alexander is Dead in Scituate," *Boston Globe*, August 29, 1941, 24.

[754] Handwritten reminiscences of a daughter of Dr. Alexander, probably Frances Johnson, probably in connection with history project of TCRIA in 1986 and 1988, copy courtesy of Paul Bowers. John J. Fitzpatrick is listed on Highland (Gilson Road) as a greenkeeper [greenskeeper] in the *1926 Directory*, and on the Driftway (where the Scituate Country Club was located) as a caretaker in the *1937 Assessors' List of Persons*. This was a house on the eastern part of the club's property, near Moorland Road.

[755] Hilda Stenbeck, "Scituate Country Club History to add to details of Scituate Herald paper of Sept. 5, 1919," June 21, 1990, SHS.

[756] Author analysis of various sources, including Assessor's Database, tax valuation lists, and Sanborn maps; David Brooks, "Spike in lumber prices hasn't translated much into higher timber value, at least not yet," *Concord Monitor* [NH], published April 10, 2021 (quoted), https://www.concordmonitor.com/lumber-wood-logging-nh-covid-coronavirus-nh-new-hampshire-39555106.

[757] Unknown author, "Was he a charter member of the Scituate Country Club?" typed notes, SHS; *1938 South Shore Social Register*, 130 (listed on Ocean Avenue, Minot/North Scituate Beach); Ann Baird (Whittemore stepdaughter), interview by author, May 16, 2016; "Presidents of Hatherly Country Club," plaque, at Hatherly Country Club; various letters, SHS.

[758] Ann Baird (Whittemore stepdaughter), interview by author, May 16, 2016.

[759] Jack Farley, interview by author, November 18, 2016; various letters, SHS; "Donald Whittemore Investment Firm Founder, 93," obituary, *Boston Globe*, September 26, 1988, 29; Donald Golden, "Condo Plan Has Scituate Abuzz," *Boston Globe*, April 14, 1984, 21–22; Scituate Golf Club by Mortgagee to Donald H. Whittemore, deed, February 11, 1946, PCRD, book 1900, page 463; David O. Whittemore and Donald H. Whittemore, Trustees of Shorelands Realty Trust to Bonwood Company, Inc., deed, July 23, 1985, PCRD, book 6395, page 178. See discussion in text below about townhouse condominiums built on part of the Scituate Country Club property.

[760] Sullivan interview (Dr. Bowers). Lowder married Meredith (Perry) Wilcox, with stepdaughters Sally O'Day, Gail Ledwig, and Diane Teuten. *Scituate Mariner*, February 22, 2001, 14.

[761] See earlier discussion in the text tracing deeds to the property. Apart from the deeds, there is a curious lack of published documentation of her presence in Scituate. According to the 1910 US census, Ruth Bailey lived

with her family in Reading, MA. Ancestry.com. 1910 United States Federal Census [database on-line]. Lehi, UT, USA: Ancestry.com Operations Inc., 2006. Original data: Thirteenth Census of the United States, 1910 (NARA microfilm publication T624, 1,178 rolls). Records of the Bureau of the Census, Record Group 29. National Archives, Washington, D.C. Enumeration district 984, sheet 23A. While there were many Baileys in town, there is no record of her or her family in the 1918 or 1926 *Harold Howard Directories*, or in the 1937 street listing of persons in Scituate, even using her married name. Nor is she listed in Scituate in the 1940 US Census. Dr. Bailey's married name was Ruth [Bailey] Gammon according to her obituary in the *Boston Globe*, February 12, 1992, page 31.

[762] Bill Giniewicz, interview by author, March 6, 2016; Dr. Ruth Bailey answers to TCRIA questionnaire about 1988 in Association's archives; 1918 Sanborn map, sheet 8.

[763] G. Robert Boggs, executor, to Ruth Bailey, deed, May 31, 1944, PCRD, book 1863, page 329; ad in *South Shore Mirror*, June 10, 1965, clipping in "Businesses — Pre-1980" file, SHS; ad in *Chimes*, Scituate High School yearbook 1969, 152, https://archive.org/details/chimes1969scit; "Dr. Bailey: 'Citizen of the Year,'" *Quincy (MA) Patriot Ledger*, November 15, 1977.

[764] Brown, et al, *Legendary Locals of Scituate, Massachusetts*, 106.

[765] Sullivan interview (Dr. Bowers); *Scituate Herald*, August 26, 1949, 2, col. 3 (pianist); Caroline S. Chapman to Albert D. Duplain and Beatrice M. Duplain of Newton, deed, February 8, 1949, PCRD, book 2031, page 177; "Albert D. Duplain, Baking Firm Owner, Philanthropist, at 63," *Boston Globe*, December 17, 1956; Town of Scituate 1959 Real EstateAssessments, 89.

[766] Paula Buckley letter to Mrs. Polly Bowers, probably 1986.

[767] Jack Farley, interview by author, November 18, 2016; Heather Dauphinee, conversation with author, October 2017; author's observations.

[768] Sullivan interview (Polly Bowers, Dr. Bowers); author's experiences.

[769] Sullivan interview (Gallagher, who arrived in 1949); Paula Buckley letter to Mrs. Polly Bowers, probably 1986.

[770] Paula Buckley letter to Mrs. Polly Bowers, probably 1986.

[771] "Spit Run," on former Historic Scituate Trails website, http://www.historicscituatetrails.org/Scituate_Historic_Bike_Trail/Spit_Run_Paddle_Trail.html.

[772] Philip W. Emery and Eleanor Emery to Peter J. Abdou and Eva B. Abdou, deed, September 26, 1949, PCRD, book 2059, page 328 (lots 219, 220, 221, bounded "Easterly by the Cliff"); Joshua Glenn, "Eva Morrison," blog at *Boston Globe* website, posted January 23, 2008, http://archive.boston.com/bostonglobe/ideas/brainiac/2008/01/eva_morrison.html; "Distance Swimmer Eva Abdou, 72; Saved Many Off Scituate Beaches," *Boston Globe*, March 18, 1985, 27; "Eva Morrison Abdou, 72, long-distance swimmer," *Quincy (MA) Patriot Ledger*, March 18, 1985, 30, copy from microfilm courtesy of Thomas Crane Public Library, Quincy, MA; handwritten reminiscences of probably Frances Johnson, probably in connection with history project of TCRIA in 1986 and 1988, copy courtesy of Paul Bowers (bell buoy); Sullivan interview. The property was sold in 1987. Lillian Clancy, under will of Peter J. Abdou, to Gary W. Cruickshank and Linda Cruickshank, deed, May 15, 1987, PCRD, book 7707, page 328.

[773] "Noted Scituate Swimmer Makes Her 49th Rescue," *Boston Globe*, May 2, 1955, 7.

[774] "Woman, Lad Save Man in Scituate," *Boston Globe*, September 18, 1967, 10; Jack Farley, interview by author, November 18, 2016 (flowers); Sullivan interview; TCRIA archives, including minutes of Executive Committee meeting, September 17, 1949, and May 14, 1950, and Annual Meeting, August 25, 1952; Howe, *The Humane Society*, 257-258.

[775] Point Place, called Point Way on a 2010 town listing, is a private way that has not been accepted by the town. *Town of Scituate Streets and Ways 2010*.

[776] George F. Welch to Chauncey W. Chamberlain, deed, July 9, 1909, PCRD, book 1027, page 425; Charles H. and Ella G. Waterman to Mary Jane MacKenzie, deed, September 7, 1933, PCRD, book 1649, page 455. It appears to have been called "Point Cottage" in a 1914 news item. "Scituate. Several Hundred Families Already at First, Second and Third Cliffs for the Season," *Boston Globe*, June 21, 1914, 6 ("At Rivermoor … George C. Scott and family of Framingham at Point cottage").

[777] Jack Farley, interview by author, November 18, 2016; Sally Rossi-Ormon, interview by author, June 26, 2016; *1938 South Shore Social Register*, 132; Sullivan interview (including Dr. Bowers, Gallagher [Prince School]).

[778] Letter from Donald Corey, September 18, 2021; photo album at Cliffsend with photos from the 1930s and later, assembled and annotated in 1980s, probably by MacKenzie's niece and later owner Peggy Long, or perhaps Peggy's daughter Betty Jane Williams, or her daughter Alison Allen ("Cliffsend photo album"); "Mary MacKenzie, 90, theater columnist," *Boston Globe*, July 30, 1974, 33; 1940 US Census; Sullivan interview (including Dr. Bowers [Shubert]).

[779] Jack Farley, interview by author, November 18, 2016; Sally Rossi-Ormon, interview by author, June 26, 2016; Sullivan interview; letter from Donald Corey, October 3, 2021.

[780] Conversation with occupants, September 12, 2021; Sullivan interview.

[781] Cliffsend photo album.

[782] Sullivan interview (Gallagher).

[783] Cliffsend photo album.

[784] Cliffsend photo album; Letter from Donald Corey, September 18, 2021; "Mary MacKenzie, 90, theater columnist," *Boston Globe*, July 30, 1974, 33; Mary J. MacKenzie by Executor to Peggy S. Long and Betty J. Williams, deed, October 20, 1977, PCRD, book 4349, page 455; letter from Donald Corey, September 18, 2021. The Assessor's Database says the house was built in 1890, but it does not show up in the late 1800s tax valuation lists for E. Parker Welch, who would have owned the property at the time.

[785] Sullivan interview (Farley).

[786] Sullivan interview; author's observations (starting 2001).

[787] Sullivan interview (Gallagher).

[788] Registrars of Scituate, *Street List of Residents Twenty Years of Age and Over in the Town of Scituate as of January 1, 1956* (Boston: printed by Spaulding-Moss Co., 1956), SHS. Such street listings were required by state law, and included names, ages, occupations, prior year residence, and nativity (place of birth). The 1956 street list was organized by street.

[789] Assessor's Database for Fiscal Year 2016, updated December 14, 2015, http://www.scituatema.gov/home/pages/online-services, and http://www.assessedvalues2.com/index.aspx?jurcode=264.

[790] "Rivermoor Folks Enjoy Dinner Dance at Country Club," *Scituate Herald*, July 13, 1950, 8.

[791] TCRIA archives, including minutes of Executive Committee meeting, September 17, 1949, and May 14, 1950, and Annual Meeting, August 25, 1952.

[792] TCRIA archives, including minutes of Executive Committee meeting, September 17, 1949, and May 14, 1950, and Annual Meeting, August 25, 1952. For title to Rivermoor beach, see deeds from E. Parker Welch to George F. Welch, August 27, 1902, PCRD, book 864, page 108; George F. Welch to Howard R. Guild, August 25, 1919, PCRD, book 1339, page 507; Amy Cheever Guild, et al, to Robert E., Rosalia, and Genevieve Preble, February 12, 1945, PCRD, book 1879, page 419; and Robert E. Preble, et al, to North and South Rivers Watershed Association, Inc., May 30, 1975, PCRD, book 4072, page 423. One of the incorporators, and vice-president, was W. [Wendell] Frank Whittemore of 18 Cliff Avenue, according to incorporation papers in the Association's records. He was not related to Donald Whittemore, according to Donald's daughter Ann Baird, telephone call by author, September 11, 2016. During the 1940s, Pop Green (or Greene), who lived on Collier across the street from 7 Lincoln, laid down the boardwalk in early June and took it up in September, according to Paula Buckley letter to Mrs. Polly Bowers, probably 1986. (Could this have been Edmund Green of 8 Lincoln Ave.? See Edmund Green and Agnes A. Green, wife, and Helen Green Martignette, to Newton Savings Bank, mortgage, June 28, 1941, PCRD, book 1809, page 116 (lots 110-114, north side of Lincoln at Collier). By 1964, the boardwalk was worn out after 30 years of use and was replaced by a new one of 26 12-foot sections, according to the Association's newsletter for 1964.

[793] Anthony Antoniello, Director, Scituate Department of Public Works, to Richard T. Bennett, Scituate Town Administrator, memo, May 21, 1980, subject: Rivermoor Barrier Beach, attaching Geotechnical Report by Asaf Ali Qazilbash P.E., Consulting Civil and Geotechnical Engineer, to Antoniello, May 15, 1980, courtesy of Skip DeBrusk; Sullivan interview; Heather Dauphinee telephone interview by author, February 27, 2016 (sand dunes at the Spit used to be "little mountains" and, near the creek used for swimming, was a pool used for swimming lessons).

[794] Town of Scituate, 1968 aerial photograph [interpositive] CGL-125, -127, and -136, 1" = 100', Town Archives, copied by author April 12, 2017 (author references IMG_0251–0255, 0259, 0260), and January 18, 2017 (author reference IMG_7618 et seq). The photos are voluminous, unwieldy, and look like large negatives. Some copied by author are on file in Town Archives in TIFF or PDF format.

[795] Jack Farley, interview by author, November 18, 2016; TCRIA, Inc., Third Cliff-Rivermoor Newsletter (Summer 1986), 5, courtesy of Gail Ledwig (tidal pool and wide creek that flowed out to the North River). Part of the creek appears to have been located inland of what is now the southern end of the seawall. See Norman T. Hornsby, Jr., Trustee of The Elizabeth G. Barthlow Trust to Alejandro R. Alvarez and Linda M. Alvarez, deed, April 22, 1999, PCRD, book 17527, page 13; 1968 aerial photo copied elsewhere in text.

[796] Sullivan interview (Dr. Bowers); conversation with Paul Bowers, October 31, 2021.

[797] Krusell and Bates, *Marshfield*, 58.

[798] Paula Buckley letter to Mrs. Polly Bowers, probably 1986; TCRIA newsletters. The Coolbroths sold their property in 1961. Norman F. & Grace N. Coolbroth to Finton J. & Marie L. Mohyde, deed, July 1, 1961, recorded July 6, 1961, PCRD, book 2863, page 268. The property is described without reference to lot 41 since the referenced original deed from George F. Welch was December 15, 1905, before the 1906 Rivermoor Plan. See also entries for Sarah E. Young, of 10 Rawson Street, South Boston, in *1905 VL*, 131, and *1906 VL*, 134.

[799] TCRIA, "Cliff Notes" newsletter, vol. 2, Spring 1999, 2, quoting Dick Sherrell to Andy Rohm, letter, February 4, 1999, both in Association archives.

[800] Jack Farley, interview by author, November 18, 2016.

[801] TCRIA, Inc., "The Heritage of Third Cliff," in Third Cliff-Rivermoor Newsletter (Summer 1986), 1, courtesy of Gail Ledwig; Paula Buckley letter to Mrs. Polly Bowers, probably 1986; see Goldberg-Zoino 1975 report (erosion of Third Cliff north of the Driftway), Goldberg-Zoino 1975 report, 6-8.

[802] TCRIA archives.

[803] Dexter ("Skip") DeBrusk to Walter [Barnard] letter, May 15, 1977, and accompanying notes, courtesy of Skip DeBrusk.

[804] Skip DeBrusk, notes of Association annual report, September 1977, courtesy of Skip DeBrusk; author's observations.

[805] Antoniello to Bennett memo, 1980; Skip DeBrusk, notes of Association meeting, September 10, 1976, courtesy of Skip DeBrusk.

[806] Gail McCracken Price, "Declaration of Easement," July 30, 1996, recorded November 12, 1996, PCRD, book 14777, page 160. Rivermoor resident Clay Shafton pursued obtaining the easement. Rights of passage to reach a beach, and rights to use a beach, have been the subject of controversies along the shores of Massachusetts; some subdivisions specifically allowed residents those rights, as shown in Anderson, *Summer Estates*, 25–26, 107-109 (Swampscott). Rights under the "public trust" doctrine are discussed in the text.

[807] TCRIA, Inc., email, June 28, 2017 (movie night featuring "Jaws" in recognition of the recent sighting of a great white shark, as noted in Rachel Antos, "Shark spotted off Scituate coast," *Scituate Mariner*, June 29, 2017); agenda for annual membership meeting of Association, May 15, 1988, courtesy of Skip DeBrusk; Association memo to neighbors with history questionnaire, summer 1988, courtesy of Skip DeBrusk; late summer 1988 newsletter of TCRIA, courtesy of Skip DeBrusk; "Silly hat paraders strut their stuff at Third Cliff," *Scituate Mariner*, July 6, 2000, page 6. The boardwalk now stretches about 500 feet, halfway to the beach, with a path leading the rest of the way, according to Google Maps/Satellite View.

[808] Sunoco, "Cape Cod and Vicinity, '65– '66," copyright by H. M. Gousha Co. (1965 ed.), author's Nancy Nyberg collection.

[809] Krusell and Bates, *Marshfield*, 37; Steve Anderson, "3-Pilgrims Highway Historic Overview," BostonRoads.com website, http://www.bostonroads.com/roads/MA-3/; Hart and Hart, *Not All Is Changed*, 383, 388–389; Wallace, "Coastal Zone Study, Phase II," App. "C": "Building Permits in Scituate's Coastal Zone, 1963–1975"; *Town of Scituate Streets and Ways 2010*; Mary Winiarz, interview by author, May 18, 2016.

[810] Richard E. Kendall, Commissioner, Massachusetts Department of Environmental Management, letter to numerous owners, March 22, 1979, Publication 11257-21-800-3-79-C. R. The protective act and order are administered by the North River Commission, http://www.northrivercommission.net/, The history of the Commission, and the NSRWA, are described in more detail in Galluzzo, *The North River*, 97-104, and in a series of articles by Jim Glinski published about 2020 on the association's website, https://www.nsrwa.org/.

[811] Kezia Bacon, "Celebrating our rivers' National Natural Landmark status," *Scituate Mariner*, August 30, 2018, B7; "National Natural Landmarks Program," National Park Service website, https://www.nps.gov/subjects/nnlandmarks/index.htm. The NNL registry available from the NPS website oddly does not mention it now, but it once said, "North and South Rivers is a large and diverse estuarine wetland system containing salt, brackish, and fresh water marshes. The two rivers are classic examples of drowned, river-mouth estuaries and support many bird and fish species."

[812] Third Cliff-Rivermoor Association archives, various documents.

[813] Goldberg-Zoino 1975 report, 6-8; William S. Zoino, Goldberg-Zoino & Associates, Inc. to Scituate Board of Selectmen, June 12, 1974, letter, re: Slope Stability-Third Cliff Proposal for Engineering Services, File PJ-1, PJ-2, Town Archives; Goldberg-Zoino & Associates, Inc., "Third Cliff Slope Stability Problem," February 3, 1976, summary, TCRIA archives; Wallace, "Coastal Zone Study, Phase II," 56-57, 116.

[814] David Ball, in "Three truly historic storms," *Scituate Mariner* website, posted February 8, 2015, http://scituate.wickedlocal.com/article/20150208/news/150208452; Rich Fahey, "A blizzard too furious to forget," *Boston Globe* website, February 7, 2008, http://archive.boston.com/news/local/articles/2008/02/07/a_blizzard_too_furious_to_forget/; "A look back at the Blizzard of 1978," *Boston Globe* website,

http://archive.boston.com/news/weather/gallery/013108_78blizzard/ (7 of 18 photos are scenes of Scituate); "The Blizzard of '78: The Storm of the Century," http://www.blizzardof78.org/; Emma Locke, "Coastal building revives storm memories," *Scituate Mariner*, March 10, 1988, TCRIA archives; *Murphy v. Conway*, 20 LCR 26a, MISC 06-317624 (Trial Court, Land Court Department, Plymouth County, 2012), at "Evolution of Third Cliff" section, Massachusetts Cases website, http://masscases.com/cases/land/20/20lcr26.html.

[815] Massachusetts Office of Coastal Zone Management (CZM), "Public Rights Along the Shoreline" (2005), Mass.gov website, https://www.mass.gov/service-details/public-rights-along-the-shoreline; Heather J. Wilson, "The Public Trust Doctrine in Massachusetts Land Law," 11 *B.C. Envtl. Aff. L. Rev.* 839 (1984), https://lawdigitalcommons.bc.edu/ealr/vol11/iss4/6; Shetterly, *Seaweed Chronicles*, 226–229; Billy Baker, "Here's the word: 'Recreation' could open up beach access," *Boston Globe*, September 10, 2021, 1. An example of a standard consent form (with limited release of liability) for the government's construction of a seawall is the one signed by Harriet H. Miller, owner of lots 206 and 207 (43 Collier), October 10, 1933, Town Archives.

[816] Boston Sand and Gravel Company to Town of Scituate, order of taking, August 12, 1975, PCRD, book 4091, page 726, referring to plan of August 1, 1975; Boston Sand and Gravel Company to Town of Scituate, deed, August 14, 1975, PCRD, book 4091, page 733; Loring H. Jacobs Co. for Town of Scituate, *Compiled Plan of Land in the Town of Scituate, Massachusetts, Located at Driftway and Stockbridge Road*, plan, 1" = 200', August 1, 1975, PCRD, plan book 18, page 594; press clippings on Widow's Walk website, http://www.widowswalkgolf.com/-press-clippings; Town of Scituate Annual Reports, various years.

[817] Paul McCarthy, "Town of Scituate Massachusetts, Historical Map & Street Directory" (n.p., 1976), author's collection; talk with Frank at Rocco's Barber Shop, November 23, 2021, https://www.roccosbarbershop.com/; Maria's Pizza and Subs Facebook page, April 23, 2021, https://www.facebook.com/MariasPizzaAndSubs/; "Robert H. Combs 1935-2020," obituary, *Scituate Mariner*, December 2020, https://www.legacy.com/us/obituaries/wickedlocal-scituate/name/robert-combs-obituary?id=7561513; "James Delaronde Goddard 1929-2021," obituary, *Boston Globe*, February 2021, https://www.legacy.com/us/obituaries/bostonglobe/name/james-goddard-obituary?id=7052152.

[818] Sullivan interview (Farley [boulders], Gallagher); conversation with Joan Foster, October 11, 2021.

[819] Marilyn Jackson and Dianna Jankowski, "Condo fight: Scituate residents believe scenic beauty of historic Third Cliff will be destroyed," *Quincy (MA) Patriot Ledger*, March 28, 1984; Julie A. Miller, "Nov. 7 decision seen on Scituate condos," *Quincy (MA) Patriot Ledger*, October 27, 1984; Third Cliff-Rivermoor Association newsletters, Association's archives, Autumn 1984 and Spring 1985; see also The Bonwood Company ("Declarant"), Master Deed of the Condominiums at the Scituate Country Club, October 25, 1988, PCRD, book 8821, page 59, and associated documents recorded therewith; Golden, "Condo Plan,"; 1996 booklet of the Scituate Country Club, SHS.

[820] 1996 booklet of the Scituate Country Club, SHS; Scituate Country Club website, http://www.scituatecc.com/club/scripts/section/section.asp?GRP=14337&NS=PG.

[821] Andrew MacLellan, "Spencers win approval for bed and breakfast," *Scituate Mariner*, November 7, 1991, 34, ad of unnamed date, and Pat Durocher, "Complaint aims to block B & B permit," [Quincy, MA] *Patriot Ledger*, November 15, 1991, all clippings in Hotels & Inns file, SHS; conversation with Shirley Hanlon, June 3, 2019.

[822] Sewer Division, Town of Scituate website, https://www.scituatema.gov/sewer-division; Third Cliff-Rivermoor Association newsletter "Cliff Notes," January 2004, courtesy of Skip DeBrusk; Anthony Antoniello, Director, Department of Public Works, April 13, 2005, letter and notice to property owners; Town of Scituate Sewer Division website, http://www.scituatema.gov/sewer-division.

[823] Robert Preer, "All aboard: Greenbush opposition has ceased as the reality approaches: Trains start rolling Wednesday, and region awaits the impact," *Boston Globe*, October 28, 2007, http://archive.boston.com/news/local/massachusetts/articles/2007/10/28/all_aboard/.

[824] Jessica Trufant, "Scituate turbine brings in $500,000 for the town in three years," *Quincy (MA) Patriot Ledger* website, posted March 3, 2015, http://www.patriotledger.com/article/20150303/NEWS/150308721; Kristi Funderburk, "Scituate seeing green with turbine," *Scituate Mariner* website, posted August 7, 2015, updated August 19, 2015, http://scituate.wickedlocal.com/article/20150807/NEWS/150807660/?Start=1; Ruth Thompson, "Neighbors of Scituate turbine call noise 'unbearable'," *Scituate Mariner* website, posted September 12, 2015, http://scituate.wickedlocal.com/article/20150912/NEWS/150919640; Jessica Bartlett, "In close call, Scituate residents vote to support wind turbine," *Boston Globe* website, posted April 11, 2013, http://archive.boston.com/yourtown/news/scituate/2013/04/in_close_call_scituate_residen.html.

[825] Ruth Thompson, "Town to buy Border Street land," *Scituate Mariner*, November 4, 1; Town of Scituate Advisory Committee, "Report and Recommendations for Special Town Meeting, October 26, 2021;" author's notes at town meeting (Beverly Westerveld remarks); Tyler Van Fleet, et al, "Chapter 61 Programs:

318

Understanding the Massachusetts Ch. 61 Current Use Tax Programs" (n.p., UMass Extension/dcr, 2014), pamphlet, https://masswoods.org/.

826 "Fourth Cliff Recreation Area: The History," website, http://fourthcliff.com/fourth%20cliff%20history.html; "Fourth Cliff Family Recreation Area," Hanscom Air Force Base Force Support Squadron website, https://www.hanscomfss.com/FourthCliff.asp.

827 Conversation with Jackie Braga, October 16, 2021.

828 Stephen Corfidi, quoted in Amanda Fiegl, "Red Sky at Night: The Science of Sunsets: A meteorologist explains why the sky is sometimes so colorful," *National Geographic* website, published October 29, 2013, https://news.nationalgeographic.com/news/2013/10/131027-sunset-sky-change-color-red-clouds-science/ (information in brackets added by author based on other sources); Brian Resnick, "Why sunsets are better in the winter," Vox.com website, November 22, 2019, https://www.vox.com/science-and-health/2019/11/22/20970563/sunset-science-explained-rayleigh-scattering. Light scattering explains why the ocean appears in cooler colors, like blue. Dicus, *Window Seat*, 55.

829 Author's observations; Bob King, "What makes Mars sunsets different from Earth's?" PhysOrg website, May 19, 2015, https://phys.org/news/2015-05-mars-sunsets-earth.html; Daniel Feldman, "Why is the sky blue? And the sunset red?" Science for Dessert website, posted September 29, 2010, https://macaulay.cuny.edu/eportfolios/sciencefordessert/2010/09/29/why-is-the-sky-blue-and-the-sunset-red/; Tony Flanders, "The Belt of Venus," *Sky & Telescope* website, February 21, 2010, http://www.skyandtelescope.com/astronomy-blogs/the-belt-of-venus/. The earth's shadow can also be seen on the eastern horizon just before sunset. Michael Douma, curator, "Earth's Shadow," Cause of Color on WebExhibits website, http://www.webexhibits.org/causesofcolor/14E.html. Third Cliff is a good location to observe and photograph other interesting astronomical features at twilight, such as zodiacal light, crepuscular rays, and Alpenglow. Harald Edens, "Sunrise and sunset phenomena: what to discover, when, and where," WeatherScapes.com website, http://www.weatherscapes.com/techniques.php?cat=optics&page=twilight. There is much useful advice for taking photos at civil, nautical, and astronomical twilight. James Brandon, "Beyond Sunset: The Different Phases of Twilight," Digital Photography School website, https://digital-photography-school.com/beyond-sunset-the-differen-phases-of-twilight/; Germán Marquès, "Understanding Golden Hour, Blue Hour and Twilights," PhotoPills website, https://www.photopills.com/articles/understanding-golden-hour-blue-hour-and-twilights. For extra credit, check out polar-mesospheric noctilucent clouds.

830 Author's observations, including USS John F. Kennedy voyage in 2007, and house on a barge, December 26, 2017; Megan Tench, "Farewell to a proud warrior; USS John F. Kennedy in last visit to Boston," *Boston Globe*, February 26, 2007.

831 Author's observations and calculations; Phil Plait, "How far away is the horizon?" *Discover* magazine online (including comments), January 15, 2009, http://blogs.discovermagazine.com/badastronomy/2009/01/15/how-far-away-is-the-horizon/; "Horizon," Wikipedia (and sources cited), https://en.wikipedia.org/wiki/Horizon; "Pilgrim Monument," Pilgrim Monument website, https://www.pilgrim-monument.org/pilgrim-monument/.

832 "The History of Race Point Lightstation," Race Point Lightstation website, http://www.racepointlighthouse.org/about-us.htm.

833 Ian Sample, ed., "Walker 'stunned' to see ship hovering high above sea off Cornwall," *The Guardian*, March 5, 2021, https://www.theguardian.com/science/2021/mar/05/ship-hovering-above-sea-cornwall-optical-illusion. Stilgoe's book *Alongshore* discusses looming.

834 Lee Billings, "New Map Shows the Dark Side of Artificial Light at Night; More than a third of humanity cannot see the Milky Way due to light pollution, and a new wave of energy-efficient lighting could make the problem much worse," *Scientific American* website, June 10, 2016, https://www.scientificamerican.com/article/new-map-shows-the-dark-side-of-artificial-light-at-night/ (noting that the trend of using blue-white LED lighting can make matters worse). See also Verlyn Klinkenborg, "Our Vanishing Night," *National Geographic*, November 2008, formerly posted on website, http://ngm.nationalgeographic.com/2008/11/light-pollution/klinkenborg-text; Ginger Pinholster, "Artificial Light Impacts Astronomy as Well as Human Health, the Environment, and World Views, Experts Say," website of American Association for the Advancement of Science, posted May 30, 2012, https://www.aaas.org/news/artificial-light-impacts-astronomy-well-human-health-environment-and-world-views-experts-say.

835 "Light Pollution," International Dark-Sky Association website, http://www.darksky.org/light-pollution/. See also Robert Lee Hotz, "Lighting at Night Has a Dark Side," *Wall Street Journal*, A12, November 24, 2017.

[836] David Owen, "The Dark Side; Making war on light pollution," *The New Yorker*, August 20, 2007, from website, http://www.newyorker.com/magazine/2007/08/20/the-dark-side-2.

[837] Denise Chow, "New interactive map shows how light pollution affects your hometown; Artificial light has been linked to health problems, and it makes life difficult for astronomers," NBC News website, March 11, 2019, https://www.nbcnews.com/mach/science/new-interactive-map-shows-how-light-pollution-affects-your-hometown-ncna981756?cid=eml_mach_20190311; Radiance Light Trends website, https://lighttrends.lightpollutionmap.info/#zoom=0&lon=0.00000&lat=33.78523.

[838] Hattie Bernstein, "The lights are going out in Massachusetts," *Boston Globe*, website, December 7, 2014, https://www.bostonglobe.com/metro/regionals/south/2014/12/07/face-sprawling-light-pollution-more-suburbs-considering-dark-skies-ordinance/6axIPVufctOimh5hPvCrgN/story.html; Thomas Farragher, "Starry, starry night? Not so much anymore," *Boston Globe*, August 22, 2021.

[839] Luis Villazon, "Why does the sea smell like the sea?" BBC *Science Focus Magazine*, https://www.sciencefocus.com/planet-earth/why-does-the-sea-smell-like-the-sea/.

[840] Author's experiences, including with his Sunfish sailboat.

[841] [*Scituate, MA (Third Cliff area)*] [map], c. 1 1/8 inch = 1000 feet, generated by author using Google Maps, Earth View, accessed November 24, 2015, https://www.google.com/maps/@42.1712548,-70.7372863,2654m/data=!3m1!1e3.

[842] Now a house on Third Cliff must have a lot size of 20,000 square feet in the Residence R-2 district or 10,000 square feet in the Residence R-3 district (R-3 being along the shore east of Gilson and east of Moorland), rather than the 5,000 square foot lots on the 1906 Rivermoor plan; also, it must be set back at least 30 feet from the road. Amory Engineers, P. C., and Dodson & Flinker, Inc. (revision), *Town of Scituate Massachusetts Zoning Map* [map], 1 inch = 1000 feet (Scituate: Town of Scituate, October 25, 2011, revised April 8, 2019), and Town of Scituate Zoning Bylaws, posted Feb. 18, 2020, 620.3 "Setback and Yard Requirements," 114, https://www.scituatema.gov/buildinginspections-department/pages/zoning-bylaw. See also Save the River View website and its links, from about early 2002, http://www.cs.bu.edu/faculty/crovella/SRV/.

[843] Assessor's Database, early tax valuation lists, internet searches for "Welch colonial," and author's analysis. The Assessor's Database lists the year each house was built. The 60 dwellings shown in the 1935 USGS map include 11 built after Welch sold The Welch Company in 1923. The average year built is 1916 using Assessor's Database, or 1914 adjusting that database for early valuation lists and news reports in the *Boston Globe*.

[844] Author's estimate based on multiple sources, primarily town tax valuation lists, Assessor's Database, and 1918 Sanborn map.

[845] Author's estimate based on review of 1968 aerial photos on file in Town Archives, and Google Earth.

[846] For example, see Miles and Galluzzo, *Beauty, Strength, Speed*; Dorothy Lawson McCall, *The Copper King's Daughter* (Portland, OR: Binfords & Mort, 1972); Hunnewell, *The Glades*. Many photos of Thomas Lawson are available, and an engraving of E. Parker Welch is in the *Biographical Review*, 398–401, but the only available image of the apparently camera-shy George Welch is a small photo in a short obituary notice in the May 31, 1931, *Boston Globe*.

[847] MACRIS inventory files on buildings in Scituate, and on buildings in Rivermoor in Scituate per author's searches; MACRIS map, March 14, 2017; Peter Stott, Preservation Planner, Massachusetts Historical Commission, to Doug Smith, Chair, Scituate Historical Commission, letter, February 16, 2017 (over 100 unfiled forms for First, Second, and Third Cliffs will be filed). The buildings listed at the end of 2016 on Third Cliff were 14 Bassin Lane, 10 Cliff Avenue, 122 and 138 Gilson Road, and 20 Town Way. The Rivermoor search then produced the same results as street-by-street searches for all Third Cliff streets, including Driftway and Gilson Road. There were three files on First Cliff. There were seven files on North Scituate Beach if searching for "North Scituate Beach," but many more are shown on the MACRIS map and on individual streets (available on street-by-street searches or on search for "Minot"), with about 84 of these in an area that was suggested for nomination as a National Register District in Turk Tracey, *2004 Survey*. In 2017, the author prepared a number of inventory forms for buildings on the cliffs, including the Daniel Ward house on First Cliff, at 6 Roberts Drive. These forms are filed in MACRIS. The author's inquiries also led to the discovery of over 100 inventory forms for buildings on the cliffs that had been submitted years before but not filed. Those forms have now been filed.

[848] Na Zhao, "Age of Housing Stock by State," NAHB Eye on Housing website, posted March 26, 2021 (based on most recent ACS survey from 2019, https://eyeonhousing.org/2021/03/age-of-housing-stock-by-state-3/; Theresa Agovino, "Inside the Land of a Thousand Teardowns," *Wall Street Journal*, December 28, 2016, B6; Jon Gorey, "What to Know When Buying an Older Home," *Boston Globe* magazine, September 9, 2018, 48 (median age was 53 years in 2015).

320

849 Author's calculations for Third Cliff homes as of the end of 2015, based on Assessor's Database and town tax valuation lists.

850 Assessor's Database, FY 2017; author's observations; Scituate Historical Commission meetings, including December 15, 2016; author's review of over 100 unfiled historical building inventory forms for Scituate's cliffs, drafted in May 2006 by Turk Tracey & Larry Architects, LLC, submitted to Massachusetts Historical Commission and later filed in MACRIS.

851 Scituate Historical Commission website, with links to the Demolition Review Bylaw, http://www.scituatema.gov/historical-commission; "Historic districts in Massachusetts by county," Wikipedia, https://en.wikipedia.org/wiki/Category:Historic_districts_in_Massachusetts; email from Doug Smith, Chairman, Scituate Historical Commission, August 19, 2018.

852 Carey Dunne, "Is It Even Possible To Design Buildings That Can Withstand 250 MPH Typhoon Winds?" November 13, 2013, *Fast Company* magazine's website, https://www.fastcompany.com/3021580/is-it-even-possible-to-design-buildings-that-can-withstand-250-mph-typh; Amanda DeMatto, "8 Ways to Protect Your Home Against Tornadoes and Hurricanes," *Popular Mechanics* website, posted after 2011, http://www.popularmechanics.com/home/interior-projects/how-to/g605/8-ways-to-protect-your-home-against-tornadoes-and-hurricanes/; McAlester, *Field Guide to American Houses*, Appendix: Approaches to Construction in the 20th and 21st Centuries, 765 et seq.

853 Jon Gorey, "They Just Don't Build 'Em Like They Used To — But Should They?" *Boston Sunday Globe*, June 3, 2018, H1; Jon Gorey, "It's not easy being Green in Massachusetts," *Boston Sunday Globe*, June 13, 2021, H1.

854 Jaci Conry, "Sustainable in Scituate: Photovoltaics on the roof and loads of insulation make this Shingle Style beauty the picture of energy efficiency," *Boston Globe*, May 12, 2013, R10.

855 Christopher Mims, "Maybe Houses Can Be Built Like iPhones," *Wall Street Journal*, July 3, 2017, B1.

856 TCRIA newsletter to residents, June 1975, in Association's archives (clam bed officially closed on Third Cliff); Krusell and Bates, *Marshfield*, 178; Patrick Ronan, "Marshfield opens shellfishing flats on North and South rivers," *Quincy (MA) Patriot Ledger* website, posted December 5, 2011, http://www.patriotledger.com/article/20111205/NEWS/312059465; "Shellfish Regulations and License," Town of Scituate website, http://www.scituatema.gov/town-clerk/pages/shellfish-regulations-license; James Kukstis, "Shellfish beds on North and South Rivers closed indefinitely by FDA," *Marshfield Mariner*, posted November 10, 2020, https://www.wickedlocal.com/story/marshfield-mariner/2020/11/10/shellfish-beds-between-marshfield-and-scituate-closed-indefinitely-by-fda/114806248/; Lori, "Help Reopen Recreational Shellfishing on the North and South Rivers," NSRWA e-newsletter, October 20, 2021, https://www.nsrwa.org/help-reopen-recreational-shellfishing-on-the-north-and-south-rivers/.

857 David Abel, "US may ease rules on plovers," *Boston Globe*, January 22, 2016, https://www.bostonglobe.com/metro/2016/01/21/beachgoers-may-get-break-plovers-rebound/cDf9WcGsBTkMV30rjLmu4N/story.html; "Piping Plover," Audubon Guide to North American Birds, https://www.audubon.org/field-guide/bird/piping-plover; "Massachusetts Piping Plover Habitat Conservation Plan Handbook, March 9, 2021," https://www.mass.gov/doc/massachusetts-piping-plover-habitat-conservation-plan-handbook/download; James T. Maughan, *Environmental Impact Analysis: Process and Methods* (Boca Raton, FL: CRC Press, 2014), 171–177 (case study on environmental impact of Scituate's sewage treatment plant at North River with maps showing adjacent Rivermoor Habitat Park), https://books.google.com/books?id=hczMBQAAQBAJ&source=gbs_navlinks_s; "Way: Rivermoor Habitat Park (29693998)," [map], website, http://www.openstreetmap.org/way/29693998. See also "BioMap2: Conserving the Biodiversity of Massachusetts in a Changing World," and associated map and information, at website of the Massachusetts Executive Office of Energy and Environmental Affairs, https://www.mass.gov/service-details/biomap2-conserving-the-biodiversity-of-massachusetts-in-a-changing-world, and the website of that agency's Natural Heritage Endangered Species Program, http://www.mass.gov/eea/agencies/dfg/dfw/natural-heritage/; Galluzzo, *The North River*, 104-106; "Site Summary: Site Summary: North River Mouth and Corridor," MassAudubon website, https://www.massaudubon.org/our-conservation-work/wildlife-research-conservation/statewide-bird-monitoring/massachusetts-important-bird-areas-iba/important-bird-area-sites/north-river-mouth-and-corridor. It is not clear how the area was designated as Rivermoor Habitat Park, but one source says it is 569 acres, owned by the Town of Scituate. "Rivermoor Habitat Park – Scituate – MA" (with map), https://www.mass-trails.org/towns/Scituate/rivermoorhabitatpark.html.

858 "Mesmerizing views and chic seaside ambiance on Scituate Harbor" in *Scituate Mariner*, August 15, 2015, cover of Community Classifieds section.

859 For example, Simons Greenhouse and Farmstand website (four generations of family farming), http://randcfarms.com/; Mullaney's Fish Markets website, http://www.mullaneysfish.com/.

860 Conversation with Jackie Braga, October 16, 2021; Review No. 7, https://usa-artmuseum.worldorgs.com/catalog/scituate/tourist-attraction/rivermoor-habitat-park.

INDEX

ACKNOWLEDGMENTS

Thanks to:

My wife Kathleen and family, who were patient, supportive, and hard-working
    (particularly editing)
My parents, whose love of books, maps, and travel filtered down to us children
Carol Miles, who was the first person to introduce me as historian
Robert Jackman, the teacher who got me started in history
Jim Conroy and Roy Harris, friends-writers-advisers on becoming a writer and author
Janet Paraschos, who offered clarity and an appreciation that God is in the details
Alix Stuart, for her wisdom, support, and insight
Garrett Kelleher, for his financial lucidity and accuracy
Gary Banks and Bill Richardson, for being such great people with such great photos
John Roman, artist, mapmaker, author
Susannah Green, designer and adviser
David Dixon and other distinguished writers, who critiqued my work and made it better
Prof. John Stilgoe, an inspiration, and a landmark in landscape history
David Noonan, an inspiration and influence in history and art
Betty Foster, for her inspiration, laughs, and advice
My friends at Scituate Town Archives and Scituate Historical Society, who are great
    resources, as well as great people
Scituate Historical Commission and Massachusetts Historical Commission,
    for their support
Michael Welch Johnson, who opened the door to his house and his ancestors;
    he will be missed
Phyllis Haskell, for her stories and photos of Cedar Camp
Vernon Woodworth and the Woodworth family, for sharing their historical photo album
Tom Whelan, writer-publisher and publishing adviser
Cynthia Krusell, for her writings and the great photo of the beach connecting the cliffs
Robert Thorndike, for being a friend and supporter

Neighbors on Third Cliff, present and past, and their descendants, who shared stories
and photos

Those whose names I may have forgotten to mention (please excuse me), and those
whose fingerprints are all over the text, photos, captions, and endnotes of this
book, including John Sullivan, Gail Ledwig, Jack Spurr, Nancy Howell, Skip &
Carolyn DeBrusk, Sue Logan, Don Corey, Sally Rossi-Ormon, Paul Bowers, Mike
Wankum, and Jack Farley

Scituate, "That's Heaven to Me" (apt song title; thank you, Sam Cooke)

I tried to be as accurate as possible. But in a work like this, with a human being like me,
it is only natural for mistakes to occur. They are my responsibility. Let me know and I
will try to fix them.

330

ABOUT THE AUTHOR

Lyle Nyberg was born near the ocean, grew up in Minnesota far from oceans, and now lives near the ocean in Scituate, Massachusetts. One of his English ancestors settled in Scituate in the 1630s and built the 38th house in town.

Lyle graduated from Dartmouth College and Boston University School of Law. He is a lawyer turned independent scholar and historian. He wrote and published *Summer Suffragists: Woman Suffrage Activists in Scituate, Massachusetts* (2020). He has documented more than 50 historic buildings in the greater Boston area, especially those relating to women's suffrage.

He is a member of the Scituate Historical Society, the Massachusetts Historical Society, and the New England Historical Association.

Lyle can be reached at www.lylenyberg.com. Selected maps and images are at his older website, http://thirdcliffdevelopment.webs.com/.